The Politics of Custom

The Politics of Custom

Chiefship, Capital, and the State in Contemporary Africa

Edited by
JOHN L. COMAROFF
JEAN COMAROFF

The University of Chicago Press
Chicago and London

The University of Chicago Press, Chicago 60637
The University of Chicago Press, Ltd., London
© 2018 by The University of Chicago
Published 2018
Printed in the United States of America

27 26 25 24 23 22 21 20 19 18   1 2 3 4 5

ISBN-13: 978-0-226-51076-7 (cloth)
ISBN-13: 978-0-226-51093-4 (paper)
ISBN-13: 978-0-226-51109-2 (e-book)
DOI: https://doi.org/10.7208/chicago/9780226511092.001.0001

Library of Congress Cataloging-in-Publication Data

Names: Comaroff, John L., 1945– editor. | Comaroff, Jean, editor.
Title: The politics of custom : chiefship, capital, and the state in contemporary
    Africa / edited by John L. Comaroff and Jean Comaroff.
Description: Chicago ; London : The University of Chicago Press, 2018. |
    Includes bibliographical references and index.
Identifiers: LCCN 2017031751 | ISBN 9780226510767 (cloth : alk. paper) |
    ISBN 9780226510934 (pbk. : alk. paper) | ISBN 9780226511092 (e-book)
Subjects: LCSH: Chiefdoms—Africa. | Africa—Politics and
    government—1960–
Classification: LCC GN492.55.P65 2018 | DDC 320.8096—dc23
LC record available at https://lccn.loc.gov/2017031751

CONTENTS

vi / Contents

EDITORIAL NOTE

How are we to explain the so-called resurgence of chiefs—or, more accurately, of indigenous sovereigns—in contemporary Africa, figures who were supposed to disappear with modernity but are a rising force in many places across the continent today? What are we to make of the increasingly assertive politics of custom, also long said to be losing its aura under the impact of Universal History? What might both of these things have to do with transformations in the state, with the workings of global political economy, with the changing social geography of the planet? These questions have pressed themselves forcibly, alike in Africa and way beyond, on scholars and social activists, on organic intellectuals and media commentators, in policy communities and digital publics. Together the contributions to this volume set out to address a counterintuitive chapter in the contemporary history of Africa, one that few mainstream social scientists would have anticipated—and to do so by locating it in world-making processes of the early twenty-first century.

A note here about translation, conceptual as well as lexical. Choosing the English terminology by which to name indigenous political offices in Africa is something of a challenge. Established usages—like chiefship or chieftaincy, traditional or customary authority—are reductively imprecise. Moreover, they carry weighty colonial baggage. For some black Africans, like Jongisilo Pokwana ka Menziwa, whom we cite in the introduction (see note 3) and who objects "to the kings [being referred to] as chiefs," they are also tinged with postcolonial racism. In many African polities, these titular offices are contained in an elaborate, more or less subtly structured lexicon; even where they are less elaborated, they do not map easily, without excess or deficit or distortion, onto conventional non-African labels. At the same time, those long known as chiefs or chieftains, traditional leaders or customary authorities, have tended to push for the continued use of these terms of address and reference, which have also entered the statute book in many countries—although in some, like South Africa, local rulers insist, wherever possible, on being called kings and queens, thus to assert their equivalence with monarchs of the global north.

Of course, as anthropologists have long noted, the "traditional" in "traditional authority" or "traditional leader" is equally problematic; so, too, is "custom," a concept notoriously disfigured by the semantics of colonial overrule. These terms, far from describing practices and institutions that have existed since time immemorial—as they are so often assumed to have done—are themselves born of modernity, marking out its ideological alterity, its "less developed" undersides. They cannot, in other words, be taken to have emerged in unalienated form from "native" discourse or practice. So-called traditional ways and means, as Hobsbawm and Ranger famously noted in *The Invention of Tradition* (1983), are *always* historically wrought phenomena, often ones of relatively recent vintage.

There is no easy resolution to the narrative issues that such terminological issues raise. So, for now, we continue, following common usage, to speak of chiefs and traditional authorities. But, in doing so, we seek to unsettle these signifiers, to emphasize that they are often contested—and do *not* necessarily mean what they did in the colonial past, either to indigenes or to colonizers. Or to anthropologists and historians. Nor do they describe a unity of form or substance in the calculus of late modern power. Patently, they have taken on different connotations by virtue of the historical processes that we shall be interrogating. We deploy them here strictly as vernacular terms of reference, never as analytic categories. At bottom, they delineate endogenous institutional frames *within* which legitimacy is managed, negotiated, and transformed—by means that are not simply ascribed by custom or by any other a priori. Like all political form(ul)ations, they are the labile creations of living history. And the peoples who make it.

JLC and JC
Cape Town and Cambridge, January 2017

ONE

Chiefs, Capital, and the State in Contemporary Africa

An Introduction

JOHN AND JEAN COMAROFF

Chieftaincy manifests itself in complex figurations . . . Each chiefly position [has] its own "grammaticality," even as we recognize that the institution has been considerably shaped by antagonistic forces . . . A new vision of the chief—global, modern, entrepreneurial—must be constructed . . . Chiefs [are] brokers of the present and the future.

—Adjaye and Misawa 2006

History often plays havoc with the certitudes of sociology. Recall the once confident prediction of many theorists of modernity, left and right, that chiefship and the customary in Africa would wither away with the rise of nationalism, democracy, and market economics? That cultural difference would recede in the face of universal advancement? That *"for the nation to live, the tribe must die"*?[1] Well, the future-then has proven obdurately otherwise in the here-and-now. So-called "traditional" offices, and the culturally distinctive species of authority they presume, continue to manifest themselves in a vibrant array of forms across the continent, coexisting in various ways—sometimes in collaboration, sometimes in contestation, sometimes in creative confusion, always in reciprocally transforming interplay—with dominant regimes of power, governance, knowledge, and capital accumulation in the late modern world.

The twenty-first century African sovereign comes in many guises. He may be a Sierra Leonean university lecturer who divides his time between his campus abode and his royal residence (chapter 6). As in parts of Ghana, he may be a professional with substantial venture capital in agriculture or mining (chapters 3, 10)—and/or an absentee landlord who lives, perhaps abroad, on rents extracted from patrimonial land that he treats as his own property. He could also be a "Nigerian chief . . . known to run huge businesses around the world and [to sit] on the boards of big companies."[2] Or, to cite a well-known South African example, he may rule as king over a platinum-rich realm *and* as the CEO of a large ethnocorporation—having been borne to his installation on a donkey cart, enrobed with a leopard skin, in a ritual staged by a major commercial events-planner (chapter 8; Comaroff and Comaroff 2009:112).

Elsewhere on the continent, he may be a migrant, an illiterate laborer, a subsistence farmer, a spirit medium, a school teacher, a lay preacher. Or a scholar, a medical doctor, a corporate lawyer. Or, like Olusegun Obasango of Nigeria, a retired national president. And, possibly, an un/common criminal, like, at the southern end of the continent, ex-King Buyelekhaya Dalindyebo of the AbaThembu, recently imprisoned for arson, assault, and homicide, *un*common because he, a former antiapartheid freedom fighter, claims—with the support of many vocal, local "traditionalists"—that the acts in question were committed under the sovereignty of custom.[3] If an indigenous ruler has long lived overseas, again as in Sierra Leone, he may be an "American chief," one believed by his people to have contacts who could be persuaded to contribute to their development. Nowadays, he also may be—increasingly *is* in some countries—a she. In fact, he may not be African at all but a former colonial officer, even, as in the case of Honorary Chief Tony Blair, an ex-British prime minister.

None of these personages is anything like the political figures described, classically, in *African Political Systems* (Fortes and Evans-Pritchard 1940), let alone in the large library of studies on chiefship published in its wake—although some features of the office detailed back then, like its structural position vis-à-vis the colonial state (e.g., Gluckman 1940a, 1940b; Busia 1951), *have* left palpable traces. As Jocelyn Alexander pithily puts it (chapter 5), "Chiefs are as varied as African states, in part because their fates are so often intimately linked . . . Chieftaincy seem[s] an extraordinarily flexible institution, never wholly of the state or of the customary but nonetheless always bound by them." Which, in turn, renders spurious an increasingly noisy debate—alike in the academy, in policy circles, and in the public media—over whether the institution is, endemically, a backward-looking, dangerous anachronism, a once noble, princely form of governance irrevocably disfigured by colonial misrule; or the authentic politicoethical embodiment of peoples with an inalienable right to their difference, their culturally validated collective will. As we shall see, it is all and none of these things, depending both on circumstance and on the angle of vision from which it is regarded.

Customary Authority in Africa

Appearances, Disappearances, Reappearances

It was not merely European social scientists who were certain that African traditional leadership was doomed to extinction. Almost a half century ago, in 1969, we encountered Kebalepile Montshiwa, chief of the Tshidi-Barolong, a Tswana polity centered at Mafeking (now Mahikeng), near the South Africa-Botswana border. A philosopher-king of sorts, the forty-ish royal was the scion of a dynasty with a venerable history: his great-grandfather, the famed Montshiwa I (1814–1896), had spent the second half of the nineteenth century dealing, skillfully if not always successfully, with Boer and British incursion (Molema 1966). Given to reflecting expansively on life under apartheid, Kebalepile was especially concerned with the political economy of the countryside, once the sovereign domain of rulers like himself. Under siege at the hands of the South African government, to which he had constantly to answer, his experience suggested to him that, six decades after the passing of his great-grandfather, *bogosi*—usually translated as "chiefship"—was finally in its death throes. Despite the claims of the British colonial and apartheid regimes to respect, recognize, and ratify "native law and custom," the office had been reduced to a shadow, a mere trace of its former self. To the degree that it survived at all, he opined, it did so in bureaucratic servitude to the purposes of the state and the industrial economy. Indeed, although he did not say so in so many words, it was the cooperation of local chiefs with the apartheid regime, willingly or under duress, that gave them such a bad name among many black South Africans, especially "young lions" committed to the struggle; Kate O'Regan (2016:111) writes of a seSotho song of liberation, *Nako e fedile, nako ya magosi* ("The time is over, the time of the chiefs"). She also recalls a statement by Chief Albert Luthuli (1962:200), African National Congress leader and Nobel Peace laureate, in which he said that the Bantu Authorities Act of 1951, a signature statute in the construction of "separate development" South African-style, "ma[de] our chiefs . . . into minor puppets and agents of the Big Dictator." Some years earlier, Govan Mbeki (1939:1, also pp. 6–7) had already spoken of their power as "vestigial," no more than an "eye-wash."[4]

A far cry, this, from Mahmood Mamdani's characterization, in *Citizen and Subject* (1996), of colonial chiefs as "decentralized despots," backed by white military might. Rather like Isaac Schapera's (1970:238) Bechuanaland *dikgosi*, some of them very powerful in the nineteenth century, who, he says, had been reduced by the 1940s to "subordinate government officers" (see Fokwang 2009:102). Or even more like Max Gluckman's (1940a; 1963:173) "intercalary" Zulu rulers, their sovereign authority "radically curtailed . . . and altered" by the late 1930s, caught haplessly between their imperial masters and their demanding subjects; this last an especially telling example, since Mamdani (1996) argues that apartheid in South Africa was the very apotheosis of colonialism—and therefore, by implication, should have epitomized his ideal typification of chiefship under European rule.[5] The internal mechanisms of Tswana democracy, which Kebalepile likened to the classical Greek *demos*—he was possessed of a lively historical sensibility—had been laid to waste, ossified.[6] In part, he asserted, this was the brute effect of overrule, in part a product of the sheer ignorance of white colonizers about how African political systems actually worked. And how they expressed the political philosophy of the peoples for whom, and by whom, they were designed. Not surprisingly, his perspective on those systems, heavily tinged with ethnostalgia and *noblesse oblige*, was unequivocally affirmative. Other, more critical black thinkers across the continent, back then as now, were much less favorably disposed toward chiefship, toward the kind of authority on which it was based and the forms of power it sanctioned (e.g., Molutsi 2004; Ntsebeza 2005; chapter 4, this volume)—although, for others, it always has had anti-imperial, counter-hegemonic potentialities precisely *because* it was seen to be founded on an/other species of sovereignty. But that story will emerge, in sharp relief, in the pages below.

Deeply depressed by the future he foresaw and forswore for his subjects, for his office, and for himself, Kebalepile died in 1971. Local legend has it that he was killed by witchcraft; this, allegedly, at the behest of Lucas Manyane Mangope, the soon-to-be president of the putatively independent ethnic "homeland" of Bophuthatswana, whose capital was built on Kebalepile's terrain. Mangope had been placed in his new position to rule over all the South African Tswana polities as proxy for the apartheid regime;[7] some, at the time, had it that he was "really" a paramount of sorts, a "decentralized despot" in fact, although the government insisted that he was not, that he was the head of a modern democratic state. In Kebalepile's view, though, his appointment had an even more thoroughgoing, sinister mandate: to do away forever with the legitimate authority of the chiefship in its "authentic" (adj., *nnete*, "real"; n., "reality, truth") customary form, leaving it "like an empty chair."[8] This image was his final epitaph for the office as he conceived of it. He was convinced that its end-time was close at hand all over Africa, albeit for different reasons in different places.

Kebalepile was not alone in his view. In 2000, the assembled kings and chiefs of South Africa walked out of a national conference on governance because, they declared, the ruling African National Congress (ANC), then under President Thabo Mbeki, had voided their sovereignty: the constitution of 1996 might have accorded them recognition, but, beyond minor perogatives provided for under statutory law, it gave them no real executive power. Quite the opposite. The Local Government Municipal Structures Act (no. 117) of 1999 had restricted them to the administration of customary law, communal land allocation, and various ceremonial activities; an amendment a year later, moreover, stipulated that they were expected to "carry out all orders given [them] . . . by competent authorities."[9] Said one of them to us, one of the most influential, most vocal: "Our history is finished. Chiefship is finished. We are just nothings." Their perception had real enough grounds. The mid-1990s, a period of deep ambivalence on the part of the ANC regime toward traditional leaders (see, e.g., Comaroff and Comaroff 2003:449; Oomen 2005:3 *et passim*), was taken by many observers to be "the nadir of [their] political legitimacy" (O'Regan 2016:112). It also rang like a coda to the script written in Europe many years before: the script according to which the ascent of rational-bureaucratic authority, under liberal democracy—the highest *political* expression of modernity—would eventually do away with all things customary, traditional, parochial, premodern. Or, if not, it would confine them within the narrow limits of tolerated cultural difference. Little wonder, then, that the country's leading cartoonist, Jonathan Shapiro (a.k.a. Zapiro) would portray a meeting, on 11 October 2000, between two traditional leaders and the Minister of Local Government, Sydney Mufamadi—whom they see as a creature from another planet, just landed in a spacecraft called "Democracy" and bearing a weaponized "power vaporizer"—in the following terms (figure 1):[10]

MUFAMADI (SAYS): *"We need to set a date . . . for local government elections."*
THE CHIEFS (HEAR): *". . . to destroy you and your culture. Do not resist."*

But appearances often their hide their obverse: phenomena taking shape, so to speak, in the interstices of the observable, just beyond the edges of public life; beyond, even, the peripheral vision of many of the South African chiefs themselves. Far from being an "empty chair," the office was already under reconstruction, being re(s)tooled, in South Africa and elsewhere on the continent, as a crucible for new forms of power, new deployments of the customary, new modes of accumulation—of which, it is clear in retrospect, "President" (Chief) Mangope had been one kind of foreshadowing; despite being a marionette-monarch, a colonial cipher, he had managed, alchemically almost, to turn *faux* political authority, *sans*

Figure 1. "Local Government Elections . . . As Seen by Traditional Leaders,"
cartoon by Zapiro (Jonathan Shapiro), *Sowetan*, 11 October 2000

any legitimacy, into various forms of hard capital (Lawrence and Manson 1994). Even before 2000, by the early 1990s in fact, it was becoming evident that African chiefship—and the customary, of which traditional authority is one element, albeit an iconic one—was a long way from "finished." Neither was it going to be confined, at the far edges of state power, to the prescribed terrain of tolerated cultural difference. Like other predictions of the end of history, this one was way off the mark.

Ever since *fin de siècle*, in sum, indigenous sovereigns across Africa—although unevenly and *not* everywhere, as Peter Geschiere shows (chapter 2, this volume; also chapters 3, 5, 6, 8, 10, 12)—have seen their fortunes grow, their authority consolidated by law, their political, cultural, economic, and moral capital accrete, their legitimacy and affective appeal enhanced, their hold over the customary and its forms of civility harden. In South Africa, again, where their powers have been incrementally redefined by statute, notably by the Traditional Leadership and Governance Framework Act (2003), the Communal Land Rights Act (2004), and the Traditional Courts Bill (2012), it has been argued that this has eventuated in a new era of chiefly despotism, resembling and extending the old order of things (e.g., Maloka and Gordon 1996; Ntsebeza 2005, 2011; LiPuma and Koelble 2009; Sibanda 2010:33; but cf., e.g., Oomen 2005; Williams 2010; Turner 2014; Krämer

2016).[11] Said Mamphela Ramphele of the Traditional Courts Bill, in a public address, "communities . . . are being held captive by chiefs . . . [W]elcome [back] apartheid in 2012" (cf. Ntsebeza 2005).[12] The point is echoed, and amplified, by Buthelezi and Skosana below (chapter 4). The passage of these statutes is often attributed to the capacity of traditional rulers to mobilize mass support, and votes, for the ANC (van Kessel and Oomen 1997; Murray 2004; du Preez 2013:179ff.; also chapter 3, this volume), persuading it to forego its earlier ambivalence toward those rulers, whose de facto following the ruling party had grossly underestimated. Another explanation lies in the claim (e.g., Crais 2006; see also Murray 2004:14) that, due to its administrative weakness, the postapartheid state eventually came to realize that it could not really do without chiefs to rule over "space[s] of ungovernance"; Lawson (n.d.:9) notes much the same thing for Africa at large.[13]

Both views have merit, if in different proportions, at different loci, under different conditions. But neither, in itself, is sufficient to account for the shifting, shifty sociology of South African—and, more generally, African—political life (chapters 2, 3, this volume). The highly labile character of chiefship in the history of the African present has complex, polyvalent determinations. They arise largely, as we shall see in detail below, out of the changing character of the global economy as it has worked its way into Africa, the political effects of which include the greater or lesser decentering of the state and the outsourcing of many of its functions; the deregulation of markets and, with it, the circumventing of national administrations by corporations, INGOs, and donor and development agencies; the pluralization of sovereignties, jurisdictions, and modes of legitimation; the privatization of public life and the empowerment of parochial authorities, communities, cultures, and identities; forces, these, that play out diversely in their encounter with microecologies of the local. It is into the spaces of possibility, the aporias of authority, opened up by such changes that indigenous rulers have pressed themselves, if in diverse ways and disparate measure. In so doing, in serving as a counter to state suzerainty, many of them have recommissioned the shards of the past to authorize new means and ends, to claim new rights and entitlements.

As this suggests, there is, on the surface of things, a bewildering degree of variance in the calculus of cause and effect surrounding the contemporary significance of chiefship in Africa. Wherever it is asserting itself, however, it is commonly portrayed in much the same way: as the *re*surgence, *re*vival, or *re*naissance of a mode of governance whose primal, generic form lies in the "customary"—which, from a Euromodernist perspective, occupies an irreducibly alien, immobile space-time. By some accounts, this "*re*surgence" is itself part of an *ur*-process increasingly dubbed "*re*traditionalization." Note the *idée (pre)fixe* here, the *re*ferential "*re*-." It points away from a linear history in favor of a different temporality, a *re*cursive one: a history of *re*petition and *re*production in which the past *re*turns in hyperbolic, intensified form. In this temporality, the sorts of sovereign power exercised in the ongoing present are at root the same as, and in direct genealogical continuity with, those of antecedent epochs; hence the adjectival recourse to the "traditional," an ideologically suspect term that, for all its apparent innocence, dehistoricizes as it essentializes, flattening out active world making into perpetual passivity (see above, p. viii). As an account of contemporary African chiefship, of its manifest emergence into the present, this talk of return, revival, resurgence is also rather too simple. It is, to be precise, a half truth—or a half of the truth—albeit an unusually illuminating one.

That half truth lies in the fact that, under colonialism, African chiefship embodied—literally, as in *The King's Two Bodies* (Kantorowicz 1957)—the very antithesis of the secular political theology on which the liberal democratic polity was founded. Or, at least it was *taken* to do so, given its association with the medieval, the feudal (cf. Smith, chapter 11, this volume); although, in fact, the doubling here resembled more closely what the medieval was to morph into, namely, "the distinction between person and office" (Kahn 2009:79; see also Lee 2016:251). In its presumptively feudal form, chiefship was, and has always remained, as Obarrio points out (chapter 12, this volume; see also above), the suppressed underside of modernity: as a form of political alterity—ever under imminent erasure, yet perpetually sustained as a sign of the uncivil African other[14]—it was a necessary element in the civilizing mission of empire. More pragmatically, the office was also an indispensable armature of colonial governance under in/direct rule; the two, direct and indirect, being "two faces of power" rather than readily distinguishable regimes of domination (Mamdani 1999:862; also chapter 2 below).[15] Consequently, customary authority, whatever its ebbs and flows across space and time—of which more in a moment—lived through the colonial epoch as if it had always been there, would always be there, always broadly the same even where/when it was obviously different. In sum, "it" was condensed into an ideal type of the sort that assimilated, into a single class of sovereigns, the likes of the Kabaka of Buganda, the Asantahene of Ashanti, the Zulu warrior kings, the heads of small polities in Central Africa, the divine monarchs of, among others, the Dogon, the Shilluk, and the Lovedu, and many other sorts of rulers besides. Hence the fact that, in *African Political Systems* (Fortes and Evans-Pritchard 1940; see above), written in the last decades of the Age of Empire, *all* forms of centralized indigenous polity, *all* forms of "customary authority," are categorized as one. And all African political life is reduced to the administration of order, devoid, ironically, of politics *sensu stricto*. From this perspective, given its conceptual infrastructure, the afterlife of that ideal type in the present day can therefore *only* be perceived as a historical continuity: as a *re*assertion of, a *re*turn to, what had always already been there, at once historically recursive and historically immanent. But now released from its colonial confines.

In short, this half truth is a product of the colonial imagination, one made (half) real, and observably concrete, by the practical mechanics of overrule. Some indigenous sovereigns deployed it—more or less deftly, at times despotically—in their dealings with both their subjects and their European masters; others were disempowered by it. To a greater or lesser degree, moreover, it colonized the consciousness of those over whom empire extended its dominion and its regimes of truth-knowledge (Comaroff and Comaroff 1989; Stoler and Cooper 1997); also much of the anthropology that was to document African political life under the long, gray shadow of colonialism. Both—anthropologists and those made to *re-cognize* themselves, as "natives" (Sartre 1963:*passim*)—came to naturalize the trope of "custom." And to valorize it, to bespeak its timeless ineffability, with scant attention to the conditions of its invention (Hobsbawm and Ranger 1983). But the other half of that truth situates the past of African chiefship: in a linear history no different in form, albeit quite different in content, from those of the global north, those given to denying Africa *its* endemic historicity. As several of the authors below note, most explicitly again Jocelyn Alexander (chapter 5), "[t]he 'return' of chiefs is a mirage, seemingly always sitting on the horizon. In fact, they never left. But their durability is *not* to do with staying the same" (our emphasis, and the emphasis of this volume as a whole). Quite the opposite.

The Historicity of the Past, Incomplete

It should go without saying, in this day and age, that the historicity of African political systems has *always* been more complex—always caught up in a counterpoint of continuity and transformation, of reproduction and structural change, of temporalities of disjunctive kinds—than is suggested by any form of binary ideal typification (see also chapter 2). After all, African history-as-discipline has accrued a large archive on the birth, rise, fall, and demise of precolonial states, including empires and kingdoms:[16] polities with hugely varying institutional interiors, more or less elaborate economies, judiciaries, militaries, and more or less extensive trade networks.[17] As cogently exemplified by Jan Vansina's (2005) history of the Nyiginya kingdom of Rwanda in the two centuries prior to the arrival of Europeans, those who established their hegemony over these states were often strikingly innovative in their elaboration of social, ritual, and economic forms, not to mention governmental practices. Often too, as in Rwanda, they laid down the lines of sociopolitical division that would later feed into patterns of colonial domination and its ethnosociological foundations—as well, sometimes tragically, as its violent postcolonial afterlife (Mosely 2016:30ff).[18] As Archie Mafeje (1971) long ago complained, such polities are hardly captured by the ideologically laden, Europrimitivist term "tribe." Some sustained themselves over the *longue durée* with high degrees of stability. Others, transformed either by their own internal workings or by the impact of external forces—or, more likely, by a combination of both (Comaroff 1982)—had shorter trajectories of growth, decline, and death. Or, if not decline and death, metamorphosis.

Like sovereignty everywhere, chiefship in Africa has, from the first, been subject to internal conflict and legitimation crises, to fluctuations in its capacity to condense power over persons and place and property, to the vicissitudes of relations with worlds outside. And, from the first, it has had to harness technologies of violence and superintend its sources of material and spiritual potency. It has also had to stave off rebellion, subversion, conquest, entropy, popular disapproval (e.g., Ayittey 1991:135ff.; Osabu-Kle 2000:18): while succession to office was, more often than not, governed by birthright, everyday *real*politik frequently eventuated in bitter struggles for sovereign authority.[19] What is more, exercise of that authority, despite preconceptions to the contrary, was never simply determined by the fixity of custom or the functional necessity of social order. High office was, in most places at most times, the *axis mundi* of dynamic *political* fields: of rivalries over rank and resources and ancestral beneficence, of exertions to sustain hegemony over territory, trade, and tribute, and, above all, of efforts to accumulate "wealth in people" (Gluckman 1941; Little 1951; Fallers 1964),[20] in their productive and reproductive capacities.

Notwithstanding the reduction of African chiefship, in the colonial imaginary, to the timelessness of tribe and tradition—to the "convenient fiction . . . of custom" (Pratt 1965:489)—its historicity during the Age of Empire was no less complex or contested, no less Gordian in its knotted trajectories, than it had been during the *longue durée* of the precolonial. For one thing, as Africanist scholars have often noted (e.g., Tosh 1973; Gartrell 1983), previously acephalous societies, "tribes without rulers" (Middleton and Tait 1958), had chiefs appointed for them by European administrations with little understanding of their political orders (see, e.g., Afigbo

1972; Dorward 1969; Beidelman 1978); in some cases of cultural mis-recognition, they had religious figures recast and ratified as secular rulers (e.g., Snyder 1982). In these situations, patently, chiefship had its genesis not in the vernacular at all but in colonialism itself—whence, also, came its legitimacy, its presumptive cultural trappings, and its political mandate. But this, the invention of chiefship *ab initio*, is the extreme instance, the null point, of a history made exogenously, projected back into mythic time, and then clothed in the "fiction of custom." Where indigenous political office already *did* exist, in all its manifold forms, the story of the colonial encounter is even more complicated.

This is not the place to tell that story, although several of the chapters below dip into the past for purposes of illuminating the present. One or two synoptic points are to be made here, however, since they will be salient as we proceed. We have already alluded to Mamdani's (highly influential, variously criticized) ideal typification of colonial chiefs as decentralized despots—and, by stark contrast, their depiction by Luthuli, Mbeki, Schapera, and Gluckman as lowly government officers, puppets really, with radically curtailed powers. In fact, neither extreme, despot or puppet, describes African chiefship, *sui generis*, under colonialism. But neither is entirely fanciful or empirically ungrounded. Each points to a partial reality, partial at once in space *and* over time. As any number of historical ethnographies show,[21] they represent end points along a continuum—immanent possibilities, that is, but rarely realized in full. Most actually existing rulers, and the actually existing offices they occupied across colonial Africa, fell somewhere in between. What is more, all alike were *moving* points on that continuum: by virtue of historical conditions—some of them exogenous, others endogenous—the magnitude of their sovereign power rose and fell, fell and rose, with varying rapidity, over the medium and long run, although *not* in the mechanistic sort of oscillating equilibrium that Edmund Leach (1954) famously described for Highland Burma.

Colonial African chiefs, in other words, were embedded in polities whose internal dynamics, indirect rule notwithstanding, determined their legitimacy to a greater or lesser degree. Sometimes by appropriating and repurposing colonial authority (see, e.g., Kuper 1970a, 1970b), sometimes by exploiting the flow of colonial capital and labor (e.g., Mbenga and Manson 2010), sometimes by maneuvering under its radar (e.g., Comaroff 1974), a number of them succeeded in accumulating and retaining fairly substantial power. Others ended up being deposed, if not by their demanding European masters, which occurred often enough—Joan Vincent (1994:280) speaks of a "rapid turnover of colonial chiefs" in, for example, Uganda—

then by their own subjects. In this latter instance it was frequently for failing to meet the vernacular requirements of good government[22] in the transformed historical circumstances of the time, with whose domestic effects they were expected to deal. If not that, then it was typically for ruling autocratically, a tendency which, in many contexts, sparked the emergence of rival factions against them. As in the past (above, p.10), succession to and incumbency of high office was decided relatively rarely by the simple application of the genealogical rules that colonial administrators, historians, and some anthropologists presumed to be "traditional" (see note 6, this chapter).

Take, again, the example of the Tswana peoples in southern Africa, the part of the continent we know best. These peoples shared a cultural universe and, broadly speaking, both a political theology and a jurisprudence. At the time of overrule in the closing decades of the nineteenth century, they were caught up in intense political turbulence, which expressed itself in recurrent succession struggles over chiefship. These struggles were exacerbated by a number of contingent conditions: among them, hostile relations with white settlers; struggles over land; and the effects of labor migration, trade competition, and other economic forces set in motion by the mineral revolution in the nearby diamond and gold fields of South Africa. All of these things fused uneasily into an entangled mess of cause and effect. As we have already intimated, a few of their sixty or so chiefs exploited these conditions to consolidate their authority—and were relatively successful in holding at bay the colonial administrations of British Bechuanaland, the Bechuanaland Protectorate, and South Africa; also in siphoning off exogenous political and material resources to their own ends. Others, particularly in South Africa, found themselves reduced to a shadow, an "empty chair"—recall Kebalepile's metaphorical lament here—if they remained in office at all. Their subjects tended to disperse, taking up residence alongside their agricultural holdings, much like an acephalous peasantry, administered by a ruler-in-little-but-name. Or, like those black South Africans so memorably documented in Colin Bundy's *The Rise and Fall of the South African Peasantry* (1979), they disappeared into the agrarian proletariat of the settler economy—all the more so after the passage of the Natives Land Act (1913), whose bitter harvest is poignantly recorded by Solomon Tshekisho Plaatje, a Tswana intellectual and organic ethnographer, in his *Native Life in South Africa* (n.d.).[23]

The point? That the fate of chiefship under colonialism, falling as it did along that moving continuum, was not simply determined by European administrations that, all alike, transformed dynamic precolonial political

systems into a monochromatic ideal type; a deformation, that is, of Weber's ([1922] 1978:215–16, 226ff.) "traditional authority" (a.k.a. "domination"), classically defined by its immutability, by the "sanctity of age-old
rules and powers" (p. 226). As we ourselves saw at first hand during the
middle years of apartheid—recall, according to Mamdani (1996; above,
p. 4), the very apotheosis of colonialism—endogenous political processes
were never entirely extirpated, or immobilized, under the impact of in/
direct rule. Not even at its most oppressive, nor even when those processes
were explicitly outlawed. The history of high office across the continent
was motivated in part by the agency of indigenous actors and institutions,
in part by the complex, colonially inflected force fields in and on which
they acted, in part by the brute, racialized lineaments of colonial capitalism. Which is why there are such obvious disparities in the chronicles of
chiefship across the polities of Africa, past and present, disparities that
also, as we shall see in the chapters below, are having a manifest impact in
the early twenty-first century.

But one thing *is* common to them all. The *imagined* past of African sovereigns, as congealed in the mythical charter of "traditional authority,"
has become, for those who reign today, an inalienable, highly productive
resource—indeed, even a form of monopoly capital. It is precisely *because*
chiefship retained its place in the colonial scheme of things by virtue of
being the suppressed underside of modernity, its negative supplement—
i.e., the literal embodiment, in perpetuity, of culture, the customary, and
difference—that it continues to have purchase. The eroding hegemony of
the liberal modernist nation-state, after all, has occasioned the return of
the suppressed, renegotiating, in the political theology of the present, the
relationship between margin and mainstream, the established and the
other. Ours, it seems, is an age that essentializes and valorizes identity,
above all racialized cultural identity: an age in which the right to that difference is both legally (if unevenly) protected and convertible (if unevenly)
into im/material property. It is this as much as anything else that has underwritten the "resurgence" of African chiefship, its presence in the present,
when it is at once the same thing it has always been and yet radically different. This and the politico-ideological infrastructure of the post–Cold War
global economy.

Customizing the Present

And so into that present. Let us pick up again on the two halves of the
truth that configure the accounts we have of contemporary African chief-

ship: of the chapter in its history, that is, that began sometime in the early 1990s or just before. The one half truth, recall, narrates it in the language of continuity, cyclicity, and reproduction, of the timeless past returned; the other situates it in linear historical time, in trajectory, transformation, and agency. This doubling is critical. On one hand, in asserting themselves as a rising force in the twenty-first century, many indigenous rulers borrow heavily from the lexicon of the eternal-customary, the transcendant ancestral, the ethnocultural, the "sanctity of age-old rules and powers." What is more, in referring itself back in time, their newfound legitimacy seeks to reclaim, and recommission, the residues of political capital past. Yet, on the other hand, as we began to note earlier, that legitimacy derives—in different degrees in different places—from sources utterly un-"traditional," sources quite different from those of yesteryear: among other things, from their capacity to serve as nodal points in the development industry between their constituencies and donors, venture capital, NGOs, and other "stakeholders"; to transform their trusteeship over territory into proprietorship, itself a refiguring of "the customary," in order to elicit rents from extractive industries, agribusiness, and even their own subjects (e.g., chapters 10, 11); to capture the value that is accruing, in many places, from the commodification of culture, its reduction into intellectual property (e.g., chapter 9); to claim the entitlements owed to their peoples by virtue of their constitutionally recognized difference; to insinuate themselves into changing forms of labor mobilization and/or the delivery of social grants and services (e.g., chapters 3, 8, 11); to act as foci of political mobilization either in collaboration with, or against, the state—or, conversely, for the state in its dealings with its citizens (e.g., chapters 4–7); to deliver electoral votes and enforce civil discipline (chapters 2, 3); and to mediate between competing religious faiths and their adherents (Nolte n.d.), between sacred legacies and the secular realities of the present (chapter 12).

These sources of legitimacy, as we outlined above, owe their animating force to a new moment in the ongoing history of the global economy, itself first made manifest in the structural adjustment programs that were coercively exported to Africa under the so-called "Washington consensus." That consensus, which was never truly consensual for those on whom it was imposed, did more than merely proclaim the primacy of the market over the state, more than just call for the privatization of many of the functions of government, more than insist on deregulation, decentralization, and the rule of law. It also demanded the delegation of responsibility for public affairs to the "local" (i.e., to "the community"), pushed hard for a culture of rights, and created the conditions for the devolution of sovereignty away from national regimes to those who would claim it in the name of culture, identity, religion, and the like. Put all these things together, and it becomes plain why and how chiefs—constitutive embodiments of cultural difference, of ancestral empowerment, of customary law—would be capacitated by them: why and how development and donor agencies, NGOs, and international corporations would find them the sorts of collaborating partners with whom they could do business in the new age of the market, why and how this might, in turn, reground their legitimacy and empower them in relation to their subjects. It is little wonder, too, that, in the circumstances, so many of them have stressed their alterity against the state: in an increasingly *poli*cultural age, an anti-*etatist* age, claims to the recognition of difference are also claims to political sovereignty (Comaroff and Comaroff 2003). Which is why so many are insisting on being seen as monarchs with "judicial immunity,"[24] not as chiefs subject to any higher authority (e.g., chapters 7, 8). And why so many African governments continue to struggle, amidst deep ambivalence, in deciding how best to deal with them and their appeal to the sanctity of custom (Logan 2008:5).

Clearly, the repositioning of indigenous rulers has created fresh sources of value for them; even more, it has afforded them a supple form of rentier capital that neither modernization nor Marxist theorists could ever have foreseen for Africa. But it has also done something else. It has (re?)affirmed the ethicoaffective centrality of the office in a world of political flux by tying the history of the present and its futures—imaginatively, if nothing else—to a known, recognizable past. Which is ironic, since, some would argue, African chiefship has, in many places, become a wholly owned subsidiary of neoliberal governance *sui generis* (e.g., chapter 12). Or, if not that, its willing broker. Recently, in June 2016, the *Washington Post* ran a story under the title "Unelected African Chiefs Make their Countries More Democratic,"[25] a contention that several scholars have contested by questioning whether customary authority and democracy can coexist at all (e.g., Molutsi 2004; Ntsebeza 2005; Logan 2008). Its author, Kate Baldwin, focusing primarily on Zambia but extending her analysis to the continent at large, makes her case by seeking to demonstrate that traditional rulers regularly "lobby for government projects" on behalf of their communities, for which they are well situated to serve as effective, and affective, representatives (cf. Williams 2004). They, more than any elected politicians, she says, are closely tied to their constituencies, have the means to discipline them, and enjoy the necessary mandate to act as their agents (see also Keulder 1998:11). But as important, Baldwin argues, indigenous authorities have been able to create this role for themselves because "most African [states] are weak," itself, in part, a corollary of the effects of structural adjustment. Whether or not chiefs today enjoy quite the measure of popular legitimacy sometimes attributed to them is open to question. As West and Kloeck-Jenson (1999:475–76) note for Mozambique—they could have made their claim more broadly—many, being no longer in any meaningful sense "traditional," are simultaneously respected and suspected by their subjects, although this does not necessarily diminish the power that a good number of them have managed to condense in their offices. Others, as Coyle (chapter 10) and Smith (chapter 11) show, are unambiguously opposed, even violently so.

Kebalepile would have been surprised at what has happened. So, we might assume, would Max Weber. Mahmood Mamdani (1996) may be as well. To his credit, Mamdani foresaw that traditional authority *would* live on after colonialism. But he thought that, in politically "conservative" African states, it would sustain itself as "decentralized despotism" while, in "radical" ones, it would be absorbed into "centralized despotism." As it has turned out, things have taken a different turn, both within and beyond nation-states—this, for all the reasons just given, because the present and future history of chiefship is not being scripted merely by gross differences between political regimes. It is being shaped by forces that lie as much in the morphing domains of economy and ecology, technology and theology, constitutional law and culture, sovereignty and property, as in ideologies of governance or the practices of official power.

Wherever African rulers have harnessed those forces, there have followed very real consequences, many of them far from positive, for the everyday lives of millions of people: for women whose equality is denied them and whose rights are restricted by chiefly patriarchy (see, e.g., on Uganda, Tripp 2001); for families that find themselves immiserated as their leaders cede their land to corporations, agribusiness, and/or foreign governments (chapters 10, 11); for ordinary citizens whose livelihoods are put at risk when they are denied official permission to move in search of jobs or to enter into trade; for those who oppose their chiefs or voice critique of their rule; for gays and lesbians who suffer violence under the sign of culture. Quite the opposite, however, for those who have capitalized on the re- or neovalorization of the customary, thus to create new sources of identity, income, or empowerment; for those alienated from an ever more remote state, one that "no longer knows them," indeed, renders them faceless by the exercise of its biopower; and for those who see little by way of sociality or moral order for themselves beyond the confines of the local. For all of these fractions of national populations, "customary" sovereignty has potent affective, spiritual, political, and material appeal. This is yet more so in places where that sovereignty is seen, positively, as an uncaptured, nonstate form of legitimate authority (see, e.g., chapters 6, 7, 12; Lawson n.d.:10)—even as a form of authority *superior* to that of the state, one that may be appealed to, and mobilized, in opposition to government and its modes of domination (see chapter 7).

But this is to talk in generalities. What of the microphysics of chiefly power, of its im/materialities, across the continent today? Exactly where is it asserting itself anew, and where not? Under what conditions? In what guises? With what effects? By what means? With what connections to the mythicohistorical past? With what relationship to the state and its sovereignty? To the global economy? And to so-called "neoliberal governance"? Let us turn, then, to the studies collected in this volume, to the problems and provocations they address. In so doing, we seek to tease out of their rich empirical archive a series of conceptual and theoretical arguments that together might inform a critical reading of the politics of custom—of chiefship, capital, and the state—in contemporary Africa.

On the Microphysics of Customary Authority

Peter Geschiere (chapter 2) begins his masterly overview of the topic, the most embracing and comparative of the contributions to the volume, with the ground-clearing reminder that the "surprising" assertiveness of chiefship since the 1990s is *not* to be read as a replay of the past. It is better described, he says, as "*neo*traditional," a creolized mix of elements at once ostensibly old and audaciously innovative; innovative above all, one might add, by refashioning the *content* of "the customary" in the very act of recommissioning it as the putatively immutable basis for the contemporary exercise of sovereign authority. To be sure, what some indigenous rulers construe these days as "traditional"—in respect, for example, of land rights and tributary extraction—bears little resemblance to practices recorded by ethnographers sixty or eighty years ago.[26] Geschiere goes on to note that while the "rebound" of chiefship in the "post–Cold War moment" (Piot 2010) has been cued by the growing privatization of the state, the devolution of public assets, and, consequently, the pluralization of power, it is by no means ubiquitous. Neither is it predictable in form or in function. Which suggests that the task of rethinking its theoretical parameters ought to begin with the questions: Why now? Why here, in this place and not another?

To answer those questions—and each chapter below addresses them in one or another way—Geschiere argues, as we have done, that it is necessary to move beyond the ideal-typical models that have long primed our conception of chiefly legitimacy: those that arise from the opposition between, for instance, primordial communities and civic publics, or between genealogically ascriptive and democratically elective office—and, by implication, between "traditional" societies caught up in cyclical, reproductive time and "modern" ones living through linear, teleological time. Nonetheless, he notes, while the terms that classically describe chiefship may misconstrue the political sociology of the African past, they remain highly significant. This may seem flatly paradoxical, but it is not at all. The dualisms in which these terms are embedded, and the temporalities they presume, constitute an *ideological* grammar of difference that undergirds all claims to customary authority today. Recall the point we made earlier: that the half truth told of the precolonial and colonial epochs—i.e., that traditional office was founded on the suprahistorical "sanctity of age-old rules and powers"— lives on in the African twenty-first century, an era in which ethnocultural difference has become an inalienable basis of identity and entitlement. To the degree that chiefship is the apotheosis of that difference, its metonymic embodiment so to speak, its legitimacy is, at least in principle, warranted in perpetuity. Which, to close the circle—power always has an element of self-referential tautology—mandates the right of officeholders to authorize the very customary practices that empower them. Thus, also, does the past manifest itself in the present as a potent residue, and as a repository, of fungible political capital.

In situating the origins of the contemporary "moment" in the 1990s— and here he rehearses further some of the implications of structural adjustment that we have spelled out—Geschiere emphasizes the degree to which decentralization has become synonymous with development. Where parochial attachments had formerly been suppressed in the interest of nation building, the dispersal of the functions of governance has encouraged a multiplication of the bases of belonging everywhere (Geschiere 2009). Not only has this energized the play of competing social and political affiliations beyond the state, a process in which chiefs are well placed to assume a catalyzing role; it has also meant taking what was once inter*national* aid, now rephrased in the entrepreneurial language of social investment, directly to "the local." Which, in turn, necessitates the identification of viable target communities, often in contexts in which populations are anything but clearly bounded or neatly defined; "community" being a chimera whose existence in the imagination far exceeds its sedimentation "on the ground." It also is taken to depend on recognizing authorities with time-honored rights to represent bona fide ethnic groups bound together in the sanctity of ancestrally sanctioned custom—authorities, moreover, who might serve as legitimate conduits for economic inputs, social programs, and, in appropriate contexts, corporate ventures (see chapters 8–11).

As Sarah Berry (chapter 3) and Mariane Ferme (chapter 6) observe, many chiefs have responded by vying to become brokers of just these sorts of resources, deploying what cultural capital they can muster from their political offices in the effort to attract local followers. And, of course, rents of various kinds. In this, they have been abetted not just by mining companies, agribusiness, and the like, but also by agencies—among them the World Bank—that seek to build "partnerships with traditional authorities" so as to promote (what they take to be) cohesion, collective action, and human capital among indigenous peoples (Woolcock 1998; Grischow 2008). Herein lies the beginnings of an answer to the questions "Why now? Why here?" Anticipated by our discussion above, that answer appears to depend on a triangulation of three axes: (1) the relative capacity of rulers to mobilize the customary as a fungible political resource in order to control flows of wealth in tangible assets, territory, and people; (2) the devolution of the functions of state and, with it, the dispersal of resources, especially where it is accompanied by an active corporate and NGO presence; and (3) the sedimentation of "local" communities of engagement around an indigenous authority, positioned to claim recognition and rights—material, social, spiritual, territorial—by virtue of inalienable cultural difference. In the measure that these things manifest themselves *together*, the "resurgence" of chiefship appears likely. Again, not everywhere, but in many places. As importantly, it may be *because* these three axes covary so widely that the predicament of customary authority in late modern Africa is at once so visible yet so variable.

The Economic Geography of Chiefly Power

Taking this a critical step further, Sara Berry (chapter 3) argues that the diverse degrees to which, and ways in which, traditional rulers are asserting themselves in sub-Saharan Africa depends largely on economic geography: specifically, on physical location and relative capacity to exert control over land and other resources—itself, in part, a function of historical positioning among various actors, all seeking to leverage the means of accumulation. Although she stresses the role of material forces in determining differences of wealth and power in local communities, communities long drawn into the wider orbit of colonial market relations, Berry cautions against facile connections between the "return" of chiefship and the rise of neoliberalism. Or between liberalization and democratization on one hand and assertions of cultural identity on the other. It is crucial in this regard, she adds, to interrogate the complex, multiply mediated processes, deeply tied to the pluralization of sovereignty, through which deregulation has opened up new arenas of contestation over territory, mobile assets, and political influence; and also, of course, over the very nature of property itself.

Berry addresses these complexities by comparing Ghana and South Africa. In both, traditional leaders have been accorded a prominent role in political and economic affairs. But, despite similarities in the legacy of colonialism and the impact of globalization, there are striking differences between them. Ghanaian chiefs hold sway over 70–80 percent of the land in the country and tend to wield power informally, using their private wealth and personal patronage for these purposes. By contrast, those in South Africa lost control over the bulk of productive real estate during colonial times. While they retain some jurisdiction over at least one-third of the country's population, they oversee less than 15 percent of its terrain, much of it relatively depleted. There are some exceptions of course, among them those—like the king of the platinum-rich Royal Bafokeng Nation (chapter 8)—who have entered the rarified universe of corporate ethnicity at its high end. Most, however, are not nearly as fortunate.

In the event, the South African chiefs, unlike their Ghanaian counterparts, have striven ceaselessly, and fairly successfully, to win legislative recognition for their administrative, judicial, and ritual authority, thus to interpolate themselves between government and their subjects. And, not incidentally, to have themselves well remunerated by the national treasury. Some—most notably the Zulu king Goodwill Zwelithini, discussed at length below by Buthelezi and Skosana—have consolidated a great deal of power in themselves, both instrumental and affective. Thus, for example, when Zwelithini commented publicly in 2015 that foreigners should be made to depart South Africa, a wave of lethal violence was unleashed (see chapter 4).[27] Less than a year before, he had announced that he was preparing a land claim—the terrain in question was said to have untapped mineral resources beneath it—that would restitute most of the province of KwaZulu-Natal to his dominion,[28] an optimistic initiative soon followed by other indigenous rulers.[29] Not all of the latter have managed to empower themselves to nearly the same degree, though; internal legitimation processes, conducted under the sign of good government, continue to affect the standing of officeholders everywhere. Nonetheless, given the deep popular emotion invested in the *office*, a fact vividly underscored by the collective effervescence surrounding the installation of a new amaXhosa king in 2015,[30] it is no wonder that the ruling ANC sees customary authorities as consequential "voter banks" (chapter 2). Or that, in return for party loyalty, it cedes to them a considerable measure of sovereign authority.

The upshot? That, where fertile land, mobile assets, and wage work are scarce, chiefs may yet build a niche for themselves as state-sanctioned gatekeepers in divers processes of certification: certification of the sort needed by their subjects to engage in licensed commerce; certification that allows access to local civil courts; certification of eligibility for social services on which so many depend for survival these days. Certification in this context, we might add, not only "authorizes the authorizers" (Sikor and Lund 2009:2). Nor does it merely yield a form of capital that may be converted into different value-yielding currencies. It also laminates the rational-legal legitimacy of modernist rule onto the customary legitimacy of chiefship, thus to "make way for a new political culture."[31] Here we see a creolization in practice—a dialectical synthesis, really—of ideal types of power; just the sort of which Geschiere speaks (chapter 2), just the sort whose performative mechanics Obarrio describes for Mozambique (chapter 12), where the pedestrian activities of local administration are spiritually endorsed by rituals of the "invisible" state.

For Berry herself, then, chiefly authority is to be understood neither as an alternative to, nor as an adjunct of, state power. It is an amalgam of both, a point made as well by Alexander (chapter 5) and Smith (chapter 11). Parenthetically, though, there *are* contexts in which it is less state power per se than brute economics that underlies the lamination of different species of legitimacy on one another. This is typified, especially, by situations in which traditional leaders are positioned to take control of proprietary rights over heritage as intellectual property, a form of "ethnoprise," of the commodification of culture, that tends to reproduce, indeed intensify, attachments to the customary. Depending on its scale, this process of commodification, like the corporate ethnicity of the Bafokeng mentioned a moment ago, may also empower chiefs politically in relation *both* to their subjects and to the state.[32] But it does so, in the first instance, through engagement with thoroughly contemporary market forces of exactly the sort that were classically held to threaten the aura of "premodern" cultural authenticity (Comaroff and Comaroff 2009).

The more general point, however, is this: in insisting on the foundational significance of economic geography in shaping contemporary African chiefship, Berry adds a significant dimension to the triangulation of axes with which we began to answer the questions "Why now? Why here?"

For it adds to the first of those axes—the capacity of chiefs to mobilize the customary as political capital—two critical qualifications. One is ecological: the sorts of resources, especially landed resources, that history has bequeathed those chiefs. The other is bureaucratic: the degree to which they may interpolate themselves directly into the operations of state by seizing its gatekeeping functions, thus transmuting an ostensibly administrative role into a political resource. Both of these qualifications are significant. They will reappear a number of times as we proceed.

Anachronizing the Present, Imperfect

Mbongiseni Buthelezi and Dineo Skosana (chapter 4) amplify Berry's analysis in a number of telling ways, although they start out from a very different point: by stressing that the transformative effects of neoliberalization may actually mask significant *continuities* in the ways in which African states have dealt with the customary. This, they suggest, is exemplified by South Africa. Because of its belated end to minority rule, many thought that the country might avoid the problem of reconciling chiefship with democracy by simply doing away with traditional authorities altogether. Since then, however, the clamor of those authorities for sovereign recognition has resonated with affectively laden calls for the return of "authentic" African modes of governance, jurisprudence, and lifeways. These calls, moreover, reach well beyond the realm of the rural, well beyond the kingdom of custom, well into urban black publics and the national electorate.

In the face of all this, Buthelezi and Skosana note, the postapartheid administration has struggled, largely in vain, to impose legislative order on a strikingly resilient institution by seeking *both* to regulate and to accommodate it. To somewhat contrarian effect. Speaking at the recent installation of the amaXhosa king (above, p. 21)—at which his presence *ex officio* was itself worthy of remark—state president Jacob Zuma proclaimed: "This coronation is also a celebration of our constitution . . . [which] provides for the recognition of traditional leadership. Today we can confirm that traditional leadership can coexist with democratic government. We view the coronation . . . as a celebration of our African identity, heritage, dignity and pride."[33] For Zuma himself, this reflected a telling inversion: the inflection of his *presidential* office, and his own political persona, with the customary; just the sort of dialectical synthesis, the manifest creolization, to which several of our chapters gesture, except from the side of state power. As a polygamous head of a liberal modernist polity, he has played heavily on "tradition" to secure his ethnically inflected base, and his populist legitimacy, in national party politics—on whose public stage he has often presented himself as a machine gun-wielding freedom fighter with a penchant for Zulu dance moves. He also relied on the customary in his criminal trial for rape in 2006, in which he insisted on testifying in isiZulu as he argued a cultural defense deeply rooted in Western constitutional jurisprudence.

By virtue of what it did *not* say, however, Jacob Zuma's amaXhosa coronation speech pointed to a lacuna at the very heart of the postapartheid dispensation: that, while South Africa's capacious bill of rights endorses both customary and democratic forms of governance, it does not address the contradictions between the principles on which, respectively, each is founded. These contradictions, long debated by critical scholars, public intellectuals, and political activists, motivate the story at the core of Buthelezi and Skosana's chapter: the deliberations of a Commission on Traditional Leadership Disputes and Claims, a.k.a. the Nhlapo Commission. Created in 2003, it was tasked with defining the functions of traditional leaders, with laying down guidelines for their recognition, and with adjudicating the competing claims to office that were proliferating wildly across the country at the time.

Rather than cleanse the Kingdom of Custom of its apartheid past, or rethink it for late modern times, the Nhlapo Commission, as Buthelezi and Skosana make plain, more or less replicated the procedures of the Bantu Affairs Department of old. Above all, it applied an inflexible, ahistoric conception of traditional authority, and of the genealogical rules held to govern it, thereby reanimating the colonial mythos of "ascriptive" chiefly legitimacy. With unintended consequences: the ratification of a claim to office by the commission appears to have emboldened royals to behave all the more autocratically. And, in the best tradition of neoliberal politics in the global north, to privatize public assets. It also emboldened them to act as if they are unaccountable to their subjects. In the case of King Goodwill, whom we encountered a few pages back, his endorsement as paramount ruler of KwaZulu-Natal made him into a constitutional monarch—an odd anomaly, this, in the deep interior of a liberal democratic national polity—and reinforced his belief that he has no obligation to answer to any superior authority either.

In short, Nhlapo et al. have reproduced the half truth on which customary authority, as a living anachronism, has been projected into the present across much of the continent. Even more, they have subverted, indeed largely erased, endogenous procedures regulating succession to, and incumbency of, high office: by failing to observe the clear vernacular distinction long drawn between chief and chiefship, office and holder (e.g., Comaroff

1974, 1978; Oomen 2005; Turner 2014; see chapter 8, this volume), they have rendered null the principles of popular accountability—the very civic democracy whose earlier demise Kebalepile so regretted. There is a major irony in this. Here is a situation in which an instrument of governance put in place by a liberal modernist state has de-democratized, by fiat, the (allegedly antidemocratic) Kingdom of Custom, thus to put its rulers in a position of latent autocracy. In so doing, in fact, the commission contradicted the landmark Constitutional Court decision in 2008, *Shilubana and Others v. Nwamitwa* (2009 [2] SA 66 [CC]), which ratified the right of indigenous political communities to s/elect chiefs according to their own cultural practices; also, to alter their rules of accession to office in response to the collective will. Nhlapo et al., it seems, created the conditions for decentralized despotism where it had only existed very unevenly, very tenuously before.

And so South Africa remains haunted by the ambiguous presence of a veritable army of chiefs and kings. By leaving intact the mythic antinomy between liberal modernist governance and indigenous authority—and by failing to address the dynamics *separating and linking* them—the commission opened up a yawning aporia in which ambitious local rulers have taken to remaking the customary in their own thoroughly contemporary image. Hence their efforts to lay proprietary claim to much of the landmass of the country. And to seize control of the commonweal of their polities, of their bureaucratic and judicial structures, of their corporate and other public assets; all this in the name of a neoliberalized, commodified "tradition" located in the new economic geography of South Africa, of Africa, and of the post-1990s global order at large. Buthelezi and Skosana's chapter, in other words, offers a cogent illustration of the general thrust of this volume: that, where the economic, political, and legal conditions for it are felicitous—*vide* our triangulated axes above—chiefship and the customary are being remade, alike substantially and substantively, in a complex counterpoint, a dialectical synthesis, of partial truths, powerful mythologies, and creolized practices born in the interstices of the past and the present.

Remade, patently, in a wide variety of ways.

Regrounding the Past, Parsing the Present

Jocelyn Alexander (chapter 5) ascribes that variance, in major part, to the protean diversity of African states, the impact of which has itself been mediated by the afterlife of colonialism. For her, the misnamed "return" of traditional authority is directly imbricated not just in unfolding struggles over resources, rights, and (especially) institution making, but in the justification of claims that legitimize those struggles. In Zimbabwe, the relationship of chiefship to the state and its operations has undergone a series of transformations. The former, chiefship, is, as she puts it, "an extraordinarily flexible institution," its politics "prickly and plastic"; it is, recall, "never wholly of the state or the customary, but . . . always bound by them" (above, p. 2). This is because, while pursuing their own ambitions, local rulers have also had perennially to respond to *both* the demands of their subjects and the imperatives of the ruling party, to its ideological orientations, its electoral strategies, its internal bureaucratic divisions. And, above all, to its deep ambivalence toward things traditional. As this suggests, for Alexander, the mutations of that "flexible institution" tend to be politically determined. But here, as elsewhere, she intimates political determinations are themselves laced through with economic cross-currents.

The latest chapter of Zimbabwean history, unfolding in the wake of the in/famous "fast track" redistribution of white-owned farmland, has seen the remaking of state institutions and administrative authority—and, with it, the cartography of governance, including "the space[s] in which chiefs work." As a result, local rulers have had to modify the application of the customary in consonance with shifts in power relations: relations that have inserted veterans of the liberation struggle, and committee structures put in place by ZANU(PF), at the hub of life in the countryside. This has made for the popular perception that chiefs only hold sway to the degree that they play into the partisan ends of government. Alexander, however, suggests that something rather more complex, more nuanced, has actually occurred. Some rulers, she says, have cooperated enthusiastically with the party; others have done so out of fear of violence or of losing the benefits of office. But, by capitalizing on the uncertainties surrounding their institutional role in rural governance, a number have succeeded in solidifying the claims of traditional authority *sui generis*, this not least by protesting their exclusion from the distribution of wealth yielded by local extractive industries. A few have managed, if ephemerally and unevenly, to confront the state by appealing to both law and the sovereignty of customary rights to land and position. What has emerged, argues Alexander (after Kyed 2013), are "highly heterogeneous constellations of power with considerable room for negotiation." Perhaps less room than has been the case in South Africa or Ghana; historically, after all, Zimbabwean chiefs have been less autonomous politically, more obviously trapped between an assertive central authority and their subjects, than those in many other African contexts. But with room nonetheless, opened up by the very ambiguities inherent in the grounding of their legitimacy at once inside and outside the customary, inside and outside government, inside and outside the party, inside and outside the extractive economy—and less caught up in a "return" than in an ongoing process of (re)positioning in the political-economic geography of the present.

A similar process of (re)positioning, of the grounding of the present in a reconfigured, recommissioned past, is evident in Mariane Ferme's account of contemporary Sierra Leone (chapter 6), where "paramount chieftaincy" enjoys "a strong hold." Like Geschiere, Alexander, and Buthelezi and Skosana, Ferme begins by demythologizing the provenance of "traditional" legitimacy by opening up to scrutiny its history-in-the-making. As she shows, British efforts to colonize the country in the nineteenth century proceeded by means of a "territorialization of the chieftaincy." This initiative sought to stabilize governable populations on terrain anchored by sovereigns who, symbolically invested by the colonial state, were authorized to collect taxes under the mandate of indirect rule. When, in the 1920s, the administration sought to rationalize its modes of governance, chiefs assumed a "preeminent role . . . in colonial modernization," ensuring that close ties of kinship linked what Martin Kilson (1966:233) called the "modern and traditional elites." Today, we are told, the fragility of party organization at the local level has contributed to the enduring imbrication of those elites—and of chiefly and national politics.

Despite some debate after the civil war about eliminating chiefs altogether—echoes, again, of South Africa—both foreign and local policy makers opted to recommission them as pivotal, culturally appropriate "partners" in the decentralization of (donor-endorsed) development and neoliberal reform; in this respect, Sierra Leone epitomized the Washington Consensus moment. As in Zimbabwe, indigenous rulers came to occupy a space in the political geography of the country alongside district councils. But, by contrast, in the *imaginative* geography of power here, they are seen by many as an alternative to state corruption and predatory governance, not complicit in it; although ambivalently so in some places, since the accumulation of wealth and authority in their hands and those of their kin—themselves often "politicians, professionals, and people of [national] influence"—brings back memories of past excesses, past conflicts, past revolts against them from colonial times. Still, the office *is* widely linked to the promise of economic melioration. This explains the phenomenon, mentioned earlier, of "American chiefs," those who, having spent time abroad, are thought able to deploy their overseas contacts as conduits for the inflow of value into their communities; also, the appointment of foreign notables, like ex-British prime minister Tony Blair, as honorary sovereigns who might do the same—something, it seems, in high demand in this day and age.

Sierra Leone seems to fuse elements of *both* South Africa and Ghana, at least as Berry contrasts them. The empowerment of its customary authorities, to the degree that it has occurred, appears to derive *at once* from their control over land *and* their interpolation between the state and their subjects—as well, says Ferme, as from "other sources of privilege, both new and old," especially sources related to "development," broadly conceived. What is more, it is not merely these authorities who have been empowered by such means. It is also those closely associated with them, those who have exploited their access to insert themselves into capital flows, thus to enable the accumulation, management, and disposition of resources. As a result the chief*ship*—the office, that is, not just its holders—has become a crucible, ensconced in a reconfigured Kingdom of Custom, for thoroughly contemporary economic and political ventures. Nor is this the case only in Sierra Leone, although the point is made very forcibly here. It is true of many parts of the continent.

Eternal Authority, Ephemeral Power

As Ferme's account underscores, the sovereignty of the state and the sovereignty of chiefship have come to relate to one another in highly complex ways, the two intersecting in labyrinthine, mutually transforming entanglement. This is especially visible in Burkina Faso, Benoît Beucher shows (chapter 7), although he points to parallels in, among other places, Côte d'Ivoire and Nigeria. Between 1987 and 2014, the Compaoré regime, which ran the country as a democratic republic, found itself paired in an awkward, often fitful *pas de deux* with the *naaba*, Mossi rulers known for their aristocratic, "apolitical" ethos and an aura of moral authority—a divinely inspired authority, as Beucher's opening vignette makes plain, seen by many far to exceed that of mere politicians, whose power is at once earthly, erratic, and ephemeral. As in other African countries, the Compaoré administration acceded in the post–Cold War years to the pressures of structural adjustment, decentralizing some of the regulatory functions of the state—thus to enable the widely trusted Mossi chiefs to take up an expanded role in local government. It also made them into a critical resource for national political elites, who appropriated their prestige and popularity, avowing respect for "tradition" in order to buttress their own legitimacy, all the more so when democracy *itself* suffered legitimation crises due to the compromised transparency of the electoral process and the creeping autocracy of the state.

This engagement of the *naaba* with the state is not a new phenomenon. *Per contra*, while it might have been augmented and inflected by the effects of structural adjustment, its origins stretch back to colonial times. From very early on, French administrators worked hard to detach their African subjects from these indigenous "despots."[34] But the Europeans underestimated both the depth of aristocratic authority and the suppleness of the customary in the face of history. They also failed to grasp the significance of the chiefs in preserving the viability of their own colonial regime, an arrangement Beucher refers to as "indirect rule that never spoke its name," this despite the *naaba* losing their formal recognition under the impact of antichiefly legislation. For their part, what the indigenous rulers learned in the process was to "recognize the importance of the symbolic and political benefits that came with their entrance into modernity and its staging," a modernity in which "[e]verything must change to stay essentially the same." Thus is the history of colonized peoples rendered at once coeval with *and* irrevocably asymmetrical to the history in which Euromodernity is ideologically inscribed. It was a lesson that the *naaba* took with them into their engagement with Blaise Compaoré and his regime, an engagement from which the influential among them were to reap substantial financial returns.

The postcolonial *pas de deux* of these *naaba* with the president and political elites, says Beucher, "coproduced" a *neo*tradition and situated it "at the heart, rather than on the margins of, the state." While Compaoré and the chiefs stressed their autonomy from one another, their coexistence-in-practice, simultaneously one of competition and complementarity, as well as mutual profit, ran deep. Expressed in the argot of the customary, it seems to have been decisive for a long time in the survival of the regime against intermittent challenge. Of greater note for present purposes, though, was the *structural* effect of this competitive complementarity: a "coalition"—we, again, prefer "dialectical synthesis"—of apparently contradictory institutions, conjoining "a republic with a kingdom," one reminiscent, at a higher level of integration, of the Zulu monarchy inside the Republic of South Africa. In the end, however, the courtship of Mossi aristocrats by the ever more authoritarian, neoliberalizing Compaoré administration could not save it from overthrow. Tellingly, it stood accused of having corrupted the *naaba* ethos. That ethos, by contrast, survives, its strength endlessly staged and mythologized, thus to preserve it in putatively timeless perpetuity.

And, no doubt, valued all the more for having allowed "escape routes" into the politics of the customary for those trapped "in a context where postcolonial powers are . . . ephemeral and subject to . . . popular uprisings."

Here, then, is a vivid instance of the ways in which the conjuncture of different species of sovereignty, mediated by the impact of deregulation and decentralization, has opened up new spaces for the politics of custom within contemporary African states, custom whose modernity depends on changing in order to stay the same, and staying the same in order to change. It is in these new spaces of engagement—some formal, some not, some in between—that public spheres and civil society are reconfigured, depending, of course, on the material possibilities and constraints of local economic geographies and affective economies. It is in these spaces, too, that indigenous rulers who have both the means and the will may seek to (re)assert a monopoly over tradition in order to draw rents, to sustain their moral authority, and to extend their political dominion.

Capital, the Customary (and the State)

Those means, Susan Cook (chapter 8) shows for South Africa, may be most available to traditional authorities where the politics of custom are coproduced less with the state than directly with capital. This mode of co-production is enhanced, in the spirit of deregulated times, by ever-greater stress on corporate social responsibility and "soft" legal compliance: both facilitate the proximate engagement of the global private sector with local institutions for purposes of leveraging material and social resources, ostensibly to mutual benefit. Cook would agree with Sarah Berry (chapter 3) that it is not simply "neoliberalism" that accounts for the "resurgence" of chiefship—although, for her, "the logic of the market" has played a critical part in shaping the various forms of legitimacy (after Krämer n.d.) enjoyed today by indigenous rulers. At the same time, she argues, in South Africa those rulers "are indispensable to the successful [economic] management of the neoliberal state . . . [largely because] their specific forms of authority offer corporations access to resources, labor, and the 'social licence to operate' in ways [government] cannot." That authority, Buthelezi and Skosana might add, has itself been augmented by the Nhlapo-infused legitimation processes described in chapter 4. More broadly, it has been buttressed by the rising global recognition of the rights of "indigenous peoples," albeit recognition honored primarily in its breach.

Recalling Max Gluckman's classic "Analysis of a Social Situation in Modern Zululand" (1940a), Cook analyzes a social situation in the North

West Province to probe the growing entanglement of traditional leaders in the high-stakes extractive economy: a mass gathering of workers held in the wake of the infamous Marikana massacre of August 2012, when thirty-four striking employees of the Lonmin platinum mine were brutally killed by the police. The state was represented by President Jacob Zuma and the Kingdom of Custom by two monarchs, Zanozuko Sigcau of the amaPondo in the Eastern Cape Province, whence most of the dead came, and Leruo Molotlegi of the Bafokeng, whose own platinum-rich capital at Phokeng abuts Marikana. When the president addressed the gathering, the restive, angry crowd—enraged by what they took to be long-time government neglect—showed him scant respect, chanting defiantly as he took hasty leave of the event. The two traditional leaders, by contrast, were treated with palpable deference, giving clear evidence of their relative standing in the eyes of the workers, evidence that recalls Beucher's account of the moral superiority of the Mossi *naaba* over Ivoirean political elites. The melodrama played out in that makeshift agora, Cook argues, made manifest the fractious interdependence of transnational capital, the present-absent state, and the sovereigns of differently empowered ethnic groups. The authority of those sovereigns, she adds, is not only a matter of their *political* positioning as "vote banks" or as legal proxies of ethnic populations and their constitutional rights, important as those things obviously are. It is political-*economic*: it derives as much as anything else from being critical nodes in the traffic between their subjects and a morphing economy, a traffic densely populated by civic organizations, fractious and faltering unions, dis/organized crime, and private contractors of diverse kinds. But their "performative legitimacy" in that traffic varies widely with their situation in the economic geography of the country (above, chapter 3).

This, too, was vividly on display at Marikana. Zanozuko Sigcau rules over a polity with high levels of poverty, food insecurity, unemployment, and ill health (Porter and Phillips-Howard 1997). His legitimacy is vested, in major part, in the brokerage of labor and the moral protection of his people, not least from the kind of exploitation that led to the meltdown at the Lonmin mine. Sigcau came to the North West primarily to assist in the removal and burial of his deceased subjects and the care of their families. Authorities of his ilk are also, in some respects, latter-day figurations of "indirect rule that never speaks its name" (above, p. 28). In addition to administering customary law and what remains of their "traditional" lands, they have perforce to deal with the consequences of the violence of contemporary labor and wage practices—and, sometimes, to quell worker unrest. By contrast, the likes of the Bafokeng king, those able to lease their mineral-rich land to mining companies in return for substantial royalties, tend to become CEO-monarchs as their polities take the shape of ethnic corporations. As the rentier wealth of the Royal Bafokeng has been redeployed to establish a large portfolio of holdings in national and international businesses, the ruler has become an influential player in the traditional-industrial complex that has developed out of this igneous bushveld region, where his state-within-a-state thrives by asserting both its cultural autonomy and its global modernity.

The difference between the platinum-rich Bafokeng king and the sovereign of the land that supplies labor to the extractive economy is captured well at the most poignant moment in Cook's narrative. It is when Sigcau says to Molotlegi, in excerpt, "it is my dream that one day my people will not be forced by poverty and desperation to travel from their homes to find work in your region. We will only achieve this when we develop our own villages instead of continuing to contribute to the wealth of yours." Both monarchs are tied into the global economy—one as an empowered rentier of land and director of companies, the other as a relatively disempowered source of exploited, disposable labor—from which each derives his legitimacy, duly performed at Marikana. Their relative presence in the world at large may be quite different, measured in terms of fungible assets. Yet the authority of both in relation to their subjects—and, more importantly, the authority and affective weight of the customary offices they hold—has come to hinge heavily on the manner in which they mediate, materially and morally, between their subjects and the protean, deregulated world in which they find themselves.

But, to reverse the order of things, chiefs may *themselves* be commodified. On the face of it, Lauren Adrover's account of the commodification of customary political authority in Ghana (chapter 9) seems a pretty bald expression of just this, of the fungible potential of chiefship-as-capital. It also shows how the branding of traditional rulers serves to fetishize their role as "natural" stewards of culture, this in the interests of transferring the allure of their sacral imprimatur to a corporate logo. The annual festival of *Fetu Afahye*, held by Fante-speaking Akan in the streets of Cape Coast, celebrates both the yam harvest and the sovereigns who preside over the region's agrarian beneficence. In a pageant of memorable proportions, the royal personages are carried through the town in palanquins, resplendent in fine ceremonial cloth, crowns, and the sumptuous accoutrements of office. In September 2011, however, the chiefs found their splendor upstaged by a much more profane event: a raucous free concert, sponsored by Tigo, the multinational telecommunications firm. In collaboration with one of the nation's leading broadcasting companies, it aimed to seize the effervescence of the fete to promote its brand and services, which range from money transfers to long-distance calls. Masses of adoring fans gathered round the latest Accra-based hiplife stars, who, as the sidelined rulers could only look on, performed with gusto on a high-tech professional stage. The corporate actors hijacked the large festival crowds—and the spirit of customary authority they had come to honor—by offering a more compelling attraction: the charisma of popular, mass-mediated celebrities, who adorned their show with a clutch of highly resonant customary invocations and props. The rulers, and the kinds of benefaction they purvey, had, it appears, been overtaken by the heady appeal of consumer culture and *its* iconic figures.

Yet is it all so simple? Does this story mark a teleological move in public culture here—an affective, aesthetic, ethical shift—from custom to customer, tradition to trademark, so to speak, thus to herald the eclipse of chiefly authority by charismatic capital? It is true that, as state support for their rituals has waned, the royals have been driven to a dangerous dependency on corporate sponsors, who threaten to extinguish their aura as they appropriate it. Tigo drew upon the widely accepted assumption that chiefs are the custodians of (vernacular) culture to position itself as analogous custodians of (consumer) culture. Or rather, it attempted to replicate, by a process of projection and identification, the kind of affinity that exists between Akan rulers and their subjects, a bond cemented by custom in its presumptively "authentic," unalienated form. Tigo, in short, also sought to capitalize, literally, on the mystique of festivals as contexts in which "people demonstrate and perform deep connections to their culture." It took pains, on the day, to display key insignia of chiefship alongside its own corporate logo, as if to infuse its brand with the aura of the customary.

Brands are queer things, however. They seldom sustain the stable identity that marketers strive to create for them. If we are to understand how they live in the world, says Constantine Nakassis (2013:110), we "require [to] situate our analyses in moments when [they are] called into question." It is at such moments that new values, new kinds of politics often emerge, "through, but in constant tension with, the brand" itself. The point applies well here: within the framing of the *Fetu Afahye* festival, the chiefs were made to compete with company advertisers to retain control over a critical site in which they perform and reproduce their political authority and popular appeal in contemporary Ghana. As the events unfolded, they complained about such things as corporate violations of "traditional protocol," countering the seizure of their symbols and their occulted power by asserting the unassimilable, transcendent charm of custom itself, hence to "(re)brand" it as their own. Commercial sponsors, here, risk either banalizing the chiefly magic they seek to tap or being declared illegitimate purveyors of royal simulacra. The potency vested in the customary, as we have noted, has long lain in defining it as "other" to rational authority—as well, of course, to the logic of capital and the commodity form. Indeed, it is precisely its elusiveness and enchantment that gives it the capacity to infuse the enterprises of state and market with spiritual legitimacy (see chapter 12).

But not always. Where contemporary statecraft makes way for the more-or-less direct engagement of chiefship with capital, each with its own species ("brand"?) of legitimacy, the rapacious tendencies of corporate enterprise, especially in extractive industries, has sometimes led to tension, even to violent conflict. Such, observes Lauren Coyle (chapter 10), is the case in and around Obuasi, in the heart of the Ashanti Region of Ghana. The town, legendary for its gold, is mined by Anglo Gold Ashanti (AGA) under state license—a signal function of the so-called "neoliberal state," parenthetically, being just this, its operation as a licensing authority, much like a franchise-holding company in the business, literally, of governance. A transnational megafirm, AGA has been widely excoriated for the brutality of its labor practices, for its exploitation of "soft" law to avoid accountability, and for its corporate social irresponsibility. These things, allege mineworkers and interested NGOs, go largely unpoliced by a national administration that has been accused of colluding in its activities, by omission if not commission. So, according to their many critics, have some local chiefs, who are said to have profited handsomely from their close ties and illicit deals with AGA. Acting as though they were its private owners— recall, again, post-Nhlapo South Africa—they are said to have ceded (some would say sold) to the company large swathes of farmland and sacred streams, which afforded adjacent communities drinking water, edible fish, and access to the many spirits that protect the sustainability of the living environment. In addition, the customary authorities are blamed for abetting the introduction of ecodestructive open-pit mining and, with it, the bitter harvest of hunger—of joblessness, violence, dispossession, despoliation, and ruin—that has followed.

Some chiefs, the "fallen chiefs" of Coyle's title, have actually been forced to flee their capitals, their mere physical presence being taken as an affront by many of their subjects. One such estranged ruler, one who appears to have had a conspicuously collusive and prodigiously profitable relationship with AGA, attempted to return home in a convoy of armored cars in 2011. His arrival sparked a bloody pitched battle between those who wished forcibly to "destool" him and those who insisted that he remain on; the latter made the case that he was their pivotal link to the ancestors, source of the vitality and productivity of his people and their lands. They did not prevail, however. He can no longer go back, under threat of death. The events that led up to this confrontation illuminate what may, often does, follow from the devolution of jurisdiction to indigenous authorities in dealings with extractive capital: it encourages the autocratic alienation of collective resources, giving rise to a "new incarnation of rentier capitalist chiefs" who are especially well positioned to take advantage of the legal ambiguities that have resulted from liberalization. These ambiguities and their exploitation by customary sovereigns, Coyle adds, exemplify the workings of what Elizabeth Rata (1999, 2011) terms "neotribal capitalism": a form of accumulation, born of revivalist, ethnicized identities, that leads to the acquisition, by ethnic elites, of communal assets embedded in newly capitalized relations of production, distribution, and alienation. Not everywhere, of course. There are chiefs who use the revenues they accrue to finance infrastructure and public institutions; also, reminiscent of the point made by Kate Baldwin (2015, above, p. 15), some lobby governmental bodies and NGOs for financial support, actively seeking venture capital from the corporate sector and development agencies for income-generating projects—or even committing their own funds to these ends.

Meanwhile, into the vacuum opened up by the fallen chiefs have stepped informal artisanal miners, galamseys, whose leaders have striven to assert a new popular sovereignty. Assisted at times by civil society activists, they have taken on many of the customary functions of governance: functions Coyle glosses as "policing, provisioning, and arbitrating." They have also sought to assume the ritual obligations of the lapsed rulers by repurposing their aura. As this suggests, the decommissioning of those rulers has not undermined the spiritual suzerainty of their office; here, too, a sharp distinction is still drawn between chiefship and incumbent. Profligate monarchs may be an abiding offense to customary authority and the promise of beneficence vested in it, but they can be removed by customary legal means. It is this that has animated grassroots struggles to recover, resignify, and reanimate, rather than abandon, "traditional" political sovereignty. And so a "slow insurgency" is being conducted "in a theater of shadows . . . [to] fashion a new cultural politics of land, labor, and citizenship," one that seeks access to a "livelihood, to a viable future, and to a just share in 'sovereign wealth.'" The moral of the story is clear. It expands further on a critical theme that keeps reappearing as we proceed. The politics of custom, at once restaged, reconfigured, and contested—not least in the ruptures forced between office and officeholders—is perhaps *the* theater in which new forms of authority and political subjectivity are being forged in the contentiously unfolding history of the present.

Artisanal miners also appear as "free radicals" in James Smith's account of customary authority, capital, and the "mining of futures" in the gold-fields of Luhwindja, South Kivu, in the Democratic Republic of the Congo (chapter 11). Like the galamseys of Obuasi, they illuminate the sorts of political struggle set in motion by clashes of sovereignty in an economic geography oriented around mineral extraction, although the alignments and oppositions here differ from those in Ghana. Artisanal diggers have long pursued precarious livelihoods along the edges of the mining indus-try across the planet, of course, sometimes in conflict, sometimes in sym-biosis, sometimes in awkward accommodation with it. Colonial extraction depended on exploiting their vernacular expertise while, at the same time, marginalizing them. Anomalously local but in no sense traditional, these organic scientists, who call themselves *geologues* (geologists) in Luhwindja, wield an autarchic knowledge-based authority of their own. During colo-nial times they relied on the indigenous rulers, *wami* ("kings"), in their bat-tles with foreign concessionaires. But, lately, those rulers have become their archenemies, allying themselves with Banro, the Canadian firm that holds the Luhwindja concession. For their part, the *geologues* declare the "law of custom" passé, a form of "false government." The historic, mutually trans-forming entanglement here of customary legitimacy, the state, capital, and local stakeholders, Smith shows, has become a multisided struggle between different technologies of power, jurisdiction, and suzerainty.

Contemporary *bwami* ("kingship") was honed largely in its relation to colonial capital, especially after the "discovery" of gold in the 1940s, which conferred upon royals new sources of wealth and authority. While the king had no rights over mineral deposits back then, the artisans who worked the goldfields by night offered him tribute in exchange for protection, thereby shoring up his "ownership" of the land. Things are very different today. Banro operates here on the assumption that the ruler, currently an unpop-ular female regent, holds the interests of her subjects in sacred trust: that, in exchange for compensation—ostensibly for them as well as her—she could legitimately cede exclusive sovereignty over the soil. But the artisanal miners think otherwise, as do the families displaced from their homes by the mine. The *bwami*, they say, has long thrived on their tribute; having been deprived of an income, they feel that they are now owed recompense. Supported by civil society activists, they oppose the regent's right to enter contracts over collective resources with Banro, protest the removal of local households, and demand that the beneficiaries of past mining deals meet their promises of payment to "the community." In one recent confrontation, residents of Luhwindja blocked the road to Banro's factory, establishing a large new artisanal town and mine on its property. They claimed to have set up a new government under the *geologues*, self-confessed "enemies of custom." This sort of popular sovereignty, like others that have arisen in Africa, has asserted itself not only against the tyranny of corporate extraction—and against the national administration that supports it—but also against the very logic of "neotribal" capitalism and its cooption of the Kingdom of Custom.

There is much to be learned from all this. *Bwami*, "kingship," notes Smith, partook of a paradox, a version of the doubling of which we spoke earlier. On one hand, it was imagined, mythically, to embody a "feudal" form of authority that, as he puts it, was the "conduit to an ontological past." On the other, its dealings with Banro have demanded of *Wami*, as legal proxy for the Kingdom of Custom, a thoroughly contemporary engagement with the world of contracts, concessions, commodities, and compensation under the Kingdom of Capital. Because neither kingdom has liberated local people from poverty, argues Smith—indeed, are its primary cause—and because *bwami* is unable to deal with the exigencies of the here and now, its subjects see no further cause for it to exist. History, for them, has overtaken ontology.

Thus it is, we are told, that Luhwindja is trapped inside a "sense of impending end . . . a shifting back and forth among alternative pasts, alternative futures, and alternative worlds"—although, Smith adds, this temporal politics is also generative of new modes of thought and action. What the role of *wami* might be in those futures remains undetermined. But this case underlines the point made by Geschiere in chapter 2: that customary authority in the age of capital is *not* everywhere "resurgent." Its fragility in Luhwindja may lie in the fact that, of the three axes we suggested in answer to "Why now, why here?," a critical one is lacking: the capacity of the reigning *mwami*, under siege from *geologues*, disaffected subjects, and attendant activists, to mobilize the customary as fungible political capital with which to control flows of wealth in tangible assets, territory, and people. Whether, in fact, the office *will* survive its current incumbent and the historical conditions of the moment, however, only time will tell. Institutions, especially mythic ones, often outlive dire predictions of their imminent demise.

The Third Moment, or Dialectical Futures

To be sure, Juan Obarrio (chapter 12) suggests that the customary is unlikely to disappear for the foreseeable future: that it persists as an immanent presence, even when it lies dormant, a "ghostly antagonist" in counterpoint to the state in Africa. And, by implication, also as a necessary supplement to its sovereignty, not to mention the sovereignty of global capital as it comes to ground in different national economies. Hence the general point, made above, that chiefship exists, like it has long done, as the suppressed underside of modernity, perpetually threatened with erasure yet perpetually sustained as a sign of African otherness—under colonialism deployed as an instrument of political domination and, in its aftermath, asserted as an authentic form of legitimacy and democratic alterity. Mozambique, of which Obarrio writes, is a case in point. As in much of Africa, precolonial power structures here were engineered by Portuguese colonizers into a system of homogenous "traditional" authorities, thus to develop a grid in terms of which local populations could be violently fixed within territories, administered and taxed, mobilized as labor, and subjected to tight disciplinary control.

But, in 1975, after the end of colonialism, the FRELIMO regime banned traditional rulers, rituals, and received lifeways, excoriating them as the detritus of an ignominious past. The mantra with which we opened this chapter, *"for the nation to live, the tribe must die,"* became the ideological cry, and the political project, of the new socialist order. And then, with liberalization, a radical shift: the dismantling and decentralization of that order, accompanied by a vigorous re-emergence of the customary and its authority figures. In 2000, the Council of Ministers officially recognized chiefs, incorporating them into local administration—which, it appears, they infused with a new spiritual legitimacy. This, coming after the colonial and socialist periods, says Obarrio, ushered in a "third moment" of articulation between state and custom, a dialectical synthesis of sorts, albeit a fraught one. Indigenous rulers and the customary have been retooled in the service of postsocialist economic policy and neoliberal governance. What had been banished forever was back, yet another mythic "eternal return of the same." In point of fact, while things indigenous *had* been outlawed, it—indigeneity, that is—had played a mobilizing role during the socialist-era civil war between FRELIMO and the Mozambican National Resistance. It had never truly been erased, merely conjured into invisibility.

Constitutional recognition of indigeneity has had the effect of (re)vitalizing a metaphysics of difference in many African nation-states. Nationalism, nativism, and neoliberalism rub up against each other under the impact of structural adjustment—and, as often as not, speculative and extractive capital—thus to decenter the hegemony of the state and either efface, deface, or interface awkwardly with the universal rights of citizenship. FRELIMO has tried to contain proliferating diversity under the single category of the customary, striving to harness it in order to produce a unified future. As Obarrio intimates, this has involved a contradictory conjuncture: of the putatively precolonial—of kinship rules, gender and generational norms, spiritual practices, and the like, as much *created* by colonizers as found in place by them—with a modernist culture of legality. On the ground, however, heterogeneity is not so easily contained. What has materialized is less a unified political order than a terrain on which alternate forms of sovereignty and citizenship jostle agonistically for expression— and for control over wealth in people, fungible assets, and im/movable property. On that terrain, a "revitalized" chiefship refuses easy encompassment by the secular rule of law precisely because it bears the traces of an older order, an otherworldly power. Perhaps *this* is the generic future of the politics of custom, and the spirit of the customary, in Africa: a perennially unresolved, shape-shifting struggle over various species of sovereignty and value in a universe of unresolvable differences.

Coda

We make no effort to draw the diversity of these various studies into what might pretend to be a unified theory, an *ur*-narrative, to explain the interplay of chiefship, capital, and the state in contemporary Africa. Indeed, the very point of this exercise lies in illuminating quite *how* diverse are the ways that, as a product of that interplay, customary authority is manifesting itself across the continent. And why. An "extraordinarily flexible institution," its politics "prickly and plastic" (above, p. 25), it has nothing like the homogeneous, ascriptive character, past or present, often ascribed to it— usually by categorical contrast to Euromodernist political office.

The chapters in this volume suggest that indigenous authority is likely to assert itself most strongly today, albeit in situationally specific ways, proportionally to the co-occurence of three conditions: synoptically, the capacity of rulers to mobilize the customary in order to authorize control over wealth in tangible assets, land, and people; the devolution of the functions of state, especially where it is accompanied by an active corporate and NGO presence; and the sedimentation of "local communities," around an indigenous office, positioned to claim recognition and rights—material, social, spiritual, territorial—by virtue of inalienable cultural difference. All of these things, plainly, are mediated by the hard facts of economic geography and by the workings of global political economy, which conduce to a form of deregulation that encourages direct engagement of capital with "the local." They are also fed by a rising politics of identity, which makes ethnicity a critical vector of mobilization, creating political brokers (i.e., "vote banks") out of many chiefs—and often embraces them in a postcolonial version of indirect rule, particularly where the reach of the state into local government is compromised for one reason or another.

Chiefship may appear to have "returned." Resoundingly, if unevenly, so. But, as we have stressed, it never actually went away, having been the perennial underside, the "ghostly other," of technorational, "enlightened" governance, colonial *and* postcolonial—either immanently or manifestly, mythically or materially, its necessary supplement. The so-called "resurgence" of indigenous rulers, where it has occurred, is often described as *neo*traditional, a mix of elements at once transcendently timeless *and* audaciously innovative, not least in its orientation to the structurally adjusted exigencies of the present. Indeed, it is by asserting their monopoly over the ostensibly eternal character of custom that those rulers are, potentially or in fact, able to refashion its content. And to capitalize on it in their effort to exercise sovereignty—in its social, economic, political, spiritual, and moral aspects—however expansive or limited that sovereignty may turn out to be. Like the sacred, which, according to Durkheim (1995:432–33), stands as perpetual other to science, so custom stands in contrast to modern government and law. And like the sacred, it is destined to be transformed but never to die. For it is perennially called upon to complete the unfinished business of secular modernity, thus to ensure the ongoing life of thinking, feeling, striving beings in the world, present and future. Thus is the historicity of the customary both recursively cyclical *and* linear, both timeless *and*, in its own way, teleological. Thus are new forms of political life, located in multiple temporalities, being fashioned across Africa.

Notes

1. This well-worn mantra is usually attributed to Samora Machel. It has recently elicited any number of counter-arguments. For one from within African/ist scholarship, see Ndlovu-Gatsheni (2008).
2. "Chief Shells Out R78m for Sky-High Luxury," Nashira Davids, *Sunday Times* (RSA), 5 April 2015, p. 7.
3. Those acts, committed in 1995–96, before the new constitution of South Africa was in place, involved the punishment of one of his subjects for a variety of alleged

infractions. He asserts, therefore, that these were sovereign acts under customary law, not common crimes; see, e.g., "Chiefs Want Free Reign," Andisiwe Makinana, *City Press*, 23 May 2016, http://city-press.news24.com/News/chiefs-want-free-reign-20160521, accessed 2 June 2016 (also note 24 below). Convicted in 2013, Dalindyebo, always a controversial figure, began serving a twelve-year sentence in December 2015; he has also been deposed as king. However, many critics of his treatment insist that it amounts to an attack on African traditional practices under the sign of "Western law," a claim that has led to a fair bit of constitutional debate. For just one analysis of the acts, facts, and arguments involved, see "A Royal Conundrum: King Dalindyebo and the Traditional Leaders Hot Potato," Marianne Thamm, *Daily Maverick*, 13 January 2010, http://www.dailymaverick.co.za/article/2016-01-13-a-royal-conundrum-king-dalindyebo-and-the-traditional-leaders-hot-potato/#.V62NXU2V8nM, accessed 3 February 2016. For an example of the support that Dalindyebo received from some black public intellectuals, see "An Affront to Customary Law," Jongisilo Pokwana ka Menziwa, *IOL News*, 5 August 2014, http://www.iol.co.za/news/an-affront-to-customary- law-1730962, accessed 7 August 2014.

4.   Mbeki's volume was published by the Xhosa-owned Verulam Press, named for the small town in which it was situated, twenty-seven kilometers north of Durban, KwaZulu-Natal. (It now falls in the eThekwini Metropolitan Area.) As a result, the press, which did not print its address in many of its books, is often listed in library catalogues—see, for example, Harvard's Hollis search engine—as n.p. (no place given), which is how we annotate it here. We should like to thank Xolela Mangcu, who alerted us to this reference.

5.   Of course, Gluckman's work was done before apartheid was formalized into state policy; however, the development of apartheid after 1948 was the culmination of a policy of segregation and "native administration" that went back many decades.

6.   On the internal dynamics of nineteenth- and twentieth-century Tswana political life—of succession to and incumbency of office, of the public negotiation of policy and chiefly legitimacy, and the like—see Comaroff (1978); also, Gulbrandsen (1995, 2012). On their (partial) ossification under apartheid, see Comaroff (1974). Similar processes have been documented elsewhere in South Africa, notably by Barbara Oomen (2005).

7.   Lucas Mangope was chief of the Bahurutshe of Motswedi in the North West Province. He was ostensibly elected by the members of what was then the Tswana Territorial Authority (TTA)—ostensibly because, as we were told during the course of our fieldwork in Mafikeng at the time, it was widely suspected that his election had been "engineered" by the apartheid regime. The TTA was the forerunner of the Bophuthatswana Legislative Assembly, of which Mangope became chief minister in 1971. In 1977, he became president of "independent" Bophuthatswana, a mythic nation-state legitimate only in the eyes of the nationalist regime in South Africa; on his rise and fall, see Lawrence and Manson (1994).

8.   Some scholarly histories suggest that Mangope "was trying to give the institution of chieftaincy a new lease of life" (Manson and Mbenga 2014:121). This is true in a limited sense. However, the *form* of chiefship that he encouraged, Kebalepile and other Tswana rulers insisted, reduced its holders to an administrative cadre subjugated to his own authority and evacuated the *democratic* character of indigenous political life.

9.   Local Government: Municipal Structures Amendment Bill (2000); see Comaroff and Comaroff (2003).

10. We should like to extend our warm thanks to Jonathan Shapiro for his permission to reproduce this cartoon here.

11. As Krämer (2016:118) notes, "the despotism perspective is based on Mamdani's (1996) arguments on 'decentralized despotism'" under colonialism. In fact, this perspective underestimates how diminished were many South African chiefs under apartheid—"minor puppets," as Chief Luthuli put it (above, p. 3). We should like to thank Mario Krämer for sharing his work with us; while he was unable to attend the conference on which this volume is based, we have learned a great deal from him.

12. For an abridged transcript of the speech, given in March 2012 at the University of Cape Town (UCT), see "Mamphela Ramphele Takes on the Traditional Courts Bill," *Sonke Gender Justice*, 16 April 2012, http://www.genderjustice.org.za/article/mamphela-ramphele-takes-on-the-traditional-courts-bill/, accessed 15 August 2014. For non-South African readers, Ms. Ramphele, a cofounder of the Black Consciousness Movement, is a past vice chancellor of UCT and managing director at the World Bank.

13. Lawson's (n.d. [2002]) paper, which is unpublished, is quoted in Logan (2008).

14. This "yet-to-be-civilized" African other recalls Homi Bhabha's (1994:122) colonial subject, s/he who was "almost . . . but not quite" (the same, sufficiently modern). But the former, the African subject—even if he was a ruler—was never even "not quite"; s/he languished some distance behind South Asians, other than those of the lowest castes, in the imperial imagination.

15. Mamdani (1999:862, also 1996) adds that indirect rule, "premised on *autonomy*," was a "more hegemonic assertion of colonial power" than direct rule, "premised on *assimilation*," this despite claims to its having been the more benign. The former, he adds, grew out of the crisis of the latter, but "never entirely displaced" it.

16. For the general reader, Wikipedia lists more than seventy African empires, defined as "states . . . with multinational structures incorporating various populations and polities into a single entity, usually through conquest"; see https://en.wikipedia.org/wiki/African_empires, accessed 25 February 2016. On kingdoms, see Vansina (1962).

17. Africanist archaeology has also made a major contribution to the study of precolonial states. For one informative overview, see Monroe (2013), who stresses, as we do, the dynamic endogenous character of those states and their interconnections with worlds beyond their own borders; he also discusses archaeological theories of their origins and the growth of their internal complexity.

18. We are indebted to Erin Mosely, a recent graduate of Harvard University, whose doctoral dissertation (2016) drew our attention to the significance of precolonial Rwanda in this respect.

19. This is also a point made, classically, by Gluckman (1963)

20. Gluckman (1941), Little (1951), and Fallers (1964), who were among the first anthropologists to use the term—which, nowadays, tends to be attributed to more recent work (e.g., Miers and Kopytoff 1977; Guyer 1993)—did not apply it specifically to precolonial contexts. But all three saw it as a generic feature of social and political life in Africa, past and contemporary.

21. We have ourselves demonstrated the point *in extenso* for the Southern Tswana (Comaroff and Comaroff 1991:chapter 4; also Comaroff 1982).

22. In many parts of Africa, the concept of "good government" was explicitly articulated, as in the Tswana and Sotho polities of southern Africa, where the vernacular term for it was *bogosi yo bontle*.

23. The publication date of this volume is not specified in its first edition, hence we cite it as (n.d.).

24. "[J]udicial immunity from criminal and civil liability arising from their decisions in the traditional courts" is what the Congress of Traditional Leaders of South Africa (CONTRALESA) has insisted on for indigenous rulers, this in an appeal to the national judiciary to have parliament pass legislation to secure their sovereign status. See "Chiefs Want Free Reign," Andisiwe Makinana (and note 3 above).

25. "Unelected African Chiefs Make their Countries More Democratic. Here's How," Kate Baldwin, *Washington Post*, 10 June 2016, https://www.washingtonpost.com/ news/monkey-cage/wp/2016/06/10/unelected-african-chiefs-make-their-countries -more-democratic-heres-how/, accessed 18 June 2016. The article is itself a synopsis of the central argument of Baldwin's (2015) recent volume on the topic.

26. To take just a single instance, this one concerning chiefly land distribution in rural Zimbabwe, compare Rambe and Mawere (2012) with Holleman (1952:12f.), and see Doré (1993:71, 306f.)—who also notes that "customary" practices described for earlier times had, in all likelihood, already been substantially transformed under the impact of colonialism.

27. Zwelithini later denied that he had called for violence against foreigners, perhaps under government pressure, although his remarks were tape-recorded; see "Zwelithini Calls for Peace," Bongani Hans, *Cape Times*, 21 April 2015, p. 1.

28. See "New Form of Dispossession: King's KZN Land Claim Signals Land Grab for Mineral Rights by Rural Elites," South African Civil Society Information Service, 10 October 2014, http://www.customcontested.co.za/new-form-dispossession-kings -kzn-land-claim-signals-land-grab-mineral-rights-rural-elites/, accessed 13 October 2014. This is also discussed in chapter 4.

29. See "Re-opened Restitution a Cover for Neo-Traditionalist Power Grab," Nomolanga Mkhize, *Custom Contested Views and Voices* [Land and Accountability Research Centre], 19 August 2014, http://www.customcontested.co.za/re-opened-restitution -cover-neo-traditionalist-power-grab/, accessed 13 October 2014.

30. This was noted by the upper echelons of the ANC administration; see "Zuma Hails amaXhosa King's Coronation as 'Historic Occasion,'" *Cape Times*, 18 May 2015, p. 7.

31. See "Radical Change Needed in Relationship Between State and Traditional Leaders," Nkosikhulule Xhawulengweni Nyembezi, *Cape Times*, 18 May 2015, p. 9.

32. As we note elsewhere (Comaroff and Comaroff 2009), the entry of ethnic groups into the market—that is, *Ethnicity, Inc.*—may also occasion bitter conflict over the disposition of income between a ruler, those close to him, and his subjects.

33. See "Zuma Hails amaXhosa King's Coronation as 'Historic Occasion.'"

34. Further to our discussion above of the putative "decentralized despotism" of chiefs under colonialism, it is notable that, in Côte d'Ivoire, French administrators believed that it was *precolonial* Mossi chiefs who were "despots." These colonizers then set about undoing their authority, quite the opposite of the general trajectory suggested by Mamdani (1996).

References

Adjaye, Joseph K., and Buba Misawa

2006   Chieftaincy at the Confluence of Tradition and Modernity: Transforming African Rulership in Ghana and Nigeria. *International Third World Studies Journal and Review* 17. http://www.unomaha.edu/itwsjr/ThirdXVII/ Chieftaincy17.htm.

Afigbo, Adiele Eberechukwu
  1972   *The Warrant Chiefs: Indirect Rule in South-Eastern Nigeria, 1891–1929.* London: Longman.
Ayittey, George B. N.
  1991   *Indigenous African Institutions.* New York: Transnational Publishers.
Baldwin, Kate
  2015   *The Paradox of Traditional Chiefs in Democratic Africa.* Cambridge: Cambridge University Press.
Beidelman, Thomas O.
  1978   Chiefship in Ukaguru: The Invention of Ethnicity and Tradition in Kaguru Colonial History. *International Journal of African Historical Studies* 11(2):227–46.
Bhabha, Homi
  1994   *The Location of Culture.* London: Routledge.
Bundy, Colin
  1979   *The Rise and Fall of the South African Peasantry.* Berkeley, CA: University of California Press.
Busia, Kofi A.
  1951   *The Position of the Chief in the Modern Political System of Ashanti: A Study of the Influence of Contemporary Social Change on Ashanti Political Institutions.* London: Oxford University Press.
Comaroff, Jean, and John Comaroff
  1991   *Of Revelation and Revolution,* vol. 1, *Christianity, Colonialism, and Consciousness in South Africa.* Chicago: University of Chicago Press.
  2003   Reflections on Liberalism, Policulturalism, and ID-ology: Citizenship and Difference in South Africa. *Social Identities* 9(4):445–74.
Comaroff, John
  1974   Chiefship in a South African 'Homeland.' *Journal of Southern African Studies* 1(1): 36–51.
  1978   Rules and Rulers: Political Processes in a Tswana Chiefdom. *Man* (n.s.) 13(1):1–20.
  1982   Dialectical Systems, History and Anthropology: Units of Study and Questions of Theory. *Journal of Southern African Studies* 8(2):143–72.
Comaroff, John, and Jean Comaroff
  1989   The Colonization of Consciousness in South Africa. *Economy and Society* 18(3): 267–96.
  2006   Law and Disorder in the Postcolony: An Introduction. In *Law and Disorder in the Postcolony,* Jean Comaroff and John L. Comaroff, eds. Chicago: University of Chicago Press.
  2009   *Ethnicity, Inc.* Chicago: University of Chicago Press.
Crais, Clifton C.
  2006   Custom and the Politics of Sovereignty in South Africa. *Journal of Social History* 39(3):721–40.
Doré, Dale
  1993   *Land Tenure and the Economics of Rural Transformation: A Study of the Strategies to Relieve Land Pressure and Poverty in the Communal Areas of Zimbabwe.* Madison, WI: University of Wisconsin Press.
Dorward, David C.
  1969   The Development of the British Colonial Administration among the Tiv, 1900–1949. *African Affairs* 68:316–33.

Du Preez, Max
  2013   A Rumour of Spring: South Africa after 20 Years of Democracy. Cape Town: Zebra Press.
Durkheim, Emile
  1995   The Elementary Forms of Religious Life, Karen E. Fields, trans. New York: The Free
          Press.
Fallers, Lloyd A.
  1964   The King's Men: Leadership and Status in Buganda on the Eve of Independence. London:
          Oxford University Press for the East African Institute of Social Research.
Fokwang, Jude
  2009   Mediating Legitimacy: Chieftaincy and Democratisation in Two African Chiefdoms.
          Mankon, Bamenda (Cameroon): Langaa Research and Publishing Company.
Fortes, Meyer, and Edward E. Evans-Pritchard, eds.
  1940   African Political Systems. London: Oxford University Press for the International Insti-
          tute of African Languages and Cultures.
Gartrell, Beverly
  1983   British Administrators, Colonial Chiefs, and the Comfort of Tradition: An Example
          from Uganda. African Studies Review 26(1):1–24.
Geschiere, Peter
  2009   Perils of Belonging: Autochthony, Citizenship, and Exclusion in Africa and Europe. Chi-
          cago: University of Chicago Press.
Gluckman, Max
  1940a   Analysis of a Social Situation in Modern Zululand. Bantu Studies 14(1):1–30.
  1940b   The Kingdom of the Zulu in South Africa. In African Political Systems, Meyer Fortes
          and Edward E. Evans-Pritchard, eds. London: Oxford University Press for the Inter-
          national Institute of African Languages and Cultures.
  1941   The Economy of the Central Barotse Plain. The Rhodes-Livingstone Papers, no.7. Man-
          chester: University of Manchester Press for the Rhodes-Livingstone Institute.
  1963   Order and Rebellion in Tribal Africa: Collected Essays with an Autobiographical Introduc-
          tion. London: Cohen & West.
Grischow, Jeff
  2008   Rural Communities, Chieftaincy, and Social Capital: The Case of Southern Ghana.
          Journal of Agrarian Change 8(1):64–93.
Gulbrandsen, Ørnulf T.
  1995   The King is King by the Grace of the People: The Exercise and Control of Power in
          Subject-Ruler Relations. Comparative Studies in Society and History 37(3):415–44.
  2012   The State and the Social: State Formation in Botswana and Its Precolonial and Colonial
          Genealogies. New York: Berghahn Books.
Guyer, Jane I.
  1993   Wealth in People and Self-Realization in Equatorial Africa. Man (n.s.) 28(2):243–65.
Hobsbawm, Eric, and Terence O. Ranger, eds.
  1983   The Invention of Tradition. Cambridge: Cambridge University Press.
Holleman, J. F.
  1952   Shona Customary Law: With Reference to Kinship, Marriage, the Family and the Estate.
          Manchester: Manchester University Press.
Kahn, Victoria
  2009   Political Theology and Fiction in The King's Two Bodies. Representations 106(1):
          77–101.

Kantorowicz, Ernst H.

1957 *The King's Two Bodies: A Study in Medieval Political Theology.* Princeton, NJ: Princeton University Press.

Keulder, Christiaan

1998 *Traditional Leaders and Local Government in Africa.* Pretoria: HSRC.

Kilson, Martin

1966 *Political Change in a West African State: A Study of the Modernization Process in Sierra Leone.* Cambridge, MA: Harvard University Press.

Krämer, Mario

2016 Neither Despotic nor Civil: The Legitimacy of Chieftaincy in its Relationship with the ANC and the State in KwaZulu-Natal (South Africa). *Journal of Modern African Studies* 54(1):117–43.

n.d. Competitive Chieftaincy, the State, and the ANC: Power and Basic Legitimacy of *Ubukhosi* in KwaZulu-Natal, South Africa. Paper presented at the African Studies Workshop, Harvard University, 9 February 2015.

Kuper, Adam

1970a Gluckman's Village Headman. *American Anthropologist* 72(2):355–58.

1970b *Kalahari Village Politics: An African Democracy.* Cambridge: Cambridge University Press.

Kyed, Helene Maria

2013 The Heterogeneous State and Legal Pluralism in Mozambique. *Journal of Southern African Studies* 39(4):989–95.

Lawrence, Michael, and Andrew Manson

1994 The 'Dog of the Boers': The Rise and Fall of Mangope in Bophuthatswana. *Journal of Southern African Studies* 20(3):447–61.

Lawson, Letitia

n.d. The House of Chiefs: Indigenizing Democracy in Africa? Paper presented to the 45th Annual Meeting of the African Studies Association, Washington, DC, 5–8 December 2002. MS.

Leach, Edmund Ronald

1954 *Political Systems of Highland Burma: A Study of Kachin Social Structure.* London: Bell.

Lee, Haiyan

2016 Mao's Two Bodies: On the Curious (Political) Art of Impersonating the Great Helmsman. In *Red Legacies in China: Cultural Afterlives of the Communist Revolution,* Jie Li and Enhua Zhang, eds. Cambridge, MA: Harvard University Asia Center, Harvard University Press.

LiPuma, Edward, and Thomas A. Koelble

2009 Deliberative Democracy and the Politics of Traditional Leadership in South Africa: A Case of Despotic Domination or Democratic Deliberation? *Journal of Contemporary African Studies* 27(2):201–23.

Little, Kenneth Lindsay

1951 *The Mende of Sierra Leone: A West African People in Transition.* London: Routledge & Kegan Paul.

Logan, Carolyn

2008 Traditional Leaders in Modern Africa: Can Democracy and the Chief Co-Exist? *Afrobarometer* Working Paper no. 93.

Luthuli, Albert John

1962 *Let My People Go.* New York: New American Library.

Mafeje, Archie
  1971   The Ideology of 'Tribalism.' *Journal of Modern African Studies* 9(2):253–61.
Maloka, Tshidiso, and David Gordon
  1996   Chieftainship, Civil Society, and the Political Transition in South Africa. *Critical Sociology* 22(3):37–55.
Mamdani, Mahmood
  1996   *Citizen and Subject: Contemporary Africa and the Legacy of Late Colonialism.* Princeton, NJ: Princeton University Press.
  1999   Historicizing Power and Responses to Power: Indirect Rule and Its Reform. *Social Research* 66(3):859–86.
Mbeki, Govan A.
  1939   *Transkei in the Making.* n.p.: Verulam Press.
Mbenga, Bernard, and Andrew Manson
  2010   *'People of the Dew': A History of the Bafokeng of Phokeng-Rustenburg Region, South Africa, from Early Times to 2000.* Johannesburg: Jacana Media.
Manson, Andrew, and Bernard K. Mbenga
  2014   *Land, Chiefs, Mining: South Africa's North-West Province Since 1840.* Johannesburg: Witwatersrand University Press.
Middleton, John, and David Tait, eds.
  1958   *Tribes without Rulers: Studies in African Segmentary Systems.* London: Routledge & Kegan Paul.
Miers, Suzanne, and Igor Kopytoff, eds.
  1977   *Slavery in Africa: Historical and Anthropological Perspectives.* Madison, WI: University of Wisconsin Press.
Molema, Silas Modiri
  1966   *Montshiwa, 1815–1896: Barolong Chief and Patriot.* Cape Town: Struik.
Molutsi, Patrick
  2004   Botswana: The Path to Democracy and Development. In *Democratic Reform in Africa: The Quality of Progress*, E. Gyimah-Boadi, ed. Boulder: Lynne Rienner Publishers.
Monroe, J. Cameron
  2013   The Archaeology of the Precolonial State in Africa. In *The Oxford Handbook of African Archaeology*, Peter Mitchell and Paul Lane, eds. Oxford: Oxford University Press.
Mosely, Erin Elizabeth
  2016   The Future of Rwanda's Past: Transitional Justice, Archival Practice, and the Remaking of History after Genocide. PhD dissertation, Harvard University.
Murray, Christina
  2004   South Africa's Troubled Royalty: Traditional Leaders after Democracy. Centre for International and Public Law, Law and Policy Paper 23. Canberra: The Federation Press in association with the Centre for International and Public Law, Faculty of Law, Australian National University.
Nakassis, Constantine V.
  2013   Brand Neoliberalism: Introduction. *Cultural Anthropology* 28(1):110.
Ndlovu-Gatsheni, Sabelo J.
  2008   'For the Nation to Live, the Tribe Must Die': The Politics of Ndebele Identity and Belonging in Zimbabwe. In *Society, State, and Identity in African History*, Bahru Zewde, ed. Addis Ababa: Forum for Social Studies.
Nolte, Insa
  n.d.   Transformations of the Customary: Christianity, Islam, and Yoruba Traditional Rulers in Southwest Nigeria. MS.

Ntsebeza, Lungisile
    2005   *Democracy Compromised: Chiefs and the Politics of Land in South Africa.* Leiden: Brill.
    2011   Traditional Authorities and Democracy: Are We Back to Apartheid? In *The Fate of the Eastern Cape: History, Politics, and Social Policy,* Greg Ruiters, ed. Scottsville: University of KwaZulu-Natal Press.

Oomen, Barbara
    2005   *Chiefs in South Africa: Law, Power, and Culture in the Post-Apartheid Era.* Oxford: James Currey.

O'Regan, Kate
    2016   Tradition and Modernity: Adjudicating a Constitutional Court Paradox. *Constitutional Court Review* 6:105–26.

Osabu-Kle, Daniel T.
    2000   *Compatible Cultural Democracy: The Key to Development in Africa.* Orchard Park, NY: Broadview Press.

Piot, Charles
    2010   *Nostalgia for the Future: West Africa after the Cold War.* Chicago: University of Chicago Press.

Plaatje, Solomon Tshekisho
    n.d.   *Native Life in South Africa: Before and Since the European War and the Boer Rebellion.* New York: The Crisis.

Porter, Gina, and Kevin Phillips-Howard
    1997   Agricultural Issues in the Former Homelands of South Africa: The Transkei. *Review of African Political Economy* 24(72):185–202.

Pratt, R. Cranford
    1965   Administration and Politics in Uganda, 1919–1945. In *History of East Africa,* vol. 11, Vincent Harlow and E. M. Chilver, eds. Oxford: Clarendon Press.

Rambe, Patient, and Munyaradzi Mawere
    2012   African Traditional Customs' Potentialities and Dilemmas: Conflict over Thanksgiving to Chiefs in Zimbabwean Rural Villages. *International Journal of Politics and Good Governance* 3(3.2):1–24.

Rata, Elizabeth
    1999   The Theory of Neotribal Capitalism. *Review: Journal of the Fernand Braudel Center* 22(3):231–88.
    2011   Encircling the Commons: Neotribal Capitalism in New Zealand since 2000. *Anthropological Theory* 11(3):327–53.

Sartre, Jean-Paul
    1963   Preface. In *The Wretched of the Earth,* Frantz Fanon. New York: Grove Press.

Schapera, Isaac
    1970   *Tribal Innovators: Tswana Chiefs and Social Change, 1795–1940.* London School of Economics Monographs on Social Anthropology, no.43. London: Athlone Press.

Sibanda, Sanele
    2010   When Is the Past Not the Past? Reflections on Customary Law under South Africa's Constitutional Dispensation. *Human Rights Brief* 17(3):31–35, 82.

Sikor, Thomas, and Christian Lund
    2009   Access and Property: A Question of Power and Authority. *Development and Change* 40(1):1–22.

Snyder, Francis G.
    1982   Colonialism and Legal Form: The Creation of 'Customary Law' in Senegal. In *Crime, Justice and Underdevelopment,* Colin Sumner, ed. London: Heinemann.

Stoler, Laura Ann, and Frederick Cooper

    1997   Between Metropole and Colony: Rethinking a Research Agenda. In *Tensions of Empire: Colonial Cultures in a Bourgeois World*, Frederick Cooper and Ann Laura Stoler, eds. Berkeley, CA: University of California Press.

Tosh, John

    1973   Colonial Chiefs in a Stateless Society: A Case-Study from Northern Uganda. *Journal of African History* 14(3):473–90.

Tripp, Aili Mari

    2001   Women's Movements, Customary Law, and Land Rights in Africa: The Case of Uganda. *African Studies Quarterly* 36(4). http://asq.africa.ufl.edu/files/Tripp-Vol-7-Issue-4.pdf.

Turner, Robin L.

    2014   Traditional, Democratic, Accountable? Navigating Citizen-Subjection in Rural South Africa. *Africa Spectrum* 49(1):27–54.

van Kessel, Ineke, and Barbara Oomen,

    1997   'One Chief, One Vote': The Revival of Traditional Authorities in Post-Apartheid South Africa. *African Affairs* 96(385):561–85.

Vansina, Jan

    1962   A Comparison of African Kingdoms. *Africa* 32(4):324–35.

    2005   *Antecedents to Modern Rwanda: The Nyiginya Kingdom*. Madison, WI: University of Wisconsin Press.

Vincent, Joan

    1994   *Anthropology and Politics: Visions, Traditions, and Trends*. Tucson, AZ: University of Arizona Press.

Weber, Max

    1978[1922]   *Economy and Society: An Outline of Interpretive Sociology*, Guenther Roth and Claus Wittich, eds. Ephraim Fischoff et al., trans. Berkeley, CA: University of California Press.

West, Harry G., and Scott Kloeck-Jenson

    1999   Betwixt and Between: 'Traditional Authority' and Democratic Decentralization in Post-War Mozambique. *African Affairs* 98(393):455–84.

Williams, J. Michael

    2004   Leading from Behind: Democratic Consolidation and the Chieftaincy in South Africa. *Journal of Modern African Studies* 42(1):113–36.

    2010   *Chieftaincy, the State, and Democracy: Political Legitimacy in Post-Apartheid South Africa*. Bloomington, IN: Indiana University Press.

Woolcock, Michael

    1998   Social Capital and Economic Development: Toward a Theoretical Synthesis and Policy Framework. *Social Theory* 27(2):151–208.

TWO

African Chiefs and the Post–Cold War Moment

Millennial Capitalism and the Struggle over Moral Authority

PETER GESCHIERE

The resilience of chieftaincy in many parts of Africa over recent decades is one of the main surprises in a continent already full of them.[1] One might even speak of its "return": despite expectations to the contrary, chiefs seem not to go away but rather to grow in importance and power. In a paradoxical way, this return of authorities that portray themselves emphatically as "traditional" echoes Pliny the Elder's famous remark, *Ex Africa semper aliquid novi*, "always something new from Africa." Their comeback in a neoliberal setting may be heavily adorned with customary trappings, but in many cases these involve audacious innovations: neotraditional might be the word to describe the phenomenon.

However, it is also necessary to emphasize from the start that the resilience, or "return," of chieftaincy is not general to the continent as a whole. Certainly, there are many examples of it. In South Africa, for instance, it is striking that traditional authority survived the transition to postapartheid so easily. Against most expectations, the institution, tarnished by its involvement with the old regime, emerged more powerful than before (Ntsebeza 2005; Oomen 2005). Or take a case that followed a very different scenario: in the forest area of South Cameroon, chieftaincy was so clearly a colonial creation that, in the first decades of nation building, it appeared to wither away, all the more so since the new government seemed intent to encourage its demise. However, after the spectacular changes around 1990—the "post–Cold War moment," to borrow a term from Charles Piot (2010)—the same government, now under President Paul Biya, who miraculously managed to survive the end of the one-party regime, made a volte face: it actively worked for a resurrection of chieftaincy, including in the southern reaches of the country. Clearly his administration had realized that customary rulers might serve as vote banks and thus could neutralize the effects of democratization and multipartyism as imposed by international donors. A consequence is that, nowadays, ministers and other politicians from these parts of Cameroon—where people used to be proud of their *egalitarian* traditions—claim royal titles that seem to be invented on the spot. Even more impressive is the recent (re)affirmation of chiefly power in places where it has flourished for quite some time, like Ghana or Nigeria. But precisely because there has been so much interest recently in the "return" of chieftaincy,[2] it is important to note that the institution has been marginalized, even to have disappeared, in some places, including ones in which it had a glorious past, among them Senegal, Mali, Guinea, Uganda, Rwanda, Burundi, and Tanzania. Moreover, where one can speak of its comeback since the post–Cold War moment of the 1990s—characterized by Piot as an enigmatic turning point, the implications of which for the continent are still far from clear—it has followed very different trajectories and had highly variable outcomes.

There are two possible approaches to deal with these differences and uncertainties. One is to look for entirely new theoretical starting points to account for the baffling dynamics of contemporary chieftaincy. The other is comparative: to try and identify recurrent patterns in what seems to be a quite unpredictable phenomenon. I propose to follow the latter, although, as we shall see, it inevitably leads to broader theoretical concerns. My preference for this alternative may stem from the fact that my own long-term research in Cameroon has forced me to take comparison seriously—both because the country evinces dazzling variety where customary authority is concerned and because the workings of the institution, in all its diversity, continue to surprise me. Even a little travel in this part of the world makes it plain that chieftaincy can mean many different things. In this respect, as in many others, Cameroon honors its self-chosen nickname as the "crossroads of Africa":

> When I started fieldwork in the forest area of East Cameroon I was little prepared for the blatantly colonial profile of *les chefs coutumiers* there. I began my research in 1971, when the memory of colonial rule was still fresh. In the Maka Mboanz district where I first settled, the *chef de canton*, Thomas Mballa, was called *la vieille machète*, "the old cleaver," because of his harsh ways in imposing forced labor in colonial days. When I visited him, he still had about eighty women living in his compound—it used to be over

a hundred—each of whom had her own "kitchen." I was impressed by its sheer size. But when he retired for the night reality turned out to be less impressive. He went to bed, accompanied by his ageing first wife, taking his very old gun with him for protection. As he explained to me: "these women turn my compound into a brothel. It is dangerous here at night. I will have the *sous-préfet* come and chase them all away." The paramount chief of the region, M. Etienne Effoudou, was even more explicit about the colonial roots of his chieftaincy. When he agreed to tell me his life story, he started quite pompously: *Moi, je suis né entre les mains des blancs* ("I was born in the hands of the whites"). The somewhat artificial (i.e., non-"authentic") character of the rulers in this area, who were known as *les chefs coutumiers*, was emphasized by the fact that both locals and people from other parts of Cameroon insisted on contrasting them with chiefs from the west (the Bamiléké) and the Islamic sultans from the north (the Foulbe)—who were seen as "the real thing." To the Bamiléké and Foulbé, the absence of "real" chiefs in the forest area of south and east Cameroon was taken to be clear proof of how backward those forest people were.

Later I did meet the "real thing." I had to sip "hot drink" (whiskey or Dutch gin) from the hands of rulers from the west and only just escaped the privilege of being blessed by their saliva. And, indeed, it *was* hard to deny that they were more "traditional" than those of the forest—and still retained a moral authority that the latter lacked. This simplistic but widespread contrast between societies *with* chiefs and those *without* was shaken in the 1990s: with the wave of democratization and decentralization that affected Cameroon, as it did the rest of Africa, the supposedly sacrosanct authority of the rulers in the West and Northwest Provinces came under heavy threat. Some had their palaces and Pajeros burned, acts of aggression that were said to be unthinkable in earlier decades; people speculated openly that they had used their special, spectral powers in collusion with witches. For these rulers, democratization and multipartyism proved to be, at least in the beginning, a direct threat: it placed them in an impossible position between their subjects, most of whom fiercely supported the opposition to the president and his clique, and the government, which paid their salaries and hence could exert concrete pressure on them. In those years their moral authority seemed to wane (Goheen 1996; Miaffo and Warnier 1993; Nyamnjoh and Rowlands 1998). This makes it all the more striking that, in the south—where chieftaincy appeared to lack traditional roots—elites developed a keen interest in claiming royal titles, titles whose historical anchorage was often highly doubtful. Equally notable is the fact that the rulers in the west survived the angry attacks of their subjects. Over the last decade, their moral authority has reinstated itself: they are seen once more as indispensable for defending the interests of their communities.

This sketch, by drawing some stark comparisons, underscores the urgent need for new theoretical starting points to make sense of chiefship in contemporary Africa. As Jean and John Comaroff emphasized, in their call for papers for the conference of which this book is a product, older Euromodernist metaphors for, and conceptions of, "traditional authority" are of limited use in understanding the institution today. It is true, of course, that many of those older conceptions characterized the office, more or less explicitly, as one that would sooner or later be superseded by modern statehood and citizenship. This is why its "resurgence," not least in places where it seemed to have withered away, came as such a surprise to many observers. Its (re)new(ed) life invites us—in step with another of the Comaroffs' challenges (2012)—to theorize it "from the South," thus to break loose of the tendency to take northern social theory as the fixed meridian from which to interpret its history in the present.

It is impossible, here, to do justice to the rich flow of recent studies on the present-day politics of custom. All I can do is to highlight general tendencies. Of special importance is the effort to move beyond the kind of binary oppositions that dominated earlier efforts to generalize about the role, and the potential, of traditional authorities. Below I shall first discuss some of those binaries, this with a view to showing that, despite their limitations, they remain significant—but in much more ambiguous ways, allowing for unexpected articulations and crossovers, than has long been assumed. Comparing the different trajectories of traditional sovereignty might help also to explore another general trend in recent studies: the stress on the variable ways in which indigenous rulers have exploited new opportunities, both economic and political, in the changing global configuration shaped by "millennial capitalism" (Comaroff and Comaroff 2000) as it has developed since the end of the Cold War. I hope to show, however, that this focus has to be balanced by ongoing attention to the *moral* aspect of chiefly authority—and the ways in which chiefs struggle to maintain that authority. Often it is precisely their management of these new forms of wealth and power that threatens their moral standing in relation to their subjects. The very different and often improvised ways in which they handle this balancing act could well be a critical factor in understanding the distinctly varied fate of the institution today.

Beyond Binaries

In retrospect, it is striking how strongly early characterizations of the role of chiefs were framed by clear, binary oppositions. Take three obvious examples. One is the contrast, more or less canonized by Fortes and Evans-Pritchard (1940) but also part and parcel of everyday discourse in many parts of Africa, between centralized and segmentary societies. An even older one in the scholarly canon differentiates colonial-era British indirect rule from French *assimilation*, with the Portuguese and Belgian models somewhere in between.[3] More recently, Mahmood Mamdani's (1996) "citizen versus subject"—an elaboration of Ekeh's (1975) distinction between two publics in postcolonial Africa, a primordial and a civic one (see also Chanock 1985)—has become widely cited in academic debate.

To start with the last one, which has been the target of much criticism, Mamdani argues that chiefs play a key role in the "bifurcated" world that African nations inherited from colonialism. In these nations, "civil society," in which people are *citizens*, coexists with a separate sphere of "decentralized despotism," in which traditional authorities rule over *subjects*. This bifurcation, he says, lies at the root of the impotence of the postcolonial state, which might only be remedied by the total abolition of customary office.[4] Perhaps because of its persuasive, direct prose, Mamdani's book is often read as a historical study based on empirical research, not as a powerful political essay. As a result, it is taken to task for separating too neatly domains whose boundaries, in practice, are constantly breached: to be sure, most Africans, in their everyday lives, are in some measure *both* subjects and citizens—and, by all manner of subterfuge, may escape the obligations of the one for the benefits of the other. Indeed, the *analytical* challenge is to understand what kind of creative strategies and transgressions people fashion to make life under the different, coexistent species of authority habitable—and, even more, to do so to their advantage.

If, however, one reads Mamdani's *Citizen and Subject* as a work of political philosophy, its merits stand out: specifically, for showing how colonial policy created this opposition, this bipolarity, in order to facilitate the governance of huge territories that, at the end of the nineteenth century, were annexed without a clear plan for their *mise en valeur*. Sara Berry (chapter 3, this volume) is certainly right to point out that chiefs were not purely a product of colonialism, that their moral authority is based both on the control of socioeconomic assets and on a form of legitimacy founded on the customary. As I have already intimated, even where they *were* very clearly colonial creations, they and their subjects went to great lengths to adorn their newfangled positions with all sorts of "traditional" trappings—and still do. These "inventions of tradition" have their own effects and cannot simply be dismissed as false consciousness. In sum, whatever the shortcomings of Mamdani's play on categorical oppositions, his emphasis on the impact of colonialism in shaping the African present is important for understanding traditional authority and the politics of custom today.

The older distinction between chiefly and stateless societies—formulated by Fortes and Evans-Pritchard in 1940 as a starting point for political anthropology as a separate branch of the discipline—has also been the target of much criticism. Edmund Leach's (1954) study of Highland Burma, another classic, might be read as a critique of this distinction; it set out to demonstrate how societies can, and do, shift between the two polarities over time. Since then many other accounts have been published to similar effect, analyzing intermediary forms and shifting patterns. But this does not render the original opposition irrelevant; after all, many Africans take it to be self-evident. An example, already mentioned, comes from Cameroon, where people commonly oppose the chiefly societies of the northern and western provinces to those of the southern and eastern forests, where there are no institutionalized customary authorities, merely a strong emphasis on equality—that is, among adult males—and on individual achievement in building up a following. An example:

> One of my most awkward moments during fieldwork was when, in the 1990s, a colleague and I traveled with a driver to a village in the extreme south, inhabited by Fang people, to discuss their reactions to a new forestry law. When we arrived we found the village in an uproar because of a big funeral at which large quantities of very strong palm wine—for which the Fang are famous—had been consumed. This climaxed in a general brawl. To my amazement our driver, a Bamiléké from the West Province who had lavishly imbibed the reddish liquid, jumped on a chair and started shouting: "Is there no chief here? How can these people have order without a chief?" The villagers were furious. "Who is this Bamiléké that he comes and tells us we need chiefs? Let him tell his own people what to do." He was violently pulled from the chair, and we were lucky to get him unscathed into the car.

In those days the conceptual opposition between chiefly and chiefless societies could easily explode into ethnic anger. Since then, there been important shifts in this respect, most notably a proliferation of chiefly titles in the segmentary societies of the forest, with urban elites claiming all sorts of honorific positions in their places of origin—and villagers celebrating the value of traditional authority for the development of their communities.[5] Nor, as we shall see in some of the chapters below, is this confined to Cameroon.

Clearly, the revival of interest in chieftaincy in the 1990s, after it had been seen as a painful relic of colonial domination, had special significance in societies formally classified as segmentary. The reasons for it varied. An important one was the competition of these societies with neighbors whose rulers served as a rallying point when ethnic tensions arose.[6] But unexpected effects of neoliberal democratization played a role as well: the reimposition of multiparty democracy around 1990 led to rising pressure on a number of politicians to celebrate their local belonging as "sons of the soil" in order to reinforce their clout at the national level (see below). So did the stress on decentralized development, which also created unexpected scope for customary chiefs to enhance their position. At the same time, the hasty, often improvised ways in which traditional authority was resurrected in areas where it was mostly a colonial creation differed markedly from situations in which it had a longer history. In the upshot, the classical distinction between chiefly and segmentary societies haunts contemporary political life in Cameroon and elsewhere.

It might be worthwhile to dwell a bit longer on the third opposition, the colonial one between British indirect rule and French direct rule, even *assimilation*. Firstly, despite being dismissed as too simplistic, this opposition still inflects present-day relations, albeit in unexpected ways. Secondly, it turns out to be relevant to the unevenly spread "resurgence" of chieftaincy across the continent. Again, here, labels taken to be self-evident confuse and obscure all sorts of intermediary forms and transformations over time.

The deeper implications of this colonial debate were already present, if implicitly, in a confrontation between Hubert Deschamps (1963) and Michael Crowder (1964) at the dawn of the postcolonial period. Deschamps, then a respected professor at the Sorbonne after a long career in the colonial service, started it by saying how he, as a young district officer in Madagascar in the 1930s, had dared challenge Lord Lugard, generally celebrated as the architect of British indirect rule. A year after he published his piece, Deschamps was attacked by Michael Crowder, then a young scholar (see Geschiere 1993). Deschamps gave his presentation the title *"Et maintenant Lord Lugard?"* ("And now Lord Lugard?"), all the more provocative since it was presented as the Lugard Lecture to the council of the International African Institute—which had been founded by Lugard himself.[7] He played at calling up the ghost of Lugard, who had died in 1945, in order to debate

him: "indirect rule" versus "assimilation." Even though he declared the result a draw, the tenor of Deschamps's text seemed different. Pride of place
was given to the idea that, by consolidating traditional chieftaincies, British indirect rule had ill prepared African societies for independence; the
French, by contrast, had allowed these institutions to wither away and thus
laid the foundation for the building of new nations. In retrospect, especially the first few pages of the prestigious lecture highlighted the extent
of French-British rivalry in colonial days. And the deep impression Lugard
had made as a great empire builder. Deschamps (1963:293) deemed it
necessary to reassure his readers that he was not calling up the

> young Lugard with his unforgettable face of a lean wolf, ... his terrible
> moustache like a Turkish sword, his black shining eyes in their deep sockets,
> and his savage energy . . . [like] a black panther.

He was talking, rather, to the ghost of the older, altogether more sedate
Lugard.

Leaving aside the pathos, Deschamps showed that the opposition was
more complex than the labels suggested. In his view *assimilation* may have
been a lofty idea, but it had never determined French colonial practice,
certainly not after the great extension of the empire at the end of the nineteenth century. It was quickly and quietly replaced by *association*, which,
he thought, largely corresponded to indirect rule. Since full assimilation
was impossible with the increasing scale of its colonial possessions, French
administrative wisdom held that it made sense to build on existing institutions; in the upshot, local chiefs became their indispensable collabora-
tors as well. For Deschamps, the difference lay in the fact that France did
not make it a policy principle to consolidate these traditional supports for
their rule, or to seal them off from the flow of changes. And so he could
conclude that "our French practice of nonchalance towards the chiefs has
proved in the end to be more positive for the building of new nations than
your [Lugard's] doctrine of allowing these old structures to follow their
own evolution" (p. 303).

It is on this point that Deschamps was taken to task by Michael
Crowder. For Crowder, speaking of French "nonchalance" toward "their"
chiefs was downright misleading, masking the often brutal and disdain-
ful way in which they dealt with these men. This is also why, for him, *association* could not be equated with indirect rule. While the British district
officers made a show of honoring local rulers, whom they often addressed
as "brother," their French counterparts, as *roitelets de la brousse* ("little kings

of the bush"), treated them as functionaries of doubtful ability to perform their required roles—and, therefore, as incumbents who could be deposed at any moment. Larger chieftaincies were cut up and outsiders were often appointed as chiefs, the main criterion for their selection and retention being the extent to which they were able *de suivre les ordres à la lettre* ("to follow orders in detail").[8] Crowder, in short, saw a quite different sort of continuity between colonial and postcolonial realities: while, in British Africa, customary authorities tended to become more powerful during the colonial period—even where, like in the Ibo region, they had to be created de novo—in French Africa they became increasingly unpopular, to the extent that they could be, and were, abolished in many Francophone countries after independence.[9]

Whichever version one prefers, recent history appears to be in line with their overall conclusions. It may be no accident that most examples of "resurgent" chiefship in this volume come primarily from Anglophone Africa, while, in many Francophone countries, it has almost disappeared or seems destined to play a more marginal role, this even where it is said to have evinced more dynamism of late.[10] The implication is that this old opposition, despite all the criticism and qualification to which it has been subjected, also remains relevant for what is occurring in Africa today.[11] But it requires to be nuanced. Already in the 1960s, Crowder had to note important exceptions, cases in which French colonial practice did not sap the chieftaincy: among them, the powerful Mossi kings in Upper Volta (now Burkina Faso; see chapter 7, this volume) and Fulani emirs in northern Cameroon. Conversely, some parts of Anglophone Africa followed the French trajectory; in countries like Tanzania and Uganda, moreover, where traditional authority boasted a longer tradition, it was readily marginalized after independence.

In retrospect, it is notable that neither Deschamps nor Crowder paid much attention to some important nuances in colonial policy. Neither, for instance, mentions the French insistence on *la politique des races* as the founding principle of their administrative order. Promulgated by William Ponty, governor-general of French West Africa at the beginning of the last century, it based the governance of their colonies on *cantons* populated by people of the same *race* (i.e., ethnicity). It was in this context that the term *autochthon* was introduced, laying the ground for the heightened relevance of ethnic politics in more recent times. A critical phrase in *Haut-Sénégal-Niger* by Maurice Delafosse ([1912] 1972:280), France's counterpart to Lugard, had it that "some *indigènes* are *autochthons*, whereas others are definitely not." In setting up a new government apparatus founded on homogeneous cantons, therefore, it was necessary to separate the *autochthons* from those others and put them in charge—one effect of which, in places such as the French Sudan, where pluralistic polities like the Foulbe and Dyula sultanates had emerged, was to free people identified as autochthonous from foreign rulers. Thus *la politique des races* meant abolishing the positions of the more powerful chiefs, some of whom had fiercely resisted French "pacification." This was more or less in line with Crowder's claim that Francophone colonial policy was intent on fragmenting larger African polities and on deploying local chiefs as "bureaucratic auxiliaries." There were exceptions, however, among them Burkina Faso, where, for practical reasons during the Scramble for Africa, France had a vested interest in sustaining the unity of the Mossi empire.[12] British support for traditional authorities in their "possessions" also varied. A significant shift that affected relations in most of its colonies—only briefly mentioned by Deschamps— was an increasing emphasis on (nonchiefly) local government, roughly after 1945. This destabilized the position of many indigenous rulers, who felt betrayed by their former protectors. Where postcolonial sovereigns tried to build directly on these late colonial institutions of local government, which they did in (formerly British) Southwest Cameroon and Tanzania, customary offices could be pushed aside more easily. But the Southwest Cameroon case underscores the fact that they could also take on renewed dynamism after 1990.

Another important intersecting factor, as in the French Sudan, was the presence and relative prominence of Islam. In Senegal, for example, France had, from 1900 onwards, sought the collaboration of the powerful *marabouts* of Muslim brotherhoods rather than the kings of the subjected Wolof and Foulbe states. Developments moved so quickly that, already by the 1920s, these Sufi leaders became useful allies for the colonial authorities, causing traditional rulers to lose their relevance (Cruise O'Brien 1971; Diouf 2013). This stands in contrast with the Islamicized reaches of the Anglophone colonies, like Northern Nigeria, where it was the emirs who could extend their powers by assuming the role of mediators between their Muslim subjects and the British.

Patently, then, received oppositions cannot simply be discarded. Their traces continue to manifest themselves in more or less complex, more or less visible ways across many parts of Africa. But it is also clear that the three binary models, singly and together, raise problems. In order to understand contemporary chiefship, in all its enigmatic dimensions, we need to identify focal points that allow us to make sense of its variations and improvisational character.

Post–Cold War: Democratization, Decentralization, and the Return of Chiefs

Why were the 1990s a turning point for so many chiefs? And to what extent do recent transformations in the politics of custom point to a more nuanced theoretical starting point for understanding the wide variations in the resurgence of traditional authority? It is clear that the upheavals of *fin de siècle*, when the existing international order seemed suddenly to lose its coherence, had a direct effect on chieftaincy, motivating its spectacular "comeback" in some of the places and cases discussed in this book—and not in others. Charles Piot (2010) introduced the concept of "the post–Cold War moment" precisely to frame the impact of this global turn on local political dynamics. The area of North Togo where he has worked consistently since the 1980s has undergone rapid and unexpected changes: the almost total absence of the state at the local level; a proliferation of NGOs to fill the gap; a return of urban elites, "sons of the soil," who are determined to take matters in "their" villages in hand but are impatient with the constraints of tradition; and, most of all, the Pentecostalization of the public sphere that reinforces their impatience with those constraints.

Elsewhere on the continent different sorts of changes mark the 1990s and the years since. In Cameroon, for instance, there has not been a similar retreat of the state. On the contrary, the former one-party regime has used the upsurge of the politics of belonging to give it new forms of control over the population: that regime has been quite successful in switching from nation building—the central theme of the first decades after independence—to a celebration of the local, this in order to circumvent the effects of multipartyism. Elsewhere on the continent, too, there has been a waxing of the politics of autochthony, itself part of a planetary "conjuncture of belonging" that has arisen in lockstep with the globalization of the world order (Geschiere 2009). But what these different contexts share, more generally, is that received conceptual frameworks appear no longer to apply to any of them, which is why "classical" characterizations of chieftaincy—situated in the binary oppositions interrogated above—seem to have been overtaken by history.

Piot asks for deeper reflection about the impact of the transformations of the 1990s. In the new global constellation, he argues, postcolonial theory no longer suffices. Of course, he acknowledges, being wide-ranging and multifaceted, it will retain its purchase; in many respects it remains essential to analyze contemporary Africa precisely because the present has been so critically shaped by the colonial past. But the post–Cold War moment calls for fresh theorizing: it is necessary to note, for instance, that the state is now only postcolonial in an attenuated sense. During the early decades of independence—for most countries a time of strenuous nation building, requiring celebration of shared citizenship and unity—ruling regimes followed in the footsteps of their European predecessors, taking over their governmental practices. This is much less true since the end of the Cold War. The extent of their control may differ, as the contrast between Togo and Cameroon makes clear, but nowhere do these regimes sustain the colonial model of autocratic command. In many contexts their authority grafts itself upon other networks and positions of power. Jean-François Bayart's (2007) model of the "rhizomatic" state, spreading its networks underground, or Beatrice Hibou's (2004) idea of its "privatization," apply especially well to current modalities of governmental command. In a similar vein, Janet Roitman (2005) emphasizes the increasing plurality of power in North Cameroon. Power, of course, has always been plural, even under the most autocratic colonial and postcolonial regimes. But colonial state authority, and the postcolonial leaders of one-party states in its slipstream, did everything to limit and deny that plurality. Since the post–Cold War moment this has changed: state authority, in many contexts, is hidden behind, or is exercised in conjunction with, other forms of domination.

These changes have affected the role of chieftaincy directly, laying the ground for the various scenarios that have characterized its "return." A few Cameroonian examples highlight those various scenarios, the range of trajectories they may take, and some of their more general implications.

Rogers Orock (2014) offers a seminal analysis of a special occasion: the reception of Cameroonian president Paul Biya in Bamenda in 2010 and his coronation as *fon* of *fons*, "chief of chiefs." Orock takes the magnanimous reception of Biya as the starting point of a fine-grained analysis of how "hosting the head of state" is becoming a key ritual in this as in other African countries.[13] Not only is it important in political competition between regional elites. It is also a context in which the president may affirm his position by a show of generosity.

Why was this so special an event? For one thing, because Bamenda, the capital of the Anglophone Northwest Province, had long been a hotbed of antagonism toward President Biya: in the early 1990s—when he, as head of an extremely autocratic one-party state since 1982, was involved in a desperate struggle to survive the transition to multipartyism—it was in here that the first opposition party emerged. It was also the staunch support of the Anglophones (notably in the Northwest) who, according to reliable sources, caused the Francophone Biya to *lose* the presidential elections of 1992. Only by drastically rigging its results and by virtue of the support of French President Mitterand did he manage to hold on to power.[14] In the following decade, Bamenda remained the scene of constant eruptions of resistance against the strenuous attempts of the regime to consolidate its power under the new circumstances.

The fact that, in 2010, Biya dared return to Bamenda with such great pomp eloquently expressed how much the situation had changed and how effective the regime had been in dividing an opposition that once seemed to be ready to take over. One of the secrets of this success was the way in which the ruling party had encouraged a vibrant politics of belonging, backing autochthons against immigrants from elsewhere who were mostly also Cameroonian citizens but not living in their area of origin. Chiefs had a vital role to play in this emergent politics of belonging—a politics, as I have already noted, that allowed the former one-party regime to neutralize the effects of open elections (Konings and Nyamnjoh 2003; Geschiere 2009; and see below).

Another reason why Biya's reception in Bamenda was so special is that, in accepting the title *"fons of fons,"* he publicly acknowledged the volte-face of his *own* policies regarding chieftaincy and citizenship. In a book published in his name in 1986, a few years prior to the transition to electoral democracy, he had dismissed customary authority as "a barrier to development," much to the indignation of elites from the west and the north; remember that the institution had a long tradition in those parts of the country. It was seen as a typical statement from someone from the south, where people had never had "real" chiefs.[15] At the time, the president's doubts about traditional office fitted well with the postindependence emphasis on the need for "nation building" and, therefore, on national citizenship and unity—in the face of which the continuing power of traditional chiefs was taken to be potentially divisive.

However, all this changed in 1989 with the passage of a law that proclaimed freedom of association. Until then, all efforts to found independent organizations were drastically punished; now government had to accept the establishment of rival parties. Under the old regime, elections had purely symbolic value. People could only vote "Yes" for the one-party list; abstentions were liable to be severely punished. With the new dispensation, the regime had to look for other ways to win a majority. Officials, who depended on salaries paid by the state, were suddenly told to take the politics of belonging seriously. Before, any politician who tried to create a following of his own in his region of origin risked being accused of subversion and under-

mining national unity. With the rise of multiparty democracy, the same people were told to do exactly this: to go home and campaign for the president
there. Clearly, the renewed politics of belonging—a complete reversal of the
earlier obsession with Cameroonian unity—was an important factor behind
the success of the Biya regime in hanging on to power against all odds.[16]

Chiefs had a crucial part in all this. During the 1980s many customary
offices, especially in the southern forest area, remained vacant due to bureaucratic obstruction. But, in the new constellation, they were quickly filled.
The salaries of local rulers were raised repeatedly and the Biya regime went
out of its way to convince them that it was in their interest to side with the
government. As Ibrahim Mouiche (2005) shows for the Bamiléké area of the
West Province, traditional authorities were eager to use the new opportunity
to reaffirm their position. By agreeing to serve as vote banks, albeit with variable success, they became indispensable allies of the ruling party. President
Biya's triumphant coronation as "chief of chiefs" by the Northwest elites was
a powerful confirmation of the success of this policy. And, indeed, the president reacted, as expected, by announcing that he would "give" Bamenda a
university (Orock 2014:240).

Similar policies have not worked everywhere in Africa. There is some
parallel with the role the ANC has wanted traditional rulers to play in
South Africa, although kings and chiefs there have become rather more demanding allies of the regime (see chapters 1 and 4, this volume). But, to reiterate, there are also parts of the continent where, under a democratic dispensation, these rulers are no longer attractive allies for governments, nor
have they always been willing or able to be, even where they have retained
substantial power. In Ghana, for instance, Sara Berry (chapter 3, this volume) emphasizes that chiefs have preferred to take up new opportunities
to go into business on their own account. In sum, different circumstances
have led to striking diversity in the way that customary office has evolved
in recent times.

That diversity came vividly to the fore at a workshop on chieftaincy during a
conference organized by the Panafrican Association of Anthropology (PAA)
in Yaoundé, all the more so since it brought together local rulers from different parts of Africa.[17] The general theme of the meeting—held at the prestigious building of the CPDM, President Biya's governing party—was "Tradition Embracing Change." An entire day was devoted to the role of customary
authorities, who, the organizers believed, were critical figures in linking tradition to change. The PAA had invited a diverse group of traditional digni-

taries: an Ewe chief from Ghana; two prominent officeholders from South Africa, one of them, a Zulu, very proud to be chairperson of the National House of Traditional Leaders there; one ruler from Benin; and a rich array from Cameroon, most of them, in line with the orientation of the host organization, from the Anglophone part of the country. As this suggests, the conference provided striking insight into the contrasts between these customary authorities.

The South African chiefs were in an advantageous position since their delegation was well financed by their government: they stayed in the Hilton Hotel and rented a Pajero with a driver. This was to the clear chagrin of the Ghanaian ruler, who, at the moment of departure from his home country, found that there was only a ticket for him, none for his assistant. He kept muttering that this was a scandal: didn't "these people" know that it is a serious insult for a chief to travel alone? The South African dignitaries also confused the audience by repeatedly changing costume. Normally they dressed according to Western fashion—three-piece suit and a tie—but for special occasions they would have themselves driven back to the Hilton in order to return in "traditional dress": half-naked, with ribbons of animal skins complemented by white sneakers, after the style of President Jacob Zuma. The contrast with the heavily robed Cameroonian and Ghanaian chiefs was stark. These chiefs, it seems, also had difficulty in dealing with the self-assured way in which their South African "brothers" claimed clear priority.

The workshop took an unexpected turn when a Cameroonian academic made an announcement: the prime minister, Ephraïm Inoni, he said, had expressed annoyance on hearing that there was an important delegation of chiefs in the capital, from all over Africa, who apparently had no intention of paying him a visit. Didn't they know that he, too, was a traditional ruler? Indeed, just a few months before, Mr. Inoni had arranged to be crowned in his native village, Bakingili, in the Southwest Province, where chieftaincy has had an uncertain history; recall what I said before about customary authority being a colonial creation in the forest zones of the country.[18] This admonition, accompanied by an invitation from the prime minister, required some urgent improvisation. The South African chiefs rushed back to the Hilton to put on their traditional dress; everybody else hurried to the PM's office. (I was admitted after some hesitation and checking.) Speeches and well wishes were exchanged. The South Africans spoke of their hope that a Panafrican House of Traditional Chiefs would soon be created, an idea for which Mr. Inoni expressed support. A general feeling of unanimity, despite obvious differences, prevailed.

Our return to the conference venue was less harmonious, however. The South Africans rushed off in their Pajero. Others were taken back in the cars of the organizers. But the Ghanaian ruler was left behind. He arrived later, fuming with rage, since he had had to take a taxi—with all of his golden paraphernalia. These were gilded copies; the originals were left at home. Still, this was seriously risky in view of the prevailing uncertainty in the city. Inevitably, complicated issues of protocol, and of hierarchy, surrounded the PAA's courageous initiative to bring together customary authorities from such different backgrounds.

Two aspects of the conference and its vicissitudes are notable here. First was the unexpected vigor with which gender entered the proceedings. The traditional authorities were clearly accustomed to dominating public gatherings; most of the day was filled with their lengthy speeches. When, however, time was finally allowed for discussion from the floor, there followed an explosion. Several female participants, all academic colleagues, rushed to the microphones. The chair tried to placate them, but to little avail. The venerable rulers present were vigorously challenged: Why had they not addressed issues of gender? How could they continue to settle inheritance disputes invariably in favor of males? One woman had brought her Bible with her: she quoted examples from the Old Testament of a fairer division between sons and daughters than currently prevailed in Cameroon. And why were there no female chiefs? The dignitaries were clearly embarrassed. For them, arguments from the Bible carried considerable weight. What is more, there was not a single woman among them or their courtiers. Africa may have a long history of female monarchs, but it was obvious—at least to the female academics in the room—that the new trajectories of chieftaincy were marked by an ever more unfavorable gender balance.

The other notable aspect, already mentioned, was the manifest popularity of claiming chiefly titles, especially among groups where the office lacks a deep history. Prime Minister Inoni, for example, was clearly happy to use the visit of his respectable "brothers" from other parts of Africa as a way to enhance his own status as chief—which remained doubtful to Cameroonians from parts of the country where chieftaincy boasts a longer tradition.

Another striking example is that of Peter Agbor Tabi, a leading politician in Cameroon—he was deputy secretary-general of the presidency before his untimely death in 2016—and at the time one of the most powerful members of the Biya cabinet. In 2011, he allowed himself to be crowned ruler of his native village, Ndekwai. This is an office of relatively low order, which tempted the district officer to make a risky joke at the crowning ceremony, referring to confusions of hierarchy: he (as DO), the administrative junior of the minister, now had "control" over the latter, his political superior, who, as a lower chief, had to take orders from him, the DO (Orock 2013). This pre-occupation with customary titles is spreading ever wider. Some colleagues at the universities in Yaounde are also developing a predilection for chiefly at-tributes, changing their desk chairs for ratan thrones and playing with elabo-rate fly-whisks when they receive visitors. It is telling that these scholars are mainly from the southern forest area; those from parts of the country where chieftaincy is more institutionalized, and thus more circumscribed by rules, turn a mocking eye on such displays of symbolic power.

As this implies, the contemporary politics of custom is blurring the distinction between the fake and the authentic. The opposition that once separated "real" chiefs—"truly traditional" ones with a precolonial pedi-gree—from those created by colonialism looks to be dissolving. Many local people have no problem recognizing that "tradition" is being newly imag-ined. Almost anything seems permissible in the cause of giving rulers the aura of the customary.

In 2013 a political scientist from Maka, Patrice Bigombe Logo, consulted me about the enthronement of a new ruler in the line of Etienne Effoudou, the Maka paramount mentioned earlier, the one who told me in 1971 that he was "born in the hands of the whites." We conducted an interview via the in-ternet. Bigombe's questions made it clear that the ceremony was to celebrate the "traditional" office in order to give a boost to an emerging Maka iden-tity, notably for the Maka Bebend, a subgroup around the village of Atok, the seat of this chieftaincy. I emphasized that my 1971 interviews with Chief Effoudou, now seen as the founder of the dynasty, made plain its colonial roots. The old ruler's own stories made it amply clear that, prior to the arrival of the Germans in 1905, it was difficult to speak at all of chieftaincy in this area. Indeed, in his personal bearing, Etienne Effoudou himself stressed this colonial background in no uncertain terms: he often dressed in khaki, the uniform that early French administrators, many from a military background, saw as fitting for the indigenous authorities they had appointed. And he re-acted with horror when I asked him if he had ever worn a helmet of monkey skin or ribbons of leopard skin, accoutrements that were held to have forti-fied warlords of old.

In 2014, during my most recent visit to Cameroon, Dr. Antang Yamo, an anthropologist from the same area who had also collaborated in preparing the ceremony, handed me an impressive brochure that had been prepared for the occasion. It contained articles, pictures, and a Maka translation of the national hymn of Cameroon (*Maka Bebend Magazine* 2013). My interview had been faithfully reprinted: no effort was made to tone down my emphasis on the colonial roots of the chieftaincy, even though this, to me at least, clashed with the stress on tradition in other contributions. It was striking, for instance, that a clear irregularity in the choice of the new chief, Bertrand Effoudou III—who could only claim descent through the daughter of Etienne Effoudou, not through his patriline—was explained by an appeal to custom. Both Bigombe and Yamo assured me that, in the olden days as well, it was "quite usual" that a sister's son, rather than a son, was chosen as successor—a statement that contradicts the heavy emphasis on patrilineal descent in Maka society in general.[19]

Telling, too, is the discrepancy in the brochure between images from colonial times and those of more recent vintage. In the older ones, Etienne Effoudou, the founder of the dynasty, is dressed in western clothes; in one photograph he has a bowler hat. By contrast, the present incumbent is pictured in a more or less improvised vest of bark cloth, worn over a western shirt. The other participants, primarily dancers and courtiers, are also attired in what was clearly meant as traditional garb of bark cloth and (pseudo) leopard skin. Bigombe explained that they had searched hard to find someone in the nearest town who was able to prepare bark in such a way that it could be used for clothing.[20] The late Etienne Effoudou would have been appalled had he had to walk around in this sort of costume. But his grandson wore it—along with an exotic looking cap of entirely novel shape—with a deep sense of solemnity.

It is precisely the lack of clearly instituted rules in such contexts that allows for experimentation with the customary. For the organizers of the enthronement, colonial and traditional practices were no longer seen as separate: acknowledging the colonial roots of chieftaincy here did not preclude an appeal to tradition—or a celebration of precolonial continuities (see Yamo n.d.). Under these conditions, the generic difference between societies with rulers and those without disappears: having one is seen to be vital for developing an authentic regional identity. Hence the immediate objective for those who have not had chiefs before is to assert, in the here and now, that they *do* have them—just like other Cameroonian societies. The question, to which I will return, is whether the more improvised character of high office in these areas leaves its mark on the emerging dynamics of customary authority.

Millennial Capitalism and Moral Authority

What does the foregoing suggest for our understanding of chieftaincy in the post–Cold War era? Can we go further than just to highlight the historical contingency of its varying trajectories in Africa since the 1990s? Clearly, democratization, decentralization, and deregulation, the shibboleths of the "structural adjustment" approach to development, stand out as the points of departure for future analyses. Each gave new impetus to contestations over belonging in which local rulers were critically placed to play a key role: there is, indeed, a direct link between the resurgence of customary authority, the politics of identity, and processes of globalization dominating the world today (Geschiere 2009). Of course, the trajectories of democratization and decentralization, neoliberal twins if you will, have varied greatly across Africa, depending on the specificities of local conditions and on negotiations among national leaders, international organizations, and expatriate donors. But it seems safe to generalize that what has happened to chieftaincy in different places—whether it has been reinforced, definitively pushed aside, or transformed—is related to the different pathways followed by the twinning of democratization and decentralization.

Another point of departure from which to make sense of the dazzling variations of chieftaincy over recent decades arises from the celebration of "tradition" under neoliberal conditions. The question that poses itself ever more urgently is why, in many parts of Africa—especially those in which development experts have a powerful presence—have post–Cold War economic policies inspired such a determined search for traditional rulers as representative of what is defined, generically, as "the" community? After all, neoliberalism, whatever it may mean, is usually taken to refer to the abstract rule of the market, not of identity or culture. Why, then, the emphasis here—paradoxically, it appears—on community and tradition? The background to this is the well-known reorientation among economists, at the World Bank and other global institutions, from a statist vision of development to a perception of the state-as-barrier. The shift began in the 1980s but had its full impact in the 1990s, in a world no longer shaped by the dictates of the Cold War. Expressed in slogans like "bypassing the state," "reaching out to civil society," and "betting on NGOS," it afforded a context for indigenous rulers to present themselves as alternatives to national governments and as champions of the local.

Sara Berry (2013:38; chapter 3, this volume) concludes that the success of Ghanaian chiefs in this respect lay in the fact that they "convinced the World Bank and other donors of their ability to bring government and development closer to 'the people,' positioning their offices as conduits for development assistance and donor-backed programs of administrative reform." She adds that these success stories "have provided inspiration for the revival of 'traditional authority' in other African countries as well as a growing chorus of international enthusiasm for the democratic potential of 'traditional' authority and customary law." Berry is certainly right that, in the 1980s, Ghana served both as a laboratory for the new approach to development and as an advertisement for its putative success. It is worth also bearing in mind here Jocelyn Alexander's point in chapter 4 below: while talk of a revival or a return of chiefship implies reversion to a stable, traditional *status quo ante*, this is "a mirage" since, even where it is durable, customary authority does not remain unchanged over time; the same point, recall, is also made in chapter 1.

What is called for might be a comparative study of the very different ways in which chiefs across Africa have used their "customary" prerogatives—often colonially derived—to position themselves as brokers in new economies of development, thus to interpolate themselves into changing flows of international funding. Of special interest, again, are those situations in which indigenous authorities had lost their significance, or had hardly been present before, only to become the object of a determined search for "traditional rulers" in the 1990s. South Cameroon is not the only case in point. Juan Obarrio (2014; chapter 12, this volume) shows how dramatic were similar processes of reversal in Mozambique, where the FRELIMO regime worked hard, after independence, to abolish chieftaincy—which it took to be an obstacle to socialist development. The post–Cold War moment witnessed an abrupt about turn. Structural adjustment demanded that the state reach out to civil society, of which traditional chiefs were seen as appropriate representatives by development experts—whose dictates under the new order had to be taken seriously by government. Already in the early 1990s, FRELIMO started a large scale research project on customary authorities. Significantly, it was given a substantial subvention from the Ford Foundation for the purpose. Researchers often had to look hard to find those authorities; many had gone underground during the socialist period. Local state officials were instructed in no uncertain terms to collaborate with these rulers. Obarrio's nostalgic study of a visit of a district officer to one of them, far out in the bush in North Mozambique, offers a fine analysis of the tentative forms of communication that emerged after the dramatic switch in policy towards the politics of custom (see chapter 12).[21]

Elsewhere, the new economic opportunities that have opened up for chiefs have played into older, more elaborate forms of customary authority—but not always in the same way. Sara Berry's seminal comparison of Ghana and South Africa (chapter 3), for example, shows that, even for established rulers, whose position was reinforced under colonialism and has continued to be under postcolonial conditions, the politico-economic configuration of the 1990s has yielded different bases of legitimacy: Ghanaian chiefs have reinforced their power by virtue of their role as "landlords," exercising their authority *"alongside* the state," while their South African counterparts have sought to secure their position by acting as the "gatekeepers" of their communities, deriving their dominion *"from* the state."[22]

But amidst all these differences and variations, what about the *moral* authority of customary rulers? At the beginning of her chapter, Berry observes that "arcane disputes over archaic rituals and prerogatives" have to be taken seriously since they are often about "highly contemporary tensions over land, money, and political power." The importance of these rituals may run yet deeper, however: arguably, they are at least as vital for affirming the very moral grounding that gives office holders the right and ability to settle disputes. It is only by maintaining moral authority, too, that they have become valuable intermediaries for politicians struggling with the effects of democratization, for development experts seeking to apply the new credo of decentralization, or for any outside intervention that seeks to bypass the state. This, in turn, raises a general question: How and to what extent does the involvement of customary rulers in the new dispensation, with its opportunities for enrichment and empowerment, affect that moral authority? The key role, here, of "archaic rituals" underscores the point: Does their eagerness to profit from their access to wealth and political power risk undermining their "traditional" standing in the eyes of their followers? And how do chiefs cope with the tensions to which this gives rise?

A brief return to some of the examples above outlines the broader relevance of this issue. It is striking in Mozambique that, after a long period of chiefly suppression under FRELIMO, the support of customary rulers could still be vital for RENAMO's success in establishing a hold over large parts of the countryside. Apparently these rulers had retained at least some moral suasion and political power, a good measure of it, as Obarrio shows (chapter 12), deriving from their ritual potency. Similarly the comeback, after their apparent demise in the early 1990s, of the Grassfields chiefs of the West and the Northwest Provinces of Cameroon. Democratization, as I have noted, put these men in a precarious position between the Biya regime on which they depended for their salaries and their subjects' deep dissatisfaction with government; in the upshot, their palaces were burned, their cars defiled. But here as well they have recovered. Some of their subjects may still be extremely unhappy with the Biya regime. But they do not blame the chiefs, who have succeeded in claiming a moral position above everyday struggles—even though no one doubts their willingness to collaborate with the state.[23]

Another, seminal analysis of chiefly resilience is to be found in one of the most original recent studies of high office in Africa, Jean-Pierre Warnier's *The Pot-King* (2007). The idea behind his enigmatic title is that, in the Grassfields of Northwest Cameroon, the ruler—his physical body, but also his palace and, in a wider sense, his realm—functions as a container for accumulating the life force vital not just for himself but also for his subjects, a life force that he must sustain in order to redistribute it ritually to his people (cf. Ferme 2001 on Sierra Leone). A key scene in the book is a ceremony during which the pot king takes a mouthful of palm wine and sprays it, mixed with saliva, over his people. The latter are supposed to feel blessed: without this recurrent rite their world would fall apart, their physical well-being be lost, and the realm disintegrate.

This book signals a reversal in Warnier's own work. A recurrent theme in that work was the exploitation of *les cadets*—mainly the young men, but also the women—by the chiefs who, prior to colonial conquest, seem to have sold their own people, especially marginalized male youth, into slavery (Warnier 1989). Even today the palace claims substantial tribute from its subjects. The heavy emphasis on polygyny among royals, moreover, meant that, until recently and in many chieftaincies, up to 30 percent of young men could never marry. In his earlier work Warnier suggested nonetheless that by the 1990s the Grassfields chieftaincies had become an "empty shell"—recall here Kebalepile's "empty chair" (chapter 1)—filled with new contents by urban elites who originated from the area. The first decades after independence (1960) had been quite hard on the chiefs. Their realms had suffered from a guerilla war by the UPC (*Union des populations du Cameroun*) against the new President Ahidjo, during which customary authorities risked being squashed between the two camps; indeed, in many places it was only due to those urban elites—mostly junior sons of royal families who had to migrate to make a career outside the chieftaincy but who typically went to great lengths to keep a base inside—that the chieftaincy had survived at all.

In *The Pot-King*, however, Warnier rejects his earlier emphasis on chiefly exploitation as a Western projection, reproaching himself for having ascribed rebellious feelings to young men and to women; this, he says, was clearly out of tune with their own perceptions of their relation to the rulers.

He portrays his reversal as a move from Marx to Foucault, defining an original approach—he refers to it as "praxeology"—that he connects directly back to Mauss (Bayart and Warnier 2004) and to "techniques of the body," which he gives a new twist with reference to the Grassfields rulers. Focusing on people's everyday "procedural knowledge" based on their corporeal experience, Warnier treats bodily movements—"sensorimotor conducts," often subconscious—as the starting point for analyzing the connections between humans and the material objects, including bodily substances, around them. This suggests a very different vision of the interaction between the rulers and their subjects, including the acquiescence of the latter to the former. To summarize all too briefly a very complex argument: it may *seem* that the chief's saliva mixed with palm wine sprayed over young men during the ceremony mentioned earlier is meager repayment for all the labor and tribute he imposes on them. But, if we take seriously the body and the effects of motor sensations, that is, of sensorimotor conducts, it becomes understandable that, in *their* experience, these young men feel adequately rewarded for their exertions by the bestowal of vital new life force upon them at the hands of their king.

Warnier has an admirable tendency to pursue his ideas to their logical conclusion. Despite the originality of *The Pot-King*, I still find it difficult to ignore the signs of rebellion among young men—and, maybe even more, among women—that had such a central place in his earlier work. Still the book demonstrates cogently why we have to take seriously rituals like the chief's spraying ceremony, an apt example, this, of Sara Berry's "arcane rituals." True, the "return" of chieftaincy in many parts of Africa has to be studied in the context of a rapidly changing global order, of its economic geography (chapter 3, this volume). But precisely the eagerness with which so many chiefs situate themselves within that order makes their struggle to retain their moral authority, and all its (neo)traditional adornments, all the more crucial. After all, holding on to customary authority ostensibly rooted in the (half) truths of the past, as we also saw in chapter 1, is indispensable for constructing, and capitalizing on, their role in the present.

Conclusion

To what extent have we succeeded in moving beyond the binary oppositions that set the terms for older studies of chieftaincy in Africa? While these oppositions appear of less avail for taking account of the (very variable) "return" of customary authority since the 1990s, could it be that it remains impossible to do without them? In this last section another binary emerged: between the new politicoeconomic dispensation of the post–Cold War moment and "traditional" moral authority. It is worth looking forward here to chapter 12, to Obarrio's exploration of "the seemingly endless conflict . . . between the 'state' and the 'customary.'" For Obarrio, this "customary"—resembling what above was labeled moral authority—stands for what FRELIMO administrators describe as "the invisible state," a "ghostly agonist" that lurks beyond the limits of the visible, official state. It is interesting to contrast this image with Joseph Tonda's vision of *Le Souverain moderne* (2005), since Tonda reproaches anthropologists for their tendency to think in terms of "a great divide": a habit of separating externally instigated developments—subjection to the modern state, the impact of the world market, conversion to Christianity—from "African culture," tradition, chiefship. In short, *le travail de dieu* as against *l'esprit sorcellaire*. Tonda argues that drawing this contrast often conduces to laying the blame for ongoing African crises on the tenacity of the local, the indigenous. For him, it is vital to see all of these elements closely intertwined in the (post) colonial moment; he invokes Castoriades's image of a stream of magma in constant flux. *L'esprit sorcellaire*, the customary, is for him not a counterpoint but part and parcel of the contemporary. Out of that stream of magma—as also argued in chapter 1, if in different terms—is born *le souverain moderne*, a Leviathan for postcolonial Africa.[24]

These differences, no doubt, are inflected by the contexts from which they derive. In Mozambique, Obarrio shows, both FRELIMO administrators and expatriate experts themselves stress the opposition between the state and the customary. For Tonda, who worked in Congo-Brazza and Gabon, this opposition is untenable precisely because of the deep, direct involvement of anything that might be called traditional in government, the market, and *le travail de Dieu*. Neither, in the abstract, obviously, is right or wrong. The question, rather, is where and when an opposition of this sort is relevant—and, even more, what work it does. In Mozambique, patently, it works for all parties involved in contemporary politics, albeit not for the same reasons. Similarly, the rich "sensorimotor conducts" that Warnier documents for Grassfields chiefs, with their elaborate rituals, yields a form of power that is starkly distinct from that of the modern state. This is very different from Gabon, where each is inseparably involved in the reproduction of the other. Similarly, the performances of Maka dance groups for the coronation of the new ruler—clad in bark cloth of unclear provenance and enacting a ceremony invented on the spot by a western-trained choreographer—may appear to offer a convincing counterpoint to the state. But the neotraditional trappings of the chieftaincy cannot hide the fact that the office is itself a product of that state. Even in areas, like the Grassfields, where customary authority has a long history and is supported by an elaborate ritual, the heavy emphasis on the customary as a separate domain does not prevent chiefs from empowering and enriching themselves under the new political-economic dispensation in which they find themselves. Precisely because there is, now more than ever, an almost global impulse to counterpose the customary—and its cognates: indigeneity, autochthony, tradition, the local—against *"the* state,*"* there is, now more than ever, reason to complicate the matter: to emphasize that these binaries are, in practice, embedded in complex crossovers, entanglements, collaboration, coreproduction. *Vide* Sara Berry's (2013:52) account of the case of a Ghanaian chief who was reputed to have been highly successful in bringing "development" to his community: "Rather than replacing 'wealth-in-people' with wealth-in things," she observes, "market liberation seems to have tightened connections between them."

Herein lies the major contribution of these various examples and explorations. The resurgence of chieftaincy in many (but not all) parts of Africa since the end of the Cold War may seem to have rendered largely superfluous all three of the older species of conceptual opposition that shaped the study of the institution. First and foremost, for those involved in the politics of custom, it seems not to matter whether the office was a colonial invention or one rooted in the precolonial past: in present-day ritual and other contexts, colonial and (neo)traditional elements are fused, not seen as antithetical. Second, the resurgence of customary authority is not restricted to former havens of British indirect rule; in some Francophone contexts, too, indigenous rulers have successfully secured their positions anew. And third, Africans across the continent manage *simultaneously* to inhabit the roles of *both* "citizen" and "subject"—which, far from being distinctive or opposed, are coimplicated—with great flair and inventiveness.

Nonetheless, these old binary oppositions *do* continue to affect the politics of the present. They do so, though, not as analytically distinct "types" of legitimacy or authority but as constructs that allow for complicated articulations. The challenge, then, is to trace the kinds of historical concatenation that facilitate or vitiate a re-empowerment of chiefs. Rather than looking for general theoretical formulas—thus to create an impression of clarity in the midst of a fascinating muddle of possibilities—it is more fruitful to look for signposts that get beyond the observation that all these variations are historically contingent. Above some stood out as helpful points of orientation: the different ways in which notions of democratization and decentralization have played out; the ways in which institutions like the World Bank have looked to "traditional chiefs" as mediators in the delivery of "development" to diverse populations; and the extent to which indigenous rulers have the capacity to use their assets—notably their control over land—for new business ventures or political enhancement.

However, perhaps the most important conclusion is that nothing is self-evident here, least of all the "traditional" authority of chiefs, which has been deeply affected by the eagerness of a good number of them to profit from new opportunities afforded to their offices. Many of their subjects are keenly conscious of this. In the upshot, what we are witnessing is not a more or less automatic "return" to a stable fund of moral legitimacy but rather a struggle over the disposition of customary power with new means under new circumstances. These circumstances oblige chiefs to walk a tightrope between seductive new forms of enrichment and empowerment on one hand and, on the other, the need to retain their moral prestige as protectors of their communities in the eyes of their followers. The outcome is still far from decided.

Notes

1. Many thanks to Sara Berry, Mariane Ferme, and Filip de Boeck for valuable advice on earlier drafts. And even greater thanks to the editors of this volume for their inspiration and for making me come back to this topic.
2. See, for instance, van Rouveroy van Nieuwaal and van Dijk (1999) and Perrot and Fauvelle-Aymar (2003). For an overview, see Buur and Kyed (2007).
3. The Portuguese gave considerable space to an elite of *assimilados* in setting up their colonial administration but treated chiefs even more harshly than did the French. The Belgians left some autonomy to the more prominent chiefs without formalizing the arrangements as indirect rule.
4. It is perhaps significant that Mamdani published this book while he was stationed in South Africa, at a time when there was fierce discussion about the place of chiefs in the postapartheid dispensation.
5. See for striking examples from Cameroon the rich collection edited by K. R. Kpwang (2011), notably the article by K. R.Kpwang and W. Samah.
6. Compare also Berry (chapter 3, this volume; 2001) and Lentz (2013) for a similar development, albeit with differences, in the Gold Coast (present-day Ghana) under British rule.
7. This institute still stages the Lugard Lecture every second year. Eight years ago its council decided to retain the name after a long debate, arguing that recognizing the colonial past was better than ignoring it.
8. See Suret-Canale (1964, 1972); the quoted phrase is from Geschiere (1982:172).
9. Compare Lentz (2013:21) on Dagara chiefship in North Ghana under the British to that in neighboring Burkina Faso, formerly under French rule, where the office has disappeared almost completely.

10. See Perrot and Fauvelle-Aymar (2003) on traditional authorities and the state in Africa.

11. This also contradicts Mamdani's (1996:82ff.) argument that the different forms of colonial rule made (and make) hardly any difference: for him, chiefs everywhere are products of the colonial creation of a bifurcated society, no matter whether they were shaped by English or French policies.

12. See Beucher (chapter 7, this volume) on the infamous 1896 expedition led by Voulet and Chanoine, who saw fit to insist on the unity of the Mossi "empire" so that one protectorate treaty could suffice for the whole region. Compare also Beucher on subsequent efforts by French administrators to marginalize the Mossi chiefs who, however, used the niche originally offered by the new colonial conquerors to the utmost.

13. See Beucher (chapter 7, this volume) on the similar coronation of President Compaoré by the Mossi "kings" in Burkina Faso.

14. Mitterand played an important role in forcing Biya to accept democratization (in line with his general policies for *Francafrique*). But the links between the two men remained very close. When the EU decided to boycott Biya's regime after the blatantly rigged 1992 election, Mitterand refused to concur. It was only due to continuing financial support from the French that the Biya regime survived the 1992 crisis.

15. President Biya is a Bulu from the South Province. Since his ascent to power in 1982, people have tended to classify the Bulu as part of a larger ethnic conglomerate for which the name Beti is usually used.

16. This and, as noted above, the unfailing support of the French government, which continued after President Mitterand stepped down.

17. The Panafrican Association of Anthropology was founded in 1987 by Professor Paul Nchoji Nkwi (University of Yaoundé I), who was also the main organizer of the 2005 annual conference.

18. At the time, in 2004, Inoni had just been appointed prime minister. He was one of a series of southwesterners in this position. In those years, the presidents' nominations were clearly dictated by the wish to divide the Anglophone opposition by playing into the old fear of southwesterners against northwesterners (see Konings and Nyamnjoh 2003; Geschiere 2009). Inoni would stay in this position for five years, long by Cameroonian standards. Three years after his release, in 2012, he was arrested on accusations of corruption. He remains in prison at the time of writing.

19. My informants have always emphasized the critical importance of the relationship between a mother's brother (*kougou*) and his sister's sons. However, maybe *because* that relationship is so powerful a counterpoint in the highly patrilineal order of the Maka, people agree that it is extremely dangerous for a sister's son (*ta*) to live with his mother's brothers. In the end, it is believed, the *ta* will bring misfortune to the *kougou*, possibly even his death. Powerful rituals are necessary to neutralize the danger.

20. Ethnographic detail on precolonial Maka clothing is lacking. According to the first colonizers, women dressed mostly in straw skirts of different sizes; men appear to have worn animal skins or a small piece of bark—but certainly *not* anything like a vest.

21. See, for other examples, Buur and Kyed (2007) and Mucanheia (n.d.), which, unfortunately, is still unpublished.

22. Berry notes that in neither case do chiefs play a key role in the crystallization of con-

flicts over belonging. In both places, local rulers are happy to welcome "strangers," not least because they stand to gain from their presence through taxation. In her view, opposition against Ghanaian and South African chiefs tends, rather, to crystallize along class lines.

23. Compare Beucher's chapter in this volume for a similar development in the case of the Mossi chiefs in Burkina Faso, who succeeded in retaining their authority, even after the fall of President Compaoré, their long-time ally.

24. Juan Obarrio's reference, in chapter 12 below, to the customary as a "small Leviathan" suggests that that he intends his view to stand in opposition to Tonda's.

References

Bayart, Jean-François

    2007   *Global Subjects: A Political Critique of Globalization.* Cambridge: Polity Press. [Translation by Andrew Brown of *Le Gouvernement du Monde,* Paris: Fayard, 2004.]

Bayart, Jean-François, and Jean-Pierre Warnier, eds.

    2004   *Matière à politique: le pouvoir, les corps et les choses.* Paris: Karthala.

Berry, Sara

    2001   *Chiefs Know Their Boundaries: Essays on Property, Power, and the Past in Asante, 1896–1996.* Portsmouth, NH: Heinemann.

    2013   Questions of Ownership: Proprietorship and Control in a Changing Rural Terrain—A Case Study from Ghana. *Africa* 83(1):36–56.

Biya, Paul

    1986   *Pour le libéralisme communautaire.* Paris: Editions Pierre-Marcel Favre.

Buur, Lars, and Helene M. Kyed, ed.

    2007   *State Recognition and Democratization in Sub-Saharan Africa: A New Dawn for Traditional Authorities?* New York: Palgrave Macmillan.

Chanock, Martin

    1985   *Law, Custom and Social Order: The Colonial Experience in Malawi and Zambia.* Cambridge: Cambridge University Press.

Comaroff, Jean, and John Comaroff

    2000   Millennial Capitalism: First Thoughts on a Second Coming. *Public Culture* 12(2): 291–344. Special issue, *Millennial Capitalism and the Culture of Neoliberalism,* eds. Jean and John Comaroff.

    2012   *Theory From the South: Or, How Euro-America Is Evolving Toward Africa.* Boulder, CO: Paradigm Publishers.

Crowder, Michael

    1964   Indirect Rule, French and British Style. *Africa* 33(4):293–306.

Cruise O'Brien, Donal

    1971   *The Mourides of Senegal: The Political and Economic Organization of an Islamic Brotherhood.* Oxford: Clarendon Press.

Delafosse, Maurice

    1972[1912]   *Haut-Sénégal-Niger.* Paris: Maisonneuve.

Deschamps, Hubert

    1963   Et maintenant, Lord Lugard? *Africa* 33(4):293–306.

Diouf, Mamadou, ed.

    2013   *Tolerance, Democracy, and Sufis in Senegal.* New York: Columbia University Press.

Ekeh, Peter P.
  1975   Colonialism and the Two Publics in Africa: A Theoretical Statement. *Comparative Studies in Society and History* 17(1):99–112.
Ferme, Mariane C.
  2001   *The Underneath of Things: Violence, History, and the Everyday in Sierra Leone.* Berkeley: University of California Press.
Fortes, Meyer, and Edward E. Evans-Pritchard, eds.
  1940   *African Political Systems.* Oxford: Oxford University Press.
Geschiere, Peter
  1982   *Village Communities and the State: Changing Relations of Authority among the Maka of Southeastern Cameroon.* London: Kegan Paul International.
  1993   Chiefs and Colonial Rule in Cameroon: Inventing Chieftaincy, French and British Style. *Africa* 63(2):151–76.
  2009   *The Perils of Belonging: Autochthony, Citizenship, and Exclusion in Africa and Europe.* Chicago: University of Chicago Press.
Goheen, Miriam
  1996   *Men Own the Fields, Women Own the Crops: Gender and Power in the Cameroon Grassfields.* Madison, WI: University of Wisconsin Press.
Hibou, Béatrice, ed.
  2004   *Privatising the State.* London: Hurst. [Translation by Jonathan Derrick of *La Privatisation des États*, Paris: Karthala, 1999.]
Konings, Piet, and Francis Nyamnjoh
  2003   *Negotiating an Anglophone Identity: A Study of the Politics of Recognition and Representation in Cameroon.* Leiden: Brill.
Kpwang, K. R., ed.
  2011   *La chefferie "traditionnelle" dans les sociétés de la grande zone forestière du Sud-Cameroun (1850-1910).* Paris: L'Harmattan
Kpwang, K. R., and W. Samah
  2011   Invention of Tradition: Chieftaincy, Adaptation, and Change in the Forest Region of Cameroon. In *La chefferie "traditionnelle" dans les sociétés de la grande zone forestière du Sud-Cameroun (1850-1910)*, K. R. Kpwang, ed. Paris: L'Harmattan.
Leach, Edmund R.
  1954   *Political Systems of Highland Burma: A Study of Kachin Social Structure.* London: Bell.
Lentz, Carola
  2013   *Land, Mobility, and Belonging in the West African Savanna.* Bloomington, IA: Indiana University Press.
Maka Bebend Magazine
  2013   *Ensemble pour le développement.* Numéro spécial 2013. Atok, Cameroun.
Mamdani, Mahmoud
  1996   *Citizen and Subject: Contemporary Africa and the Legacy of Late Colonialism.* Princeton, NJ: Princeton University Press.
Miaffo, Dieudonné, and Jean-Pierre Warnier
  1993   Accumulation et ethos de la notabilité chez les Bamiléké. In *Pathways to Accumulation in Cameroon / Itinéraires d'accumulation au Cameroun*, Peter Geschiere and Piet Konings, eds. Paris: Karthala.
Mouiche, Ibrahim
  2005   *Autorités traditionnelles et démocratisation au Cameroun: Entre centralité de l'Etat et logiques de terroir.* Munster: LIT.

Mucanheia, Francisco Ussene

n.d.   Democratization and the Revival of Chieftaincy in Mozambique. Unpublished paper, University of Leiden, 2005.

Ntsebeza, Lungisile

2005   *Democracy Compromised: Chiefs and the Politics of the Land in South Africa.* Leiden: Brill.

Nyamnjoh, Francis, and Michael Rowlands

1998   Elite Associations and the Politics of Belonging in Cameroon. *Africa* 68(3): 320–37.

Obarrio, Juan

2014   *The Spirit of the Laws in Mozambique.* Chicago: University of Chicago Press.

Oomen, Barbara

2005   *Chiefs in South Africa: Law, Power and Culture in the Post-Apartheid Era.* Oxford: James Currey.

Orock, Rogers

2013   Rethinking Democracy and Development in Cameroon's Patrimonial State: An Anthropology of Political Elites. PhD dissertation, University of Aarhus.

2014   Welcoming the 'Fon of Fons': Anglophone Elites and the Politics of Hosting Cameroon's Head of State. *Africa* 84(2):226–45.

Perrot, Claude-Hélène, and François Xavier Fauvelle-Aymar

2003   *Le retour des roi: Les autorités traditionnelles et l'État en Afrique contemporaine.* Paris: Karthala.

Piot, Charles

2010   *Nostalgia for the Future: West Africa after the Cold War.* Chicago: University of Chicago Press.

Roitman, Janet

2005   *Fiscal Disobedience: An Anthropology of Economic Regulation in Central Africa.* Princeton, NJ: Princeton University Press.

Suret-Canale, Jean

1964   *Afrique noire occidentale et centrale II: L'Ere coloniale (1900–1945).* Paris: Éditions sociales.

1972   *Afrique noire occidentale et centrale III: De la colonisation aux indépendances (1945–1960).* Paris: Éditions sociales.

Tonda, Joseph

2005   *Le Souverain moderne: Le corps du pouvoir en Afrique centrale (Congo, Gabon).* Paris: Karthala.

Van Rouveroy van Nieuwaal, Emile Adriaan Benvenuto, and Rijk van Dijk, eds.

1999   *African Chieftaincy in a New Socio-political Landscape.* Hamburg: LIT Verlag.

Warnier, Jean-Pierre

1989   Traite sans raids au Cameroun. *Cahiers d'études africaines* 29(113):5–32.

2007   *The Pot-King: The Body and Technologies of Power.* Leiden: Brill.

Yamo, Antang

n.d.   (Re)penser la chefferie traditionnelle aujourd'hui: Concilier tradition et modernité? Unpublished paper, Yaoundé, 2014.

THREE

Chieftaincy, Land, and the State in Ghana and South Africa

SARA BERRY

Introduction

Recent literature has drawn attention to an apparent resurgence of tradi-tional authority across sub-Saharan Africa in the late twentieth and early twenty-first centuries, prompting debates over the sources of chiefly influ-ence and its significance for development and democracy (see chapter 1 above).[1] In the present chapter, I compare two countries—Ghana and South Africa—where chiefs play a prominent role in contemporary politi-cal and economic affairs. Since, in many respects, the modern histories of these two countries have been strikingly different, the prevalence of chiefly influence in both appears to confirm Mahmood Mamdani's influential argument that, far from an exception, South African apartheid provides a template for understanding the colonial legacy of "decentralized despo-tisms" throughout the continent. While indirect rule certainly helped to lay the groundwork for enduring chiefly influence after independence, a closer examination of chieftaincy in postindependence Ghana and South Africa suggests that, far from a uniform institution or mode of governance, chief-taincy has worked differently in different contexts, with varied implications for the distribution and exercise of power in different countries.

In the following pages, I argue that the way chiefs have exercised influ-ence depends not only on legal and constitutional arrangements that de-fine and regulate their roles in government, but also on their control over territory and material resources—and their ability to influence who gets access to them, on what terms. Chieftaincy is not simply a relic of legal and administrative institutions created under colonial and/or white-minority rule, but one element in ongoing, multifaceted struggles among local, na-tional, and international actors over practices and meanings of ownership, authority, and belonging in postcolonial Africa. As the following comparison of Ghana and South Africa illustrates, chiefs' ability to control citizens' access not just to material and financial resources, but also to the state, has allowed them to wield influence beyond the social and territorial boundaries of their "customary" jurisdictions.[2]

Drawing primarily on existing scholarly literature on chieftaincy in both countries, supplemented with examples from my own research in Ghana, this chapter is intended as a preliminary foray into comparative studies of chieftaincy in different parts of postcolonial Africa. While Ghana never experienced the draconian forms of racial segregation imposed by the state in South Africa, in both cases, colonial/white-minority regimes worked to incorporate customary rules and institutions into the administrative and judicial architecture of the state, leaving legacies of legal and institutional pluralism that continue to figure, albeit differently, in contemporary political and economic affairs.

At the time of independence, newly elected governments in both countries committed themselves to replacing colonial or apartheid-era hierarchies with democratic systems of rule, but were also anxious to consolidate their power by courting (or at least not alienating) potentially influential supporters, including traditional chiefs. In Ghana, Nkrumah and the Convention People's Party (CPP) dismantled the colonially constructed apparatus of Native Administration (including "native treasuries" and customary courts). However, the party concentrated its attacks on chiefs who had opposed the CPP in elections leading up to independence while, at the same time, actively courting those who backed Nkrumah and the CPP (Allman 1993; Dunn and Robertson 1973; Rathbone 2000). In South Africa, ANC activists opposed to customs such as hereditary rule and the subordination of women were overruled by those who agreed with Mandela that the ANC needed all the support it could get—including that of the newly created Congress of Traditional Leaders of South Africa (CONTRALESA)—in its struggle to win votes from the Zulu-based Inkatha Freedom Party and put an end to National Party rule (Ntsebeza 2005; van Kessel and Oomen 1997; Oomen 2005; Murray 2004; see also chapter 4, this volume).

At the same time, there are significant differences in the way chiefs acquire and wield political influence in the two countries. In South Africa, while chiefs have understandably downplayed their former subservience to the apartheid regime, they have worked hard to reconstitute themselves as *official* players in the new South African state, holding seats in the national assembly but also seeking "recognition as [a] tier of government," separate from and independent of the district councils established under the new constitution (Cousins 2011:15). In Ghana, on the other hand, chiefs tend to exercise power informally. Constitutionally barred from standing for elective office, traditional authorities have not sought formal recognition as local government institutions—parallel to, much less in place of, the district assemblies and local administrations established under the Fourth Republic. Instead, many have built private businesses and/or professional careers, gaining contracts, wealth, and expertise and reinvesting them in networks of access and patronage with citizens, politicians, officials, corporations, and a variety of nongovernmental organizations at home and abroad. Long recognized as custodians of Ghana's cultural heritage, chiefs today claim equal recognition as leading agents of economic and social development.

Differences in chiefs' political practices and their relations with the state are, in turn, related to differences in the economic and territorial resources of traditional jurisdictions in the two countries. In Ghana, studies estimate that chiefs exercise some form of jurisdiction over 70–80 percent of the national territory (Deininger 2003; Yirrah n.d.), in contrast to South Africa, where the former homelands over which chiefs presided during (and before) the era of apartheid comprise just 13 percent of the national territory. Not only are chiefly territories more extensive in Ghana but, since the early twentieth century, they have included the most dynamic sectors of the Ghanaian economy—cocoa farming, timber, mining, food crop production, and, especially in recent decades, Ghana's rapidly expanding cities and periurban settlements. Invoking their customary authority over stool and skin lands, Ghanaian chiefs have succeeded in garnering a significant share of the country's gains from economic growth from colonial times to the present.[3]

In South Africa, on the other hand, where roughly one-third of the population remains attached to the former homelands, traditional leaders' overcrowded domains constitute some of the poorest areas in the country.[4] With some exceptions—notably, chiefdoms located in the platinum belt of the North West Province—South Africa's chiefs have had to look beyond the natural and agricultural resources of the traditional areas in their efforts to reestablish and consolidate their influence in the new South Africa.

The rest of this chapter is organized as follows. Following a brief review of recent literature on the rise of chiefly authority in contemporary Africa and a historical overview of official policies toward customary authorities in Ghana and South Africa, I discuss the roles chiefs play in land allocation and local administration in Ghana and South Africa and their implications for chiefs' strategies of accumulation and governance, their relations to the state, and the place of chieftaincy politics in the recent economic and political histories of both countries.

Literature Review

Since its publication in 1996, *Citizen and Subject: The Legacy of Late Colonialism in Contemporary Africa*, Mamdani's incisive critique of the political and institutional aftermath of colonial rule, has framed debates over chieftaincy in the postcolonial era. Arguing that colonial policies of indirect rule divided rural Africa into petty fiefdoms presided over by chiefs who were little more than subordinate agents of the colonial state, Mamdani concludes that indirect rule left postcolonial Africa with a legacy of "decentralized despotisms" that obstructed the development of meaningful democracy, even in countries with universal adult suffrage and multiparty elections. Apartheid in South Africa, he argues, should be seen as a template for the rest of the continent, rather than as an exceptional case (see chapter 1, this volume).

In laying out his argument, Mamdani recants his own earlier emphasis on labor and materialist history, arguing that "the specificity of the African experience" owes more to colonial laws and governing institutions than to capitalist exploitation or "the uncaptured peasantry" (Mamdani 1996:13). Treating cities as centers of emerging commerce, industry, and modern governance separated from the traditional ways of the countryside, colonial rulers left behind a continent of "bifurcated states," split between "free peasants closeted in separate ethnic containers, each . . . guarded over by a Native Authority" and "a civil society bounded by the modern laws of the modern state" (ibid.:61).

Deservedly influential for its forceful analysis of colonial powers' role in institutionalizing authoritarian modes of governance in twentieth-century Africa, *Citizen and Subject* both underplays the importance of economic resources in enabling the accumulation and exercise of power and overplays the separation of rural from urban areas. Mamdani's depiction of traditional authorities wielding virtually absolute dominion over colonially constructed tribal societies—isolated from one another and from the cities, where nationalist politics are more important than tribal divisions—sidesteps the history of internal migration that has woven dense, if shifting and unequal, webs of economic, social, and political connection between city and countryside throughout the twentieth century, and before.[5] Since the late nineteenth century, Ghanaians have moved within and beyond the country's borders to work, trade, farm, attend school, or seek spiritual guidance and protection, establishing or maintaining connections with relatives and associates across space and time. In South Africa, restrictions on Africans' residential rights and their forcible removal from land set aside for whites to cramped and impoverished reserves prompted steady, often illegal movement away from the reserves by Africans unable to eke out a livelihood within them. As road transportation facilities expanded during and after the colonial era, not only did rates of mobility increase, intensifying connections between rural and urban areas, but movements of people, commodities, and ideas also reconfigured the contours and social dynamics of rural and urban life, disrupting lines of division between them and reshaping the political and economic terrain of chiefly influence (see also chapter 6, this volume).

Mamdani's arguments have helped to stimulate both academic and public debate over the apparent resurgence of chieftaincy in the late twentieth century. Some scholars attribute chiefs' enduring influence to Africans' deep-seated respect for tradition, arguing that traditional authorities are often more accessible to, and trusted by, ordinary citizens than either state officials or elected politicians—adding that long-standing methods of removing abusive chiefs from office constitute a kind of protodemocracy that offsets the legacy of colonial regimes and has been reawakened by recent moves to democratize and decentralize African governments.[6] Others suggest that modernity in Africa is only skin-deep: traditional institutions such as chieftaincy survive because markets and states are weak. In an argument reminiscent of Mamdani's bifurcated state, Jeffrey Herbst (2000) maintains that African states' inability to enforce their authority outside of major urban centers has left chiefs free to wield power in the countryside with little interference from national government. In a similar vein, Jean-Philippe Platteau exhorts policy makers to look "behind the market stage [to the place] where real societies exist" if they want to understand African political economies (Platteau 1994a, 1994b, cited in Grischow 2008).

Another interpretation links the recent resurgence of chieftaincy to the hegemony of neoliberalism in the late twentieth century. In pressuring African governments to deregulate prices and exchange rates, open their doors to global markets and investors, privatize assets and enterprises, and incorporate Western models into their laws and governing institutions, international "donors" precipitated a kind of African identity crisis, leading people to ask how best to assert their Africanness in the face of homogenizing globalization. Reinforced by economic decline and fears of political marginalization, anxieties over identity rekindled ethnic and sectional tensions that had arisen under colonial strategies of divide and rule but subsided amid the upsurge of nationalist optimism that accompanied the advent of independence (van Rouveroy van Nieuwaal and van Dijk 1999; Williams 2010). A more nuanced version argues that market liberalization and the reestablishment of multiparty elections served to intensify competition over land, economic resources, and political influence, in which chiefs jockey with professionals, politicians, businesses, and NGOs, provoking ethnic, religious, and intrafamilial tensions in the process.[7]

In several recent publications, Catherine Boone draws on these and other case studies to compare patterns of land-related conflict under different constitutional arrangements and "land regimes" (by which she means both land tenure arrangements and rules of citizenship and authority) in different jurisdictional domains (Boone 2013:190). Distinguishing broadly between central (i.e., state) and "local" authority, Boone provides a framework for predicting lines of conflict and identifying likely losers in areas where competition over land is increasing. Using evidence from Ghana and northern Cameroon she concludes (as do I—see below) that strong chiefly authority tends to keep conflict over land at the local level, but her analysis does not directly address the situation in South Africa, where chiefs have organized themselves as political players at the national level.[8]

Building on these insights, this chapter argues that chiefly authority is neither an alternative to nor an adjunct of state power but a combination of both, and that the extent of chiefs' influence and modalities of chiefly interaction with the state have as much to do with patterns of mobility, resource allocation, and territorial jurisdiction as with colonial law, postcolonial states' "weakness," or the cultural politics of globalization. What often appear to be arcane disputes over archaic rituals and prerogatives are driven by contemporary tensions over land, money, legitimacy, and power.

State Policy and Chiefly Prerogative in the Twentieth Century: The Question of Land

In both Ghana and South Africa, control over land figured centrally in the constitution of chiefly authority under colonial and postcolonial rule. Beginning with the Glen Grey Act of 1894, the South African state waged an intensifying campaign to displace Africans from land they had occupied for many years, in order to make room for whites who would supposedly use it more productively. Africans were relegated to small tribal reserves, presided over by traditional authorities who owed their positions to the state.[9] In 1913, the Natives Land Act set aside a mere 7 percent of the national territory for Africans, who made up approximately 80 percent of the population.[10] Beginning in 1936, parcels of land acquired from white owners were gradually added to the tribal areas, expanding them from 7 percent to 13 percent of the national territory. Africans were not able to own land outright, however, even in the reserves. By law, parcels of land could be purchased only from willing sellers, and lands so acquired were not turned over to African owners but held in a trust managed by the state on behalf of various tribes. Within the reserves, chiefs and headmen heard disputes and "exercise[d] considerable authority [though not independent control] over the distribution of land" (Beinart and Bundy 1988:112; Ntsebeza 2005; Beall et al. 2005).

In Ghana, where few Europeans were interested in becoming settlers, colonial authorities made an early attempt to claim all "waste land" for the Crown but backed down in the face of protests from Western-trained African lawyers who argued that the land was already owned—by the people as represented by their "native" rulers—so there was nothing for the Crown to claim (Mensah Sarbah 1897). By the 1910s, colonial officials had abandoned their earlier efforts to promote private land ownership among Africans, deciding instead that preserving the custom of tribal ownership would be less disruptive. As land values rose, chiefs built on state endorsement of custom to claim tribute from strangers who found something of value on stool land. Applied initially to game killed by itinerant hunters and "treasure" (principally, gold dust and nuggets) that a traveler might stumble upon, this customary precept became the basis for chiefs to demand substantial rents from the thousands of migrant farmers who had planted cocoa on their stool lands. Having encouraged appeals to custom as a stabilizing force, colonial officials found themselves struggling to forestall social unrest brought on by exorbitant chiefly demands (Dunn and Robertson 1973; Berry 2001; Boni 2005; Austin 2005).

In South Africa, state restrictions on where and how Africans could hold land mushroomed into full-blown racial segregation after the National Party took power in 1948. Desirable urban neighborhoods and "black spots" (rural lands outside the "homelands" that were still owned by blacks) were cleared for exclusive occupation by whites, and occupants of both were forcibly "removed" to the reserves, renamed "homelands" or bantustans. Officially portrayed as rural enclaves where ethnically homogeneous "tribes" followed "customary" lifeways, the bantustans became human dumping grounds, filled with people of varied ethnic backgrounds who lived crowded together in sprawling, impoverished rural slums (Murray 1992; Platzky and Walker 1985). Nominally in charge of these "traditional" African communities, chiefs served at the pleasure of state officials, allocating small plots of land for residential homesteads, adjudicating disputes, and issuing (or denying) the all-important passes that allowed people to leave the homelands legally to work in white-controlled sectors of the economy. Thus empowered, chiefs did exercise a kind of "decentralized despotism," but only within lines set for them by the state (Mamdani 1996; Beall et al. 2005; Ntsebeza 2005).[11]

As South Africa became a segregated police state in the 1950s, Ghana gained international renown as one of the first African nations to achieve independence from colonial rule. With an elected parliamentary government and a president, Kwame Nkrumah, who was widely hailed as an African liberator, the new country enjoyed a few years of prosperity but soon slid into economic instability, as export prices declined and the state's revenues fell increasingly short of its ambitions for centrally managed development. Ousted by a military coup in 1966, Nkrumah's government was followed by a series of military and civilian regimes that struggled to stabilize and develop the economy, without much success.[12] Saddled with unmanageable levels of foreign and domestic debt, aggravated by a severe drought and the sudden expulsion of up to a million Ghanaians from Nigeria in 1983, the economy fell into deep crisis, forcing the then-military regime of Jerry John Rawlings to abandon its plans for socialist transformation and sign on to neoliberal market reforms in exchange for debt restructuring and loans from the IMF and the World Bank.

Chiefs were both suppressed and courted by Nkrumah and the CPP. Stung by the vigorous opposition of the Asante-based National Liberation Movement during preindependence elections in 1954–56, once in power, Nkrumah moved swiftly to punish his opponents, confiscating land held by the Kumasi Traditional Council and deposing and eventually imprisoning senior chiefs who had actively supported the NLM.[13] At the same time, he was not above donning chiefly regalia to enhance his public image, and he actively courted chiefs who shared his dislike of the Asantehene and other leading members of the Asante Confederacy Council.[14] In 1962, Parliament approved laws that authorized government to acquire land needed "for public purposes" and placed all stool lands under state authority to manage on behalf of the people.[15] But the regime stopped short of abrogating the colonially sanctioned precept that stool lands were vested in the office of the stool. Following Nkrumah's ouster in 1966, his successors reinstated chiefs who had been deposed by the CPP, and traditional authorities gradually extended their influence under both military and civilian rule (Arhin 2001). In 1979, the constitution of the short-lived Third Republic extended recognition of traditional authorities' control over land to the northern regions (where land had previously been vested in the state). Billed as a measure to standardize land arrangements throughout Ghana, the new dispensation intensified contestation over land, pushing up land prices and strengthening traditional authority across the region (Aryeetey et al. 2007; Lund 2008; Talton 2010; Lentz 2013).[16]

While Ghana was absorbed in regime changes and economic malaise from the late 1960s to the early 1980s, the South African state found its massive project of socially engineered apartheid increasingly at odds with industries' rising demand for skilled workers to keep pace with changing technology. Struggling to meet their needs for skilled labor from the available pool of qualified whites, South African industries began to press for relaxation of some of the stringent limitations placed on black and "colored" workers' access to urban housing, as well as secondary and higher education. Meeting little encouragement from the government, some of South Africa's leading industrialists began their own discussions with the exiled ANC. In 1986, a group of executives led by Gavin Relly, the chairman of Anglo American, South Africa's largest conglomerate, travelled to Lusaka to meet with ANC leaders (*New York Times*, 13 January 1999). Not long afterward, government repealed the pass laws, freeing Africans to seek work outside the homelands without official permission.[17]

Deprived of a key source of leverage over homeland residents and fearing political marginalization in a future democratic South Africa, a group of traditional authorities led by Chiefs Holomisa and Nonkanyana established the Congress of Traditional Leaders of South Africa (CONTRALESA), a political organization dedicated to securing a place for traditional authority in a future democratic South Africa (see chapter 4, this volume).[18] After an initial period of cooperation with the Zulu-based Inkatha Freedom Party led by Chief Gatsha Buthelezi, the two organizations split. While Inkatha made a direct, and ultimately unsuccessful, bid to outpoll the ANC and take power in the postapartheid government, CONTRALESA worked to gain power by strengthening its ties to the ANC. Over the objections of Govan Mbeki and others who argued that CONTRALESA was basically a continuation of the Bantu Authorities created under apartheid, Nelson Mandela insisted that the ANC needed to mobilize broad support to overcome Chief Buthelezi's bid for national power and should work with CONTRALESA to this end.[19]

Once in power in 1994, the ANC made good on its promise by writing traditional leadership into the new constitution.[20] Under the Traditional Leadership and Governance Framework Act of 2003, chiefs and traditional councils were recognized as legitimate authorities in their respective tribal areas. Legally, their authority is subordinate to that of the new, democratically elected municipal and rural councils established by the postapartheid state. Since the boundaries of the traditional areas coincide with those of the new local governments, however, disputes over their respective spheres of authority are inevitable. Lacking any mechanism for insuring chiefly accountability, the TLGF Act "risks interposing traditional councils between communities and their democratically elected representatives" (Murray 2004:18; chapter 4, this volume). A new Traditional Affairs Bill, soon to be introduced in Parliament, to replace the TLGFA has been criticized by researchers at the University of Cape Town as even more undemocratic than its predecessor.

The published version of the bill re-entrenches the controversial bantustan boundaries adopted by the Framework Act, thereby locking people living in the former bantustans into ascribed tribal identities. At the same time, the Traditional Affairs Bill redefines "traditional community" in a way that makes it considerably more difficult for groupings to qualify for official recognition and shuts out ordinary people from important consultative processes that influence governance in these communities.[21]

In Ghana, the return to civilian rule in 1992 came in the midst of structural adjustment reforms designed to replace state-owned firms and market controls with deregulated markets and private enterprise. Propelled by the acute economic and environmental crises of 1983, Ghana's turn toward market liberalization deepened in subsequent years, with significant implications for both land arrangements and the role of traditional authorities in economic development and governance. Comprised increasingly of men and women with secondary or tertiary education and careers in business or the professions, Ghanaian chiefs were well positioned to take advantage of the new dispensation (Arhin 2001; Lentz 2000).

Reaffirmed in the new constitution, chiefs' control over stool lands laid the groundwork for an accumulation of land- and resource-based wealth that muted political rivalries between "traditional" office holders and "modern" elites, enabling many chiefs to achieve the same levels of education, pursue the same occupations as their nonroyal counterparts, and extend their influence in public affairs. Collectively, traditional authorities in Ghana have established themselves as active players in the constitution of property relations and the development of both public services and private enterprise, as well as influential voices in public debates over politics and policy decisions. Since its establishment in 1969, the National House of Chiefs has sent representatives to bodies charged with drafting each of the country's constitutions, ensuring that they not only reaffirmed chiefs' allodial titles to stool lands but also guaranteed the institution of chieftaincy and barred government from intervening in matters of chiefly succession and destoolment (Constitution of the Republic of Ghana 1992, Article 270 [1,2]).[22] Unlike most other African governments, Ghanaian officials have left the negotiation of recent large-scale commercial leases of rural land to the chiefs, citing their statutory commitment to keep government hands off of chieftaincy affairs (Vermeulen and Cotula 2010; German et al. 2013).

Traditional Authority in Modern Times

While chiefs play active and influential roles in public affairs in both Ghana and South Africa, their modes of political engagement differ. These differences, I argue, reflect historical differences in the economic geography of chiefly jurisdiction as well as the legal and institutional underpinnings of chiefly authority in the two cases.

In Ghana, British efforts to incorporate customary rules and structures of authority into the apparatus of the colonial state created an opportunity for chiefs, claiming expertise in matters of custom, to put forth interpretations of tradition and historical precedents that were consistent with their interests and challenge those that were not (Rathbone 2000; Amanor 1999; Allman and Tashjian 2000; Berry 1992, 2001; Lund 2009; Lentz 2013). Although chiefs' formal administrative and judicial powers were sharply curtailed after independence, the CPP stopped short of abrogating their authority over stool land. Thus, they were able to share handsomely in the gains from rising cocoa and timber prices in the 1950s and early 1960s, as well as the revival of gold mining under structural adjustment and the rapid growth of demand for urban and periurban land in the 1990s and the first decade of the twenty-first century (Boni 2005, 2006; Kasanga and Woodman 2004; Hilson and Banchirigah 2009; see chapter 10, this volume).

Deploying their authority over land allocation and local supporters, chiefs rebuilt their political influence after Nkrumah's ouster in 1966, cultivating ties with both military and civilian regimes that struggled to muster popular support during the economically straitened times that followed the years of postwar prosperity (Arhin 2001). Like Nkrumah, Rawlings inveighed against hierarchical institutions such as chieftaincy but modified his stance for political advantage, developing cordial relations with chiefs who supported his neoliberal policies in the late 1980s and 1990s and his bids for the presidency in 1992 and 1996.[23]

In addition to conflicts with migrant farmers over the amounts of tribute demanded by chiefs, their use of revenues from the lease of stool lands has been a point of contention between them and their local constituents since cocoa farming spread across southeastern Ghana and into Asante in the early twentieth century. Colonial officials tried to mediate these disputes and argued about how to channel stool revenues into community services (Berry 2001). Since independence, the state's role has been one of omission: chiefs are supposed to turn over land revenue to the Office of Stool Land Administration, but with no legal mechanism requiring chiefs to report what they collect, the office had little power to enforce the rules. With Customary Land Secretariats (most of which were established under the Land Administration Reform Program after 2003) slated to "take over and extend" the work of the stool land administrator, it seems unlikely that chiefs' land revenues will become more transparent in the near future (Boone and Duku 2012:680; Bugri n.d.; Boamah 2014).

As Ghana moved to comply with economic and political conditionalities imposed by the IMF and the World Bank, some chiefs took the opportunity to refashion themselves as forward-looking agents of development. Combining business experience and professional expertise with public advocacy for their constituencies,[24] enterprising chiefs have spearheaded development and infrastructure projects in their traditional areas. Invoking their customary prerogative to mobilize communal (i.e., unpaid) labor, they enlisted local residents to dig ditches, clear roads, or begin construction on a building, then touted these efforts as evidence of their ability to inspire "local participation" in an effort to leverage additional resources from donors and the state and build their own reputations for "progressive" traditional leadership (Berry 2013;. Wiemers 2012). The present Asantehene has been especially successful in attracting support from international donors (World Bank 2007; Knierzinger 2011).

Ghanaian chiefs' treatment of strangers has varied from one area to another, depending on local patterns of land use. In some rural areas of the Western Region, chiefs are using Customary Land Secretariats to register all migrant farmers as tenants, effectively downgrading their right to farmland that they or their forebears purchased in the 1950s and 1960s. By ceding authority to the Customary Land Secretariat, Boone and Duku (2012:682) argue, the government has played a central role "in shoring up . . . the customary powers of Ghana's traditional chiefs" (see also Alhassan and Manuh 2005).[25]

In other areas chiefs have sometimes favored strangers at the expense of locals, seeking to strengthen their own authority, especially in relation to land. In periurban areas, chiefs often sell building plots to the highest bidder, regardless of where s/he comes from, explaining that local residents must "make way for development" even if this means relinquishing claims to land their families have held for generations. In one case, a chief in eastern Asante encouraged immigrant farmers from the north to settle on disputed stool lands, asking for no initial payment and only token amounts of annual tribute from the settlers. By treating the strangers well, many of whom were cultivating food crops very successfully, the chief secured their loyalty, effectively colonizing the land and preempting would-be challengers among his own constituents and from neighboring stools (Berry 2001). In another case, the chief of a stool on the outskirts of Kumasi who had allocated numerous building plots to strangers set aside a number of smaller, less expensive plots for "natives" of the town, earning their appreciation as well as that of the strangers, who were attracted by the town's location near Kumasi and its reputation as "peaceful" (Berry 2006, 2009).

As these examples suggest, Ghanaian chiefs have reinforced and expanded their power in recent years primarily through informal networks, linking them to politicians, civil servants, and NGOs as well as businesses and professional agencies, rather than seeking formal incorporation into the governing structures of the state. As "stool holding became an alternative means of securing political influence by those unable or unwilling to engage in national party politics," traditional offices attracted better educated candidates than they did in the past. At the turn of the millennium, Arhin writes, "nearly all the major stool holders are successful professionals who command considerable resources" (Arhin 2001:74–75). Beginning in the 1980s, many invested in agriculture, mining, and timber ventures on their own account, joining the growing number of "middle-class" Ghanaians (Ninsin 1989). The professionalization of the chiefly class has, in turn, facilitated informal networking between traditional office holders and officers of the state. Recognizing the influence of powerful paramount chiefs, district and regional officials make a point of consulting them on land use planning and other local projects and frequently appear together with traditional authorities at public function (Berry 2013; see also Ubink 2008:94ff., 148–49; Lund 2008:chap. 4; Odotei and Awedoba 2006). In matters of land allocation, chiefs' authority has become virtually unchecked: in recent large-scale acquisitions of rural land, buyers negotiated directly with paramount and divisional chiefs, while government officials stood aside, invoking the constitutionally recognized principle of noninterference in chiefly affairs (German et al. 2013).

Moving easily in business, professional, and official circles, many Ghanaian chiefs have explicitly avoided closer incorporation into national politics and the state. While some object that the constitutional ban on chiefs' participation in elections relegates them to a kind of second-class citizenship, others emphatically disagree. As more than one Asante chief explained to me, "What if a chief were to stand for election and lose? What would happen to the sacred dignity of the stool?" The Asantehene, arguably the most influential traditional ruler in Ghana today, is firmly opposed to lifting the ban, and so far, the majority of his colleagues appear to agree (Yankah 2002, cited in Boafo-Arthur 2003). When President Jerry Rawlings, seeking to bolster his chances of reelection, suggested in 1996 that the constitution be amended to allow chiefs to stand for elected office, thereby placing them on an equal footing with other citizens, a majority in the National House of Chiefs chose to decline the offer (Tettey et al. 2003:14). Together with Ghana's long history of vigorous contestation over stool boundaries and traditional histories, this incident betokens a degree of comfort with informal power and inconclusive debate that contrasts with South African chiefs' preoccupation with gaining statutory recognition for their control over land in the Communal Areas, their status as autonomous local government agencies, and their right to official representation in parliament and party politics.

In contrast to Ghanaian chiefs' reliance on informal networking, traditional leaders in South Africa have lobbied hard for legislative endorsement of chiefly authority in the postapartheid order. Feeling threatened by the demise of a regime that had secured the authority of traditional rulers who complied with the dictates of the apartheid state, traditional leaders have worked to reestablish themselves as *official* participants in the new South Africa at both local and national levels of government. Legally subject to the newly established municipalities, chiefs have maintained effective power in the Communal Areas in part by retaining de facto control over residents' access to state services.[26] Recently established, the elected municipal councils are often poorly funded and are hampered in their daily work by insufficient facilities and inexperienced staff. Traditional leaders, on the other hand, continue to receive salaries from the state and have also retained the offices, vehicle allowances, staff, and other perquisites they held under the old regime.[27]

For people living in the Communal Areas, chiefs and headmen are often the only local officials authorized to sign the letters of residence required to certify their eligibility for state services, such as pensions and child welfare grants, on which their livelihoods depend (Reynolds 2013). Facing slow and uneven responses from beleaguered municipal officials, residents turn to chiefs, subchiefs, headmen, and headwomen for the all-important "papers" on which their livelihoods depend. Repeated requests serve, in turn, to reinforce the chiefs' authority—bearing out Christian Lund's astute observation that frequent appeals for authorization work to authorize the authorizers, whether or not their positions are official (Lund 2002).

Not content with de facto local power, however, South African chiefs have lobbied vigorously for legislation that spells out the extent of their powers and guarantees their autonomy from Municipal and Rural Councils.[28] One of the most contentious pieces of postapartheid legislation was the Communal Land Rights Act of 2004, enacted, ostensibly, to secure citizens' rights to land in the Communal Areas. Approved hastily, after what opponents charged were last minute, closed-door revisions that gave chiefs effective control over rural land allocation, the act was challenged in court by four rural communities who claimed that it deprived them of rights guaranteed under the new constitution.[29] The law was overturned in 2010, but the court ruled on procedural rather than constitutional grounds, leaving unresolved the question of who owns land in the Communal Areas.

Instead of reworking the law, in 2014 Parliament turned to another plank in the ANC's postapartheid land reform plans, passing an amendment to the Restitution of Land Rights Act (1994) to reopen the window for people to file claims for land taken away from them after 1913 by the state. Although the time for filing such claims originally ended in 1998, over 20,000 claims filed before that deadline remain unresolved, leading some to suggest that the RLR Amendment Act is largely a symbolic gesture intended to deflect mounting popular criticism of the government's failure to do more to reduce unemployment and alleviate poverty. As noted in chapter 1 above, and again in chapter 4 below, King Goodwill Zwelithini, encouraged by President Zuma, has declared his intention to file a claim to most of KwaZulu-Natal Province, on the grounds that colonial authorities took the kingdom away from his ancestors in the nineteenth century, and other traditional leaders have intimated that they intend to follow suit.[30]

The contrasting styles of political engagement between chiefs and state in South Africa and Ghana reflect differences in economic geography as well as in the legal and political histories of chieftaincy in the two countries. In Ghana where, historically, chiefs' territorial jurisdictions encompassed many of the most dynamic areas of the economy, much of their influence, as well as their revenues, stemmed from their ability to control access to valuable land and natural resources. In South Africa, where land values in the former homelands have been curtailed by poverty, chiefs derived much of their influence from their control over access to administrative services that, in turn, enabled access to the means of livelihood for people constrained to reside in the countryside. Under apartheid, chiefs controlled residents' access to passes that allowed them to seek employment outside of the homelands. Today, chiefs provide proof of residence and other documents needed for access to state pensions and child welfare grants (Cousins et al. 2011).

As Villalon (1995) has argued, *à propos* Senegal, the power to grant formal authorization is especially valuable in poor countries, where governing authorities have few material resources to dispense in exchange for political support. In South Africa, where a large proportion of the black population remains economically marginalized and unable to secure stable jobs or sufficient income to support their families, traditional leaders' authority affects roughly one-third of the population, crowded onto less than 15 percent of the land. With little land and limited material resources to allocate to their constituents, chiefs have relied on their authority over access to state resources to wield influence over their constituents. Like the state in Senegal, traditional leadership in South Africa "maintain[ed] its appeal in large part by its monopoly over the satisfaction of needs which would not themselves exist without the state" (Villalon 1995:103). While the rich history of popular protest against corrupt and abusive chiefs in South Africa suggests that "appeal" is not quite the right word, bureaucratic control *has* worked to enhance the power of traditional authorities even if their domains yielded little in the way of material gain.

Reflections and Some Tentative Conclusions

Landlords and Gatekeepers

In Ghana, where chiefly influence reflects a history of advantageous positioning in expanding markets, traditional authorities have built on the incomes and assets of their predecessors, gaining educational credentials, establishing businesses, and investing in social and political as well as economic capital. In addition to the rents and royalties chiefs have collected from cash crop farmers and mines, they have also gained from the rising value of stool lands on the periphery of expanding towns and cities and, most recently, from large-scale acquisitions of farmland from international agribusiness firms (Ubink 2008; Berry 2006; Lund 2008; World Bank 2010; Vermeulen and Cotula 2010; Tsikata and Yaro n.d.). Chiefs' control of land and wealth has allowed them to work *alongside* the state, negotiating influence with officials and politicians, rather than seeking to guarantee their power through formal incorporation into state institutions.

In South Africa, where traditional authorities were consigned to preside over impoverished rural homelands crowded with "surplus people," for whom the homelands provided neither jobs nor enough land to support themselves and their dependents, much of chiefs' power derived *from* the state. As Villalon (1995, esp. chap. 3) observes, a state with few resources to distribute can wield considerable power over its citizens by putting up bureaucratic hurdles and gateways in every domain of social and economic life. South Africa as a whole is not a poor country, but decades of state-sanctioned discrimination produced yawning disparities in income and wealth between races, classes, and spaces that universal suffrage has done little to dispel. For traditional leaders whose authority is grounded in some of its poorest areas, obtaining official control over bureaucratic resources remains a high priority.

Differences in what chiefs have to allocate have, in turn, been associated with different modalities of political practice. Traditional leaders in South Africa have been preoccupied with securing official recognition through laws that extend their formal power, while their counterparts in Ghana, where chiefs' official roles and political activities are more narrowly drawn, have been able to use their economic power to build informal political networks and cultivate legal and institutional ambiguities that allow them to work effectively beside rather than through the law.

Traditional leaders' reliance on formal participation in politics and bureaucracy does not mean, of course, that they have not also looked for ways to derive wealth from their domains, and recent developments suggest that their efforts have been increasingly successful. Chiefdoms in the mineral rich "platinum belt" of the North West Province have litigated successfully for shares of the assets and revenues of mining companies that work in their domains and have also capitalized on the growing international market for cultural tourism. One of the best-known examples, discussed in chapter 8 below, is the Royal Bafokeng Nation (RBN), a small kingdom near the border with Botswana, which is home to some of the richest platinum reserves in the country. After years of litigation, it gained control of a block of shares in Implats, the largest mining company in the area, as well as some 20 percent of revenue from the mines. Shrewdly investing the resulting gains in a diverse portfolio of industrial and service enterprises, the Royal Bafokeng Nation morphed rapidly into a conglomerate corporation, amassing wealth while, at the same time, using its status as a "public" authority to avoid paying corporate taxes (Comaroff and Comaroff 2009; Cook 2011; Capps 2012a, 2012b; Manson 2013; Mbenga n.d.; Royal Bafokeng Holdings, Ltd., 2014).

Inspired by Bafokeng's success, chiefs in other parts of the platinum belt have also claimed the right to issue leases to mining companies and share in the resulting wealth (Custom Contested 2014). Encouraged by advocates of market-based development, traditional leaders—especially those whose domains are not endowed with minerals—have turned to tourism, marketing both wildlife and traditional culture to affluent visitors eager to experience lifeways different from their own (Comaroff and Comaroff 2009). In both countries, chiefs face popular pressure to use wealth derived from the natural and cultural resources of their jurisdictions for the benefit of their constituents, and those who fail to do so risk losing some of the moral authority that makes them valuable to the state. As Peter Geschiere astutely points out, chiefs today celebrate archaic rituals not only to attract tourists but also to reaffirm their moral authority against accusations of hoarding or misuse of community resources (chapter 2, this volume; see also chapters 9 and 12). Taking a cue from neoliberal rhetoric, some chiefs are also working to position themselves as leading promoters of development (see, e.g., Cook 2011; Comaroff and Comaroff 2009; Berry 2013). Whether their increasing success in turning customary prerogative to pecuniary advantage will also bring the *political* practices of South African chiefs closer to those of their counterparts in Ghana remains to be seen.

Chieftaincy, Land, and Political Stability

Studies of the recent wave of commercial "land grabs" in Africa point out that while, in most cases, it is African governments who negotiate lucrative land deals with international investors, in Ghana officials steer clear of these deals as if reluctant to offend potential chiefly supporters by infringing on their allodial titles to marketable rural land. I would take the argument a step further and suggest that decades of litigation and sometimes violent popular protests over chiefly claims to land and traditional office have, paradoxically, contributed to political stability at the national level, at least since Ghana's last transition to democracy in 1992. By decentralizing competition over control of wealth and property, land and chieftaincy disputes—which are legion—may have deflected popular discontent with economic inequality and lack of political accountability away from the state to traditional authorities. Rather than devolving power to the people, strengthening chieftaincy has worked to decentralize popular political energy.[31]

In South Africa, on the other hand, to the extent that traditional leaders are seen to benefit from the profound economic and social inequalities that pervade the entire country, resentment against their privileges may converge with growing popular discontent over the ANC's inability or unwillingness to bring more prosperity to the majority of the population who voted them into office. While some chiefs have long been seen as symbols of resistance—against Nguni invaders, Boer settlers, the Native Lands Act, etc.—directing popular anger toward individual ones who abuse their authority rather than against chieftaincy in general (Delius 2008; Williams 2010), grassroots groups have also played a significant role in opposing recent legislative measures designed to extend chiefly authority. Parliament's recent abandonment of the Traditional Courts Bill, which would have given tribal courts exclusive jurisdiction over a variety of civil cases, was in part a response to widespread grassroots protest (Alliance for Rural Democracy, 21 February 2014, www.customcontested.ac.za). The wildcat strike at Marikana of 2012, described in chapter 8 below, underscored popular dissatisfaction with persistent economic inequality and *all* those who are seen to reap disproportionate gains from the country's natural resources (BBC News Magazine, 20 April 2013). Mounting popular resentment over the meager results of the ANC's land reform program is another example (African National Congress 2012; Atuahene 2011).

In further support of this argument, recall the difference in constitutional provisions relating to chiefs' participation in electoral politics. By barring chiefs from direct participation in national elections, the Ghanaian constitution gives statutory and political weight to perceptions that chiefly authority is local. In South Africa, on the other hand, chiefs have sought and, in some cases, won seats in Parliament—further associating them in public perception with power and privilege at national as well as local levels of political agency.

Chiefs and Strangers

Finally, I suggest that these histories of chiefs' interactions with the state in the late twentieth century complicate arguments about the revival of chieftaincy as a by-product of heightened tensions between indigenes and strangers over access to land. Competition over land has certainly fostered social divisions, along lines of gender and generation as well as ethnicity, in both Ghana and South Africa.[32] Unlike Côte d'Ivoire or Kenya, however, where ethnic tensions over land have been inflamed by national politicians seeking to galvanize popular support in their own quest for power, in

Ghana and South Africa popular anger at chiefs' appropriation of stool or communal land and the proceeds of land transactions has not necessarily divided along ethnic lines.

In Ghana, natives (often referred to as citizens) of a town or traditional area may be wary of strangers, but chiefs stand to gain from them—as tribute-paying sojourners and potentially loyal clients. Chiefly influence has been used, in turn, to redefine ethnic compatriots as strangers, in order to justify demanding that they pay tribute or rent (Boni 2006). As Boone and Duku (2012) remind us in their paper on rural southwestern Ghana, while the state has played a central role in reinforcing chiefly power, the way chiefs use their influence varies from one area to another, with varied implications for the definition and treatment of strangers vis-à-vis indigenes or natives. In South Africa, where the indiscriminate dumping of surplus people made a mockery of the apartheid regime's rhetoric of preserving tribal societies in the homelands, tensions today over chieftaincy and land rights may also divide rural residents along lines of class, rather than those of origin or ethnicity (Cousins et al. 2011). Or, as we shall see in chapter 4, it may reinforce the latter. Whether newly found mineral wealth will lead South African chiefs to seek additional legislative gains, move toward more informal modes of political networking, or both remains to be seen.

Notes

1. Warm thanks to Aninka Claassens, Ben Cousins, John Comaroff, Peter Geshciere, Pauline Peters, panelists at the Institute of African Studies, Legon and the Law and Society Association, and participants in the African Seminar at Johns Hopkins University for their very helpful comments on earlier drafts of this chapter. I am entirely responsible for the use I have made of their generosity.
2. Throughout this essay, the terms "custom" and "customary" should be understood as institutions and practices, framed in terms of timeless tradition, that have been reworked in response to changing social, political, and economic conditions. Quotation marks will not be used in the rest of the text.
3. Chiefly offices are referred to as "stools" in much of southern and central Ghana and as "skins" in parts of the northern regions believed to have been under centralized rule in precolonial times. During the colonial period, land in the Northern Territories was considered the property of the British Crown and was taken over by the government after independence. In 1979, the constitution of the newly installed Third Republic overturned this arrangement, declaring that henceforth all land in Ghana would be subject to the same laws. De facto privatization gave rise to a flood of claims from chiefs, institutions, individuals, and earth priests (ritual custodians of the earth's fertility and natural resources)—all arguing that they were the original or historic owners of portions of northern land. The ensuing years of litigation and sometimes violent conflict among rival claimants have arguably served to consoli-

date chiefs' authority and raise the stakes in contests over chiefly succession in many parts of the north (Lund 2008; Lentz 2013; Talton 2010).

4. In a recent study of one rural district in KwaZulu-Natal, Cousins et al. (2011) found that most land allocations consisted of homesteads of a few acres each, for which a chief or *induna* might receive as little as R15 or as much as R100—a significant amount of money for many rural residents but hardly a windfall for the traditional leaders.

5. For a stimulating analysis of Africans' mobility within and outside the continent over the *longue durée*, see Larson (n.d.).

6. See Ray (1996), Skalnik (1996), Ray and Reddy (2003), Ray et al. (2005), and Williams (2010). Much the same argument was used to justify indirect rule during the colonial era; see, e.g., Berry (1998, 2001).

7. For examples of the extensive literature on this subject, see Bierschenk et al. (1998), Bierschenk and Olivier de Sardan (2000), Le Meur et al. (1999), Geschiere (2009), and Lentz (2013), among others. As many of these authors attest, the quest for outside resources as a way to recruit followers has led many local "development brokers" to develop ties with national and even international organizations. Early in the first decade of the twenty-first century, the World Bank announced its intention to "promote partnerships with traditional authorities"—a strategy designed to harness "social capital," the "cohesion" or "social glue" that enables collective action on the part of "traditional communities" (Woolcock 1998; Grischow 2008; see also Lyon 2000).

8. See Boone (2014, 2007) and Boone and Duku (2012). More extended treatment of particular countries or localities may be found in Bierschenk and Olivier de Sardan (2000), Chauveau and Richards (2008), Geschiere (2009), Goheen (1992), Spear (2003), Vaughan (2005), West and Kloeck Jensen (1999), and Obarrio (2010), among others. For in-depth historical analyses of traditional authority in South Africa, see Delius (1996), Hamilton (1998), Ntsebeza (2005), Oomen (2005), and van Kessel and Oomen (1997). In Ghana, important studies include Amanor (1999), Arhin (2001), Baku (2006), Lund (2008), Lentz (2000, 2013), Rathbone (2000), Sackeyfio-Lenoch (2014), Talton (2010), Ubink (2008), and Ubink and Amanor (2008). A variety of views on chieftaincy in Ghana appear in Odotei and Awedoba (2006).

9. Initiated by Cecil Rhodes, the Glen Grey Act not only limited the amount of land allocated to Africans to about three hectares per man but also declared all land so allocated to be held under communal rather than individual tenure, thus preventing Africans from acquiring the property they would need to qualify for the franchise (Ntsebeza 2005:64ff.).

10. The Natives Land Act did not immediately evict Africans who owned land outside the newly constituted "reserves," but it meant that from 1913 on, they could not acquire land *except* in the reserves—thus earmarking 93 percent of the national territory for eventual white ownership (Worden 2000:55–57).

11. Chiefs who challenged state authority were disciplined or dismissed but admired by many of their constituents (Delius 1996; Oomen 2005).

12. On macroeconomic and political conditions during this period see, inter alia, Killick (2010), Chazan (1983), Rimmer (1992), and Hansen and Ninsin (1989).

13. See Rathbone (2000) and Arhin (1993). For the best account of the rise and decline of the NLM in the mid-1950s, see Allman (1993).

14. Relevant studies include Dunn and Robertson (1973), Rathbone (2000), Arhin (1993, 2001), Baku (2006), and Kwarteng (2012).
15. The State Lands Act (125) and the Administration of Lands Act (123), respectively. Beginning with the constitution of the Second Republic (1969), successive Ghanaian constitutions have reaffirmed the principle that "all stool and skin lands are vested in their respective stools and skins" (Constitution of Ghana 1992, Art. 267 [1]). In 1983, the Administration of Lands Act was amended to classify all stool land managed by government as "public land." In effect, this amendment extinguished communal allodial titles, but "in practice those rights continue to be exercised today, with the acquiescence of the Lands Commission." Since "the state does not enforce its rights . . . for practical purposes the allodial title still exists" (Woodman 1996, quoted in Aryeetey et al. 2007).
16. In some areas of the north, the state's divestment of lands revived the claims of *tindaanas* (ritual guardians of the land) that they, rather than chiefs, were the true owners (Lund 2008; Lentz 2000). Elsewhere, the state's recognition of stools and skins as "owners" of land led historically chiefless people, such as the Konkomba, to demand their own paramount chief, in order to claim ownership of the land they occupied and repudiate their colonial-era subordination to the historically centralized Dagomba (Talton 2010, esp. chap. 5).
17. The effect of this measure was to substitute segregation by the market for segregation enforced by the state. Rather than provide substandard but subsidized housing in the black townships for Africans who obtained urban jobs, the state deregulated the housing market, opening township residence to anyone who could afford it. In effect, township residence was still limited to those who had jobs, but the state saved the trouble and expense of enforcement, and businesses who needed to recruit skilled black workers could offer housing allowances and/or living conditions that surpassed those of the squatter settlements that held the inevitable overflow of unemployed and casual workers trying to escape destitution in the homelands (Murray 1992).
18. The term "traditional leader" distances contemporary chiefs and headmen rhetorically from the widely despised traditional or bantu authorities of the homelands, but many argue that, substantively, not much has changed (Ntsebeza 2005; Delius 2008; Claassens 2008; cf. Williams 2010).
19. For informative accounts of debates within the ANC over the role of traditional leadership in the new South Africa, see Murray (2004), Ntsebeza (2005), van Kessel and Oomen (1997), Düsing (2002), and Oomen (2005).
20. "The institution and role of traditional leadership, according to indigenous law, shall be recognized and protected in the Constitution. Indigenous law . . . shall be recognized and applied in the courts, subject to the fundamental rights [of democracy and equality] contained in the Constitution." Final Constitution, quoted in Ntsebeza (2005:271).
21. See "Traditional Affairs Bill (TAB)," 2013, www.customcontested.co.za. See also Legal Resources Center (2015).
22. In effect, Article 270, which prohibits the long-standing practice of state intervention in matters of chiefly succession, represents an advance in chiefs' autonomy from state oversight. Its significance was pointed out to me by a senior chief who had participated in the Consultative Assembly and claimed responsibility for seeing to it that Article 270 was included in the final draft.
23. See Nugent (1996, 1999). Although many chiefs in Asante and Akyem supported

the main opposition party, the NPP (New Patriotic Party), when political competition reopened in the 1990s, Rawlings's NDC (National Democratic Congress) enjoyed wide support in the rest of the country, buoyed, in part, by sizeable state investments in roads and rural electrification, which began under Rawlings's military regime and continued during his presidency of the Second Republic.

24. Since traditional authorities are not popularly elected but are chosen through a combination of off-stage politicking, closed door ritual, and public performance, "constituents" is something of a misnomer but is preferable to "subjects"—the term used during the colonial era to denote ties of allegiance and willing service believed to define commoners' relations with their customary overlords. Chiefs sometimes use the term "subjects" to remind listeners of their time-honored prerogatives, but I have never heard Ghanaian citizens refer to themselves as subjects of a traditional ruler.

25. As Boone and Duku explain, the terms "immigrant" or "stranger" refer to anyone whose ancestors migrated into the local area from somewhere else, regardless of ethnic affiliation. In Sefwi Wiawso and the Wassa Districts, between one- and two-thirds of all farmers are Akan, having moved there in the 1950s from Ashanti or the Eastern Region to acquire tracts of old growth forest for growing cocoa (Alhassan and Manuh 2005, quoted in Boone and Duku 2012:676). These findings provide an important corrective to studies such as Quisumbing et al. (2004), who conclude that there is no significant difference in landed assets between indigenes and migrants by assuming, erroneously, that all Akans are "indigenous" to their survey area.

26. Formally established in 1998, municipalities were designed, in part, to pool land and resources of formerly all-white towns and cities with those of poorer black townships and their adjacent rural districts. In some cases, the boundaries of a municipality overlap with one or more Traditional Council areas, creating numerous occasions for dispute over their respective jurisdictions (Oomen 2005; Ntsebeza 2005; Williams 2010).

27. Paramount chiefs receive government salaries higher than those paid to members of Parliament and, in many cases, inherited well-equipped offices, staff, and vehicles established for them under apartheid (Maloka and Gordon 1996; Oomen 2000, 2005).

28. In contrast to Williams's argument that because rural South Africans regard both traditional and democratic norms as legitimate, "chieftaincy and democratic institutions . . . are blending together in complex ways to create new types of norms, rules and processes that are distinct and unique," chiefs' ongoing efforts to push through laws that give them the upper hand suggest that mutual accommodation is hardly the norm in relations between traditional authority and local government (Williams 2010:133, cf. Beall et al. 2005; Ntsebeza 2005; Claassens and Cousins 2008).

29. Before the CLRA was overturned, chiefs were using it to control the definition of "community"—defined in the Act as the basic land-holding unit in the Communal Areas (Claassens and Cousins 2008:chaps. 12, 13). Whether exercised formally or informally, power to define the boundaries of local jurisdictions has served as an important source of tenurial and political leverage in both Ghana and South Africa. I intend to do more work on this issue in the future.

30. See Custom Contested (2014). Apparently, King Zwelethini does not feel constrained by the fact that restitution applies only to land taken after passage of the Natives Land Act of 1913.

31. Boone (2014) makes a similar point *à propos* areas with strong chiefly authority.
32. By requiring that land ownership be legally vested in communities—defined as those under the jurisdiction of a traditional authority—rather than households or individuals, the Communal Land Rights Act threatened to aggravate rather than ameliorate tensions between preexisting groups. See Cousins (2007, 2011); also Lentz (2013), Boone and Lund (2013), Cousins et al. (2011), and Claassens and Cousins (2008).

References

African National Congress
  2012   Land Reform Policy Discussion Document. http://www.anc.org.za/docs/pol/2012/landpolicyproposals_june2012v.pdf.
Alhassan, Osman, and Takyiwaa Manuh
  2005   Land Registration in Eastern and Western Regions, Ghana. Securing Land Rights in Africa. Research report no.5. London: IIED.
Allman, Jean Marie
  1993   *The Quills of the Porcupine: Asante Nationalism in an Emergent Ghana*. Madison, WI: University of Wisconsin Press.
Allman, Jean, and Victoria Tashjian
  2000   *'I Will Not Eat Stone': A Women's History of Colonial Asante*. Portsmouth, NH: Heinemann.
Amanor, Kojo S.
  1999   *Global Restructuring and Land Rights in Ghana: Forest Food Chains, Timber and Rural Livelihoods*. Research Report No. 108. Uppsala: Nordic African Institute.
Arhin, Kwame, ed.
  1993   *The Life and Work of Kwame Nkrumah*. Legon: University of Ghana, Institute of African Studies.
Arhin, Kwame (a.k.a. Arhin Brempong)
  2001   *Transformations in Traditional Rule in Ghana (1951–1996)*. Accra: Sedco.
Aryeetey, Ernest, et al.
  2007   *The Politics of Land Tenure Reform in Ghana: From the Crown Lands Bills to the Land Administration Project*. Technical Publication no. 7. Legon: University of Ghana, ISSER.
Atuahene, Bernadette
  2011   South Africa's Land Reform Crisis: Eliminating the Legacy of Apartheid. *Foreign Affairs* 90(4):121–29.
Austin, Gareth
  2005   *Land, Labor, and Capital in Ghana: From Slavery to Free Labor in Asante, 1807–1956*. Rochester, NY: University of Rochester Press.
Baku, Kofi
  2006   Contesting and Appropriating the Local Terrain: Chieftaincy and National Politics in Wenchi, Ghana. In *Chieftaincy in Ghana: Culture, Governance and Development*, Irene Odotei and Albert Awedoba, eds. Accra: Sub-Saharan Publishers.
Beall, Jo, Sibongiseni Mkhize, and Shahid Vawda
  2005   Emergent Democracy and 'Resurgent' Tradition: Institutions, Chieftaincy and Transition in KwaZulu-Natal. *Journal of Southern African Studies* 31 (4):755–71.
Beinart, William, and Colin Bundy
  1988   *Hidden Struggles in Rural South Africa: Politics and Popular Movements in the Transkei and Eastern Cape, 1890–1930*. Berkeley, CA: University of California Press.

Berry, Sara
    1992   Hegemony on a Shoestring: Indirect Rule and Access to Agricultural Land. *Africa*
            62(3):327–55.
    1998   Unsettled Accounts: Stool Debts, Chieftaincy Disputes and the Question of Asante
            Constitutionalism. *Journal of African History* 39(1):39–62.
    2001   *Chiefs Know their Boundaries: Essays on Property, Power, and the Past in Asante, 1896–
            1996.* Portsmouth, NH: Heinemann.
    2006   'Natives' and 'Strangers' on the Outskirts of Kumasi. *Ghana Studies* 9:25–59.
    2009   Property, Authority, and Citizenship: Land Claims, Politics and the Dynamics of
            Social Division in West Africa. *Development and Change* 40(1):23–45.
    2013   Questions of Ownership: Proprietorship and Control in a Changing Rural Terrain—
            A Case Study from Ghana. *Africa* 83(1):36–56.
Bierschenk, Thomas, Jean-Pierre Chavreau, and Jean-Pierre Olivier de Sardan, eds.
    2000   *Courtiers en développement: Le villages africans en quête de projects.* Paris: Karthala.
Bierschenk, Thomas, and Jean-Pierre Olivier de Sardan, eds.
    1998   *Les pouvoirs au village: Le Bénin entre démocratisation et decentralisation.* Paris: Karthala.
Boafo-Arthur, Kwame
    2003   Chieftaincy in Ghana: Challenges and Prospects in the 21st Century. *African and
            Asian Studies* 2(2):125–53.
Boamah, Festus
    2014   How and Why Chiefs Formalize Land Use in Recent Times: The Politics of Dispos-
            session through Biofuels Investments in Ghana. *Review of African Political Economy*
            40(141):406–23.
Boni, Stefano
    2005   *Clearing the Ghanaian Forest: Theories and Practices of Acquisition, Transfer, and Utiliza-
            tion of Farming Titles in the Sefwi-Akan Area.* Legon: Institute of African Studies.
    2006   Indigenous Blood and Foreign Labor: The Ancestralization of Land Rights in Sefwi
            (Ghana). In *Land and the Politics of Belonging in West Africa,* Richard Kuba and
            Carola Lentz, eds. Leiden: Brill.
Boone, Catherine
    2007   Property and Constitutional Order: Land Tenure Reform and the Future of the Afri-
            can State. *African Affairs* 106:557–86.
    2013   Land Regimes and the Structure of Politics: Patterns of Land-Related Conflict. *Africa*
            83(1):188–203.
    2014   *Property and Political Order: Land Rights and the Structure of Politics.* Cambridge: Cam-
            bridge University Press.
Boone, Catherine, and Dennis Kwame Duku
    2012   Ethnic Land Rights in Western Ghana: Landlord-Stranger Relations in the Demo-
            cratic Era. *Development and Change* 43(3):671–94.
Bugri, John
    n.d.   Sustaining Customary Land Secretariats for Improved Interactive Land Governance in
            Ghana. World Bank Conference on Land and Poverty, Washington, DC, 23–26 April
            2012. http://www.landandpoverty.com/agenda/pdfs/paper/bugri_full_paper.pdf.
Capps, Gavin
    2012a   A Bourgeois Reform with Social Justice? The Contradictions of the Minerals De-
            velopment Bill and Black Economic Empowerment in the South African Platinum
            Mining Industry. *Review of African Political Economy* 39(132): 315–33.
    2012b   Victim of Its Own Success? The Platinum Mining Industry and the Apartheid Min-

eral Property System in South Africa's Political Transition. *Review of African Political Economy* 39(131):63–84.

Center for Law and Society, University of Cape Town

2015   Notes on the 2013 Draft Traditional Affairs Bill. February.

Chauveau, Jean-Pierre, and Paul Richards

2008   West African Insurgencies in Agrarian Perspective: Côte d'Ivoire and Sierra Leone Compared. *Journal of Agrarian Change* 8(4):515–52.

Chazan, Naomi

1983   *An Anatomy of Ghanaian Politics: Managing Recession, 1969–1982.* Boulder, CO: Westview Press.

Claassens, Aninka

2008   Power, Accountability and Apartheid Borders: The Impact of Recent Laws on Struggles over Land Rights. In *Land, Power and Custom: Controversies Generated by South Africa's Communal Land Rights Act,* Aninka Claassens and Ben Cousins, eds. Cape Town: University of Cape Town Press.

Claassens, Aninka, and Ben Cousins, eds.

2008   *Land, Power and Custom: Controversies Generated by South Africa's Communal Land Rights Act.* Cape Town: University of Cape Town Press.

Comaroff, John, and Jean Comaroff

2009   *Ethnicity, Inc.* Chicago: University of Chicago Press.

Cook, Susan

2011   The Business of Being Bafokeng: The Corporatization of a Tribal Authority in South Africa. *Current Anthropology* 52(S3):S149–59.

Cousins, Ben

2007   More than Socially Embedded: The Distinctive Character of 'Communal Tenure' Regimes in South Africa and Its Implications for Land Policy. *Journal of Agrarian Change* 7(3):281–315.

2011   *Land as Property, Land as Territory: Contested Boundaries in Msinga, Kwazulu-Natal.* Cape Town: PLAAS, University of the Western Cape.

Cousins, Ben et al.

2011   *Imithetho yomhlaba yaseMsinga*: The Living Law of Land in Msinga, KwaZulu-Natal. Research report no. 43. Cape Town: PLAAS, University of the Western Cape.

Custom Contested, Land Accountability Research Centre, University of Cape Town

2013   Traditional Courts Bill (TAB). *Custom Contested: Views and Voices,* http://www.custom contested.co.za/law-and-policy-tracker/traditional-courts-bill-b1-2012/.

2014   *Custom Contested: View and Voices,* http://www.customcontested.co.za/tag/2014 -election/.

Deininger, Klaus

2003   *Land Policies for Growth and Poverty Reduction.* Washington, DC: World Bank.

2011   Challenges Posed by the New Wave of Farmland Investment. *Journal of Peasant Studies* 38(2):217–47.

Delius, Peter

1996   *A Lion amongst the Cattle: Reconstruction and Resistance in the Northern Transvaal.* Portsmouth, NH: Heinemann.

2008   Contested Terrain: Land Rights and Chiefly Power in Historical Perspective. In *Land, Power and Custom: Controversies Generated by South Africa's Communal Land Rights Act,* Aninka Claassens and Ben Cousins, eds. Cape Town: University of Cape Town Press.

Dunn, John, and A. F. Robertson
  1973   *Dependence and Opportunity: Political Change in Ahafo.* Cambridge: Cambridge University Press.
Düsing, Sandra
  2002   *Traditional Leadership and Democratisation in Southern Africa: A Comparative Study of Botswana, Namibia, and South Africa.* Münster: Lit Verlag.
German, Laura, George Schoneveld, and Esther Mwangi
  2013   Contemporary Processes of Large-Scale Land Acquisition in Sub-Saharan Africa: Legal Deficiency of Elite Capture of the Rule of Law? *World Development* 48(c):1–18.
Geschiere, Peter
  2009   *The Perils of Belonging: Autochthony, Citizenship, and Exclusion in Africa and Europe.* Chicago: University of Chicago Press.
Ghana, Republic of
  1992   Constitution of the Republic of Ghana, http://www.ghana.gov.gh/images/documents/ constitution_ghana.pdf.
  1999   National Land Policy. Accra: Ministry of Lands and Forestry.
Goheen, Mitzi
  1992   Chiefs, Sub-Chiefs, and Local Control: Negotiations over Land, Struggles over Meaning. *Africa* 62(3):389–412.
Grischow, Jeff
  2008   Rural Communities, Chieftaincy, and Social Capital: The Case of Southern Ghana. *Journal of Agrarian Change* 8(1):64–93.
Hamilton, Carolyn
  1998   *Terrific Majesty: The Powers of Shaka Zulu and the Limits of Historical Invention.* Cambridge, MA: Harvard University Press.
Hansen, Emmanuel, and Kwame Ninsin, eds.
  1989   *The State, Development and Politics in Ghana.* London: CODESRIA.
Herbst, Jeffrey
  2000   *States and Power in Africa: Comparative Lessons in Authority and Control.* Princeton, NJ: Princeton University Press.
Hilson, Gavin, and S. M. Banchirigah
  2009   Are Alternative Livelihood Projects Alleviating Poverty in Mining Communities? Experiences from Ghana. *Journal of Development Studies* 45(2):172–96.
Kasanga, Kasim, and Gordon R. Woodman
  2004   Kumasi, Ghana. In *Local Land Law and Globalization: A Comparative Study of Peri-Urban Areas in Benin, Ghana and Tanzania*, Gordon Woodman, Ulrike Wanitzek, and Harald Sippel, eds. Münster: LIT.
Killick, Tony
  2010   *Development Economics in Action: A Study of Economic Policies in Africa.* Second edition. London: Taylor & Francis.
Knierzinger, Johannes
  2011   Chieftaincy and Development in Ghana: From Political Intermediaries to Neotraditional Development Brokers. Working paper no.124. Department of Anthropology and African Studies, Johannes Gutenberg University, Mainz.
Kwarteng, Kwame Osei
  2012   Ahafo: Big Men, Small Boys and the Politics of Regionalism in Ghana from 1896–1986. *Journal of History and Cultures* 1:37–50.
Larson, Pier
  n.d.   African Diasporas and the Atlantic. Unpublished manuscript.

Le Meur, Pierre-Yves et al.

    1999   *Paysans, Etat et ONG au Bénin.* Working Papers on African Societies, no. 33. Berlin: Das Arabische Buch.

Lentz, Carola

    2000   'Chieftaincy Has Come to Stay': La chefferie dans les sociétiés acéphales du Nord-Ouest Ghana. *Cahiers D'études Africaines* 159:593–613.

    2013   *Land, Mobility, and Belonging in West Africa.* Bloomington, IN: Indiana University Press.

Lund, Christian

    2002   Negotiating Property Institutions: On the Symbiosis of Property and Authority in Africa. In *Negotiating Property in Africa*, K. Juul and C. Lund, eds. Portsmouth, NH: Heinemann.

    2008   *Local Politics and the Dynamics of Property in Africa.* Cambridge: Cambridge University Press.

Lund, Christian, and Catherine Boone

    2013   Introduction: Land Politics in Africa—Constituting Authority over Territory, Property, and Persons. *Africa* 83(1):1–13.

Lyon, Fergus

    2000   Trust, Networks and Norms: The Creation of Social Capital in Agricultural Economies in Ghana. *World Development* 28(4):663–81.

Maloka, Tshidiso, and David Gordon

    1996   Chieftainship, Civil Society, and the Political Transition in South Africa. *Critical Sociology* 22:37–55.

Mamdani, Mahmood

    1996   *Citizen and Subject: Contemporary Africa and the Legacy of Late Colonialism.* Princeton, NJ: Princeton University Press.

Manson, Andrew

    2013   Mining and 'Traditional Communities' in South Africa's 'Platinum Belt': Contestations over Land, Leadership and Assets in North-West Province c. 1996–2012. *Journal of Southern African Studies* 39(2):409–23.

Mbenga, Bernard K

    n.d.   Impact of Mineral Wealth upon the Bakgatla ba Kgafela of Rustenberg District, South Africa. Paper presented to the annual meetings of the African Studies Association, Baltimore, MD, November 2013.

Mensah Sarbah, John

    1897   *Fanti Customary Laws: A Brief Introduction.* London: William Clowes & Sons.

Murray, Christina

    2004   South Africa's Troubled Royalty: Traditional Leaders under Democracy. Centre for International and Public Law, Law and Policy Paper no. 23. Canberra: Federation Press.

Murray, Colin

    1992   *Black Mountain: Land, Class and Power in the Eastern Orange Free State, 1880s to 1980s.* Edinburgh: University of Edinburgh Press.

Ninsin, Kwame

    1989   The Land Question since the 1950s. In *The State, Development, and Politics in Ghana*, Emmanuel Hansen and Kwame Ninsin, eds. London: CODESRIA.

Ntsebeza, Lungisile

    2005   *Democracy Compromised: Chiefs and the Politics of the Land in South Africa.* Leiden: Brill.

Nugent, Paul
1996 *Big Men, Small Boys and Politics in Ghana: Power, Ideology and the Burden of History, 1982–1994.* London: Pinter.
1999 Living in the Past: Urban, Rural and Ethnic Themes in the 1992 and 1996 Elections in Ghana. *Journal of Modern African Studies* 37(2):287–319.
Obarrio, Juan
2010 Remains: To be Seen. Third Encounter between State and 'Customary' in Northern Mozambique. *Cultural Anthropology* 25(2):263–300.
Odotei, Irene, and Albert Awedoba, eds.
2006 *Chieftaincy in Ghana: Culture, Governance and Development.* Accra: Sub-Saharan Publishers.
Oomen, Barbara
2000 *Tradition on the Move: Chiefs, Democracy and Change in Rural South Africa.* Amsterdam: Netherlands Institute for Southern Africa.
2005 *Chiefs in South Africa: Law, Power and Culture in the Post-Apartheid Era.* Oxford: James Currey.
Platteau, Jean-Philippe
1994a Behind the Market Stage Where Real Societies Exist—Part I: The Role of Public and Private Order Institutions. *Journal of Development Studies* 30(3):533–77.
1994b Behind the Market Stage Where Real Societies Exist—Part II: The Role of Moral Norms. *Journal of Development Studies* 30(3):753–817.
Platzky, Laurine, and Cherryl Walker
1985 *The Surplus People: Forced Removals in South Africa.* Johannesburg: Ravan Press.
Quisumbing, Agnes, Jonna P. Estudillo, and Keijiro Otsuko
2004 *Land and Schooling: Transferring Wealth across Generations.* Baltimore, MD: Johns Hopkins University Press for The International Food Policy Research Institute.
Rathbone, Richard
2000 *Nkrumah and the Chiefs: The Politics of Chieftaincy in Ghana, 1951–60.* Athens, OH: Ohio University Press.
Ray, Donald I.
1996 Divided Sovereignty: Traditional Authority and the State in Ghana. *Journal of Legal Pluralism and Unofficial Law* 37–38:181–202.
Ray, Donald I, Tim Quinlan, Keshav Sharma, and Tacita Clarke, eds.
2005 *Reinventing African Chieftaincy in the Age of AIDS, Gender, and Development.* Calgary: University of Calgary Press.
Ray, Donald I., and P. S. Reddy, eds.
2003 *Grassroots Governance? Chiefs in Africa and the Afro-Caribbean.* Calgary: University of Calgary Press.
Reynolds, Lindsey J.
2013 Categories, Care, and Kin: Constructing the Vulnerable Child in KwaZulu-Natal, South Africa. PhD dissertation, Johns Hopkins University.
Rimmer, Douglas
1992 *Staying Poor: Ghana's Political Economy, 1950–1990.* New York: Pergamon Press for the World Bank.
Royal Bafokeng Holdings, Ltd.
2014 Royal Bafokeng Holdings, Ltd., www.bafokengholdings.com.
Sackeyfio-Lenoch, Naaborko
2014 *The Politics of Chieftaincy: Authority and Property in Colonial Ghana, 1920–1950.* Rochester: University of Rochester Press.

Schoneveld, George C.
  2011   Anatomy of Large-Scale Farmland Acquisitions in Sub-Saharan Africa. Working Paper no. 85. Bogor, Indonesia: Center for International Forestry Research.
Skalnik, Peter
  1996   Authority versus Power: Democracy in Africa Must Include Original African Institutions. *Journal of Legal Pluralism* 37–38:109–21.
Spear, Thomas
  2003   Neo-Traditionalism and the Limits of Invention in British Colonial Africa. *Journal of African History* 44(1):3–27.
Talton, Benjamin
  2010   *Politics of Social Change in Ghana: The Konkomba Struggle for Political Equality.* New York: Palgrave Macmillan.
Tettey, Wisdom J., Korbla Puplampu, and Bruce Berman, eds.
  2003   *Critical Perspectives on Politics and Socio-economic Development in Ghana.* Leiden: Brill.
Tsikata, Dzodzi, and Joseph Awetori Yaro
  n.d.   Land Market Liberalization and Trans-National Commercial Land Deals in Ghana since the 1990s. Paper presented to the International Conference on Global Land Grabbing, Institute for Development Studies, University of Sussex, 6–8 April 2011.
Ubink, Janine
  2008   *In the Land of the Chiefs: Customary Law, Land Conflicts, and the Role of the State in Peri-Urban Ghana.* Leiden: Leiden University Press.
Ubink, Janine, and Kojo Amanor, eds.
  2008   *Contesting Land and Custom in Ghana: State, Chief, and the Citizen.* Leiden: Leiden University Press.
van Kessel, Ineke, and Barbara Oomen
  1997   'One Chief, One Vote': The Revival of Traditional Authorities in Post-Apartheid South Africa. *African Affairs* 96:561–85.
Van Rouveroy van Nieuwaal, Emile Adnaan Benvenuto, and Rijk van Dijk, eds.
  1999   *African Chieftaincy in a New Socio-political Landscape.* Münster: Lit Verlag.
Vaughan, Olufemi, ed.
  2005   *Tradition and Politics: Indigenous Political Structures in Africa.* Trenton, NJ: Africa World Press.
Vermeulen, Sonja, and Lorenzo Cotula
  2010   Over the Heads of Local People: Consultation, Consent, and Recompense in Large-Scale Land Deals for Biofuels Projects in Africa. *Journal of Peasant Studies* 37(4): 899–916.
Villalón, Leonardo
  1995   *Islamic Society and State Power in Senegal: Disciples and Citizens in Fatick.* Cambridge: Cambridge University Press.
West, Harry, and Scott Kloeck-Jensen
  1999   Betwixt and Between: 'Traditional Authority' and Democratic Decentralization in Post-War Mozambique. *African Affairs* 98(393):455–84.
Wiemers, Alice
  2012   Help Them Help Us: Development, Authority, and Family in a Northern Ghanaian town, 1942–1992. PhD dissertation, Johns Hopkins University.
Williams, J. Michael
  2010   *Chieftaincy, the State, and Democracy: Political Legitimacy in Post-Apartheid South Africa.* Bloomington, IN: Indiana University Press.

Woodman, Gordon
1996 *Customary Land Law in the Ghanaian Courts.* Accra: Ghana Universities Press.
Woolcock, Michael
1998 Social Capital and Economic Development: Toward a Theoretical Synthesis and Policy Framework. *Theory and Society* 27(2):151–208.
Worden, Nigel
2000 *The Making of Modern South Africa: Conquest, Segregation, and Apartheid.* Third edition. Malden, MA: Blackwell.
World Bank
2007 Ghana—Promoting Partnerships with Traditional Authorities Project. Implementation Completion and Results Report, no. ICR000095, http://documents.worldbank.org/curated/en/446151468029960657/pdf/ICR000095.pdf.
2010 *Rising Global Interest in Farmland: Can It Yield Sustainable and Equitable Benefits?* Washington, DC: World Bank.
Yankah, Kojo
2002 Osei Tutu II: Tradition in Modern Times. *West Africa* 29 April–5 May.
Yirrah, Nana Ama
n.d. Improving Customary Land Administration in Ghana: The Role of Customary Land Secretariats. World Bank Conference on Land and Poverty, Washington, DC, 23–26 April 2012, http://siteresources.worldbank.org/INTIE/Resources/475495–1302790806106/GOV5abstracts.pdf.

FOUR

The Salience of Chiefs in Postapartheid South Africa

Reflections on the Nhlapo Commission

MBONGISENI BUTHELEZI AND DINEO SKOSANA

South Africa is the latest in a series of decolonizing African nations to grapple with how to accommodate traditional authorities in a democratic state. Its late entry into postcoloniality had led some observers to anticipate that it would avoid the problem by doing away with chiefs altogether, taking lessons from other African countries (van Kessel and Oomen 1997:561–85).[1] However, as the form of the state and its various constitutive elements have been worked out since the early 1990s, traditional authorities progressively have been accommodated, no longer as pawns of indirect rule and apartheid but as an assertive force that demands to be heard and recognized. The Commission on Traditional Leadership Disputes and Claims, colloquially known as the Nhlapo Commission after its first chairperson, Thandabantu Nhlapo, is the latest attempt to resolve the position of customary authorities.[2] It was tasked with cleansing the institution of its colonial and apartheid accretions and with determining who is a legitimate customary authority—by contrast to those who owe their position to colonial or apartheid authorities (see, e.g., Peires 2014).

This chapter examines the work of the Nhlapo Commission in KwaZulu-Natal and Limpopo provinces. It aims to analyze the ongoing attempts of customary authorities to carve out a place for themselves in democratic South Africa by perpetuating the institutional practices of the apartheid era, thus extending the history of the ethnic homelands of the past into the present and future. Among other things, two become especially clear when we interrogate this history: the first are the similarities in the moves by successive governments—those of the Union of South Africa, of the apartheid years, and of the postapartheid dispensation—to bring "traditional authorities" firmly under the control of the state; indeed, to *make* them "the state" at the local level. Second are the contradictions inherent in the efforts of the government, through the Nhlapo Commission, to reverse engineer chieftaincy, a strategy that has yielded competing claims, infighting, and much litigation, all of which seem destined to continue for the foreseeable future. This raises several questions: What is the state actually trying to achieve with the Nhlapo Commission? Is it likely to succeed? What do chiefs themselves want? And what are the prospects for chieftaincy going forward?

An analysis of chieftaincy over time illustrates customary leaders' ongoing efforts to negotiate and assert their legitimacy, to adapt to an evolving state, and to deal with changing political and economic conditions. The argument here is that the politics of custom demonstrate continuity within the institution of traditional leadership—contrary to much contemporary literature, which draws attention to its unexpected resurrection. The chiefs' exertions were not instigated suddenly at the dawn of democracy but have been continuously tailored to various moments of interaction with different forms of government administration since the advent of colonialism in the nineteenth century. The manner in which they have adapted their claims for recognition is to be observed in the way they present those claims—mobilizing aspects of the past that position them as rightful heirs of (often) revered historic leaders—as arguments for a role in institutions of state. They assert that they would have been sovereign over their dominions had it not been for the violent imposition of colonial rule. Successful claims, documented in letters of appointment or certificates of recognition, confer political and material benefits. This is especially the case in a province such as Limpopo, which contains some of the largest mineral reserves in South Africa. KwaZulu-Natal is different and unique in that there is a recognized king of the whole province, Goodwill Zwelithini kaBhekuzulu, under whom all chiefs fall and in whose Ingonyama Trust is vested all land of the former apartheid-era KwaZulu homeland. Benefits from mining seem to flow to the trust, although this remains opaque.[3]

Homelands in Perspective

Laurence Piper (2002:77) observes that the homelands had been conceived in order to territorialize racial segregation. Drawing on Mahmood Mamdani's (1996) "bifurcation" between direct and indirect rule in colonial and postcolonial Africa,[4] Piper describes these "bantustans" as "self-governing territories"—they comprised 13 percent of the total land mass

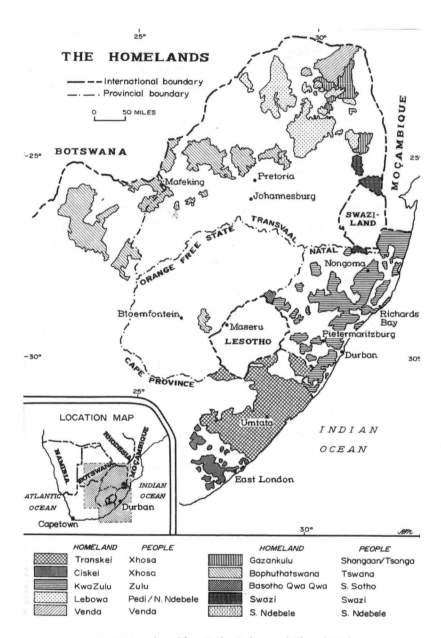

THE HOMELANDS

——— —International boundary
——.——. Provincial boundary

0   50 MILES

HOMELAND	PEOPLE		HOMELAND	PEOPLE
Transkei	Xhosa		Gazankulu	Shangaan/Tsonga
Ciskei	Xhosa		Bophuthatswana	Tswana
KwaZulu	Zulu		Basotho Qwa Qwa	S. Sotho
Lebowa	Pedi / N. Ndebele		Swazi	Swazi
Venda	Venda		S. Ndebele	S. Ndebele

Map 1. Map adapted from Butler, Rotberg, and Adams (1977)

of South Africa—in which the black population was ruled by "'traditional' authorities" under "customary law." The other 87 percent of the country—urban areas and farmland—was defined as "white South Africa" where people were governed by democratic institutions and European law. From 1959, Piper adds, under National Party leader and Prime Minister Hendrik Verwoerd, the "homelands" were conceptualized as nation-states with power devolved at three levels: first a local and, second, a regional level, both ruled almost exclusively by chiefs; the third level had a legislative assembly, an executive, and an administration, of which the legislative assembly and executive were partly populated by them. Many of the homeland leaders claimed to be traditional authorities, although the electoral procedures were typically odd hybrids.

Thus, in the main, the ethnic homelands in which the National Party government attempted to retribalize the African population came to be governed largely by chiefly elites even at the level of legislative assemblies and government. These pseudodemocracies mainly were one-party arrangements in which opposition parties were not permitted and liberation movements like the African National Congress (ANC) were violently suppressed. In most of them there were no effective accountability mechanisms, leaving many chiefs to act in despotic ways.

Although chiefs were perceived as appendages of the apartheid administration, in some places they were symbols of resistance. Bank and Southall (1996:418) note that "in the rural areas of the former Transvaal province, chiefs, commoners and migrants joined forces in the 1950s and 1960s to oppose the implementation of Bantu Authorities and agricultural 'betterment' schemes. In some areas, such as Sekhukuneland in the north and Marico in the west, rural people mobilised behind their chiefs to reject the creation of tribal authority structures." This resistance was crushed in the 1960s when chiefs were finally co-opted into the bantustan system and new forms of tribal government were imposed. Between the 1960s and the 1980s, they asserted and retained their authority by using the new powers devolved to them by the apartheid state and by actively seeking alliances with local elites—who, in turn, were dependent on them for access to resources. This patronage system, which allowed many chiefs to exclude ordinary people from participating in rural governance and helped them deal with potential rivals, was duplicated elsewhere in this and other bantustans (Keenan 1988; Delius 1990; van Kessel 1993).

In the 1980s, youths aligned to the United Democratic Front (UDF) revolted against the authority of chiefs. From about 1950, the ANC had turned the focus of its mobilization to urban areas, no longer perceiving traditional rulers as potential allies by 1960 (van Kessel and Oomen 1997:564). By then, most of those in the bantustans had become functionaries of state with little popular legitimacy. Many collaborated with the security forces in trying to suppress protests, organizing vigilante groups armed by the South African Defense Force that fought bloody battles against members of civic organizations (ibid.:567–58). CONTRALESA, the Congress of Traditional Leaders of South Africa, emerged out of this maelstrom as an alliance of progressive rulers and quickly aligned itself with the liberation movements. The dilemma that followed about the place of chiefs in the anti-apartheid alliance was resolved when the ANC shifted to focusing on a negotiated settlement as a military victory seemed less and less likely. Thus, "[w]ith the promise of delivering the 'block vote,' chiefs assumed a new role: no longer relics of a feudal past, but strategic allies in the conquest of state power" (p. 571; see chapter 1, this volume).

It was to take until 2004, ten years after the end of apartheid, for the state to define and legislate the place of traditional leaders in the democratic dispensation. As Beall, Mkhize, and Vawda (2005:763) remind us, with the rushing through Parliament of the much contested Traditional Leadership and Governance Framework Act (TLGFA) ahead of the election in 2003, the state finally validated the role of customary authorities in local government: they would be leaders of traditional councils in the rural areas of South Africa, where they would work alongside elected representatives. For them (ibid.), the effect of this law was to "significantly entrench the authority of traditional leaders . . . mean[ing], in effect, that legislation introduced in the 21st century will give perpetual life to a system of 'indirect rule' dating back to the colonial era and ossified under apartheid."[5]

The Return of State Legitimation: The Nhlapo Commission

The Nhlapo Commission was established by the Traditional Leadership and Governance Framework Act of 2003, later replaced by the Traditional and Khoi-San Leadership (TKL) Bill of 2015, which, like its predecessor, lays out the guidelines for the recognition of traditional leadership and attempts to define the functions of chiefs within a political context that endorses customary and democratic forms of governance. Both pieces of legislation employ rigid conceptions of traditional leadership, succession, community, and history. The Nhlapo Commission was instituted to, among other things, investigate:

(i) a case where there is doubt as to whether a kingship or principal traditional leadership, senior traditional leadership or headmanship was
established in accordance with customary law and customs; [. . .]

(iii) a traditional leadership position where the title or right of the incumbent
is contested; [. . .]

(viii) all traditional leadership claims and disputes dating from 1 September
1927 to the coming into operation of provincial legislation dealing with
traditional leadership and governance matters.

The commission was established following years of inability by the ANC
to take decisive legislative action on the role of chiefs in the postapartheid
state, a point to which we return below. The immediate precedent for it
came in the form of two earlier commissions in the Venda homeland. The
Mushasha Commission—appointed by the then-military ruler Gabriel Ramushwana in 1990—abolished Venda kingship. This for two reasons: first,
that Ramushwana did not want to be subject to the king, who would, according to Republic of Venda legislation, be head of state;[6] second, that the
kingship was an apartheid invention, created to advance the broader seg-
regationist project. The other precedent was the Ralushai Provincial Commission, established in 1996 to investigate disputes relating to irregularities and malpractices in the appointment of certain traditional leaders; it
is said to have found, contrary to Mushasha, that the Venda kingship *was*
legitimate, but its report was never made public.

Amidst an increasing number of thorny chieftaincy disputes across
South Africa, the Nhlapo Commission received 1,322 submissions,[7] conducted many investigations and hearings, and published a report on paramountcies in its five-year life span. By the end of its term, it had not resolved all the claims and disputes before it, leading to one claimant,
Melizwe Dlamini of the Nhlangwini in southern KwaZulu-Natal, to challenge the president of South Africa in court to extend its term so that his
suit could be resolved. The result was the establishment of a new commission in 2011.

The limitations of the TLGFA that established the Nhlapo Commission have been laid bare (Centre for Law and Society 2013). Two defects of
the commission itself are of relevance to this chapter. First, the manner in
which it conceptualized what was under investigation was vague and circu-
lar. The act states in Chapter 1 (Section 1), for example, that "senior traditional leadership means the position held by a senior traditional leader,"
this last term being loosely defined as "any person who, in terms of custom-

ary law of the traditional community concerned, holds a traditional leadership position, and is recognized in terms of this Act." The same conceptual shortcomings are to be observed in the vague definitions of customary institutions or structures, kingship, and traditional communities. Not only do these limitations and lacunae pose interpretative challenges, they also create problems for implementation. One obvious, unanswered question is whether claimants to office themselves, or their would-be subjects, employ these terms in a similar manner. While the commission was charged to investigate "whether kingship, senior traditional leadership or headmanship was established in accordance with customary law and customs" (see above), it is clear from its report that it relied on a one-size-fits-all model to which societies with very different vocabularies for leadership positions have been compelled to conform. In almost all contexts, the terms used by the commissioners for those positions—king, principal and senior traditional leader, and headman—are hollow and do not align with the ways in which traditional authority is conceptualized in their vernacular contexts. Although, in most cases, those who bring claims are represented by highly educated advocates, the challenge is to articulate their arguments in the official language required to make them legible on the commission's terms. Failure to do so easily results in an unsuccessful claim.[8]

Even more important here, second, is the apparatus employed by the commission to adjudicate disputes, based on formal rules governing succession to office. Amongst these rules is the prescription of male primogeniture, a fundamental criterion for arbitrating the many claims that have been brought. The assumption of the commissioners is that, by virtue of identifying the "rightful" male successor to any office, the dispute surrounding it is effectively resolved. But the reality is that there are much more intricate dynamics involved in succession disputes (see chapter 1, this volume). This is well illustrated by one involving the Valoyi people in Limpopo. In 2001, its ruling family, and the community at large, resolved—under the democratic dispensation—that a woman, Mrs. Tinyiko Shilubana, who would have followed her father as chief in 1968 had it not been for the rule of male primogeniture, should assume the office instead of Sidwell Nwamitwa, her father's younger brother's son. Because the late chief had no male offspring, his younger brother, Sidwell's father, had succeeded him, but had died in 2001, making way for Sidwell, who defied the decision that Mrs. Shilubana, incidentally an ANC member of Parliament, accede to the chieftaincy. He took his case to the South African courts, arguing that the custom of male primogeniture was legally protected, and won. The Valoyi royal family appealed the decision, countering that they and their community had decided to reverse past gender prejudices to meet the demands of the South African Constitution. The Constitutional Court eventually overturned the original decision and paved the way for Mrs. Shilubana's appointment.

Apart from obvious shortcomings in the ways that the commission implemented succession rules, its decisions actually contradicted its own project: the reliance on ascribed rules and preconceived notions of culture replicated the colonial and apartheid management of traditional leadership, much of it at odds with the 1996 Constitution. One of the best critiques of the ways in which custom was deployed by the commissioners to make their determinations has been advanced by Jeff Peires (2014). Writing as a historian and himself a former member of the commission, Peires demonstrates how its approach to the culture of claimants and disputants sat awkwardly with both constitutional imperatives and the legislation that established the commission itself, leading it to make up its own criteria to arrive at its findings. Using Western Mpondoland and the Transvaal Ndebele as examples, he shows how the state's attempts during the Mbeki era to "cleanse" chiefship of its colonial accretions—in order to "officially recognise traditional leaders as shining lights of pre-colonial African democracy"—has yielded results so illogical in some places that the whole enterprise is called into question (p. 8). Thus, while the TLGFA set 1 September 1927, the date of the promulgation of the Black Administration Act No. 38, as the cut-off for disputed claims to chiefship, the cases on which Peires focuses actually go "back to the pre-colonial period or the period before any kind of colonial intervention was demonstrably present" (ibid.). He shows that, in both the Western Mpondo and the Ndebele instances, the commission sought to give neat (i.e., ascriptive) accounts of how rulers ascended to their offices and how political power was passed among them. Both the leadership of Ndamase in Western Mpondoland and that of the Ndzundza Ndebele were deemed not to be kingships because the commissioners did not recognize the splintering of Faku's and Manala's kingdoms in the nineteenth and (possibly) the seventeenth centuries, respectively, maintaining that there was only *one* senior royal house—and that the hereditary principle of succession had been followed.

In criticizing the single-minded focus on male primogeniture of the line of questioning directed at the Western Mpondo representative before the commission, Peires (2014:18) argues:

> During the pre-colonial era there were no constraints of land, water and nat-ural resources to tie traditional communities down, no territorial boundaries

to constrain political expansion and innovation, no overarching national state to set out norms and standards or to demand transformation in line with constitutional imperatives. There was no [Traditional Leadership and Governance] Framework Act Clause 8 to reduce the great diversity of traditional institutions into three categories only [i.e., kingship, senior traditional leadership, and headmanship]. And no Commission either.

What he demonstrates is that, in their attempts to adjudicate events that took place in the precolonial past, the commissioners relied on tools unequal to the task; nor did they take enough care to make those tools applicable. Only in exceptional cases, where it would not have been politically expedient, did they depart from their one-size-fits-all approach to custom and tradition. And so Peires (pp. 17–18) asks of the Zulu kingdom:

> What would have happened, for example, if the Commission had applied its version of customary law to the well known case of the Zulu kingdom? Ignoring the 1927 cut-off date, as it usually did, the Commission would have had no difficulty going back to 1840, some years before British colonial authority was imposed on the colony of Natal. That was the year in which Mpande fled his homeland to enlist the support of the Voortrekker leader, Andries Pretorius. In February 1840, the Boers destroyed the army of Dingane and proclaimed Mpande King of the amaZulu. The Commission should have asked whether that was in accordance with Zulu customary law. By the criterion of customary law, all the descendants of Mpande onwards can only be seen as illegitimate, and the Commission is duty bound to replace Zwelithini with a more legitimate incumbent. But who? Mpande's predecessor, according to customary law, was his brother Dingane. But Dingane had murdered his own predecessor, Shaka, another clear contravention of Zulu custom. Further research by the Commission would have revealed that Shaka himself had usurped the chiefship of his father Senzangakhona, leaving the Commission with no option but to identify the most senior descendant of Sigujana, Senzangakhona's rightful heir, and to place him on the Zulu throne.

He then proceeds to argue forcefully that "[n]o historical event of the precolonial period should be adjudicated by the criteria of the post-colonial period, because the circumstances of the pre-colonial period were so fundamentally different that the fundamental assumptions of the present simply do not apply" (p. 18). Peires's conclusion is that "[a]lthough the mantra of 'custom' is frequently invoked as a universal panacea to solve all problems and cure all ills, the experience of the Nhlapo Commission shows the extent to which it serves as a mask, or even a blunt instrument, to facilitate outcomes that are the very reverse of customary" (p. 19).

The commission's determinations thus followed a line of reasoning that fixed what would have been fluid political developments in the past—in which, as shown by the Zulu case, succession processes involved usurpation, war, and the legitimation over time of a political order that came into being through what would have been considered illegitimate means (cf. Comaroff and Roberts 1981; Landau 2010). In so doing, they disregarded the very different results that may have been, in some cases were, yielded by the very indigenous political processes on which the commissioners purported to base their findings. More importantly, in limiting the positions available to contemporary traditional authorities to kingship or queenship, senior traditional leadership, and headmanship, the founding legislation constrains the commission to a schema that bears little resemblance to the forms of independent polity that existed prior to colonialism. This straitjacket, as we have intimated, bears uncanny resemblance to the management of chiefship under British colonial overrule, the Union of South Africa, and the apartheid regime.

The commission ignores the fact that, as John Comaroff (1974) has demonstrated for the Tshidi (Tswana) chiefdom of the former Bophuthatswana, "customary" descriptions of formal succession arrangements present an "idealized picture" of chiefship. Beyond that idealized picture occur political processes in which competition for influence and legitimacy take place on an ongoing basis: Comaroff shows that "the rules governing access to positions of authority are all founded upon birth, and yet the Tshidi perpetually emphasize that political power depends upon individual ability" (pp. 38–39). Hence a leader reigns as long as he has political support. What is more, there are institutional arrangements by means of which he may be removed if he is no longer considered legitimate by his subjects, an eventuality usually occasioned by autocratic or ineffective governance. Under these conditions, his genealogical status is typically questioned, since "biological and jural parentage need not coincide" according to a Tswana rule that "any man who dies without an heir should have one raised in his name" by a close kinsman. In that way (p. 41),

> a royal who attempts to accede to the chiefship will exploit the flexibilities of
> the secondary rules in order to assert his jural seniority within the ruling lin-
> eage. One corollary of a successful campaign is that his version of the royal
> genealogy becomes publicly accepted. If the campaign is aimed against an

incumbent (rather than at the vacant office), it follows that this man is now recognized as having been junior to his rival.

Hence a chief can be removed from office once a popularly supported rival successfully argues that the incumbent was always only a regent. The Nhlapo Commission swept aside all such intricacies, however, and went for tracing clear genealogical lines going as far back as possible to determine who should be recognized in the present. This is precisely what the Ethnology Section of the Bantu Affairs Department did during apartheid: it published ethnological surveys that were intended to determine the "rightful" rulers of the tribes of South Africa.

Nhlapo Commission Determinations

Limpopo

In Limpopo, claims for recognition of paramountcies were submitted by the Bapedi ba ga Sekhukhune and VhaVenda. In its long-awaited final report on paramountcies (2010), the commission recognized the late King Victor Thulare Sekhukhune III and dismissed Kenneth Kgakgudi Sekhukhune's claim;[9] Toni Mphephu-Ramabulana was found to be the legitimate king of VhaVenda. Recording the aura of anxiety and the significance of a succession determination, Sizwe Yende wrote, in a report entitled "Buried as King or Commoner?"[10]

> The funeral of senior Bapedi ba ga Sekhukhune royal house member Thulare Sekhukhune III has been delayed by four weeks while his family tries to ensure he is posthumously bestowed the kingship. Sekhukhune III (60) died from diabetes on December 27 at Montana Private Hospital in Tshwane amid a tug-of-war with his half-brother to be declared the king of the tribe. He had made presentations to the presidential Commission on Traditional Leadership Disputes and Claims.

Sekhukhune III's spokesperson, Dimo Morwamoche, said the funeral had been moved to February 11 while the commission was being requested to release its findings before he was buried: "We want the commission to release the report before his burial so that the Bapedi people can know the truth. If he is the heir to the throne, he should be given that right, even after death" (see note 10).

Although Sekhukhune III did not live to see his recognition as the king of Bapedi Nation, Mphephu-Ramabulana was able to celebrate the day after a court battle that lasted for two years. He enjoyed victory over three local chiefs—Kennedy Tshivhase, Musiiwa Gole Mphaphuli, and Tshidziwelele Nephawe—who had gone to the high court to challenge his Venda kingship. Following his success, Ramabulana took the headlines when "he made a grand entrance exhibited opulence and the lavish lifestyle befitting royalty, arriving in a Rolls-Royce Phantom. A fleet of expensive vehicles, including a Porsche Cayenne and Panamera, a convertible Ferrari California and Range Rovers, formed part of his long convoy."[11]

What is evident in the Bapedi ba ga Sekhukhune, VhaVenda, and other determinations, in sum, is the commission's repeated tendency, as discussed above, to employ fixed ascriptive conceptions of rank and status in which the king assumes the position of supreme ruler over a particular "ethnic nation," not taking into account variations within polities, such as the Pedi, whose history is not simply tied to that of a paramountcy or a monarchy.

KwaZulu-Natal

In KwaZulu-Natal, claims for recognition as paramountcies and for their leaders as kings were received from the Hlubi, Ndwandwe, Nhlangwini, and Zulu. In its final report, the commission recognized Goodwill Zwelithini as king of the amaZulu and dismissed the Hlubi claim. The Nhlangwini action was not finalized (see above, note 7). The Ndwandwe initiative ran into various difficulties—including infighting and the intimidation of those who had lodged it—that resulted in a largely incoherent case: various people with differing investments in the recognition of a Ndwandwe kingdom presented conflicting evidence to the commission. Moreover, there was vocal opposition, even threats, against claimants from King Goodwill Zwelithini's defenders, who saw other kingship claims as a sign of disrespect for the Zulu monarch.

Jabulani Sithole (2009) has noted that eleven of the 705 applications received by the Nhlapho Commission by the end of June 2007 were from KwaZulu-Natal. Some of them used the new legislation to assert that they had never been subjects of Zulu kings. A number of the claimants had longstanding disputes with the homeland rulers, dating back to the 1970s and 1980s. The official response was swift and tough: "Goodwill Zwelithini publicly condemned the submissions, dismissing them as mischievous challenges, not only to the authority of the Zulu king, but to the Zulu nation as a whole" (p. xv). In a show of force, he presided over gatherings near the territories of two would-be kings at which he vowed to deal with the alleged impostors. Some claimants, including a certain Sakhile Shadrack Ndwandwe who had submitted a case on behalf of the "amaNguni," were cowed into withdrawing. Moreover, both the Provincial House of Traditional Leaders and the KwaZulu-Natal government threw their weight behind the Zulu ruler (p. xvi).

In the end, the struggles over the various kingship claims have effectively resulted in the recognition of Goodwill as the only king in the province. His affirmation as the sole paramount by the commission, and his elevation by successive provincial governments, has in effect made KwaZulu-Natal into a constitutional monarchy; this since the advent of democracy in the country. Each year the king officially opens the provincial legislature. He has a unit dedicated to his protection within the South African Police Service, the Royal Protection Unit. And provincial and national politicians fall over themselves to placate him each time he expresses displeasure at the government.[12] This was most visible in 2015, when he made statements that led to xenophobic violence against immigrants. Malusi Gigaba, the national minister of home affairs, publicly criticized him, after which Zwelithini retorted as an insulted party. Gigaba promptly met the monarch behind closed doors and reportedly apologized.[13]

In bolstering the position of the Zulu monarch, the overall effect of the Nhlapo Commission has been to embolden him to advance even more claims. When the national land restitution program was reopened in July 2014 under the Restitution of Land Rights Amendment Act 15 of 2014—it had closed in December 1998—Zwelithini announced that he would demand back the land his people had lost since 1838.[14] 1838 was the year in which the first Afrikaner trekkers from the Cape arrived east of the Drakensberg Mountains and hence the beginning of Boer settlement and the dispossession of African land in today's KwaZulu-Natal region. Opposition to the king's impending action has been met with threatening rebuttals by people associated with the Ingonyama Trust; recall, the structure formed in 1994 that controls a third of the land in KwaZulu-Natal, whose sole trustee is the Zulu monarch.[15]

The commission has proven to be one more route to state recognition, and the centralization of authority, for those whose claims are successful. The Zulu king's success has strengthened his hand in imposing his rule across rural KwaZulu-Natal, where he appoints local rulers who are aligned with him. To date, chiefs in the province number in the region of 300. With appointment by the monarch and a recognition certificate from the premier's office come rewards such as a state-funded salary, a vehicle, a mobile phone, and travel allowances. Popular legitimacy counts for little.

Implications of the Commission's Findings: Struggles for Position

The commission dismissed many claims and recognized a king per province in most instances. Yet many cases remain unresolved. One, in Limpopo, is the Kekana chieftaincy dispute, which intensified in 2001 following the regent Kekana's death. This dispute, like many others, has seen families and communities split into factions, each in support of its own candidate. The competing claimants and their followers challenge their rivals' genealogical status and adherence to local custom. It is the one best able to substantiate his right to office, the one who has the strongest backing or who is most closely aligned to influential state actors, who often turns out to be successful.

After Chief Alfred's death in 2001, the Kekana royal family proposed different candidates to succeed him. Vaaltyn I, born in 1964, son of Chief Alfred and a contested principal wife, was supported by one faction of the Kekana traditional council. Another faction supported Vaaltyn II, born in 1974, son of Chief Alfred's uncle Molalakgori, who was once a regent due to the ruler's ill health. In 2003, the local Mogalakwena municipality and the Limpopo provincial government conducted interviews with the divided Kekana traditional council/s and decided to award the office to Vaaltyn II. Some council members recall filling in forms that asked about their genealogy.[16] A councilor of the current chief believes that they won because they answered the questions "exceptionally well"—and because "he is the rightful leader."[17] The unsuccessful faction argued that Vaaltyn II was appointed only because his father had good relations with the apartheid administration and later the Transitional Local Council (TLC).[18] According to this account, his father, Molalakgori, was improperly cozy with the land affairs commissioner and was a tyrannical leader, which resulted in him and his contested principal wife being chased away from the village when Vaaltyn II was three months old. As a result, he did not grow up in the royal village, nor did he speak Northern Ndebele fluently when he was called to become chief from Johannesburg, where he worked as a driver for the car rental company.

Members of Vaaltyn I's traditional council wrote to the Nhlapo Commission, but their appeal was never investigated. Their attempts to have the 2003 decision reversed landed them in financial distress, unable to pay their legal costs. A 2013 high court ruling records that they launched their application for review in 2004; there is no explanation for why it was abandoned. When they were finally able to organize legal representation, they lost the case. In dismissing it, the court noted that "there is no explanation as to the inordinate delay from 2006 until the beginning of 2012 to launch the present review application."[19] Its judgment didn't take into consideration that Vaaltyn I is relatively popular amongst the residents of villages surrounding his homestead.[20]

Is a Chief the Chief of the People or the Chief of the State? Contestations over Legitimacy

Donald Ray (1996) advances one of the best analyses of the dual basis of chiefly authority—and of its implications for democratization and development—in African states. Focusing on Ghana, his premise is that traditional rulers here and in "many other African countries derive their authority and legitimacy from two sources: the imposed European colonial states and the pre-colonial African polities" (p. 183). He contends that the sacred political bases of chiefship in a contemporary, postcolonial nation like Ghana are rooted in the precolonial period. Consequently, customary authorities draw their sovereignty from roots other than those of the state, which was a creation of, and a successor to, its colonial antecedent. Chiefs, therefore, form a parallel power to government, a fact that raises a number of political and conceptual problems yet to be adequately addressed, let alone resolved. Ray observes that "in Ghana the post-colonial state is sovereign in nearly all powers, but it appears to coexist with another entity, traditional authority, which has distinct claims to sovereignty, legitimacy, authority and power. . . . a very asymmetrical division" (p. 198; see also chapter 3, this volume).

What Ray's argument suggests for us here is that, prior to colonization, popular support from the people[21] was an adequate basis for chiefly authority. However, this later changed as chiefs and the colonial state competed over sovereignty. For the latter, an effective way to weaken traditional rulers was to appoint ones who were willing to collaborate with them. An expansive literature demonstrates a commonly shared conclusion in this respect: that the British colonial regime and the apartheid administration both used indigenous leaders to preserve their system of overrule. Hence Mamdani's (1996:17) assertion that "direct rule was an initial response to the problem of administering colonies while indirect rule was in practice the reintegration and domination of the natives in the institutional context of semi-servile and semi-capitalist agrarian relations." One of the first pieces of legislation to alter the institution of traditional leadership in the Union of South Africa was the Natives Administration Act of 1927, which declared the governor-general to be "the supreme chief of all the natives . . . and allowed him to delegate powers to any administrative officials"; he could also "appoint any person as a chief or a headman in charge of a tribe or location; could overthrow any chief or headmen and was authorized to define their powers, duties and privileges" (Delius 2008:223). This compromised the institution, as not everyone who was appointed by the governor-general was a popularly legitimate ruler. The appointment of officeholders was decided mainly on the basis of their willingness to cooperate with the government.

Under the successor to the Natives Administration Act, the Bantu Authorities Act of 1951—which, recall, introduced the ethnic homelands, in which Africans were to live separately under Tribal Authorities—chiefs could once more be handpicked to rule within particular jurisdictions, this time by the Department of Bantu Affairs. They were trapped yet again in a contradictory position: accountable at once to their own subjects and to the apartheid regime. What this meant was that, increasingly, state recognition became *the* prerequisite for the survival of the institution. Local rulers, legitimate and illegitimate alike, were now competing for ratification, mostly at the expense of their people, which ultimately tarnished and threatened the office.

Succession Disputes: A Resurgence of Chieftaincy in Postapartheid South Africa?

Given its chequered history, as we noted earlier, it was expected that chiefship would not survive its way into the democratic dispensation. Some argued that it should not, that it was incompatible with the principles espoused by the constitution (Ntsebeza 2005; Bank and Southall 1996). As a result, its renewed vigor after 1994 was seen by some as a "resurgence" (e.g., Oomen 2002). Ntsebeza (2005) argues that three factors together led to its reemergence: first, the indecision of ANC policies on its role in the postapartheid era; second, the perception of the ANC and the National Party, at the time of the transition, that the Inkatha Freedom Party (IFP), with its strong Zulu following and its close connections to traditional authority, would remain politically significant after 1994; and lastly, the political and economic circumstances in which the South African transition was taking place, itself influenced by global and continental trends. Barbara Oomen (2002:6) picks up on this last point, suggesting that traditional leaders staged their comeback in the context of broader planetary developments, among them, the fragmentation of nation-states; the emergence of an alternative politics that operates at once locally, transnationally, and internationally; and the growing centrality of collective rights and culture as a means to engage with modernity (cf. chapter 1, this volume); all factors that sat well with the idea that customary authority would not, could not, be demolished at any time soon—indeed, that facilitated its "resurrection."

Research on chieftaincy has revealed continuities and discontinuities that are highly pertinent to the understanding of African societies today, yet many scholars continue to write about it as if it were only a product of colonial rule in Africa (Bodley 2001:197–98). Once more, Donald Ray's (1996) work is relevant here when he observes that "chiefs may have been modified to greater or lesser extents by the colonial and postcolonial states, but traditional authority's legitimacy predates the latter two state forms." To understand chieftaincy more than simply as an "artefact of modernist projects of colonial rule, missionary activity and postcolonial state formation" (Ngubane 2005) offers a way to interpret claims to the office[22] as continuous efforts aimed at negotiating legitimacy within an evolving state under prevailing political and economic conditions.[23] Often these claims are crafted in a language of "authentic" customs and traditions—ostensibly restoring these to what they were before, but usually referring to a period in which chieftaincy was fabricated by colonial administrations.

State recognition, as we have noted, offers political and economic benefits to those in office. In KwaZulu, for instance, in the 2011–2012 financial year King Zwelithini's Royal Household Trust was allocated R12m (approximately US$1.4m) from the R55m budget of the Royal Household Department; that sum was overspent by R5.1m.[24] Further, concerned about reports that "King Zwelithini and his entourage stayed at an exclusive Durban hotel at a reported cost of R150,000 to the taxpayer," the leader of CONTRALESA, Phathekile Holomisa, was told to "stay out of the king's business. . . . If it is good for Prince Harry to splash millions of pounds on luxury hotels, why is it wrong for our king to spend the night in a five-star hotel?"[25]

City Press newspaper gave an acute analysis of the stakes involved in contemporary chieftaincy disputes when it noted, during the Sekhukhune kingship determination, that

> The two families are not at each other's throats for nothing, as the stakes are significant. Not only will the winner be recognized as king, he will get an annual budget from the provincial government, like other South African royalty. But even more lucrative are the vast platinum deposits in the Sekhukhune region, and the more than 20 mines in which the winner will become an immediate shareholder.[26]

In the Kekana case, recognition provides otherwise unavailable access to resources, status, and security.[27] According to the Traditional Council Minute Book—the council, that is, of the pretender to office who failed to become chief (see above)—the Plat-Reef Resources mining company held prospecting negotiations with the royal family as early as the 1980s. It has been suggested, too, that the mine is paying for the house in which the current chief resides. This proved difficult to validate, but a record of agreement between the ruler and Plat-Reef confirms that Vaaltyn II received R30,000 monthly from the company during the prospecting process.[28] His uncle revealed, during an interview, that the Canadian-owned mine bought the costly leopard skin that he wore during his inauguration in 2003.

The Traditional Council Minute Book also notes that a series of meetings took place in 2000–2001 between Plat-Reef and *both* rival traditional councils to negotiate prospecting rights. It appears that both believed that the presence of the mine would create employment and generate infrastructural development for the local community. A cosy relationship seemed to have grown up between the councils and Plat-Reef; this may be read off letters of invitation from the company for occasions such as *braais* (barbecues), the acceptance of those invitations, and subsequently a letter from the royal family expressing gratitude for the gracious way in which they had been received by Plat-Reef. The minutes also detail the contribution of the mine to Chief Alfred Kekana's burial.[29]

The rift seems to have opened up when the royal family split and the mine began to negotiate only with the recognized chief and his traditional council. His opponent, along with his followers, complained that they were no longer included in economically and politically binding decisions that pertained to their community. *"Bahaijeke ubukhosi bakaMughombani. Bayabubulala,"* they lamented; "they have hijacked Mokopane's chieftaincy, they are killing it."[30] Their actions were not just calculated to gain state recognition; they were also part of an ongoing struggle to restore the Kekana chieftaincy. This is not a struggle that began at the dawn of democracy. It is merely the latest chapter in a drawn-out battle to adapt to "different moments of interaction" (Esterhuysen 2015) with the colonial and apartheid administrations.

Toward a Conclusion

The Nhlapo Commission, then, is an institutionalized apparatus through which traditional leaders across the provinces of South Africa have reclaimed their legitimacy under the democratic dispensation. The self-assertion of chiefs, not least through institutions of state, is not new, however. At different moments during colonial and apartheid South Africa, some rulers aligned themselves with the government for strategic purposes. Attempts to keep their place by customary authorities have taken a variety of forms and deployed a wide range of strategies and tactics. When the state goes the route of instituting commissions, they have had to adapt their claims to fit the goals, rationales, and procedures of contemporary administrations, presenting them in defensive, resistant, or assertive modes depending on the orientations and attitudes of the regimes (and commissions) with which they have to engage. And many have done so quite skillfully. This is what is to be observed in the case of the Nhlapo Commission: an adaptation of time-honored methods of contestation—and of chieftaincy itself—to changing historical contexts.

The periods before and during the country's transition, and after the first democratic elections, have witnessed a continuity in the tactical means by which traditional leaders negotiate their place on the political landscape. The mobilization of constructed notions of culture, custom, and tradition is one way in which they have called for state recognition. Elsewhere, particularly in the mineral-rich parts of South Africa, like Limpopo and the North West, chiefs have positioned themselves at the center of their local economies; however, the sheer magnitude of the political and financial stakes involved have led to an increase and an intensification of disputes over succession to high office.

Unlike in the past, postapartheid calls for the recognition of chieftaincy have been resolute, even confrontational: the advent of a government led by Africans has created an environment in which demands for a return to African forms of governance, and African cultural practices—violently disrupted by colonial rule and apartheid—may be advanced forcefully and justified constitutionally (see chapter 1, this volume). In contemporary South Africa, the Nhlapo Commission assumed its inordinate significance precisely because it was empowered to determine who might benefit from state recognition—which, arguably, has become more important to claimants than popular support for them and for the institution of chieftaincy. However, many cases submitted to the commission remain unresolved. As a result, several provinces, including Limpopo, have set up their own commissions in an effort to make conclusive determinations.

In this chapter we have discussed two sides, two dimensions, of the continuity of chieftaincy in South Africa. The first is a continuity in the tactics employed by traditional authorities to gain recognition, and secure their place, within ever-changing political and economic landscapes. The second are the mechanisms used by state commissions, in this case by the Nhlapo Commission, which perpetuate some of the practices of old regime—of the Ethnology Section of the Bantu Affairs Department, that is—in applying rigid genealogical rules to decide rights to office. It is in light of both of these things that customary leadership has remained salient in the democratic era. The Nhlapo Commission has merely opened up another arena of contestation for office. That contestation will go on for the foreseeable future as the state attempts to resolve the complicated, ambiguous role of chiefs in postapartheid governance.

Notes

1. Tellingly, discussion of lessons from other postcolonial African contexts has been markedly absent from South African public discussion, lawmaking, and, to an extent, scholarship.
2. The Traditional and Khoi-San Leadership Bill is another such effort. It has been before Parliament since September 2015.
3. The workings of the Ingonyama Trust are so opaque that, when it accounts to Parliament each year, it is regularly criticized for the inadequacy of its reports and accused of hiding what it does with money raised from residents in areas that fall under it. The trust was established in the dying days of apartheid, with the land transferred to it just a few days before the first democratic elections in 1994. The Zulu king is its sole trustee. For a critical look at chiefs' attempts to capture land and mineral wealth see http://www.customcontested.co.za/south-africas-mining-boom-double -dispossession-rural-poor/.
4. As Geschiere makes clear in his chapter in this volume, Mamdani's work has been critiqued extensively.
5. Chieftaincy was recognized in Chapter 12 of the 1996 constitution. However, chiefs, through CONTRALESA and the Houses of Traditional Leaders, vociferously complain that this grants them no real power or status, merely hollow recognition of their office. The TLGFA established a National House of Traditional Leaders as well as provincial and district-level houses.
6. See "Second Destruction of Venda Kingship," under "Venda Kingship," Luonde VhaVenda History, http://luonde.co.za/venda-kingship/, accessed 16 August 2015.
7. See "Commission on Traditional Leadership Disputes and Claims," Department of Traditional Affairs, Republic of South Africa, 29 March 2011, http://www.dta.gov.za/ index.php/entities/52-commission-on-traditional-leadership-disputes-and-claims .html, replaced by http://pmg-assets.s3-website-eu-west-1.amazonaws.com/docs/11 1101dta-edit_0.pdf.
8. Adam Ashforth (1990) offers a useful view of official commissions that partially applies to the Nhlapo Commission. He portrays them as "symbolic rituals" through which agents of the state "seek to apprehend and master" reality (p. 8).
9. The dispute over the Bapedi kingship had been deadlocked for decades, until 2005, when the government appointed the Nhlapo Commission.
10. "Buried as King or Commoner?," Sizwe Sama Yende, *City Press*, n.d., http:// m24arg02.naspers.com/argief/berigte/citypress/2007/01/07/CP/7/sysekhukhune .html, accessed 11 August 2015 (no longer available online).

11. "Euphoria as King Toni Returns Home a Conquering Hero," Moloko Moloto, *Star*, 25 September 2012, http://www.iol.co.za/the-star/euphoria-as-king-toni-returns-home -a-conquering-hero-1389242, accessed 14 August 2015.

12. See "King's Budget Reeks of Favouritism," Monica De Souza, *Mercury*, 27 August 2015, http://www.iol.co.za/mercury/king-s-budget-reeks-of-favouritism-1.1906476, accessed 27 August 2015.

13. "Gigaba Meets with Zulu King," Bongani Hans, *IOL News*, 14 April 2015, http://www .iol.co.za/news/politics/gigaba-meets-with-zulu-king-1844671, accessed 15 March 2016.

14. "King Zwelithi's Land Claim: What Does the King Want?" Stephen Coan, *Witness*, 14 July 2014, http://www.customcontested.co.za/king-want/, accessed 26 August 2015.

15. "Bayede Newspaper, Traditional Leaders and Mining Deals in KwaZulu-Natal," Stha Yeni, Custom Contested (Centre for Law and Society, University of Cape Town), 25 August 2015, http://www.customcontested.co.za/bayede-newspaper-traditional -leaders-and-mining-deals-in-kwazulu-natal/, accessed 26 August 2015.

16. Klass Kekana, interviewed by Dineo Skosana and Philip Bonner, Vaaltyn, 15 August 2009.

17. Joseph Kekana, interviewed by Dineo Skosana, Vaaltyn, 15 September 2011.

18. Abraham Kekana, unrecognized tribal council, interviewed by Dineo Skosana, Amanda Esterhuysen, Phil Bonner, and Sekibakiba Lekgoathi, Vaaltyn, 16 August 2009.

19. Mokopane Royal Council, Polokwane Circuit Court of the North Gauteng High Court, judgment, March 2013.

20. Community members, interviewed by Dineo Skosana, Magogwa, 14 August 2011.

21. In Sesotho, this general principle is captured in the idiom *kgosi ke kgosi ya batho*, "a chief is a chief of the people."

22. Succession disputes in precolonial Africa, arguably, were about asserting control and power—and, in some instances, about rectifying diversions from the rules of succession.

23. After 1994, the Department of Rural Development and Land Reform formally took over the management of land affairs in the former homeland territories. But chiefs in some parts of South Africa, as in the cases discussed here, remain key actors in the administration of land and in decision-making processes regarding economic activities; see, e.g., Manson and Mbenga (2003).

24. "Zulu King Needs More Money," Nathi Olifant, *IOL News*, 28 October 2012, http://www .iol.co.za/news/politics/zulu-king-needs-more-money-1412431, accessed 16 March 2016. During 2012, the value of the South African rand varied from ZAR 0.113561 to 0.130807 to the US dollar.

25. "King Goodwill Zwelithini Favoured—Report," SAPA, *News 24*, 24 September 2012, http://www.news24.com/SouthAfrica/Politics/King-Goodwill-Zwelithini-favoured -report-20120924, accessed 24 August 2015.

26. "Battle Royale Hits Limpopo Royals," *City Press*, 29 September 2012, http://www .news24.com/Archives/City-Press/Battle-royale-hits-Limpopo-royals-20150429, ac- cessed 24 August 2015.

27. As noted above, Limpopo contains the largest concentration of platinum reserves in the country. Mogalakwena Municipality, which falls into the Bushveld Igneous Complex, is said to have one of the richest ore deposits on earth. The reserves of chromium, platinum, palladium, osmium, iridium, rhodium, and ruthenium are

the world's most extensive. The Bushveld Igneous Complex is over 66,000 square kilometers in extent; see Cawood and Minnitt (1998).

28. Although it is generally believed that rural communities in South Africa draw much of their local livelihoods from agriculture, they are increasingly embraced in the growing mining economy, particularly in Limpopo, the North West, and Mpumalanga; see, for details, Capps (2012:71).

29. Unrecognized traditional council, interviewed by Dineo Skosana, Amanda Esterhuysen, Philip Bonner, and Sekibakiba Lekgoathi, Vaaltyn, 1 August 2009.

30. Unrecognized traditional council, interviewed by Dineo Skosana, Amanda Esterhuysen, Philip Bonner, and Sekibakiba Lekgoathi, Vaaltyn, 1 August 2009.

References

Ashforth, Adam
  1990   Reckoning Schemes of Legitimation: On Commissions of Inquiry as Power/Knowledge Forms. *Journal of Historical Sociology* 3(1):1–22.
Bank, Leslie, and Roger Southall
  1996   Traditional Leaders in South Africa's New Democracy. *Journal of Legal Pluralism and Unofficial Law* 28(37–38):407–30.
Beall, Jo, Sibongeni Mkhize, and Shahid Vawda
  2005   Emergent Democracy and 'Resurgent' Tradition: Institutions, Chieftaincy, and Transition in KwaZulu-Natal. *Journal of Southern African Studies* 31(4):755–71.
Bodley, John H.
  2001   *Anthropology and Contemporary Human Problems.* Fourth edition. Mountain View, CA: Mayfield Publishing Company.
Butler, Jeffrey, Robert Rotberg, and John Adams
  1977   *The Black Homelands of South Africa: The Political and Economic Development of Bophuthatswana and Kwa-Zulu.* Berkeley, CA: University of California Press.
Capps, Gavin
  2012   Victim of Its Own Success? The Platinum Mining Industry and the Apartheid Mineral Property System in South Africa's Political Transition. *Review of African Political Economy* 39(131):63–84.
Cawood, F. T., and R. C. A. Minnitt
  1998   A Historical Perspective on the Economics of the Ownership of Mineral Rights Ownership. *Journal of South Africa Institute of Mining and Metallurgy* 98(7):369–76.
Centre for Law and Society, University of Cape Town
  2013   Questioning the Legal Status of Traditional Councils in South Africa. http://www.cls.uct.ac.za/usr/lrg/downloads/CLS_TCStatus_Factsheet_Aug2013.pdf.
Comaroff, John L.
  1974   Chiefship in a South African Homeland: A Case Study of the Tshidi Chiefdom of Bophuthatswana. *Journal of Southern African Studies* 1(1):36–51.
Comaroff, John L., and Simon A. Roberts
  1981   *Rules and Processes: The Cultural Logic of Dispute in an African Context.* Chicago: University of Chicago Press.
Cope, Nicholas
  1990   The Zulu Petit Bourgeoisie and Zulu Nationalism in the 1920s: Origins of Inkatha. *Journal of Southern African Studies* 16(3):431–51.

Delius, Peter

  1990   Migrants, Comrades and Rural Revolt: Sekhukhuneland 1950–1987. *Transformation* 13:2–26.

  2008   Contested Terrain: Land Rights and Chiefly Power in Historical Perspective. In *Land, Power and Custom: Controversies Generated by South Africa's Communal Land Rights Act,* Aninka Claassens and Ben Cousins, eds. Athens, OH: Ohio University Press.

Esterhuysen Amanda

  2015   Margins of Difference: A Study of the Collapse and Restoration of the Kekana Chiefdom under the Rule of Chief Mugombane. In *Materializing Colonial Encounters: Archaeologies of African Experience,* Francois G. Richard, ed. New York: Springer Press.

Geschiere, Peter

  1993   Chiefs and Colonial Rule in Cameroon: Inventing Chieftaincy, French and British Style. *Africa* 63(2):151–75.

Hiemstra, V. G.

  1985   Report on Trans-border Clashes between Subjects of Gazankulu and Lebowa. Pretoria: Republic of South Africa.

James, Deborah

  1990   A Question of Ethnicity: Ndzundza Ndebele in a Lebowa Village. *Journal of Southern African Studies* 16(1):33–54.

Keenan, Jeremy

  1988   Counter Revolution as Reform: Struggle in the Bantustans. In *Popular Struggles in South Africa,* William Cobbett and Robin Cohen, eds. Johannesburg: Ravan Press.

Khunou, S. F.

  2009   Traditional Leadership and Independent Bantustans of South Africa: Some Milestones of Transformative Constitutionalism beyond Apartheid. *Potchefstroomse Elektroniese Regsblad* 12(4), http://www.saflii.org/za/journals/PER/2009/19.html.

Klopper, Sandra

  1996   'He Is My King, but He Is Also My Child': Inkatha, the African National Congress and the Struggle for Control over Zulu Cultural Symbols. *Oxford Art Journal* 19(1): 53–66.

Landau, Paul S.

  2010   *Popular Politics in the History of South Africa, 1400–1948.* New York: Cambridge University Press.

Mamdani, Mahmood

  1996   *Citizen and Subject: Contemporary Africa and the Legacy of Late Colonialism.* Princeton, NJ: Princeton University Press.

Manson, Andrew, and Bernard Mbenga

  2003   'The Richest Tribe in Africa': Platinum Mining and the Bafokeng in South Africa's North West Province, 1965–1999. *Journal of Southern African Studies* 29(1):25–47.

Marks, Shula

  1986   *The Ambiguities of Dependence in South Africa: Class, Nationalism and the State in Twentieth-Century Natal.* Johannesburg: Ravan Press.

Myers, Jason C.

  2008   *Indirect Rule in South Africa: Tradition, Modernity, and the Costuming of Political Power.* Rochester: University of Rochester Press.

Ngubane, M.

  2005   Sources of Succession Disputes in Respect of *Ubukhosi*: Chieftainship with Regard to the Cele and amaNgwane Chiefdoms, Kwazulu-Natal. Master's thesis, University of Zululand.

Ntsebeza, Lungisile
  2005 *Democracy Compromised: Chiefs and the Politics of the Land in South Africa*. Leiden: Brill.
Omer-Cooper, J. D.
  1966 *The Zulu Aftermath: A Nineteenth-Century Revolution in Bantu Africa*: London: Longman.
Oomen, Barbara
  2000 *Tradition on the Move: Chiefs, Democracy and Change in Rural South Africa*. Amsterdam: Netherlands Institute for Southern Africa.
  2002 *Chiefs! Law, Power and Culture in Contemporary South Africa*. Leiden: University of Leiden Press.
Peires, Jeff
  1995 Matiwane's Road to Mbholompo: A Reprieve for the *Mfecane?* In *Mfecane Aftermath: Reconstructive Debates in Southern African History*, Carolyn Hamilton, ed. Johannesburg: University of Witwatersrand Press.
  2014 History versus Customary Law: Commission on Traditional Leadership: Disputes and Claims. *South African Crime Quarterly* 49:7–20.
Piper, Laurence
  2002 Nationalism without a Nation: The Rise and Fall of Zulu Nationalism in South Africa's Transition to Democracy, 1975–99. *Nations and Nationalism* 8(1):73–94.
Ramutsindela, Maano, and David Simon
  1999 The Politics of Territory and Place in Post-Apartheid South Africa: The Disputed Area of Bushbuckridge. *Journal of Southern African Studies* 25(3):479–98.
Ray, Donald I.
  1996 Divided Sovereignty: Traditional Authority and the State in Ghana. *Journal of Legal Pluralism and Unofficial Law* 37–38:181–202.
Sithole, Jabulani
  2009 Preface: Zuluness in South Africa: From 'Struggle' Debate to Democratic Transformation. In *Zulu Identities: Being Zulu, Past and Present*, Benedict Carton, John Laband, and Jabulani Sithole, eds. Scottsville: University of KwaZulu-Natal Press.
South African Institute of Race Relations (SAIRR)
  1957 *Annual Report, 1956–1957*. Johannesburg: SAIRR.
van Kessel, Ineke
  1993 From Confusion to Lusaka: The Youth Revolt in Sekhukhuneland. *Journal of Southern African Studies* 19(4):593–614.
van Kessel, Ineke, and Barbara Oomen
  1997 'One Chief, One Vote': The Revival of Traditional Authorities in Post-Apartheid South Africa. *African Affairs* 96:561–85.

FIVE

The Politics of States and Chiefs in Zimbabwe

JOCELYN ALEXANDER

Chiefs in Africa are as varied as African states, in part because their fates are so often intimately linked. When I first set out to try to understand the history of rural state making in Zimbabwe, I struggled to find any single model of chieftaincy in either the archives or oral histories. Chiefs were very different as individuals. There were decrepit, drunken, and illiterate chiefs; young, educated nationalists; homebodies and well-travelled labor migrants; Christians and spirit mediums; cattle barons and failing farmers; nurses and teachers. Their relation to the state was founded and performed in diverse ways and their routes to office were rooted in different claims to authority—bureaucratic, political, and spiritual. Some chiefs ruled over long-standing communities while others managed a hodgepodge of evictees and migrants with no common identity, products of the turbulent nineteenth and twentieth centuries. Some chiefs became outspoken opponents of the Rhodesian state, making common cause with nationalism. A small number made their way to the guerrilla camps in Zambia and Mozambique. Others went on state-sponsored tours of empire, robed in invented costumes and embodying newly created institutions and constituencies.

Chieftaincy seemed an extraordinarily flexible institution, never wholly of the state or the customary but nonetheless always bound by them. This is not far off the description of the intercalary or Janus-faced customary figure of classic anthropological accounts. There are good reasons why that is a perennial image in the literature: even if there was little that bound chiefs as individuals together, they nonetheless shared the task of making authority, and they had to interact with both state institutions and their constituencies in doing so. Too often, however, more recent analyses have cast chieftaincy more rigidly, and vapidly, as a neutral pivot caught between easily identifiable opposing demands, an empty vessel filled exclusively by variations on the customary, or simply a repressive tool of a monolithic state. The fluid and promiscuous possibilities of the "intercalary" and of custom are missed in debates over the progressive or regressive charge of chieftaincy, whether one viewed "custom" in negative terms as constituting an ethnic block to citizenship (Mamdani 1996) or in a positive light as the cultural foundation of community, compatible with a donor-driven vision of decentralized democracy (see Obarrio 2010; Alexander 1997; Oomen 2005). The always contradictory and changing interests and demands of state institutions are likewise occluded in these accounts.

Neither chiefs nor state institutions operate only within a customary register. Chiefs' politics have ranged far beyond traditional appeals as they mediated the desires of their constituencies—nationalists, migrant laborers, Christians, and farmers among them. State actors have often cast chiefs as customary first and foremost, but they have also called upon them to implement technocratic edicts or enforce partisan loyalties. These demands create contradictions, reflections of the heterogeneous claims to authority of state institutions themselves, which leave space for chiefs to imagine their own political projects and relations to the state in varied ways. They cannot be reduced to Mamdani's "decentralized despots," clad in faux-tribal garb, just as they cannot be captured by the notion of inclusive and culturally authentic community representatives.

Chiefs combine a prickly and plastic politics with a perennial appeal to states—and a desire to be afforded recognition by them. They require careful unpicking not least because the stakes of office are high: chieftaincy has very often played a central role in shaping the spheres of property relations and citizenship. In this, the binaries that have so often been used to describe chiefs—they are the traditional, ethnic, or informal mirror of the modern, civic, or formal—have provided a powerful means of constructing (as well as dismissing) their authority. But to say so is not to go far enough. The work done by inscribing these binaries, their shifting content and relation to the actual practices of states and chiefs, needs to be explored in order to make sense of the persistent urge to "return" powers to chiefs across radically different times and regimes and the consequences of doing so.[1] While the act of "return" is often authorized as a step back in time, tapping into something ancient and resilient, at its core are struggles over resources, rights, and institution making that are very much of the present (see chapter 1, this volume).[2]

To explore the politics of states and chiefs, I focus on chieftaincy in the tumultuous times of settler-ruled Rhodesia and independent Zimbabwe, from the 1960s to the first decade of the twenty-first century. I cover the period up to 2000 with broad brushstrokes and focus in more depth on the extraordinary upheavals in rural state making after that year as it has been explored in a recent literature. Across this period, there were three dominant, though not exclusive, bases on which assertions of rural authority were constructed and in which chieftaincy played divergent roles: custom, technocracy, and nationalism. In each of these, assertions of authority encompassed particular claims to rights and resources, almost always in tension with other claims; in each, local struggles shaped ambitious state-making projects that sought both domination and legitimacy and that did so through the construction of institutions that were ideologically and functionally heterogeneous.[3]

Chiefs in Rhodesia: Remaking and Returning Power

The 1960s were a turbulent time for chieftaincy in Rhodesia and make a fitting starting point for detailing the varied roles states and chiefs imagined and played prior to independence. As in much of British colonial Africa, the post–World War II period heralded a concerted effort at state-planned "'modernization." Famously characterized as the "second colonial occupation," it drew on an empire-wide set of ideas that emphasized technical solutions and required state intervention in an expanding set of fields, from welfare and the environment to production (Low and Lonsdale 1976; Cooper 1996). The Southern Rhodesian (soon to be Rhodesian) settler state was particularly ambitious in this regard: it was exceptionally centralized, bureaucratic, and capable in comparison to any of its neighbors barring South Africa. In the name of modernization, it had developed a powerful set of expert bureaucracies in the 1940s and 1950s, their authority founded in scientific knowledge (Drinkwater 1991). These institutions swept aside the suddenly backward-seeming rural rule of the Native Affairs Department with its vague claims to customary expertise and reliance on hands-on methods of "knowing the native." As the state's ambitions and institutions changed, so too did the role of chieftaincy within it and so also the possibilities of chiefly politics.

Southern Rhodesia's modernist ambitions were most dramatically expressed in the Native Land Husbandry Act of 1951. The act mirrored postwar interventions in other colonies, and it echoed earlier visions of a reordered rural world rooted in missionary aesthetics and ideas, expounded most notably in Rhodesia by the ebullient American missionary and agriculturalist E. D. Alvord (McGregor 1991; Drinkwater 1991). The Land Husbandry Act set out to realize a vision of development in which African men would be transformed from rural "tribesmen" and temporary urban migrants—both cast as backward, inefficient, and morally suspect—into full-time, modern workers and farmers. These men would head nuclear families and embody a newly disciplined productivity alongside reformed gender relations and citizenship.[4] Political stability and economic growth would seamlessly follow. There was scant room for custom in this project but there was plenty of room for chiefs and the hierarchy of headmen and village heads beneath them. They were to implement rural modernity at the behest of the small army of expert extension workers who overran the "reserves." Much to the consternation of native commissioners, these new experts set about determining who had a right to land, demarcated fields and conservation works, cut cattle numbers, and demanded people settle in straight lines, all with scant reference to custom or customary authority. Chiefs' authority was to be replaced by individual rights to the land, monitored by the expert state. Chieftaincy itself was to be "rationalized" so as to make bureaucratic sense of the chaos caused by land alienation and eviction: demotions and wholesale deletions were planned, regardless of the niceties of custom.

The result of attempting to implement this vision of modernity was neither stability nor growth but a rural revolt in concert with a rapid expansion of African nationalism. This revolt drew on the anger of the many migrant workers who entered the ranks of the "landless unemployed"— those whose claims to land in the reserves were denied under the act and who at the same time failed to find urban employment in a contracting market. It built on outrage over a postwar wave of evictions from "white" farms that affected tens of thousands. And it drew on widespread resistance to what rapidly turned into coercive interventions in people's lives and production in the reserves, measures that required labor-intensive conservation works and reduced field sizes and cattle numbers, outraging the poor and the wealthy alike, as well as no small number of chiefs (e.g., Machingaidze 1991; Maxwell 1999; Ranger 1985). These constituencies remade nationalism in a confrontational and popular mode that shook the state's confidence in its developmental project. The official response was to meet nationalism with repression and to court chiefs with an elaboration and authorization of custom.

In this context, the Native Affairs Department and its claims to customary expertise made a comeback against its overweening technocratic brethren. It constructed a narrative that saved everyone's blushes: the Land Husbandry Act had provoked resistance for no more complicated reason than that Africans were not ready to become modern citizens (no matter the highly circumscribed offer). The route to restoring political stability lay in rule by "tribal authorities," a move that insisted on the essential cultural difference of Africans and gave it institutional form. Native commissioners touted the failure to recognize this essential difference as the great error of otherwise well-meaning technical experts who had, as a result, been unable to build rural authority. The 1960s saw a concerted program of courting chiefs, establishing more prestigious institutions for them from district to national level so that they might represent Africans in place of the nationalists and offering them a "return" of powers over the land and law—in effect remaking property relations and the delineations of citizenship once more.

This was not a smooth transition. State institutions were far from being of one mind and chiefs had their own agendas, based on particular histories of eviction, migrant worker demands, political allegiance, and interpretations of custom, as well as their own interests in wealth and office. A battle among bureaucracies ensued, fought out in the medium of expert commissions. Most importantly, against the demands made in the name of custom by Native Affairs, the agrarian experts did not want chiefs to have unfettered powers over land allocation while the law department was horrified by the lack of proper legal procedure, records, and the like in the mooted chiefs' courts. The offer of a "return" to customary authority was in the end much qualified. The response of chiefs further complicated the matter. While some embraced their new powers and perks, others adopted a nationalist rhetoric to challenge the inadequacy of a "return" of customary powers over the land without the return of the "lost lands" themselves, that is, their historic lands now alienated to white settlers. In those reserves where the Land Husbandry Act had been implemented, chiefs held that it had created such confusion and conflict over tenure that they could not reassert customary authority. The individual land rights of the Land Husbandry Act were jealously guarded while those labor migrants who had been denied land under the act continued to insist on the validity of their claims. Chiefs could not satisfy both, and the state's new customary regime offered no solution. Some chiefs also denounced what they saw as the pathetically limited offer of judicial powers, hedged in as they were by the exclusion of certain categories of crime, limits on punishments, and possibility of appeal to magistrate's courts, concessions demanded by the law department in defense of Africans' legal rights (see Karekwaivanane 2012).

As many chiefs grasped all too well, much of what they were being asked to do in the name of custom was to enforce the same set of punitive restrictions on land use as the technocrats of the Land Husbandry Act had envisioned while also standing as a justification for the denial of national-ist demands for a return of alienated land and for a rights-based citizen-ship. Versions of the latter had long been debated in nationalist circles, but they were now on display in the newly independent countries to the north of Rhodesia and so far more difficult to dismiss. None of this deterred the Native Affairs Department from developing a belief that where chiefs failed to exercise authority as intended it was because they were not "properly" customary, a view that led to the production of hundreds of voluminous "delineation reports" on chiefs and headmen and that would embroil na-tive commissioners in labyrinthine efforts to discover "real" traditional au-thorities over the next decade. Such projects were echoed in neighboring South Africa where the Department of Ethnological Affairs's experts pro-duced "blue books" on "tribes" as a basis for legitimating rule (chapter 4, this volume). The Rhodesian version relied less on ethnographic expertise and more on amateur investigation by administrators in search of a usable hierarchy.

The district of Chimanimani, situated on the Mozambican border, of-fers an apposite example of the ways in which chiefs used official attempts to build authority on the back of custom for their own ends.[5] As elsewhere, the delineation teams of the early 1960s found Chimanimani's chiefs sus-picious of land allocation powers and vehement proponents of a return of alienated land. Everywhere, the teams struggled to find the bounded, homogenous communities that chiefs were supposed to rule. Chiefly fol-lowers were often in fact dispersed on white-owned farms and over the Mo-zambican border, beyond the ordering capacities of custom. In addition, the state's embrace proved a problem. For example, the official promotion of one of Chimanimani's chiefs to a prestigious new post at national level had the worrying effect of undermining his authority locally to the extent that he took to carrying a loaded pistol with him at all times. Chimani-mani's native (later district) commissioner spent much of the 1960s and 1970s attempting to solve these and other problems through seeking out "authentic" traditional authorities. Vast files were produced on every rec-ognized chieftaincy, reaching all the way down an imagined hierarchy to "village" level (see Ranger 2001:42–45).

In the case of the Mutambara chiefs, the incumbent, one Dindikwa Mutambara, used his newly granted powers to obstruct administrative and agricultural policy. The frustrated district commissioner moved to depose him, claiming with the collusion of two of his brothers and a spirit me-dium that his installation had been flawed in customary terms. Dindikwa at first defended himself in the language of custom, mobilizing his own spiritual experts and kin, and then openly allied himself with the nationalist cause, a move that pleased a popular constituency unhappy with state taxes and agricultural controls. When the district commissioner finally managed to depose Dindikwa for "not following proper custom" the brother appointed in his place promptly took up a stance of noncooperation while his younger brother, Samuel, used networks he had built as a Methodist evangelist to recruit students for the guerrilla struggle, work that landed him in a nationalist-filled detention center in 1974. The result of all this effort was state paralysis born of a failure to remake custom as the basis of rural power.

By the time of Samuel's detention, the Native Affairs Department (now Internal Affairs) was fast becoming a militarized arm of the state in the face of an expanding guerrilla war mounted from across Rhodesia's borders. As the 1970s progressed, chiefs faced an existential crisis. In this era, to serve the state, as chiefs did in many guerrillas' eyes, was to be a sellout, and to be a sellout was a capital crime. Armed young men and nationalist party committees began to displace chiefs' authority in the rural areas, along with the rest of the Rhodesian state's civilian representatives, from extension workers and dip tank attendants to school teachers. They instituted new regimes of justice and mobilization that focused on the production and enforcement of political loyalty. Many chiefs were killed (by both guerrillas and security forces), reduced to living behind barbed wire, or forced to flee to the towns. Their fate echoed that of chiefs elsewhere in the region at moments of political rupture: Oomen (2005:130) records how, in Sekhukhune's rural revolt of 1986, chiefs were "burnt, chased away, or killed." Chiefs' politics in South Africa nonetheless remained highly varied, as they did elsewhere.[6] In Zimbabwe, some chiefs joined the nationalists, winding up in nationalist party committees, in the guerrilla camps in Mozambique and Zambia, or, as with Samuel Mutambara, in detention.

During the war, chiefs often lost the capacity to function as intercalary figures, much as was the case elsewhere in the region in periods of violent revolt. The war years did not, however, end chiefs' desire for state recognition or close debates among nationalists or within the Rhodesian state over chiefly authority. Rhodesian attempts to use the legitimating power of custom continued throughout the war, and guerrillas of different ideological stripes were more or less sympathetic to chiefs and mediums. While some guerrillas' demands for the return of ancestral lands echoed those of chiefs, other guerrillas based their claims to land and political change in democratic or Marxist principles.[7] However, a powerful element in Zimbabwean nationalism remained deeply distrustful of chieftaincy as an insufficiently modern and progressive form of rule, over and above the problem of its entanglement with the Rhodesian state (Ranger 2001:45–47).

Building Rural Authority in Independent Zimbabwe

At independence in 1980, state attempts to build rural authority played out in new but not unfamiliar ways. ZANU(PF) won Zimbabwe's first elections and faced a daunting task of state making in the country's war-ravaged rural areas.[8] There were huge challenges due to the widespread displacement of people and destruction of infrastructure. There were also great difficulties due to the fact that rural institutions of rule ranged from the moribund councils to the often deeply distrusted official chiefs to the fiercely independent "structures" of ZANU(PF)'s own rural committees and, far worse from ZANU(PF)'s point of view, those of its only real political rival, the nationalist party ZAPU. In this context, the customary seemed at first to lose out, but in the end there would be a "return"—or "returns"—to chiefs once again, as new battles over land and citizenship were ignited.

In its first few years in power, ZANU(PF) sought to, first, centralize control over the rural party structures and mute their demands, not least for "lost lands" and political authority, and, second, create new institutions of rural rule on a "modern" model—both goals that reflected powerful strands of nationalism. ZAPU was militarily crushed and then absorbed into ZANU(PF) under the Unity Accord of 1987.[9] ZANU(PF)'s rural committees were more gently marginalized and coopted. Their demands were contained through the institution of an elected hierarchy of village development committees (vidcos) and district councils, alongside elected presiding officers in rural courts. The vidcos were based on the rational-seeming unit of 100 households. Land and judicial powers were transferred from traditional leaders to the councils and presiding officers, though recognized chiefs kept their state salaries. ZANU(PF)'s new ministers glossed this as nationalist respect for African culture. Such recognition did not, however, extend to spirit mediums or to chiefs who had been deposed owing to land alienation or nationalist sympathies.[10] The Ministry of Local Government, successor to the Native Affairs Department, made it clear that the administrative understanding of traditional authority would remain unchanged. Political loyalty and settler injustices held no sway. The delineation reports and the voluminous files they had spawned still formed the basis for laborious—and once again often unresolved—efforts to establish claims to chiefly office. Chiefly aspirants did not take all this with equanimity: some launched court cases contesting their exclusion from titles;

many exercised the powers they claimed despite lacking state recognition.[11] Everywhere, achieving state recognition was an important goal for chiefs (see also chapter 3, this volume).

In the 1980s, a vision of nationalism as modernizing development held sway. It encompassed state-delivered redistribution and an end to racial discrimination alongside a large dose of familiar technocracy. The experts who had—in part—been pushed aside in the 1960s returned to center stage. They proposed for the former reserves, now known as communal areas, something very like the Land Husbandry Act (and in fact they drew directly on the plans left behind by their Rhodesian predecessors) but called it land use planning. They also instituted direct state rule in the new resettlement areas, that is, the formerly "white" large-scale farms acquired by the state and redistributed to black smallholders. On the resettlement schemes, official authority took the shape of the resettlement officer, unmediated in theory at least by traditional authorities or indeed any form of elected representation. Claims to land based on historical restitution, ancestral traditions, or local versions of democratic process—the varied constituents of popular nationalism—had no place in this state vision.

The new government cast this modernist vision against a traditional world imagined and condemned as backward, unproductive, and undemocratic. These were the familiar binaries by which rural rule had so often been constructed and authorized, claiming control over property and delineating the rights of citizens in the process. As in the past, however, such discursive divides fell apart in practice. Often it was traditional leaders, though not necessarily those identified via the delineation reports, who were elected onto the new model vidcos and as presiding officers in the remade courts. This outcome underlined a different idea of the requirements of justice and representation than that of the 100-household vidco or magistrate-trained presiding officer. Where traditional leaders were entirely excluded, there was often paralyzing conflict as the authority-making power of elections tout court was vigorously challenged.

The content of the state's categories and intentions was confounded in other ways too. When traditional leaders objected to technocratic land use plans they did not do so only due to their affront to custom but also because they threatened livelihoods: they might require people to move and rebuild homes, or prevent cultivation of fertile wetlands, for example. As importantly, they flew in the face of rural nationalism. Opposition to settling in lines and building contour ridges, measures coercively enforced by Rhodesian governments and reintroduced in the 1980s, had stood at the heart of decades of rural protest. Similarly, when chiefs railed against the rule of resettlement officers on redistributed land they did so because it was their land to govern, customarily speaking, but also because rural nationalism had called for historical restitution, a demand the new government pointedly refused. Chiefs also found a popular constituency for their "customary" views on gender and generational relations, now challenged by progressive legislation granting women new rights, and they defended such views in official and unofficial courts. Both the nature of citizenship and the shape of rural development was heatedly contested in these debates—though not in the form of the state's imagined binaries—and acted as a source of instability for rural authorities.

There were great ructions over these and other matters in the 1980s. Nonetheless, party chairmen and many traditional authorities (categories that were not exclusive) were to a significant extent channeled into the new model vidcos, councils, and courts. As in earlier eras, the state's initiatives shaped the spaces in which chiefs could act. Once made part of these institutions, chiefs and others found that they had scant control over decision making and resources, laboring rather as implementers of centrally made policy, again in an echo of previous decades. This proved tolerable for many so long as ZANU(PF) delivered schools, clinics, infrastructure, and grain depots—the far from trivial benefits of government by a capable bureaucracy intent on development. None of this applied to the ZAPU-supporting regions of Matabeleland and the Midlands to anything like the same extent, however. In these regions, violent repression produced developmental neglect and the distinct claims of ZAPU's nationalism remained influential. Rural institutions of rule had a tenuous grasp on authority as a result. But even in ZANU(PF) strongholds there were dissonant voices. A good many ZANU(PF) MPs and provincial governors (the powerful political appointees who oversaw the bureaucratic state in the provinces) sided against administrators and technocrats in order to back, in populist mode, rural versions of nationalism that called for decentralized power, land restitution, and recognition for local versions of custom. ZANU(PF) politicians did so because they wanted to win elections, but they were also genuinely divided over what version of nationalism should hold sway. In the 1980s, politicians' support for the large-scale "squatter" occupations of formerly "white" land against the authority of law and the aims of the official resettlement program was their most visible protest against the definition of nationalism as top-down, modernizing development.

In the late 1980s, the tensions in rural as well as urban areas found new voice as the violent demise of ZAPU opened up political space. This trend was greatly amplified in the 1990s when ZANU(PF)'s adoption of a structural adjustment program undercut state bureaucrats' ability to deliver on the material promises of modernizing development. In the rural areas, disaffection and conflict over resources—including land—spread, as did a language of rights that echoed nationalist claims but which had a new set of proponents among NGOs, civic associations, and trade unions, all increasingly hostile to ZANU(PF). In the mid- and late 1990s, ZANU(PF)'s rule was threatened in unprecedented ways. Rural disaffection sat side by side with trade union strikes and war veteran protests (which were met with economically disastrous but politically productive state largesse). A powerful new opposition party, the Movement for Democratic Change (MDC), was launched on the backs of the unions and civics in 1999 and was rapidly followed by the shock of the ruling party's constitutional referendum defeat in early 2000.

In the 1990s, ZANU(PF)'s response to rural disaffection had at first taken a page from its Rhodesian predecessors in diagnosing the problem as too much modernity: technocratic and democratic institutions could not gain a foothold in a society where customary powers and allegiances still held such sway. It was an explanation that struggled to disguise the fact that, in the era of structural adjustment (much as in the 1960s), technocracy had become too expensive and unpopular while democracy had grown too fractious, opening space for opposition movements and angry condemnations of abuses of power and corruption. Moves were made once more to "return" powers to chiefs. As in the 1960s, this process was deeply contested among state bureaucracies and delayed by the cogitations of expert commissions. The Land Tenure Commission of 1994, with its mixed bag of recommendations, is a case in point. Its report called for recognition of the "traditional village" as the "basic unit of social organization." This unit was to be represented by elected committees bearing traditional names, which would then be subjected to the discipline of surveys, mapping, and fencing.[12] The Traditional Leaders Act, passed in 1998, promised chiefs a (limited) set of powers over land and in courts while the Ministry of Local Government elaborated a system under which ward and village "assemblies" would be headed by chiefs and headmen (Ranger 2001:31–32). In this iteration, the "return" to chiefs did not untether "custom" from the long-standing and unpopular tasks of governance stipulated from on high—enforcing conservation rules, tax collection, reporting crime, and the like—that flowed from the insertion of chiefs into a bureaucratic state. The implementation of these measures was, however, overtaken by a second, very different response from the ruling party to its rural political vulnerability. This would bring chiefs into a relationship not with a bureaucratic state but with a newly partisan set of institutions.

This second response followed from the ascent of a radical faction within ZANU(PF).[13] This group had been unable to override those in the party and state who had imagined nationalism as modernizing development in the 1980s, but it did far better in the face of the popular discontents and weakened state bureaucracy of the structural adjustment era of the 1990s. In the late 1990s, this shift began to tip the scales in favor of a long-standing strand of nationalist discourse that put fighting men, land redistribution, and race at the center of claims to rule. It revived a wartime language of sellouts and enemies—threats to the revolution—alongside violent practices intended to discipline them. Dubbed the "Third *Chimurenga*," thereby placing it as the successor to armed revolt against conquest and then the liberation struggle of the 1970s, it was at first most dramatically expressed in war veteran-led occupations of the large-scale farm sector, land often still in white hands. This was a messy process—and much contested within ZANU(PF)—but it would nonetheless lead on to a dramatic remaking of the state and chiefs' role in it.[14]

In what follows, I focus on the remaking of rural authority on the vast swaths of land that were redistributed under "Fast Track resettlement," as the land occupations came to be known. These spaces offered a particularly revealing view of the reshaping of the relationship between chiefs and the state in yet another moment of dramatic upheaval.

"Fast Track" Resettlement and Rural Authority in the Twenty-First Century

It would be difficult to dispute that Fast Track resettlement transformed Zimbabwe after 2000. Over the next years, the vast majority of largely white-owned, large-scale farms was transferred to black households, mostly smallholders who (in theory) held land on the basis of a state-issued offer letter. This process has been described as "repeasantization," although there was much differentiation within it. The scale and rapidity of change was stunning. According to Moyo (2011:942), the large-scale sector dropped from 4,956 farms on 8.7 million hectares in 2000 to 1,371 farms on just over a million hectares in 2010. The (black) small- and medium-scale sector (including the communal areas) jumped from about 1.13 million households on 21.4 million hectares to 1.35 million households, an increase of some 218,000, on over 30 million hectares. Within this, the medium-scale sector grew by around 20,000 farms. In addition, some large-scale farms were taken over intact by black owners outside the official bounds of Fast Track.[15] That this transformation went hand in hand with a re-making of the political sphere is widely agreed. How to understand this process and its implications for chiefs and the state, has, however, been hotly disputed.

Let me start by briefly setting out two different approaches. An influential view propounded by leading leftist scholars of agrarian change cast Fast Track resettlement as economically costly and politically compromised by ZANU(PF)'s "oppressive, corrupt, and desperate" regime, but nonetheless as a "significant *and* 'objectively progressive' expression of a (new) agrarian question of labor." The occupations, they argued, addressed the reproductive struggles of the "worker-peasant" and redressed the "'unfinished business' of national democratic revolution" by undoing the legacy of territorial segregation.[16] In this approach, the remaking of rural authority was evaluated in terms of its class politics. Sam Moyo noted the role that traditional leaders had played in the early days of the occupations—very much in keeping with previous decades—in expressing demands for land "on the basis of its sacred or cultural value in addition to its productive potential." However, he identified a trend toward their displacement by "informal movements" led by war veterans and urban workers with an "anticolonial" ideology based on "combining self-reliance with surplus production and sales" (2001:326–27).

A few years later, Moyo, writing with Paris Yeros, found that the revolutionary momentum of this movement had been "interrupted" as the occupations had brought about no more than a "temporary suspension" of the bureaucratic state (2007:108). The land occupiers had ultimately failed to "prepare the semi-proletariat organizationally against the reassertion of the black bourgeoisie." ZANU(PF) leaders used the state to divide urban and rural workers, repressing urban trade unionists, allocating land to an urban petty bourgeoisie and to black elites, and allying with traditional authorities (see Moyo and Yeros 2005:192–93, 201). In this view, chiefs' land demands embodied patriarchal and "ethnoregional" biases and their links to the state allowed personal accumulation on the model of a "lower tier 'policy elite'" (Moyo and Yeros 2007:110–11). Ultimately, in Moyo and Yeros's account, chiefs constituted an obstacle to progressive class politics because they represented "social organization on the basis of kinship rather than economic interest" and served to extend the bourgeois state's power into the rural areas (2007:119).

Another strand of writing interpreted the remaking of rural authority through "moral geographies" of identity and belonging (Dande and Mujere n.d.:3), often taking a view from the state's "margins" and focusing on the political dynamics of particular chieftaincies.[17] This work rejected the notion of a homogenous constituency of traditional leaders amenable to state manipulation, seeing rather a cacophony of potentially subversive, historically and spiritually rooted claims that sought state recognition if not a remade state. For Joost Fontein, the post-2000 state was not unmade by the truncated struggles of the worker-peasant but through the resurgence of the ancestors. Focusing on war veterans and spirit mediums in southern Masvingo, an area of relatively recent evictions and return to ancestral lands under Fast Track, he found "profoundly alternative and radical imaginings of the way the postcolonial state should operate." These were based in a shared historical narrative of cooperation between mediums and guerrillas during the liberation struggle and expressed in the performance of ceremonies linking the living and the dead through which a "moral conviviality" was made (Fontein 2006a:194; also see Lan 1985). The shared desire for a restitution of the land among traditional leaders, war veterans, and some state officials offered a "reopened access to the process of state making, revitalizing the possibility, at least for these particular groups, of making the state towards their interests," a project that had the "ongoing legacy of ancestrally-guided struggle" at its heart (Fontein 2009:17–19).

Innocent Dande and Joseph Mujere's work (n.d.:4) echoes Fontein's in emphasizing the importance of "traditional" readings of Fast Track in which a central role is played by chiefs' historical and spiritual claims to land. Their case study of chiefs in Makoni District in the eastern Manicaland Province is, however, less about mediums and veterans acting in concert with chiefs and more about the conflicts among chiefs' claims and their efforts to use a variety of state institutions and ZANU(PF) leaders, deploying a wide range of strategies, to gain political advantage. Their point is that chiefs were not "stooges" of the state or ruling party. Instead, they regularly challenged and circumvented both, primarily through drawing on histories of identity and belonging that presented exclusive kin and ethnic claims going back to precolonial days. As in Mazarire (2008) and Mujere's work (2011) in Masvingo, these contestations brought chiefs and their allies into intensive interactions with state institutions in which traditionalist claims held great sway, but were far from the only means by which claims for authority were made and did not evince any uniform or even easily identifiable political position.

These depictions of rural state making are a far cry from Moyo and Yeros's concerns over the threat that an alliance between chiefs and a bourgeois state might pose to peasant-worker struggles. Both approaches find compelling stories of struggle rooted in histories of dispossession, but they offer very different interpretations of what sort of rural state was being created and the role of chieftaincy within it. It is useful to take a step back in order to ask in more detail how state institutions were remade after 2000. As we have seen, rural authority had for many decades been powerfully shaped by the central state and its shifting visions of agrarian development and citizenship. In this process, chiefs' politics and practices were highly variable and not limited to the sphere of custom. Though custom was always a part of their claim to authority and of state institutions' claims on them, the technocratic and nationalist also shaped both sides of this interaction. How did these processes shift in the midst of the dramatic transformation of the state's legitimating ideas and practices after 2000?

In part, the answer to this question flows from how one understands post-2000 politics. Perhaps the most striking aspect of the third *Chimurenga* was the championing of a particular version of liberation war-era nationalism from the very top of the ZANU(PF) government to the land occupiers. While there was much variation, a historically rooted set of practices and ideas formed the basis for new forms of authority that challenged a powerful array of long-standing claims to legitimacy, such as those of the technocratic bureaucracies, administrative constructions of custom, and the rule of law, as well as the newer challenge of the MDC's politics. Over the 2000s, the bureaucratic state was not "suspended" for a brief moment and then reanimated, as in Moyo and Yeros's account. Rather, it was transformed through a logic of partisan patronage and violence. To enable this process, ZANU(PF) created new institutions and agents such as the youth militia and relied on veterans to enforce loyalty inside and outside state institutions.[18] Crucial for Fast Track resettlement were the newly created district and provincial land committees that, as we shall see, displaced and remade bureaucratic authority. ZANU(PF) also introduced new forms of governance exemplified by the "operation," a means of implementing policy that evaded and destabilized the bureaucratic state.[19] These shifts blurred lines between the state and ZANU(PF) from top to bottom. They created new constituencies while alienating others, and they remained contested not only by the MDC but also by many of the bureaucratic state's cadres. These latter partook in the remaking of state institutions by participating in partisan practices and patronage networks even as they objected to them or hoped one day they would end, owing both to the high price of refusal (the threat of coercion or job loss) and to the need to survive—or indeed the desire to accumulate—amidst economic collapse.[20]

Though writers on Fast Track have acknowledged the role of partisan and violent politics they have less often taken into account the ways in which state institutions were remade.[21] The institutional context in which power was generated had changed; new actors were able to make new rules and new claims—amidst great uncertainty—as a result. Just as in the eras of technocratic dominance or the upheavals of the liberation struggle, this inevitably reshaped the space in which chiefs worked and meant, as Martin Chanock (1991:63) noted for South Africa, that custom would to some extent "take on its content in application from the dominant political directions and discourses."[22] Most accounts of the early years of the land occupations in Zimbabwe stressed their diverse motives and constituents,[23] but it is also clear that loyalty to ZANU(PF) rapidly became necessary, if not necessarily sufficient, to making and defending claims to land and authority on Fast Track farms. Customary leaders had no choice but to engage with the "dominant political directions and discourses" of the third *Chimurenga*.

A vivid account of the early stages of the occupations in Chiredzi District illustrated these shifts in power (Chaumba et al. 2003).[24] Chiefs are present in this account, but neither they nor custom stood at the center of the remaking of the state. A host of other actors and claims to legitimacy came into play. On Fair Range Ranch, for example, veterans led an occupation in early 2000 in which they consulted chiefs about historical claims, the army supplied tents, and the police dismissed the white farm owner's appeals to law (Chaumba et al. 2003:589). In a nod to technocratic authority the occupiers pegged out fifty hectare plots, but they rejected efforts to control their engagement in a host of illegal activities, from stock and wire theft to fire setting and the blocking of roads. In 2001 the ranch owner was ordered out and state extension agents pegged plots. In this process, custom constituted an influential claim to land but more important were "political connections and a pro-ZANU(PF) reputation" (Chaumba et al. 2003:593). Governance on these farms was initially constructed on a remembered model of ZANU(PF)'s liberation war-era practices that was far more suited to a military view of authority than an alliance with the ancestors. Veterans stood at the heart of this politics: they "deliberately echoed the language and symbols of the liberation war," its categories of enemies and sellouts, its use of youth, and its night time meetings. Farms were a "no go" area for the MDC. Access was "strictly policed" and "base camps" had a "highly militarized organizational structure" through which roll calls, drills, and meetings were time-tabled and punishments meted out (Chaumba et al. 2003:589–97).

These authorities had the capacity to discipline and demand performances of loyalty. Identifying and excluding people associated with the MDC from Fast Track farms was possible because ZANU(PF) and veterans had rural committee structures on the farms and in communal areas that were able to perform surveillance and information-gathering activities. They were also able to draw on traditional leaders and councilors, at times calling upon them to provide letters verifying occupiers' ZANU(PF) credentials.[25] As Zamchiya (2011:1117) emphasizes, the most important "vehicle" for defending land claims was political allegiance: an explicit discourse from veterans on the farms and from senior ZANU(PF) politicians justified partisan land allocation. This discourse continued unabated through a multitude of political vicissitudes. A full ten years after the launch of Fast Track, a veteran in Chipinge District explained: "Those who were supporting the MDC must go and get their land in Britain. The land is for sons of the soil not sellouts" (Zamchiya 2011:1114). In his study of Mazowe District, Matondi (2012:216) similarly found that, a decade in, Fast Track farmers "assumed that everyone belonged to ZANU-PF and expected everyone to conform to the dictates of the party." This required ongoing demonstrations of loyalty to ZANU(PF) through, for example, attending national celebrations or donating money, food, and labor.

How were these ideas about authority, belonging, and land institutionalized and what role did chiefs play in the process? Authority on the farms at first most often took the form of war veteran-led "committees of seven." These usually incorporated traditional leaders alongside ZANU(PF) activists, youth, and women representatives. They were paralleled by the creation of district and provincial land committees. These were state institutions, but they were firmly under ZANU(PF)'s partisan control and they entrenched a rejection of technocratic and legal authority.[26] Chaired by district administrators, themselves increasingly overtly partisan (where their credentials were suspect they were at times literally chased away by veterans), they were dominated by ZANU(PF) leaders and veterans and incorporated chiefs alongside officials from the security, agricultural, and welfare arms of state. For Moyo and Yeros (2007:108–9) the land committees played the "most influential" role in structuring the occupations, directing and monitoring line ministries, identifying beneficiaries and farms for acquisition, resolving disputes, and eventually introducing procedures and paperwork—even if their work was regularly disrupted by differently minded local veterans, more senior and powerful state and ZANU(PF) officials, and, on occasion, technocrats (Matondi 2012:90).

This is the context in which traditional leaders made their "return." Unsurprisingly, a number of authors have portrayed traditional leaders as influential only insofar as they subordinated themselves to ZANU(PF)'s partisan project. Moyo and Yeros (2007:110) note chiefs' consistent lobbying for land restitution but stress that "their capacity to overcome the influence of [Land Committees'] other members is doubtful." Matondi (2012:217–18) refers to chiefs as an "appendage" of the District Land Committee in Mazowe: "In many cases, their views, as representatives of the people, were overruled in the committees, thus rendering their social power worthless." Chaumba et al. depict chiefs as "part of the state's attempt to extend its hegemony deeper into rural areas at a time of political discontent. Chiefs and headmen are back—but only on ZANU(PF)'s terms" (2003:599; also see Murisa 2013:10; Zamchiya 2011:1119). While veterans and ZANU(PF) leaders might well support ancestral claims to land and engage chiefs in, for example, the identification of graves or sacred places, they only did so "as long as they toe the party line," as veterans in Chiredzi stressed (Chaumba et al. 2003:599). This subordination of chiefs' customary claims echoed a long-standing strand in ZANU(PF) nationalism and land policy that rejected particularist demands for restitution in favor of invoking land as "a marker of sovereignty. Land reform is about returning the land stolen by whites to 'the people'" (Chaumba et al. 2003:595). Casting the righting of historical injustice as a state task left ZANU(PF) in a position to opt for other grounds for land distribution. This was not an unpopular position amongst the significant constituency of land occupiers and veterans who were, in chiefs' eyes, illegitimate interlopers, foreigners, or "strangers" on their land.[27]

In their interactions with the partisan state, the chiefs' role was not of course limited to making claims to land. Over the first decade of the twenty-first century, their roles in both the communal areas and the Fast Track farms expanded to encompass duties such as political mobilization, surveillance, and punishment, notably during and after elections, and the partisan dispersal of state resources. The ambitious Chiefs' Council president Fortune Charumbira regularly asserted the necessity of all chiefs' allegiance to ZANU(PF).[28] Some traditional leaders took on partisan roles with genuine gusto; others acted out of fear of violence or of a loss of access to the expanding array of official perks offered chiefs, including improved salaries, vehicles, agricultural inputs, farms, and higher political office.[29] As Matondi (2012:217) writes, chiefs became "semi-politicians whereas, as traditional leaders, they were supposed to be apolitical" (see also chapter 7, this volume). There were significant material effects to these politics, as Phillan Zamchiya (2011, 2013) has shown in Chipinge. The partisan networks in which chiefs engaged played a decisive role in determining not only who got hold of land but who gained access to free and subsidized fuel, state tillage, seeds, and fertilizer, all of which made a substantial difference to the fortunes of farmers.[30] The binding of chiefs to a state remade as partisan has taken on new forms as the threat posed by the MDC receded in the aftermath of the 2013 elections and the battle for dominance among factions within ZANU(PF) took center stage. Following the ouster of the faction associated with former Vice President Joice Mujuru in December 2014, her supporters were expelled not only from the party itself but—reportedly—also from the ranks of traditional leaders who, having associated themselves with senior politicians, were deemed to be "loyalists" in one camp or another.[31]

Amidst all this there remained a great uncertainty regarding the ultimate basis of rural authority. In the day-to-day administration of Fast Track land, authors reported diverse practices. In his study of Gutu, Mujere (2011:1131–32, 1135–37) found that the committees of seven had been transformed into "village committees" but remained dominated by veterans and ZANU(PF) "activists" who had a "complete disregard for the authority of traditional leaders." Matondi's study (2012:218) of Mazowe found "village heads" had been appointed by chiefs in some cases while in others people "had chosen their own village heads, either someone in a position of political influence or a War Veteran." Tendai Murisa's study (2013:13–14) in the districts surrounding Harare found that village headmen, who might be appointed by chiefs or elected, had taken up leadership roles on village committees otherwise made up of a mixed bag of elected members and veterans. These were referred to as "vidcos," somewhat ironically in that they were dominated by leaders construed as "traditional" and so were a far cry from the intentions of the 100-household modernizing model of the 1980s' originals. In terms of their practice, however, they echoed their namesakes in that they "mostly focused on ensuring that government directives on agrarian reform are implemented at a local level," enforcing for example prohibitions on tree cutting or subletting plots. For Murisa (2013:17), this use of traditional leaders marked their "resuscitation" as "a crucial cog of local government and control."

A number of writers have identified a "contradiction between a simultaneously reinvigorated and disempowered chieftaincy" (Chaumba et al. 2003:600). However, the "return" of powers to chiefs by the state has always been double-edged: the terms of return constrained customary authority—in this case in partisan mode—but the "intercalary" nature of chieftaincy and the diverse agendas of chiefs meant that they could use their state-sanctioned position to contest the terms of office and to play on the contradictions and divisions within state and party. In some places chiefs emerged as outspoken critics of elite accumulation, notably where elites used their positions in the state and ZANU(PF) to ride roughshod over local land claims or to monopolize mining resources (e.g., Mkodzongwi 2016; Mawowa 2013; Moyo and Yeros 2007:110; Chaumba et al. 2003:602). At times they played on the ruling party's promises to "indigenize" mining wealth in an attempt to hold it to account. Chief Zimunya, speaking to an NGO audience in July 2015, complained bitterly over the exclusion of chiefs from the distribution of diamond riches supposedly gathered for their followers under the Marange-Zimunya Community Share Ownership Trust: "We have no say over resources within our own communities, so tell me what is our role as chiefs?" Zimunya asked.[32] The successes that chiefs enjoyed in confrontations with state and party were uneven and often ephemeral, dependent on their alliances with politicians whose fortunes rose and fell, as well as civil servants, local institutions of government, churches, NGOs, and diaspora groups. They appealed to the law and they mobilized followers in acts of disobedience and, as they long had, they constructed elaborate historical narratives legitimating customary claims to office and land. As a rich literature has documented, fifteen years into the third *Chimurenga* there is a vast array of ongoing conflicts among traditional authorities and between them and other authorities over position, powers, land claims, boundaries, belonging, custom itself, and a host of other matters that continues to disrupt the state's construction of customary authority and its partisan—and bureaucratic—use.[33]

The long decade of ZANU(PF)'s third *Chimurenga* left it with few challengers to its overall control but with many challenges to its authority from within and outside the state and party. Partisan and patronage relationships, rooted in a reimagined wartime nationalism rather than the developmental and modernizing promises of bureaucratic rule, stood at the heart of the rural state. These relationships had delivered a dramatic redistribution of the land and offered a means to discipline political loyalties through a redefinition of citizenship. The ZANU(PF) state had, however, lost much of its bureaucratic capacity and expertise (though the appeal of technocratic rule remained and regularly resurfaced) while its partisan institutions had worrying tendencies to dissonance and autonomy—on the part of veterans and chiefs incorporated into the bottom rungs of the state, as well as of elites seeking to defend or extend new modes of power and accumulation through the upper levels of state institutions.

Returning to the Desire to "Return" Chiefly Powers

This brings us back to a consideration of the durable nature of the relationship between rural state making and chiefs. As Helene Kyed (2013) has recently argued, the boom in southern African states' uses of the customary has resulted in highly heterogeneous constellations of power with considerable room for negotiation. As we have seen in Zimbabwe, customary and technocratic ideas were mixed in institutional practice and their content was sufficiently malleable to be able to legitimate at one and the same time state intervention and resistance to it, while nationalism was a central arbiter before and after independence of the authority of both the customary and the technocratic. It is in grasping the interplay over time of these different claims to authority, their institutional expressions, and their practical politics that we begin to see more clearly the manifold and sometimes surprising possibilities of chiefs in their relationship to states. The "return" of chiefs is a mirage, seemingly always sitting on the horizon. In fact, they never left. But their durability is not to do with staying the same: they have been as changeable and contradictory as state institutions themselves, always bound by the state's shifting demands and always rooted in versions of custom but never wholly defined by either of them.

Notes

1. In emphasizing the practices of states I build on a recent strand of anthropological scholarship that focuses on the "actual functioning" of the state apparatus (see Bierschenk and Olivier de Sardan 2014) as well as long-standing historical approaches to studying the colonial state that insist on its heterogeneity.
2. There are a great many insightful works in this area. For a variety of approaches, see Berry (1993, 2000); Comaroff (2001),Hellweg (2004), Kyed (2013), Leach (2004), Lund (2006), Obarrio (2014), and Oomen (2005).
3. I develop the historical case in detail in *The Unsettled Land* (2006). For further considerations of the relationship between chiefs, state, law, and rural politics (among other things), see Alexander et al. (2000), Maxwell (1999), Mazarire (2008), Moore (2005), Munro (1998), Ranger (1999), and Tshuma (1997).
4. A bald-faced expression of this vision can be found in Government of Southern Rhodesia (1955). Also see the seminal report of the Godlonton Commission (Government of Southern Rhodesia 1944). On the tensions in colonial promises of modernity, see Comaroff (2002).
5. See Alexander (2006:93–98) for Chimanimani. Also see, for example, Maxwell (1999), Ranger (1982), and Moore (2005).
6. See for example the accounts of Suttner (2003:185) on South Africa and Nyamnjoh (2003) on Botswana.
7. For a range of interpretations of the shifting views of ZANU's guerrillas on chiefs and spirit mediums in eastern Zimbabwe and in the Mozambican camps, see Max-

well (1999), Lan (1985), and McLaughlin (1991). On ZAPU's guerrillas in Matabeleland, see Alexander et al. (2000); on views on chiefs among detained nationalists, see Alexander (2011).

8. ZANU(PF) is the Zimbabwe African National Union (Patriotic Front), known as
ZANU before 1980. ZANU was formed in 1963 as a breakaway from ZAPU, the
Zimbabwe African People's Union. Both parties formed guerrilla armies and con-
tested Zimbabwe's first elections.

9. On the repression of ZAPU see Alexander et al. (2000) and Alexander (2006) for
accounts specifically of the effects of the 1980s' violence on rural authority.

10. See, e.g., Fontein (2006b), Dande and Mujere (n.d.:2–3), and Alexander (2006).

11. Gerald Mazarire has begun to explore the extensive use of courts and lawyers by
disgruntled chiefs in the 1980s; personal communication, 1 April 2015. Chiefs' capacity to undermine state efforts to constrain what they deem to be their customary
powers is dramatically illustrated in the South African case (Oomen 2005).

12. See Ranger (2001:48–49); Land Tenure Commission (1994).

13. Few have subjected to scrutiny the battles within ZANU(PF) in the 1980s and 1990s
and their repercussions for land inter alia. For a range of views, see Moyo (2001),
Moyo and Yeros (2007), Helliker et al. (2008), Selby (2006), and Sadomba (2011).
Much of ZANU(PF)'s internal politics in this period and after remains opaque. See
Tendi (2013).

14. Some of the best work on this period as a whole is in Hammar et al. (2003) and
Raftopoulos and Mlambo (2009). For more recent work, see Alexander et al. (2013).

15. All figures need to be treated with a large grain of salt and are complicated by the
occupations, reoccupations, and evictions of black and white farmers that have continued since 2010, though not on the scale of the first years of Fast Track.

16. Bernstein (2003:220). For other key contributions, see Moyo (2001), Moyo and
Yeros (2005), and Helliker et al. (2008).

17. See the detailed rural studies of Fontein (2006a, 2009), Mazarire (2008), and Mujere
(2011). Fontein explicitly draws on a wider anthropological literature, especially
Das and Poole (2004) and Hansen and Stepputat (2001), which seeks to explore
the state through its margins.

18. Veterans played an autonomous role at times, but their capacity to sustain autonomy from ZANU(PF) was limited; see Sadomba (2011) and Kriger's critique (2013).

19. See Alexander (2013:811–813) and literature discussed therein, contributions to Alexander et al. (2013), and Raftopoulos and Mlambo (2009).

20. The best discussion of these processes within the agriculture-related ministries is
Marongwe (2008); for fascinating studies on the early partisan attacks on bureaucracy and meritocracy in local government, see McGregor (2002), Chaumba et al.
(2003:603–604), and Hammar (2003). For the longer-term battles between civil
servants who deemed themselves to be "professional" and their partisan colleagues
within the judiciary, see Verheul (2013), and for the prison service, see Alexander
(2013).

21. See, e.g., discussions of partisan and violent politics in Moyo and Yeros (2007:117),
Fontein (2009), and the influential study by Scoones et al. (2010). For critiques of
the latter on this score, see Rutherford (2012), Hammar (2012), and Kriger (2013).
For the broader debate among left scholars over the value and fate of economic
and political rights under the third *Chimurenga*, see Hammar et al. (2003), Moyo
and Yeros (2005), Raftopoulos and Phimister (2004), Moore (2004), Helliker et al.
(2008), Bond and Manyanya (2002), and Sadomba (2011).

22. Chanock is quoted in Oomen (2005:87). I draw on her wider insights here.
23. See accounts in Matondi (2012:chap. 3), Marongwe (2003), Moyo (2001:323–24), Zamchiya (2013:1117), and Mujere (2011:1127).
24. For regional variations, compare this case to the detailed accounts in Marongwe (2008) and Zamchiya (2012), which refer to areas of Mashonaland and Manicaland.
25. A range of examples can be found in Chaumba et al. (2003:597–98), Zamchiya (2011, 2013), Human Rights Watch (2002), Alexander (2006), and Matondi (2012).
26. The committees of seven and land committees have been written about by a range of authors, with some variation in emphasis. For detailed accounts, see Mujere (2011:1133), Zamchiya (2011:1103–6; 2013:941), Murisa (2013:12–14), Marongwe (2003:187), Chaumba et al. (2003:598), and Alexander (2006:188).
27. In his study area of Gutu, for example, Mujere (2011:1130–31) found that most occupiers were not going "home," i.e., they had no historical claim to the land, while veterans held that productive capacity, not custom, was the correct basis for claiming land. See also Dande and Mujere (n.d.) and Mazarire (2008).
28. See Fontein (2009:29n83) for some background on Charumbira.
29. See Fontein (2006a:198n8), Chaumba et al. (2003:599n29), Moyo and Yeros (2007:110), and Murisa (2013:10). As many authors note, accusation of any association with the MDC could lead to loss of land, office, and worse; see, e.g., Chaumba et al. (2003:602).
30. Others also document these practices as part of not just an elite form of partisan patronage politics but as part of the day-to-day politics of ordinary peoples' struggles to survive. See, e.g., Mujere (2011:1132) and Chaumba et al. (2003:597).
31. "Mnangagwa Faction Purges Traditional Leaders," *Zimbabwean*, 13 May 2015, http://www.zimbabwesituation.com/news/zimsit-m-mnangagwa-faction-purges-traditional-leaders/; "Chombo Threatens Chiefs over Mliswa," *Newsday Zimbabwe*, 15 April 2015, http://www.zimbabwesituation.com/news/zimsit-m-chombo-threatens-chiefs-over-mliswa-newsday-zimbabwe/.
32. Reported in "Chiefs Now Powerless Says Zimunya," *Zimbabwean*, 17 July 2015, http://www.zimbabwesituation.com/news/zimsit-m-chiefs-now-powerless-says-zimunya/. Also see especially Mkodzongwi (2016) on chiefs' claims with regard to Community Share Ownership Trusts and platinum mining.
33. There are detailed accounts of such cases and their labyrinthine ups and downs in Mujere (2011), Dande and Mujere (n.d.), Mazarire (2008), and Ngulube (2015).

References

Alexander, Jocelyn
  1997   The Local State in Post-War Mozambique: Political Practice and Ideas about Authority. *Africa* 67(1):1–26.
  2006   *The Unsettled Land: State-Making and the Politics of Land in Zimbabwe, 1893–2003.* Oxford: James Currey.
  2011   Nationalism and Self-Government in Rhodesian Detention: Gonakudzingwa, 1964–1974. *Journal of Southern African Studies* 37(3):551–70.
  2013   Militarisation and State Institutions: 'Professionals' and 'Soldiers' Inside the Zimbabwe Prison Service. *Journal of Southern African Studies* 39(4):807–28.
Alexander, Jocelyn, JoAnn McGregor, and Terence Ranger
  2000   *Violence and Memory: One Hundred Years in the 'Dark Forests' of Matabeleland.* Oxford: James Currey.

Alexander, Jocelyn, JoAnn McGregor, and Blessing-Miles Tendi, eds.
    2013   Special Issue: Politics, Patronage and Violence in Zimbabwe. *Journal of Southern African Studies* 39(4):749–988.
Bernstein, Henry
    2003   Land Reform in Southern Africa in World Historical Perspective. *Review of African Political Economy* 30(96):203–26.
Berry, Sara
    1993   *No Condition is Permanent: The Social Dynamics of Agrarian Change in Sub-Saharan Africa.* Madison, WI: University of Wisconsin Press.
    2000   *Chiefs Know Their Boundaries: Essays on Power, Property, and the Past in Asante, 1896–1996.* London: Heinemann.
Bierschenk, Thomas, and Jean-Pierre Olivier de Sardan, eds.
    2014   *States at Work: Dynamics of African Bureaucracies.* Leiden: Brill.
Bond, Patrick, and Masimba Manyanya
    2002   *Zimbabwe's Plunge: Exhausted Nationalism, Neoliberalism and the Search for Social Justice.* Scottsville, SA: University of Natal Press.
Chanock, Martin
    1991   Law, State and Culture: Thinking about 'Customary Law' after Apartheid. *Acta Juridica* 10:52–70.
Chaumba, Joseph, Ian Scoones, and William Wolmer
    2003   New Politics, New Livelihoods: Agrarian Change in Zimbabwe. *Review of African Political Economy* 30(98):585–608.
Comaroff, John L.
    2001   Colonialism, Culture, and the Law: A Foreword. *Law and Social Inquiry* 26(2):305–14.
    2002   Governmentality, Materiality, Legality, Modernity: On the Colonial State in Africa. In *African Modernities*, Jan-Georg Deutsch, Peter Probst, and Heike Schmidt, eds. Oxford: James Currey.
Cooper, Frederick
    1996   *Decolonization and African Society: The Labor Question in French and British Africa.* New York: Cambridge University Press.
Dande, Innocent, and Joseph Mujere
    n.d.   Reclaiming Ancestral Lands: The Fast Track Land Reform Programme and Boundary Politics in Makoni District, Eastern Zimbabwe, 2000–2011. Paper presented at the First Biennial Faculty of Arts Conference, University of Zimbabwe, 13–15 August 2014.
Das, Veena, and Deborah Poole, eds.
    2004   *Anthropology in the Margins of the State.* Oxford: James Currey.
Drinkwater, Michael
    1991   *The State and Agrarian Change in Zimbabwe's Communal Areas.* Houndsmills: Macmillan.
Fontein, Joost
    2006a   Shared Legacies of the War: Spirit Mediums and War Veterans in Southern Zimbabwe. *Journal of Religion in Africa* 36(2):167–99.
    2006b   *The Silence of Great Zimbabwe: Contested Landscapes and the Power of Heritage.* New York: UCL Press.
    2009   'We Want to Belong to Our Roots and We Want to Be Modern People': New Farmers, Old Claims around Lake Mutirikwi, Southern Zimbabwe. *African Studies Quarterly* 10(4):1–35.

Government of Southern Rhodesia

  1944   *Report of the Native Production and Trade Commission* [Godlonton Commission]. Chairman W. A. Godlonton.

  1955   *What the Native Land Husbandry Act Means to the Rural African and to Southern Rhodesia.* Salisbury: Government Printer.

Hammar, Amanda

  2003   The Making and Unma(s)king of Local Government in Zimbabwe. In *Zimbabwe's Unfinished Business: Rethinking Land, State and Nation in the Context of Crisis,* Amanda Hammar, Brian Raftopoulos, and Stig Jensen, eds. Harare: Weaver Press.

  2012   Review of *Zimbabwe's Land Reform Myths and Realities,* I. Scoones et al. *African Studies Review* 55(1):219–21.

Hammar, Amanda, Brian Raftopoulos, and Stig Jensen, eds.

  2003   *Zimbabwe's Unfinished Business: Rethinking Land, State and Nation in the Context of Crisis.* Harare: Weaver Press.

Hansen, Thomas Blom, and Finn Stepputat, eds.

  2001   *States of Imagination: Ethnographic Explorations of the Postcolonial State.* Durham, NC: Duke University Press.

Helliker, Kirk, Tendai Murisa, and Sam Moyo

  2008   Introduction. In *Contested Terrain: Land Reform and Civil Society in Contemporary Zimbabwe,* Sam Moyo, Kirk Helliker, and Tendai Murisa, eds. Pietermaritzburg: S&S Publishers.

Hellweg, Joseph

  2004   Encompassing the State: Sacrifice and Security in the Hunters' Movement of Côte d'Ivoire. *Africa Today* 50(4):3–28.

Human Rights Watch

  2002   Fast Track Land Reform in Zimbabwe. *Human Rights Watch* 14(1):1–44.

Karekwaivanane, George

  2012   Legal Encounters: Law, State and Society in Zimbabwe, c. 1950–1990. PhD dissertation, University of Oxford.

Kriger, Norma

  2013   Review Essay: Human Rights and the Zimbabwe Land Debate. *African Studies* 72(2):176–91.

Kyed, Helene Maria

  2013   The Heterogeneous State and Legal Pluralism in Mozambique. *Journal of Southern African Studies* 39(4):989–95.

Lan, David

  1985   *Guns and Rain: Guerrillas and Spirit Mediums in Zimbabwe.* Harare: Zimbabwe Publishing House.

Land Tenure Commission

  1994   *Report of the Commission of Inquiry into Appropriate Agricultural Land Tenure Systems,* vol. 1. Harare: Government Printers.

Leach, Melissa

  2004   Introduction to Special Issue: Security, Socioecology, Polity: Mande Hunters, Civil Society, and Nation-States in Contemporary West Africa. *Africa Today* 50(4):vii–xvi.

Low, D. A., and John Lonsdale

  1976   Introduction: Towards the New Order, 1945–1963. In *History of East Africa,* vol. 3, D. A. Low and A. Smith, eds. Oxford: Oxford University Press.

Lund, Christian

  2006   Twilight Institutions: An Introduction. *Development and Change* 37(4):673–84.

Machingaidze, V. E. M.
   1991   Agrarian Change from Above: The Southern Rhodesian Native Land Husbandry Act
          and African Response. *International Journal of African Historical Studies* 24(3):557–88.
Mamdani, Mahmood
   1996   *Citizen and Subject: Contemporary Africa and the Legacy of Late Colonialism.* Princeton,
          NJ: Princeton University Press.
Marongwe, Nelson
   2003   Farm Occupations and Occupiers in the New Politics of Land in Zimbabwe. In *Zim-
          babwe's Unfinished Business: Rethinking Land, State, and Nation in the Context of Crisis,*
          Amanda Hammar, Brian Raftopoulos, and Stig Jensen, eds. Harare: Weaver Press.
   2008   Interrogating Zimbabwe's Fast Track Land Reform and Resettlement Programme: A
          Focus on Beneficiary Selection. PhD dissertation, University of the Western Cape.
Matondi, Prosper
   2012   *Zimbabwe's Fast Track Land Reform.* London: Zed Books.
Mawowa, Showers
   2013   The Political Economy of Artisanal and Small-Scale Gold Mining in Central Zimba-
          bwe. *Journal of Southern African Studies* 39(4):921–36.
Maxwell, David
   1999   *Christians and Chiefs in Zimbabwe: A Social History of the Hwesa People, c.1870s–1990s.*
          Edinburgh: Edinburgh University Press.
Mazarire, Gerald C.
   2008   'The Chishanga Waters Have Their Owners': Water Politics and Development in
          Southern Zimbabwe. *Journal of Southern African Studies* 34(4):757–84.
McGregor, JoAnn
   1991   Woodland Resources: Ecology, Policy and Ideology: An Historical Case Study of
          Woodland Use in Shurugwi Communal Area, Zimbabwe. PhD dissertation, Lough-
          borough University.
   2002   The Politics of Disruption: War Veterans and the Local State in Zimbabwe. *African
          Affairs* 101(402):9–37.
McLaughlin, Janice
   1991   The Catholic Church and the War of Liberation. PhD dissertation, University of
          Zimbabwe.
Mkodzongwi, Grasian
   2016   'I Am a Paramount Chief, This Land Belongs to My Ancestors': The Reconfiguration
          of Rural Authority after Zimbabwe's Land Reform. *Review of African Political Economy*
          43(1)99–114.
Moore, David
   2004   Marxism and Marxist Intellectuals in Schizophrenic Zimbabwe: How Many Rights
          for Zimbabwe's Left? A Comment. *Historical Materialism* 12(4):405–26.
Moore, Donald S.
   2005   *Suffering for Territory: Race, Place, and Power in Zimbabwe.* Durham, NC: Duke Uni-
          versity Press.
Moyo, Sam
   2001   The Land Occupation Movement and Democratisation in Zimbabwe: Contradic-
          tions of Neoliberalism. *Millennium: Journal of International Studies* 30(2):311–30.
   2011   Changing Agrarian Relations after Redistributive Land Reform in Zimbabwe. *Journal
          of Peasant Studies* 38(5):939–66.
Moyo, Sam, and Paris Yeros
   2005   Land Occupations and Land Reform in Zimbabwe: Towards the National Demo-

cratic Revolution. In *Reclaiming the Land: The Resurgence of Rural Movements in Africa, Asia and Latin America*, Sam Moyo and Paris Yeros, eds. London: Zed Books.

2007   The Radicalised State: Zimbabwe's Interrupted Revolution. *Review of African Political Economy* 34(111):103–21.

Mujere, Joseph
2011   Land, Graves and Belonging: Land Reform and the Politics of Belonging in Newly Resettled Farms in Gutu, 2000–2009. *Journal of Peasant Studies* 38(5):1123–44.

Munro, William
1998   *The Moral Economy of the State: Conservation, Community Development, and State-Making in Zimbabwe*. Athens, OH: Ohio University Press.

Murisa, Tendai
2013   Democratisation and Control: Fast Track and Local Government Reforms in Zimbabwe. *Journal of Contemporary African Studies* 32(1):1–21.

Ngulube, Mbongeni
2015   Let Them Eat Cake: A Victory on Maleme Farm. *Zimbabwe Review* 15(2):1–2.

Nyamnjoh, Francis B.
2003   Chieftaincy and the Negotiation of Might and Right in Botswana's Democracy. In *Limits to Liberation in Southern Africa: The Unfinished Business of Democratic Consolidation*, Henning Melber, ed. Cape Town: HSRC Press.

Obarrio, Juan M.
2010   Remains: To Be Seen. Third Encounter between State and 'Customary' in Northern Mozambique. *Cultural Anthropology* 25(2):263–300.

2014   *The Spirit of the Laws in Mozambique*. Chicago: University of Chicago Press.

Oomen, Barbara
2005   *Chiefs in South Africa: Law, Power and Culture in the Post-Apartheid Era*. Oxford: James Currey.

Raftopoulos, Brian, and Alois Mlambo, eds.
2009   *Becoming Zimbabwe: A History from the Pre-Colonial Period to 2008*. Harare: Weaver Press.

Raftopoulos, Brian, and Ian Phimister
2004   Zimbabwe Now: The Political Economy of Crisis and Coercion. *Historical Materialism* 12(4):355–82.

Ranger, Terence O.
1982   Tradition and Travesty: Chiefs and the Administration in Makoni District, Zimbabwe, 1960–1980. *Africa* 52(3):20–41.

1985   *Peasant Consciousness and Guerrilla War in Zimbabwe*. Harare: Zimbabwe Publishing House.

1999   *Voices from the Rocks: Nature, Culture and History in the Matopos Hills of Zimbabwe*. Oxford: James Currey.

2001   Democracy and Traditional Political Structures in Zimbabwe, 1890–1999. In *The Historical Dimensions of Democracy and Human Rights in Zimbabwe*, vol. 1, *Pre-Colonial and Colonial Legacies*, Ngwabi Bhebe and Terence Ranger, eds. Harare: University of Zimbabwe Press.

Rutherford, Blair
2008   Conditional Belonging: Farm Workers and the Cultural Politics of Recognition in Zimbabwe. *Development and Change* 39(1):73–99.

2012   Shifting the Debate on Land Reform, Poverty and Inequality in Zimbabwe, an Engagement with *Zimbabwe's Land Reform: Myths and Realities*. *Journal of Contemporary African Studies* 30(1):147–57.

Sadomba, Zvakanyorwa Wilbert
2011   *War Veterans in Zimbabwe's Revolution: Challenging Neo-Colonialism and Settler and International Capital.* Oxford: James Currey.

Scoones, Ian, Nelson Marongwe, Blasio Mavedzenge, Felix Murimbarimba, Jacob Mahenehene, and Chrispen Sukume
2010   *Zimbabwe's Land Reform: Myths and Realities.* Oxford: James Currey.

Selby, Angus
2006   Commercial Farmers and the State: Interest Group Politics and Land Reform in Zimbabwe. PhD dissertation, University of Oxford.

Suttner, Raymond
2003   Culture(s) of the African National Congress of South Africa: Imprint of Exile Experiences. In *Limits to Liberation in Southern Africa: The Unfinished Business of Democratic Consolidation,* Henning Melber, ed. Cape Town: HSRC Press.

Tendi, Blessing-Miles
2013   Ideology, Civilian Authority and the Zimbabwean Military. *Journal of Southern African Studies* 39(4):829–43.

Tshuma, Lawrence
1997   *A Matter of (In)justice: Law, State, and the Agrarian Question in Zimbabwe.* Harare: SAPES Books.

Verheul, Susanne
2013   'Rebels' and 'Good Boys': Patronage, Intimidation and Resistance in Zimbabwe's Attorney General's Office after 2000. *Journal of Southern African Studies* 39(4):765–82.

Zamchiya, Phillan
2011   A Synopsis of Land and Agrarian Change in Chipinge District, Zimbabwe. *Journal of Peasant Studies* 38(5):1093–122.

2012   Agrarian Change in Zimbabwe: Politics, Production and Accumulation. PhD dissertation, University of Oxford.

2013   The Role of Politics and State Practices in Shaping Rural Differentiation: A Study of Resettled Small-Scale Farmers in South-Eastern Zimbabwe. *Journal of Southern African Studies* 39(4):937–53.

SIX

Paramount Chiefs, Land, and Local-National Politics in Sierra Leone

MARIANE FERME

While chieftaincy has enjoyed a "renaissance" in much of Africa since the turn of the second millennium, this has often followed times in which the institution had been marginalized, contested, or even outlawed, because of its "undemocratic" or "colonial" entanglements—as happened in Ghana under Kwame Nkrumah (Rathbone 2000:3–4, 66), for instance, or, more recently, in South Africa in the immediate postapartheid years (Berry 2000, 2004; chapter 3, this volume; Comaroff and Comaroff 2012:70). Sierra Leone has been represented in the scholarly literature as an exception to this pattern on account of the strength and resilience of the chieftaincy there, even during and after the transition to independence in 1961 (e.g., Bayart 1993:126; Kilson 1966). This chapter explores the nature and the basis of this exceptionalism: not only the resilience of the chieftaincy in Sierra Leone when it was being called into question elsewhere, but also the changes it has undergone since the 1991–2002 civil war, when its future was seriously brought into question.

Among the reasons that the civil war proved to be a watershed in this history is the fact that some 40 percent of the country's 149 chieftaincies were left vacant when it ended in 2002. During the course of the conflict, the insecurity and displacement of the population prevented the selection of successors to the paramount chiefs who had died or were killed by rebel forces that targeted them because of complaints about abuses of power (Smith et al. 2004). Indeed, popular discontent with them was held to be one of the grievances that fueled the war—at least, in the view of postconflict transitional institutions ranging from the Truth and Reconciliation Commission through NGOs devoted to governance reform to well-reputed scholars.

The fact that, by and large, paramount chiefs supported incumbent regimes in central government—particularly the undemocratic, single-party rule of the All Peoples' Congress (APC) that preceded the civil war—made them targets of harassment once those regimes came to an end. This was also the case with the two military regimes that introduced reform agendas during different phases of the war: the National Provisional Ruling Council, or NPRC, which overthrew the APC government in 1992, and the military-rebel junta that ruled for nine months in 1997. When the conflict came to an end, the prospect of eliminating the chieftaincy was seriously debated among young and educated citizens—many of whom no longer lived under chiefly jurisdiction—and also by scholars, policy makers, activists, and rural aid organizations, such as the World Bank and the UK Department for International Development, or DfID (P. Jackson 2005:53–55; Kamara 2008; Mokuwa et al. 2011; Richards and Chauveau 2007:30–31; also Fanthorpe 2004). The majority of those living in chiefdoms, however, even those (like women, youth, and "strangers") of marginal status, focused on finding more effective chiefly successors, rather than seeking to eliminate the office tout court.

In this chapter, I examine Sierra Leone's ostensibly "atypical" history of chieftaincy. I focus, in particular, on the transitions that followed the civil war, thus shedding light not only on the administrative and political prominence of the institution in the country's system of governance but also on the ways in which that institution is itself changing. I argue that it is critical to take account of the policies established under British colonial rule in order to understand one distinctive aspect of the strength of chieftaincy here, namely, its unusual degree of imbrication with national politics. Colonial-era reforms also shed light on a second strand of my argument, which concerns the relationship of chieftaincy to land and territory and the implementation of dynastic principles of succession that continue to inform the selection of paramount chiefs today. These features are critical both to establishing the principles of chiefly legitimacy and to chiefly control over natural and mineral resources in the present (see chapter 1, this volume).

As we shall see through an examination of specific cases, control over chiefdom resources is today among the factors leading to what I will call the "decentralization of political conflict," arguably a key feature of contemporary Sierra Leonean politics. In many ways this shift provides an instance of a broader and more encompassing tendency observed elsewhere in contemporary Africa: one in which the chieftaincy becomes the target of "popular discontent with economic inequality and lack of political accountability" as political conflict moves "away from the state [and] to traditional authorities" (see chapter 3, this volume).

In the case of Sierra Leone, the decentralization of political conflict is related to the fact that much of the country's wealth and population are concentrated in largely rural chiefdoms—that is, in the domain of paramount chiefs. But, paradoxically, this decentralization has resulted, too, from postconflict reforms aimed at democratizing local governance, thus stemming the excessive concentration of state power and economic resources, which were among the grievances that fueled the civil war (Collier and Hoeffler 2004).

Fixers-in-Chief: The Everyday Life of Paramounts

First, I offer a brief overview of a paramount chieftaincy, past and present. Whereas precolonial chiefs have been described as powerful, nomadic warriors who eschewed identification with specific territorial locations in favor of "personal-amorphous" polities mobilized in an ad-hoc manner (Abraham 1978:33–37), the British saw the deployment and systematization of the paramount chieftaincy as key to the processes of territorialization that established the Sierra Leonean colonial state. The colonizers aimed to root populations in space and immobilize them by way of the symbols and apparatus of customary office. They provided salaries for paramounts, formalized their treasuries and court systems, and required that they rule in collaboration with tribal authorities, that is, "councilors and men of note elected by the people according to native law and custom" (quoted in Fanthorpe 2001:380). Significantly, the British administration initially encouraged the proliferation, rather than the containment, of chiefdoms, using the recognition of rulers as a way to secure allies. But, by the late 1920s, they sought to reverse the process through amalgamation, a policy pursued, despite local resistance, until independence in 1961. Although since then there have been splits and amalgamations, for the past several decades the number of chiefdoms has remained around 149, the number that exist today.

In contemporary Sierra Leone, the duties of paramount chiefs include attending meetings to hear about government policies, briefing officials from the capital or provincial headquarters about local issues, and resolving disagreements within their own domains and with neighboring chiefdoms on everything from territorial boundaries and land allocation to the timing of regional weekly markets. They also are responsible for collecting an annual income tax from their subjects, the receipt for which helps establish residency and other rights. This tax receipt can also be used to travel outside of the chiefdom without being harassed by the police; in the absence of other identity documents, it serves to link their bearer to a particular place. Thus chiefs are guarantors of citizenship and territorial belonging and can exercise control over the mobility of their subjects beyond the borders of their domains. Their attendance invests occasions—like funerals or meetings to launch political or economic ventures—with authority. Paramounts also must take care of the needs of their large extended families, the latter being a key element, as we shall see, in their ability to span multiple political, socioeconomic, and spatial domains.

In Mende, the predominant language of southeastern Sierra Leone, the word used for the chief's engagement in social, political, and economic arrangements is *hugbatɛ*, literally "making (from the) inside," the act of reaching a thorough, complete solution to a problem. *Hugbatɛ* is a feature of everyone's life in the country: *muaa hugbatɛ*, in Mende—or *wi go arrange am*, "we will arrange them (things)" in the country's Krio lingua franca—is an expression that peppers ordinary conversation, especially among the wealthy and powerful, who have more dependents and complicated arrangements to oversee. It is the very essence, specifically, of chiefly work: his or her title is *mahɛi*, to "sit on" or take command of an occasion, being the "fixer in chief" as well as a mediator and an administrator. *Hugbatɛ*, the meeting to arrange things, is historically the main vehicle for a ruler's work of mediation and encompasses both secular and religious domains. The fact that, among the Mende, paramounts—and not lower-level chiefs—"sit on the land" (*ndolo mahɛi*) points to a feature of their role that is increasingly central to the office throughout the country: the arrangement of important land transactions.

On the secular level, a *hugbatɛ* brings together people to deliberate, reach solutions, and plan. In the religious domain, in addition to vesting key rites in their realms with the authority of their presence, some paramounts are also ritual specialists—Qur'anic scholars, Christian pastors, diviners—and officiate in that capacity at public functions. By and large, however, Mende rulers have been characterized, somewhat imprecisely, as "secular figures" (Little 1967b:184), in that the office itself is not invested with the same sacredness as it is in the Temne-speaking north. There, the election, installation, and burial of paramounts are supervised by one of several secret societies, especially the *Ragbenle* (Dorjahn 1959:157), a function recognized by the state. The Chieftaincy Act of 2009, for instance, specifies that electors include a "Ceremonial Chief (where the paramount chieftaincy in the chiefdom is by customary law linked with secret societies)."[1] The link between male secret societies and the chieftaincy in Temne and other ethnic areas in northern Sierra Leone is said to be the reason why women cannot become paramounts there, whereas they have historically done so in the southeast (Day 2012; Hoffer 1974).

The activities of paramount chiefs come to the fore at times of succession, when the mutual imbrication of local and national politics becomes visible—all the more so when valuable resources are at stake. I turn, now, to the contested succession in Wunde Chiefdom, one of many seats left vacant at the end of the civil war. Then, by adding insights drawn from nearby polities whose assets have been coveted by outside investors in recent years, I discuss why developments in the broader Sierra Leonean political economy and beyond have raised the stakes of chieftancy itself—and of succession struggles like the one witnessed in Wunde.

The Politics and Territory of Chiefly Succession

During the 1991–2002 civil war many chiefs, often along with their subjects, fled the conflict either for the relative safety of refugee and internally displaced peoples' camps, or to join their families abroad. The evacuation of rural chiefdoms led to an unmooring of the chieftaincy from the land, whose oversight has long been among the key responsibilities of indigenous office.

This process was especially evident in Wunde, whose long-ruling paramount succumbed to illness in 1998, after going into hiding from the Armed Forces Revolutionary Council-Revolutionary United Front; the AFRC-RUF junta had ruled the country since May 1997 and had persecuted chiefs suspected of supporting the former, elected government. Once the population of the chiefdom had returned in significant numbers after the end of the civil war, the contentious business of selecting the next paramount began. While the office had remained vacant, two factions had vested recognition in different regents, and at one point a third one was recognized as well. Two of these regents did not even reside in Wunde Chiefdom. In fact, for most daily administrative needs, some local people often ignored the reigning regent; they went instead to the late chief's family compound to seek advice from his surviving brother, who had been a trusted advisor and representative of the previous ruler and was widely respected both for his deep knowledge of local issues and for his skills in dispute resolution. Clearly, it is not always the formal officeholder who, in practice, officiates on the ground; for some, kinship ties to the ruling dynasty carried more weight than did variously sanctioned regents.

Since the early twentieth century, new paramounts have been selected through a mix of hereditary and democratic principles, in part because candidates represent ruling houses; extended kin groups, that is, that have held political office in the history of particular chiefdoms. In Sierra Leone, the basis for accession to chiefship at all levels—from the village through the section to the chiefdom at large[2]—was lineal descent from a founding settler, usually a hunter or a warrior, who is held to have turned "virgin country" into sedentary farming communities (Little 1967b:176, 1967a). It is on the basis of these widely known genealogies, regularly discussed in public gatherings, that particular paramounts represent themselves as having definitive ties to the territory—whether or not they reside in it or even return to it from abroad to contest the succession.

When an office becomes vacant, members of recognized ruling houses[3] present candidates; given that more than one individual from any house may want to become paramount, and that multiple houses usually offer up candidates, what follows is typically fairly fractious. During the selection process that began in Wunde in 2002, many relatives of the deceased paramount, along with eleven pretenders from the chiefdom's two other ruling houses, initially put themselves forward. Eventually, each of the ruling houses reaches an agreement to support a particular candidate,[4] this by way of deliberations (*hugbates*) and also by consulting religious specialists to help arrive at consensus. In the meantime, lists of electors known as TAs (tribal authorities) are prepared, each representing twenty taxpayers: herein lies the more "democratic" aspect of chiefly succession. Wunde Chiefdom had 197 TAs at the time of the 2002–2003 chieftaincy elections. These lists are often challenged, but, once finalized, the TAs gather to vote in the presence of local government representatives—if necessary over multiple rounds—until one candidate secures a majority.

Officials from the Ministry of Local Government confirm election results, but the Wunde case illustrates how state-chiefdom politics are intertwined at even the most capillary level of governance. During the 2002 election, Paramount Chief Mohamed Tshombe Kargoi II, the eventual winner, maintained that he had been asked by a high-ranking official from the provincial secretariat not to run against the man's "relative"—the candidate of the Dabo ruling house. In a small country, where traditional and national elites have intermarried and created familial bonds over many decades, it is common to find state officials with kin involved in chiefly politics. Many take sides during succession battles, even if this is in conflict with their putative impartiality. The stakes are high, since a paramount holds office for life unless he or she is deposed for abusing power or for criminal misconduct.

Many candidates who stood for election as paramount chiefs in the years following the war were more cosmopolitan and better educated than their predecessors had been, and the chieftaincy was not their main occupation. The new Wunde paramount, Chief Kargoi, was a lecturer at Njala University and lived between his home in the provincial center of Bo and his house in a village along the partly paved Bo-Pujehun road. Even after his election, he did not take up permanent residence at the historic headquarters of the chiefdom at Gboyama.[5] When he retired from his teaching post some years later, he began to spend more time in the village—rather than at Gboyama. He explained that this was due to the better cell phone coverage in the village; in the decade following the end of the war, cell phones had become crucial in linking chiefly authorities with government officials, NGOs, and anyone wanting to do business with the chiefdom.

Not only did Chief Kargoi choose to exercise his duties from a new location, at a remove from the chiefdom's administrative center. He also differed from his predecessor by spending more time living and working in Bo, the district capital. This unmoored the chieftaincy from its territorial seat, even while potentially allowing for more control over its territory by virtue of proximity to the administrative, political, and business centers where decisions consequential to his subjects were made. Kargoi also pointed out that he had a strong, trusted speaker (note 2, above) representing him when he was absent.

Several paramounts elected after 2002 came from the diaspora. Some, like Ali Marah, a relatively young man elected in the northern Sengbe Chiefdom, had spent the war years in the United States (M. Jackson 2005: 2ff.). Others, such as the late Paramount Chief Jeremiah Yovoni of Kamajei Chiefdom, stood for office when he retired in Sierra Leone after a long career abroad. As I have already intimated, the fact that these rulers had tenuous physical ties to their polities was balanced by their membership of powerful chiefly houses, which invariably included trusted local representatives. In addition, as I was told in Wunde, "American" chiefs—chiefs who had spent time, or were resident, in the United States—could benefit their constituencies, even if based in far-flung cities, by capitalizing on their connections there to secure aid and business deals. But absentee rulers also had drawbacks: they left space for local intrigue on the part of relatives and other political actors.

Since the end of the civil war, paramount chiefs, in their capacity as caretakers of the land, have become key brokers in business arrangements involving the expanding exploitation of rural resources. Since 2004, a series of policy reforms has been crafted to bring Sierra Leone in line with "poverty reduction" targets outlined in the Millennium Development Goals, as well as in projects underwritten by the United Nations, particularly through its Food and Agriculture Organization (FAO), and by donors like the World Bank. These reforms have sought to launch public-private partnerships designed to move development from the domain of aid to that of business. The state increasingly devolves economic stimulus programs and rent-generating activities to the local level, especially in the countryside, by encouraging investors to pursue commercial opportunities by making direct contact with paramount chiefs.[6] And although laws were drafted to regulate and monitor foreign direct investment in the decade after the civil war, enforcement mechanisms remain weak or nonexistent.

Exploiting Local Resources

In 2012, I visited neighboring villages on the main road connecting the two provincial headquarters of Bo and Pujehun, a visit conducted against the background noise of power chainsaws unceasingly at work in the nearby bush.[7] Loggers from outside the chiefdom, accompanied by someone claiming to be an emissary of the paramount, were turning trees into boards. Fueled by a construction boom that greatly increased the demand for sand, wood, cement, gravel, and water,[8] these artisanal logging ventures were only one of many commercial agricultural and extractive activities going on in Pujehun; nearly 82 percent of the district's arable land was now under contract with agribusiness corporations, mostly for large-scale biofuel and palm-oil plantations.[9] Elsewhere in the country, rice, forestry, and other commercial farming and mining leases continue to be negotiated. In all of these arrangements, paramounts must be consulted, and their signatures affixed to contracts, along with those of their council members and section and village leaders. The chiefs are also key intermediaries for distributing the rents paid under the terms of these leases, although in some cases companies prefer to distribute the funds directly to named landowning lineages, whose heads are also contract signatories.

By 2011, the government had granted a 6,500-hectare lease for an oil palm plantation,[10] with possible expansion to 30,000 hectares, in the Sahn Malen Chiefdom, which borders the chiefdom where I had witnessed logging activities; its beneficiary was Socfin Agricultural Company (SAC), a corporation based in Belgium and Luxembourg. This area comprised roughly the whole chiefdom of some twenty-seven or thirty villages, whose

residents had mostly, until then, been engaged in subsistence rice production. Later that year, some local farmers employed in the new plantation
scheme mounted a protest against low wages and inadequate compensation for their lost land and crops. The protest turned violent when gun-
shots were fired at company employees, which in turn elicited a heavy-
handed response from the police, who imprisoned a number of villagers
without due process. The workers also claimed that about half the compensation they received went in fees and taxes to the district council and
the paramount chief, who had been "bribed" with a new vehicle to facilitate the deal.[11]

The farmers also protested the fact that the massive clearing operation to
prepare the ground for the new plantation in Sahn Malen had eliminated
all the natural features marking the boundaries between the ancestral lands
of the local patrilineages. A survey had been promised but not undertaken,
and it was feared that nobody would remember who had rights in which
plots once the leases expired in fifty or more years.[12] Such landmarks, including planted trees, waterways, paths, hills, and rock formations, had
formerly provided the basis for establishing claims in land disputes.[13] In
colonial and postcolonial times, one of the paramount chief's main duties had been to resolve those disputes in consultation with elders whose
accounts of the history of particular features of the terrain, often narrated
while "walking the land" during court cases, were the basis of final arbitra-
tions. In the absence of durable documentation, the homogenization of
the landscape by mechanized plowing and monoculture seems certain to
lead to future conflicts—amidst a radical restructuring of the agrarian political economy, and of people's livelihoods, in Sierra Leone.

The result of these transformations is likely to be the wholesale replacement of small-scale agriculture—hitherto the norm in much of rural Sierra Leone—with wage labor on large plantations in a countryside that has
seen little commercial farming in the past. This would mean, too, a shift
away from cultivation as a socially integrated activity in which males and
females of all ages collaborate to plant and harvest a range of subsistence
and cash crops on fields owned by extended households (Ferme 2001:40–
47; Richards 1986:chap. 4). Instead, the able-bodied will labor on huge
holdings devoted to single cash crops, where wages will have to provide for
other displaced family members. This move toward agricultural commer-
cialization is part of a global trend in the name of achieving food security,
particularly in Africa. While changing demographics might appear to justify it, aid-dependent governments like that of Sierra Leone concur less as

a result of their own strategic planning than in order to access funds from the FAO, the World Bank, and other donors.[14]

These projects address the technical challenge of increasing the productivity of rural lands, either through commercial farming or the extraction of valuable resources. But they seldom anticipate the myriad ways in which their interventions become politicized and foster new levels of conflict in rural chiefdoms. Thus, in Sahn Malen, not only are some lineages in sharp disagreement with the paramount chief, whom they feel has cheated and "harassed" them, but the drive to clarify the identity of legitimate landowners has opened up unprecedented disputes between patrons and their unrelated dependents; only the former are entitled to compensation and rents, although the latter often provide crucial agrarian labor. Those dependents, whose families have been established in chiefdoms for generations—and have married into landowning lineages—are being redefined as "foreigners."[15] For their part, paramount chiefs, their own beneficence now in question, are being drawn into the disputes in their capacity as officeholders authorized to validate identity and provide residency papers.

In this transformed scenario, the basis of chiefly legitimacy no longer vests mainly in their historical role as trustees of land held for the lineages of their chiefdoms. It lies as much in other practices of governance, among them the authorization of identities, seeking rents, and fiscal surveillance.

Fiscal Regulation, Electoral Politics, and Dynastic Strategies

For the present, despite some resistance to the part played by chiefs in the economic transformations afoot in the countryside, the power of their office persists, as does their importance in national politics. From the outset, paramounts have been considered lynchpins in the fiscal viability of the administration, tasked with collecting taxes where the state has had only a weak presence. Since the establishment, in 1954, of a House of Representatives, each of the country's twelve districts elects a paramount chief as its delegate, with full voting rights. Some of them have held ministerial posts in the governments of postcolonial Sierra Leone and continue to do so today.[16]

A key feature of the close proximity between local and national politics in Sierra Leone is that parties—which were introduced in the 1950s, when independence loomed—have never been strongly organized in the rural areas, where the majority of the population has lived; as many as 89 percent until the decade preceding the 1991–2002 civil war. Early on, paramounts became key intermediaries in securing votes in national elections. Chiefly politics, in turn, has molded party loyalties and alliances:

> Factions joined parties because they hoped to secure outside help in the pursuit of chiefdom goals, namely, to acquire or retain chiefdom office. The central government's ultimate control over the office of Paramount Chief ensured that national politics would be of crucial importance for the members of chiefdom conflict groups. (Tangri 1978:166)

This relationship affects the outcome of conflicts in arenas in which the national and the local, the state and the customary, merge. Recall the case discussed earlier, in which opponents of the Sahn Malen paramount called for his removal after he leased virtually all of the chiefdom's farmland to a foreign company: his adversaries attributed his survival in office to the fact that he was a staunch supporter of the ruling APC party, and hence enjoyed government backing. By contrast, his supporters pointed out that one of the leading spokespersons for MALOA—the association of landowners who signed protest petitions—had been a member of parliament for an opposition party until he lost his seat in 2012, the implication being that his actions had more to do with electoral politics than local land rights. In the end, the paramount retained his office despite the fact that, since the unrest in the chiefdom began, he had not been locally accessible to the majority of his subjects.[17]

The mutual imbrication of party and chiefly politics has been made possible by the ties of kinship and sociality linking the leadership in these distinct spheres. Consider once again the situation in Wunde. In the decade before the civil war, the brother of Paramount Chief Mohamed Kaifala Dabo II had been a member of parliament and representative of the APC for the political constituency that encompassed this and the neighboring chiefdom. An Oxford graduate with a German medical degree, he was based in Freetown, and exemplifies the trend that Kilson (1966:232–33) observed regarding the emergence of modern Sierra Leonean "elites" out of traditional rural upper classes. But the MP lost his seat to the brother of a local section chief in the 1986 parliamentary election (Ferme 1999), a political contest that profoundly divided the paramounts' subjects, many of whom had begun to rebel against his authority.

Paramount Chief Dabo II's staying power in those turbulent prewar years was tied in part to the marriages he entered into over his long reign. Like many traditional rulers at the time, he claimed to have so many wives that he had trouble counting them—one of the ways in which a political aesthetics of superfluity constitutes "big" persons and chiefly status here (Ferme 2001:171).[18] Among those wives was a female paramount chief of the neighboring Bo chiefdom, which encompassed Blama, a large market town on one of the country's main highways. Between his own political networks and hers, Chief Dabo managed to resist calls for his replacement from a growing number of his subjects during the conflicts surrounding the 1986 election, the one lost by his brother. Among his siblings, children, and nephews were officers in the national army and the police, as well as high-ranking functionaries in various government ministries. During the civil war, he used his extensive networks to secure shelter and protection for many who had been displaced by rebel attacks on his realm, thereby gaining back the favor of a majority of his subjects.

Postwar Reconstruction and Decentralization

In 2000, the Sierra Leonean government launched the Paramount Chiefs' Restoration Project, later renamed the Chiefdom Governance Reform Programme, with support from the UK Department for International Development (DfID), other international donors, and NGOs. British policy advisors planned to go beyond restoring indigenous rulers or electing new ones, aiming rather to reform the office within a broader reorganization of local governance that included the revival of elected district councils. In practice, the most visible outcome of the project was a DfID program to rebuild "chiefdom houses," a literalization of the project of postwar reconstruction.

These new chiefdom houses were intended to standardize the official residences of paramount chiefs that, before the war, had taken a variety of forms, many of them wattle-and-daub structures with thatched roofs. In some cases, the rebuilding project provided an opportunity to move the seat of the paramount to a site considered more central, geographically, to his or her jurisdiction. The hope was that these residences would not be seen to belong to particular incumbents and their extended families, as had previously been the case; instead, they would be regarded as the collective property of the people of their chiefdoms, to be occupied by a ruler only for the duration of his or her term in office. The program was plagued by controversy, however. It exceeded projected costs and lacked participation on the part of key stakeholders. Among its controversial aspects was a plan to rely on the "volunteer labor" of chiefly subjects to build the houses, which smacked of the *corvée* labor that, in the past, had been one of the most resented prerogatives of customary authorities. By June 2002, the project budget had been depleted, not least because of the need to employ paid workers: only fifty new residences had been built. Many rulers refused to move into them, finding them small in comparison to the expansive compounds they associated with chieftaincy, compounds that accommodated extended families, numerous dependents, and large staffs.[19] Ironically, this post–civil war British intervention to securely reestablish the chieftaincy in its territorial base—to cement it there, as it were—was shaped by classic, rather static notions of sovereignty that no longer corresponded with the practices of the officeholders for whom it was being designed.

As I mentioned above, the reform of chiefly governance was seen as one element in a broader scheme to encourage decentralization in postwar Sierra Leone, thus distributing development initiatives, business investments, and tax revenue collection across the country and at different administrative levels. These things had previously been concentrated in the hands of elites and their patrimonial networks, leading to popular discontent and civic conflict (e.g., Bayart et al. 2009; Reno 2000). The UK government, along with other global donors, also contributed to a parallel effort to promote political devolution: particularly favored by the World Bank, the object, also noted earlier, was to revive elected district and municipal councils, "local councils" in common parlance, these being the same bodies that, having proved largely ineffective, were abolished with the transition to single-party rule in 1972. The expectation now was that these renewed local councils, whose members were to stand for office in elections every four years, would raise taxes in their jurisdictions, thus funding services formerly provided by the central government.[20] They were also to benefit from a share of rents levied on mining, agribusiness, and other commercial operations dependent on rural lands, revenues whose collection was left to paramount chiefs and their counselors; they, too, were to receive a share (Government of Sierra Leone 2004:33; also Sawyer 2008:402). The law did not specify how the income was to be apportioned between chiefdom and district administrations, however, thus opening up further possibilities of conflict and abuse (P. Jackson 2005:56).

The solvency and survival of these new, liberalized administrative structures thus depends in large part on paramount chiefs, as was the case when district councils were first introduced unsuccessfully in the 1950s. In colonial times, these councils were never able to raise sufficient revenues to fund services that ranged from road maintenance to education, in part because local rulers underreported tax collections to keep enough for their own operations. This history led some to argue, in the post–civil war deliberations on decentralization, that "post-war re-bureaucratization should have started at chiefdom rather than the district level (especially in respect to revenue collection)" (Fanthorpe 2006:44–45); they advocated paying paramounts much higher salaries, increasing their accountability to their subjects, and subjecting their business and fiscal practices to auditing (P. Jackson 2007:100). Higher pay, in this view, would put an end to the arbitrary exploitation of rural subjects, exploitation driven, above all else, by the need to support patronage networks, staffs, and the general trappings of office (Archibald and Richards 2002; Mokuwa et al. 2011).

Conclusion

As the evidence presented in this chapter makes plain, the paramount chieftaincy continues to exercise a strong hold on Sierra Leoneans everywhere. In the aftermath of the civil war, it became an attractive, "culturally appropriate" institution, poised to help bolster policies of political decentralization and governance reform alongside newly instituted, elected district councils. On the one hand, customary office has been seen by those supporting efforts to reform it as a viable alternative to the corruption and predatory practices associated with the state. The active role of chiefs in national politics also gives them a robust, high-level platform from which to advance their own collective interests and those of their constituencies. On the other hand, the accumulation of power by these rulers and their extended families—which invariably include professionals, politicians, and people of influence on the national scene—can lead to abuses that provoke resentment and rebelliousness among their subjects. And, with them, the public recollection of past revolts. In spite of the widespread perception that chiefs have far too much control over land and resources—*vide* the conflict in Sahn Malen discussed above—rural Sierra Leoneans have thus far supported the institution: for all its historical roots in colonial times, it is deeply etched into their collective imaginary.

At the same time, there are signs that its future may lie less directly in the control it affords over land and natural resources than in other sources of privilege, both new and old. While there is considerable evidence of rulers taking rents from the opening of their domains to commerce, there are also signs that the reform of their offices may be serving as a way for the state to devolve their powers in contentious circumstances. Historically, chiefdoms were reconfigured through internal splits and amalgamations; this, along with the institution of new forms of local government, continues to inform politics in the present. At the same time, the policies put in place to bolster reform of customary authority run the risk of further politicizing the selection of incumbents and, with it, of increasing conflict at the local level. This also underscores the fact that, despite phenomena such as absentee or part-time paramounts, the rooting of chieftaincy in a particular territory, in ruling dynasties, and in emblems of sovereignty[21] remains important for making legitimate claims to high office.

District councils are one institution that, in future, may offer a different kind of politics, and a different kind of authority, to chieftaincy, one more open to democratic dialogue and brokerage. Among those elected to the Bo District Council, under whose jurisdiction Wunde falls, for example, is a member of the Dabo family, the historic ruling line of the chiefdom. Like many of his kin, he is active in oppositional party politics and with NGOs—including some dedicated to governance reform—and works well with the current paramount, despite the contentious circumstances of his election some twelve years ago. This shows how, despite the heated rhetoric of elections, chiefs and district councils are able to operate without undermining each other's authority; also, that they are open to consultations not only with formally appointed chiefdom councils, but informally, with the growing population of "relatives" in the world beyond, people who maintain political, economic, and kinship ties to their rural homelands.

Rather than a lessening of chiefly control over their territories, then, perhaps it would be more accurate to speak of a multiplication of powerful brokers with interests in the chiefdom, brokers who work alongside the paramount in negotiations involving collective resources. This is made manifest by the fact that the symbols of office are increasingly given nowadays to persons with no connection at all to the land. Since 2002, honorary chieftaincies have been conferred on foreign dignitaries, a phenomenon with a longer history in other West African countries but relatively new in Sierra Leone (e.g., Barnes 1996:22–23; Nyamnjoh 2003:234–35). A notable recipient is former British Prime Minister Tony Blair, who was awarded the honor for his government's support of Sierra Leone during the civil war.[22]

On the occasion of their investiture, long-standing chiefly regalia are put on display, along with new ones commissioned by government since the fiftieth anniversary of independence in 2011—as if to rebrand the chieftaincy (see, on Ghana in this respect, chapter 9, this volume). Among the new logos are those that now adorn the vehicles in which today's more mobile paramounts are driven to their engagements. These synthesize older images, like the chiefly staff of office, the drum, and the elephant tusk horn

Figure 2. Investiture of Tony Blair as honorary paramount chief of Mahera Chiefdom, Sierra Leone, May 2007 (courtesy of Stefan Rousseau/PA Archive/PA Images)

that was once used to announce the arrival of the ruler and to summon his subjects to *hugbatɛs*, gatherings to "make arrangements" (above, p. 165).

In sum, the power of paramount chiefs still lies in mobilizing alliances and, hence, in the political capacity to persuade followers to align with issues and interests that go beyond the specificity of particular rural villages or sections or even chiefdoms. These issues—as the Sahn Malen oil plantation and other farming and mining ventures make plain—increasingly involve large-scale commercial interests of the sort that are transforming Sierra Leone's social and geophysical landscape in unprecedented ways. Local rulers will continue to have an important role to play in mediating these processes as the national government encourages investors to engage directly with political authorities in the countryside, where the resources that draw them are principally located.

Acknowledgments

I am grateful to Jean and John Comaroff for their invitation to present a draft of this material at Harvard University's African Studies Workshop in September 2014, for their robust critical engagement, and for their insightful comments. Pauline Peters provided a thoughtful response to my presentation, and participants in the workshop further enriched the conversation. Thanks also to Brittany Young for research assistance and to Hadji Dabo both for filling in gaps in his family history and for periodically providing news of the Wunde Chiefdom. He has been a generous friend on both American and Sierra Leonean shores. This material is based upon work supported by a Mellon Project Grant from UC-Berkeley and by the National Science Foundation under grant no. BCS-1430959. The views expressed in this chapter are those of the author and do not necessarily reflect the views of the National Science Foundation.

Notes

1. Government of Sierra Leone (2009:3, Article 4.1.a.v.).
2. At each level of the nesting order of the chiefdom—paramount, section, and village—the office of chief is flanked by that of speaker. Several villages constitute a section, and varying numbers of sections comprise a chiefdom.
3. On the eve of independence in 1961, the British colonial administration established a list of ruling houses whose members could legitimately claim the paramount chieftaincy in each chiefdom. That list is still the key document in establishing a claimant's legitimacy.
4. In the Wunde case, the fact that eventually two of the three ruling houses backed a single candidate, rather than each presenting one of their own, suggests a determination to disrupt the long incumbency of the Dabo house, whose two paramount chiefs—father and son—had held office over the span of some sixty years.
5. He later attributed his decision in part to the appearance of a mysterious being in the middle of the night before his installation in January 2003. This apparition called him out of the house where he was sleeping and told him that, for the next seven years, he was not to sleep for more than seven consecutive nights in the chiefdom (Bo, Sierra Leone, 23 October 2015).
6. See, for instance, the website of the Sierra Leone Investment and Export Promotion Agency, or SLIEPA, at http://www.sliepa.org, whose messaging includes a running banner advertising "arable land in abundance . . . significant untapped mineral deposits . . . opportunities for oil and gas investors." See also Sierra Leone Ministry of Trade and Industry, "Leasing Agricultural Land in Sierra Leone, Information for Investors," March 2010, *SLIEPA*, http://www.eds-sl.com/docs/SL_agrilandleasing _09March(2).pdf.
7. See also "Factsheet on Large-Scale Agri-Investments in Pujehun District, Sierra Leone," Green Scenery, Freetown, April 2013, http://www.greenscenery.org/content/factsheet -large-scale-agri-investments-pujehun-district-sierra-leone. This logging directly con-

travened an official, nationwide moratorium on the practice, aimed at stemming rapid environmental degradation and soil erosion; see "Sierra Leone: Timber!," *Africa Investigates, Aljazeera,* 26 November 2011, http://www.aljazeera.com/programmes/africainvestigates/2011/11/20111123134340348960.html.

8. In 2012, the country's gross domestic product doubled after a new bauxite mine opened in the north and substantial oil deposits were found offshore; see "Research-Based Evidence in African Policy Debates, Case Study 4: Chieftaincy Reform in Sierra Leone," Emma Broadbent, Overseas Development Institute, June 2012, http://www.odi.org/sites/odi.org.uk/files/odi-assets/publications-opinion-files/9120.pdf. These enterprises and many others, including agribusiness, invested in infrastructure, company housing for expatriate and local employees, factories, and roads to get their commodities to market.

9. Of the main companies in Pujehun at the time, two were foreign and one national; see "Understanding Land Investment Deals in Africa. Country Report: Sierra Leone," Oakland Institute, 2011, http://www.oaklandinstitute.org/sites/oaklandinstitute.org/files/OI_SierraLeone_Land_Investment_report_0.pdf. The leases taken out by these corporations have not always led to productive activities. Some agribusiness deals hide mineral or oil prospecting ventures and are left unexploited if deposits are not found. Most contracts are voided after a specified number of years elapse without evidence of efforts by investors to establish productive operations, and they explicitly prohibit activities not specified in the lease.

10. "Who is Benefitting? The Social and Economic Impact of Three Large-Scale Land Investments in Sierra Leone: A Cost-Benefit Analysis," Joan Baxter, July 2013, p. 23, http://www.christianaid.org.uk/images/who-is-benefitting-Sierra-Leone-report.pdf.

11. "Understanding Land Investment Deals in Africa"; see note 9 above.

12. Ibid.

13. In a shifting cultivation economy like the one that had been prevalent in these areas, only a portion of a lineage's land is in use at any given time, the rest remaining fallow to regenerate soil nutrients. As the forest grows back, identifying boundaries becomes more of a challenge.

14. See, for instance, FAO's Food Security through Commercial Agriculture Program in West Africa. In Sierra Leone, food and fuel crises in 2008 led to the drafting of a National Agricultural Response Program in order to achieve a measure of food security. Among other things, it established an Agricultural Business Center in every Sierra Leonean chiefdom as a potential hub for commercial farming ventures and the sale of produce; see "Understanding Land Investment Deals in Africa," note 9.

15. In this respect, Sierra Leone may, like other parts of Africa (e.g., Chauveau 2000; Geschiere 2009), see conflicts over land in future between autochthonous and settler populations.

16. For an example, see my discussion of the manner in which Paramount Chief B. A. Foday-Kai straddled the domains of chiefly and national politics as a former member of parliament (Ferme 1999).

17. Since most of the country's postcolonial history has been dominated by APC rule—except for fifteen years between 1992 and 2007—supporters of the paramount chiefs have tended to be APC loyalists; opposing factions have tended covertly to support the banned Sierra Leone Peoples' Party (SLPP), which oversaw the 1961 transition to independence. See Ferme (1999) for an account of how these alliances played out in Wunde during the 1986 parliamentary elections, the last under APC rule before the 1991–2002 civil war.

18. For an analysis of the dynamics of "excess" informing political power in the African postcolony more generally, see Mbembe (2001).
19. Consultation on Chiefdom Governance Reform Programme, Department for International Development (DfID) headquarters, attended in London, June 2002.
20. Last minute additions to the 2004 Local Government Act subordinated the councils to resident ministers, appointed by the central government, thus undermining the goal of decentralization (see P. Jackson 2005:52). However, the clear intention of international donors to channel development aid, private investment, and the provision of services through these democratically elected local councils—rather than through paramount chiefs and their administrations—had prompted "some international agency staff . . . [to predict] the final demise of chiefdom administration as soon as this funding stream reach[ed] the grassroots" (Fanthorpe 2006:36).
21. The staff of office, in particular, is the core emblem of the chiefdom and is recognized as such by the state in matters of legitimacy and succession. To wit: "No later than one month after the death or removal of a Paramount Chief, the Provincial Secretary or an officer deputed by him in that behalf, shall retrieve the Staff of Office from the family of the Paramount Chief or from him, as the case may be" (Government of Sierra Leone 2009:14).
22. "Sierra Leone Makes Blair 'Chief of Peace,'" David Blair, *Telegraph*, London, 31 May 2007, http://www.telegraph.co.uk/news/uknews/1553167/Sierra-Leone-makes-Blair-Chief-of-Peace.html.

References

Abraham, Arthur
    1978   *Mende Government and Politics under Colonial Rule: A Historical Study of Political Change in Sierra Leone, 1890–1937.* Freetown: Sierra Leone University Press.
Archibald, Steven, and Paul Richards
    2002   Converts to Human Rights? Popular Debate about War and Justice in Rural Central Sierra Leone. *Africa* 72(3):339–67.
Barnes, Sandra T.
    1996   Political Ritual and the Public Sphere in Contemporary Africa. In *The Politics of Cultural Performance*, D. Parkin, L. Caplan, and H. Fisher, eds. Oxford: Berghahn.
Bayart, Jean-François
    1993   *The State in Africa: The Politics of the Belly.* M. Harper and E. Harrison, trans. London: Longman.
Bayart, Jean-François, Stephen Ellis, and Béatrice Hibou
    2009   *The Criminalization of the State in Africa.* Bloomington, IN: Indiana University Press.
Berry, Sara
    2000   *Chiefs Know their Boundaries: Essays on Property, Power, and the Past in Asante, 1896–1996.* London: Heinemann.
    2004   Reinventing the Local? Privatization, Decentralization and the Politics of Resource Management: Examples from Africa. *African Study Monographs* 25(2):79–101.
Chauveau, Jean-Pierre
    2000   Question foncière et construction nationale en Côte d'Ivoire: Les enjeux silencieux d'un coup d'État. *Politique africaine* 78:94–125.
Collier, Paul, and Anke Hoeffler
    2004   Greed and Grievance in Civil War. *Oxford Economic Papers* 56:563–95.

Comaroff, Jean, and John L. Comaroff.
   2012   *Theory from the South: Or, How Euro-America is Evolving toward Africa.* Boulder, CO: Paradigm Publishers.
Day, Lynda
   2012   *Gender and Power in Sierra Leone: Women Chiefs of the Last Two Centuries.* New York: Palgrave Macmillan.
Dorjahn, Vernon R.
   1959   The Organization and Functions of the 'Ragbenle' Society of the Temne. *Africa* 29(2):156–70.
Fanthorpe, Richard
   2001   Neither Citizen nor Subject? 'Lumpen' Agency and the Legacy of Native Administration in Sierra Leone. *African Affairs* 100(400):363–86.
   2004   Chiefdom Governance Reform Programme Public Workshops: An Analysis of the Facilitators' Reports. DFID/SSR Research Project R8095 Report. www.dfid.gov.uk/r4d/PDF/Outputs/Mis_SPC/R8095a.pdf.
   2006   On the Limits of Liberal Peace: Chiefs and Democratic Decentralization in Post-War Sierra Leone. *African Affairs* 105(418):27–49.
Ferme, Mariane C.
   1998   The Violence of Numbers: Consensus, Competition, and the Negotiation of Disputes in Sierra Leone. *Cahiers d'études africaines* 38(150/152):555–80.
   1999   Staging *Politisi*: The Dialogics of Publicity and Secrecy in Sierra Leone. In *Civil Society and the Political Imagination in Africa: Critical Perspectives,* J. L. Comaroff and J. Comaroff, eds. Chicago: University of Chicago Press.
   2001   *The Underneath of Things: Violence, History, and the Everyday in Sierra Leone.* Berkeley, CA: University of California Press.
   2003   Flexible Sovereignty? Paramount Chiefs, Deterritorialization and Political Mediations in Sierra Leone. *Cambridge Anthropology* 23(2):21–35.
Geschiere, Peter
   2009   *The Perils of Belonging: Autochthony, Citizenship, and Exclusion in Africa and Europe.* Chicago: University of Chicago Press.
Government of Sierra Leone
   2004   The Local Government Act 2004. *Supplement to the Sierra Leone Gazette Extraordinary,* vol. 135, no. 14. Freetown: Government Printing Office.
   2009   The Chieftaincy Act, 2009, No. 10. Freetown, Sierra Leone: Government Printing Department.
Hoffer, Carol P.
   1974   Madam Yoko: Ruler of the Kpa Mende Confederacy. In *Woman, Culture, and Society,* M. Z. Rosaldo and L. Lamphere, eds. Stanford, CA: Stanford University Press.
Jackson, Michael
   2005   *Existential Anthropology: Events, Exigencies, and Effects.* New York and Oxford: Berghahn Books.
Jackson, Paul
   2005   Chiefs, Money and Politicians: Rebuilding Local Government in Post-War Sierra Leone. *Public Administration and Development* 25(1):49–58.
   2007   Reshuffling an Old Deck of Cards? The Politics of Local Government Reform in Sierra Leone. *African Affairs* 106(422):95–111.
Kamara, Kortor
   2008   The Institution of Chieftaincy: The Last Bastion of Underdevelopment in Sierra Leone, http://www.thepatrioticvanguard.com/the-institution-of-chieftaincy-the-last

-bastion-of-underdevelopment-in-sierra-leone. *Patriotic Vanguard*, 21 October 2008. Freetown, Sierra Leone.

Kilson, Martin
1966   *Political Change in a West African State: A Study of the Modernization Process in Sierra Leone*. Cambridge, MA: Harvard University Press.

Little, Kenneth
1967a   The Mende Chiefdom of Sierra Leone. In *West African Kingdoms in the Nineteenth Century*, D. Forde and P. Kaberry, eds. Oxford: Oxford University Press.
1967b[1951]   *The Mende of Sierra Leone: A West African People in Transition*. London: Routledge & K. Paul.

Mbembe, Achille
2001   *On the Postcolony*. Berkeley, CA: University of California Press.

Mokuwa, Esther, Maarten Voors, Erwin Bulte, and Paul Richards.
2011   Peasant Grievance and Insurgency in Sierra Leone: Judicial Serfdom as a Driver of Conflict. *African Affairs* 110(440):339–66.

Nyamnjoh, Francis B.
2003   Chieftaincy and the Negotiation of Might and Right in Botswana Democracy. *Journal of Contemporary African Studies* 21(2):233–50.

Rathbone, Richard
2000   *Nkrumah and the Chiefs: The Politics of Chieftaincy in Ghana, 1951–60*. Athens, OH: Ohio University Press.

Reno, W.
2000   Commercial Agendas in Civil Wars. In *Greed and Grievance: Economic Agendas in Civil Wars*, M. Berdal and D. Malone, eds.. Boulder, CO: Lynne Rienner Press.

Richards, Paul
1986   *Coping with Hunger: Hazard and Experiment in an African Rice-Farming System*. London: Allen and Unwin.

Richards, Paul, and Jean-Pierre Chauveau
2007   Land, Agricultural Change and Conflict in West Africa: Regional Issues from Sierra Leone, Liberia and Côte d'Ivoire. Club du Sahel Paper no. SAH/D(2007)568, February.

Sawyer, Edward
2008   Remove or Reform? A Case for (Restructuring) Chiefdom Governance in Post-Conflict Sierra Leone. *African Affairs* 107:387–403.

Smith, Alison, Catherine Gambette, and Thomas Longley
2004   *Conflict Mapping in Sierra Leone: Violations of International Humanitarian Law from 1991 to 2002*. Freetown, Sierra Leone: No Peace Without Justice. http://www.npwj.org/ICC/Conflict-Mapping-Sierra-Leone-Violations-International-Humanitarian-Law-1991-2002.html.

Tangri, Roger
1978   Central-Local Politics in Contemporary Sierra Leone. *African Affairs* 77(307):165–73.

SEVEN

Republic of Kings

Neotraditionalism, Aristocratic Ethos, and Authoritarianism in Burkina Faso*

BENOÎT BEUCHER

In 2009, Yannick Somda expressed his indignation in *Le Pays*, the Burkinabe daily. His expression of outrage was directed against the award by President Compaoré, in power since 1987, of the highest national honor to the *Moogo Naaba*, one of the Mossi's main monarchs.[1] It was scandalous, Somda said, for the president to decorate the king, rather than the other way around. To prove his point, he asked: "Would the British have accepted Queen Elizabeth being decorated by her prime minister?"[2]

This incident is not mere happenstance. At a casual glance it may seem to refer to an accidental collision of two radically distinct historical pathways leading to, and contained in, Burkina Faso's statehood:[3] one of them is precolonial and is embodied by the *naaba*, Mossi chiefs;[4] the other is more recent, dating to the 1950s, when Upper Volta was granted autonomy before becoming a republic and then gaining independence. Blaise Compaoré, as president, personified the latter and its institutions of state that, logically, ought not to coexist with customary kingdoms. I argue, however, that this conjuncture of apparently contradictory political institutions and historical trajectories actually exemplifies a state whose history and modes of operation occlude it being seen as a mere European colonial import. In addition, I shall argue that this conjuncture has had to be constantly readjusted and renegotiated by those who manage it, namely the elites in power and the Mossi nobility. I shall also show that the rise of the Compaoré regime, born in the ashes of the revolution of the charismatic Captain Thomas Sankara (1983–1987),[5] opened up an informal political space for (non-legally recognized) chieftaincy. Based on colonial government practice, this regime created a comfortable framework for ongoing material and symbolic transactions between the president and "his" kings—and

for the mutual development of neotraditionalism, which exploited a noble
Mossi ethos of honor and morality.[6] That ethos—founded on a modesty
of lifestyle, a proper sense of proportion, a desire for consensus, and self-
sacrifice in the cause of social well-being—generally worked in favor of
Compaoré's party. This was especially so when his administration, which
paid lip service to "good governance" but was in fact highly authoritarian,
came under increasing challenge; it would eventually be brought down by
a popular uprising in October 2014 (see chapter 2, this volume).[7]

As in many parts of Africa, this form of neotraditionalism is not a total
invention.[8] On the contrary, it is integral to government practices of long
standing, notably those based originally in the "discharge" of the colonial regime's regulatory and coercive functions to local intermediaries[9]—
arrangements that were favorable to the construction of sites of informal
political negotiation at the very heart of the state. In postcolonial times,
the goal behind the reactivation of the aristocratic Mossi ethos has been to
legitimize a ruling regime voted in at every election but ever more sharply
criticized. Also at stake in this has been the problematic fact that the president and the chiefs, all of whom seek a measure of independence from
each other, are caught up in simultaneously competitive and complemen-
tary relations.

The "Discharge": From Revolutionary Idealism
to Postrevolutionary Pragmatism

When History Catches Up on Revolution

In 1983, Blaise Compaoré was one of the four insurgents—the others being Thomas Sankara, Jean-Baptiste Lingani, and Henry Zongo—who, as the
Conseil national de la Révolution (CNR), assumed executive power in Upper Volta on the highly symbolic date of 4 August. Two centuries earlier in
revolutionary France, on that day, the nobility and clergy in France relin-
quished their privileges, a fortuitous coincidence that pleased these four
men. All in their thirties, they were determined to build a new society, devoid of the "archaisms" and forms of "oppression" that had long burdened
farmers, women, and all those still considered as subjects—some of whom
were the descendants of slaves. Paradoxically, although he denounced colonialism and its "scars," President Sankara, leader of the *Révolution démocratique et populaire* (RDP), intended to put in place "antifeudal" policies
that were very similar to those tried a hundred year earlier by the French

colonial administrator Louis Carrier, himself also an admirer of the French Revolution.

Sankara's intention was to make Year 1 of the Revolution into Year 0 of the country's history. Amongst those on the vague list of "enemies of the revolution," and thus of the new nation, were the "traditional chiefs.[10]" These men, according to *Discours d'Orientation politique*, a publication that served as Burkina Faso's *Little Red Book*, procured their "power from traditional feudal-like structures"[11] that debased their "subjects"—who had yet to claim their status as full citizens more than twenty years after independence in 1960. In so doing, Sankara sought to put an end to both the cumbersome colonial legacy of a recurring oscillation between direct and indirect rule and the capacity of chiefs to straddle the public and private spheres. The government set out, with no more resources than had the colonial administration, to neuter the indigenous authorities politically by confining them purely to the realm of the cultural—itself destined to be swept away by revolutionary modernity.

Sankara seems to have been unaware of earlier attempts by some colonial officers to remove the chiefs, let alone the reasons for their failure. He grasped neither the complexities of "tradition" nor the fact that it is not simply the opposite of what is understood by modernity,[12] this in spite of the bitter lessons learned from French administrators, one of whom, Louis Carrier, had headed the "Mossi circle"[13] in 1907. Carrier developed a policy described as "antifeudal" to detach local people from their rulers, particularly by encouraging the denunciation of *naaba* accused of despotism. He also humiliated them publicly, either by imposing prison sentences on them or by relieving them of their functions—which, in Mossi country, amounted to driving them to social or even physical death.[14] But Carrier had underestimated their importance in preserving colonial order and their role in the operations of his branch of government. It led to his transfer far away from this part of the country and, after the Mossi revolt of 1908, to the repudiation of his policy. From then on, the colonial regime was careful to establish closer, more respectful relationships with the chiefs, albeit still considering them mere auxiliaries of the administration.[15] The paths of accommodation that followed were consolidated during the 1920s, when the most influential *naaba*—including the king of Ouagadougou, *Naaba* Koom II—put their weight behind economic development, notably through cotton cultivation; this mode of intensive agricultural production relied on a large workforce whose recruitment, without chiefly intervention, would have been impossible.

Catholic missionaries liked to point out that Carrier did not achieve a "Mossi 1789."[16] Sankara, however, was convinced that his determination alone would suffice. It was as if he could erase precolonial history at the stroke of a pen—without even knowing it very well. Asking young revolutionary comrades to "do the most with the least," the young captain busied himself building a strong symbolic universe around the nation.[17] The country was renamed Burkina Faso in 1984 (see note 3); First Republic symbols were replaced. The middlemen between state power and civil society—chiefs, unions, political parties—were replaced by Committees for the Defense of the Revolution (CDR), made up of ordinary people who were not professional politicians. These CDRs had the responsibility of building the nation "from the bottom up," of "banalizing" it in order to make it so ordinary that it would seem self-evident;[18] this is also the meaning that Mossi give to the word *rog-n-miki*—today commonly translated as "tradition"—literally, "what we came to find at birth." At least to a certain extent, the revolutionary authority created its own reality, its own social model.[19] A few years later, one of its architects, Basile Guissou, recognized that "Our error was to think that we could do without the chiefs. We were mistaken. We denied the socio-historical reality of the country."[20] In their eagerness to be new, they recreated the old, repeating the errors of colonial administrators. They also slapped Western-derived arrangements onto complex social realities, specifically the Marxian understanding of "feudality." They did not see the danger represented by the "temporal disassociation" from which Mossi royalty had benefited since the French conquest: by the fact that, throughout decades of incomplete domination by colonial and postcolonial rulers, this nobility had been sustained by a rich mythology of power founded on an aristocratic ethos, by a sensitivity for managing political and social change, and by its experience of processes of state building acquired over centuries. All the while, it had regular dealings with ephemeral, unstable regimes and with men who were obliged to create their own symbolic universe, their own legitimizing myths: the "civilizing mission,"[21] economic "development," postcolonial national construction.

Blaise Compaoré paid close attention to the misguided ways of the Revolution, of which he was a main figure. In private, he was quick to criticize Sankara's idealism. The shift taken by the revolutionary process in 1985–1986 had a lasting influence on his attitude toward the Mossi nobility and "tradition." While not a reader of Hobsbawm and Ranger, he believed that tradition can be invented, albeit within strict parameters; it is not that easy to deviate from the historical paths either of the state or of social identity, which develop over the long term.

The Organization of an Informal Political Space
between the President and the Chiefs

A conference convened in 1986 to evaluate the CDRs took the form of a collective "moral purification," focusing on the "power-hungry maniacs" and "chameleon tight-rope walkers"[22] who had worked their way in among the revolutionaries to sully their ideals. It is true that CDRs were open to young people, many of whom were inexperienced and some of whom abused their positions for personal ends. Others united with the *naaba* through matrimonial links, which enabled the nobility to infiltrate these vital organs of the Revolution.[23] A few months earlier, a number of administration officials, including Dô Alexis Sanou, High Commissioner for Mouhoun Province, said they were willing to take a few liberties with Sankara's "antifeudal" line and collaborate with public figures from his region. Sanou considered them to be both "wells of wisdom"[24] and able to ease tensions caused by the attempts to carry out major changes in Burkinabe society.

The collapse of the Revolution in 1987 at the hands of a counter-coup brought palpable relief for many Burkinabe: for husbands asked to go the market instead of women; for revolutionary comrades obliged to take part in weekly sporting activities; for thousands of civil servants deprived of beer and kebab breaks while at work; for trade unions and the ordinary people investigated by the CDRs; and for the regularly humiliated *naaba*. Once again, the Mossi nobility had witnessed the disintegration of an authority that saw itself as legal, legitimate, and hegemonic.

At first, Blaise Compaoré's authority was seen to be fragile because it was born of violence: namely, the assassination of Sankara and then, in 1989, of Jean-Baptiste Lingani and Henri Zongo, who were accused of a plot against the state; both had been involved in the Sankara regime *and* the coup against it (above, p. 183). Lacking a clear political direction or a strong base, Compaoré had to find ways to legitimatize himself, if possible through consent, institutionalization—and neotraditionalism. And so the new head of state set about unraveling the Revolution whilst at the same time normalizing his state-of-emergency regime, the *Front Populaire* (FP). At the time, his intention was to organize presidential and general elections after the introduction of a Fourth Republic. In order to "hold," his authority required an historical anchoring deep enough for its founding crimes to be overlooked; over the long term, he believed, they would be forgotten. This recalls the strategy of the first colonists in Mossi country, which could not be sustainably "pacified" without hijacking the mythology and history of its royalty;[25] hence, in 1896, instead of looking to destroy the Mossi state by military means, they created a protectorate and reinvented traditions intended to fashion a bespoke nobility, one capable of ending the fighting and enabling the establishment of a regular administration. Similarly, at the beginning of the 1990s, soon after his (violent) coup, Compaoré also sought to "pacify" the country with the help of the *naaba*, indigenous moral authorities who, he hoped, might ensure the legitimacy of his regime. The *bonnets rouges* (red caps), a distinctive sign of Mossi nobility, began to appear in official photos reproduced in the progovernment press, thus to disseminate the subliminal message—in a format that even the illiterate could access—that the president and the *naaba* were coming together.

The resort of the FP to neotraditionalism expressed its desire, initially, to hold the Burkinabe within state-controlled frameworks. Compaoré did not want to present himself as a "solitary builder."[26] The ruling regime sought, rather, to create a national consensus, drawing all political stakeholders into a constellation around him; but this required channeling them into established (preferably conservative and loyal) bodies—which, in turn, involved recognizing those who represented, among others, youth, the elderly, women, and farmers. The net effect was to put chiefs on the path to official rehabilitation. Their influence over those whom I would categorize as "subject-citizens" remained substantial, particularly in rural areas.[27] Compaoré relied on them to ensure victory in elections from 1991 onward. The majority supported his candidacy that year: they included the chief of Kaya, *Naaba* Karfo, who gave his public support to the president and his party, *Organisation pour la démocratie populaire/Mouvement du travail* (ODP-MT, Organization for Popular Democracy/Workers' Movement), on condition that they "remember his region."[28] The chiefs of Zabré were just as enthusiastic but insisted that their area be linked by direct telephone to the presidency.[29] An unofficial space of negotiation was being forged between the political elite and the chiefs, whose status was never formally recognized. Just as in 1946, when the French authorities supported the Voltaic Union—a party created by the Mossi King Naaba Saaga II (1942–1957) to thwart the growth of the *Rassemblement démocratique africain* (RDA, African Democratic Assembly or African Democratic Rally), judged anti-French and communist by the colonial authorities[30]—a section of the Mossi nobility entered the 1990s electoral arena by demanding concrete political, symbolic, and material returns for themselves from the state. Their influence contributed greatly to the magnitude of Blaise Compaoré's win in the 1991 presidential ballot: 86 percent of the vote, despite a low voter turnout of approximately 25 percent.[31] In the same year, the ODP-MT became the majority party in parliament, a victory repeated at the local level in the 1995 municipal elections,[32] again with massive support from the *naaba*.

From 1996 onwards, Compaoré's ruling party, an avatar of ODP-MT, was the *Congrès pour la démocratie et le progrès* (CDP, Congress for Democracy and Progress), known also as the "juggernaut." Given the numerous votes he owed them, the consistently reelected president's gratitude toward the *naaba* seems quite restrained: their office was not recognized in the Constitution of the Fourth Republic and they received no public reward for their services to government. But their key role in the workings of the CDP-state[33] was constantly affirmed, both by official protocol, which always gave them front-row seats at official events alongside religious authorities, and by progovernment media. Of course, not all *naaba* desired formal status. They were aware that the constitutional recognition of chiefs in Nkrumah's Ghana (1957–1966) had been used by the ruling regime to suffocate those indigenous authorities.[34] In similar vein, many *naaba* feared that they would be restricted to the—politically neutral/ized—cultural sphere in which their Ugandan counterparts had been placed following the restoration of the monarchy by President Yoweri Museveni in the 1990s.[35] The informal nature of their relationship with the state was one to which they had accommodated themselves effectively almost all the way through colonial times. It had allowed them, and still allows them, to act with a degree of freedom—as long as the ratio of power with respect to the ruling elite is broadly in their favor.

Some royals managed to do especially well out of their collusion with the Compaoré regime. A handful of them consolidated their legitimacy, in its various forms, through a process of "social straddling,"[36] breaching the boundaries, that is, between existing social statuses, most notably those between old and new elites. Victor Tiendrébéogo is a striking example. A former bank officer who was enthroned as Larlé *Naaba* in 1990 and was one of the main dignitaries of the Ouagadougou court, he entered politics in 1992 with the backing of Roch Marc Christian Kaboré, an aide to the president. A royal and a servant of the king, Larlé *Naaba* joined parliament as a member of the ruling party and held his seat until 2012. During that time, he was a magazine director, an economic and identity entrepreneur, and a supervisor of model farms. He also headed various charity and cultural associations, as well as maintaining an impressive diplomatic and financial network that enabled him to build a solid client base.[37] These positions ensured access for his king to the president, giving the king a discrete presence at the forefront of the national political scene. The Larlé *Naaba* is one of a long line of princes who, during the colonial period, particularly

from the 1920s onward, were able to ensure that the frontiers between ancient and modern elites were porous. Such was also the case of Baloum
Naaba (1910–1950), a Palatine high dignitary, a politician, and a key actor
in the "development" of the Upper Volta territory in the 1940s.

These men contributed to pushing the limits of acceptable change at
the heart of the nobility, thus giving shape to a "conservative modernization."[38] They are also architects of the *re*invention of a tradition that has rekindled Mossi hegemonic dispositions, dispositions observed long before
the colonial conquest. All, or nearly all, has had to change to conserve the
essential: namely, the *naam*, the political-religious power, inherited from
the founding ancestors.

The Resurgence of an Imperial African Myth

In 2004, the main national dailies reported a quarrel among historians
regarding the hypothetical existence of a Mossi empire.[39] This debate, at
first circumscribed to the academy, took on a national aspect. For good
reason: the origin of this myth clearly refers to the role that the nobility,
especially that of Ouagadougou, believe they played in the construction of
the state, not only in Mossi country but in Burkina at large. At the time of
its formation, at the turn of the fifteenth and sixteenth centuries, the *Moogo*
was dominated by five independent kingdoms, around which local leaders
with varying degrees of autonomy gravitated. According to Michel Izard,
the precolonial history of the *Moogo* involved a permanent tension between order and the prospect of disorder, between a fantasy of oneness and
a more diverse reality.[40] The kingdom of Ouagadougou aspired to become
the established hegemon in the *Moogo*. But, lacking the necessary military
means, it did not realize its ambition before the colonial conquest.

When Ouagadougou was occupied in 1896, the officers responsible for
the French conquest were obliged to collect ethnographic materials in order to justify—in the eyes of their European rivals—the incorporation of *all*
of the *Moogo* under Francophone influence.[41] The objective, to prove the existence of a unified Mossi empire under the *naaba* from Ouagadougou, was
expedited by having to sign a single protectorate treaty with the sovereign,
rather than one with each *naaba*, such treaties being crucial in the context of the Scramble for Africa. The officers' surveys were carried out mostly
within the court of the king, who provided information most favorable to
his interests. And so the fantasy of the oneness of the Mossi of the Central
Plateau (Ouagadougou) found a new lease of life, and translation into the
language of the law, with the protectorate treaty "on the Mossi" in 1897;[42]

the drawing of the colonial borders conserved *Moogo* entirely. Thereafter, the *Moogo Naaba* became the main indigenous representative to the French authorities, at first for the Mossi and then for the Upper Volta colony created in 1919. Ouagadougou, the heart of the monarchic power, became the administrative center of the colony and then the capital of the independent state; its rise, while not linear, was no less remarkable.[43]

During the 1920s in particular, and then during the 1940s and 1950s, the French authorities considered the "Mossi country" as a hub of civilization, connected to a scattering of "archaic" lineage societies. During the short-lived partition of Upper Volta (1932–1947), which took place mostly for economic reasons, the monarchy did all it could to ensure the consolidation of the territory, which had become more than simply an administrative creation. From the 1950s, the idea took hold among Mossi nobility that it was the true *fons et origo* of the nation-state.[44] For his part, Sankara set about dispelling this version of the country's history, but Blaise Compaoré, himself Mossi, reinstated it, hoping for the approval of the *Moogo Naaba* and the Mossi from the Central Plateau, whose demographic weight was electorally significant.[45] At the same time, he had no intention of restoring a kingdom that might take on the appearance of a "quasi-state" as had occurred in Buganda (Uganda).[46] It is no wonder, in the circumstances, that the debate around the existence of the Mossi empire should have become so impassioned. Or that the authority of the state and the authority of the *naaba* should have become so embroiled in each other.

Under President Compaoré, for example, King Baongho II used seals that included the unofficial title "Emperor of the Mossi." He became the president of the *Conseil Supérieur des Chefs Coutumiers et Traditionnels du Burkina Faso* (Burkina Faso Board of Customary and Traditional Chiefs), establishing himself as the spokesperson of a polity that, in reality, is very heterogeneous. Compaoré turned to him to facilitate campaigns for birth and voter registration, for the national census, against excision and forced marriage, and the like; the monarch was also one of his main supporters in dealing with the acute social and political tensions that peppered his presidency. In other words, the president perpetuated the colonial practice of governing by discharge. Like his French predecessors, however, he had constantly to find ways of curbing the ambitions of the Mossi nobility—and protect the independence of his power from their purview.

During the 1990s, a policy of decentralization was put in place in order "gently" to reduce the influence, and especially the independence, of the Mossi rulers. It emerged timidly under the Revolution before being visibly strengthened during the Fourth Republic.[47] This contrasts, at least on paper, with colonial centralization. During that era there were two faces of power in Ouagadougou: one European, embodied by the French bureaucracy, and the other African, centered on the Mossi royal court. From the first decade of the twenty-first century onward, with the push for decentralization accelerated and broadened, new "development brokers"[48] have emerged—among them local elected officials, the presidents and members of village community associations, women, and youth—along with new forms of "associative clientelism."[49] At face value, this looked likely to challenge the authority of (especially lower-level) *naaba*. But decentralization has not led to their demise: some of them have become stakeholders in the process, not least by having themselves elected as mayors of rural municipalities.[50] The main danger they seem to have faced—given the fragile legitimacy of their authority and its critical need for historical anchoring—is the "vampirization" of their symbolic universe, on which their power is ultimately founded.

Neotraditionalism: The Limits of "Historical Vampirization"

The "Mossification" of Blaise's Power

Although the Revolution proclaimed the creation of a new society, built on a new relationship with time, history, and modernity, it also went through its own quest for authenticity, its own neotraditionalization. In 1985, for example, the terms "law," "decree," and "order" stopped being used. They were replaced by *zatu, kiti,* and *raabo* in Moore, which were described by the state press as "authentic popular *terroir* expressions."[51] At the same time, Burkina Faso was being "banalized" through the promotion of a local gastronomy (especially *to* or millet gruel) and the wearing of traditional costumes known as *Faso Dan Fani*. Such acts of national construction pretend that these signifiers are precisely what they are not: symbols of "disidentification" intended to enter a consensual national heritage, rather than reference any particular culture. This process continued after Sankara's assassination. From the end of the 1980s, the FP started to take some liberties with "tradition" in order to legitimize it: the young regime wanted to encourage the emergence of a neotradition that it could control without being prisoner to vernacular representations and affectations rooted in the long term.

At the end of the 1980s, the ruling regime openly supported agricultural cooperatives known as the "*naam* groupings," founded in 1967 by Bernard

Lédéa Ouédraogo in the north of Mossi country. The intention was not to honor the *naam*, the source of Mossi noble authority; Ouédraogo believed the royal *naam* to be tyrannical, whereas his own creation was intended to ensure "equality among members" and manifest a "perfect traditional format."[52] Better yet, according to the minister for farmer cooperative action, these groupings were a "parallel power to the existing feudal power."[53] Membership was not totally closed to the Mossi nobility—as long as they left "their prince's coat . . . at the door."[54] In reality, the mythos of royal power was harnessed by Ouédraogo; the criteria to select applicants were based on a moral code very close to the Mossi aristocratic ethos. Candidates were expected to strive, like the *naaba*, to speak little but with knowledge, to "control their stomach" thus to devote themselves to their community, and to be capable of curbing their "desires for love."[55] These cooperatives were supported by a ruling regime whose own official communications emphasized a spirit of solidarity and sacrifice for the benefit of the nation-state, economic development, and, of course, presidential power.

During the first decade of the twenty-first century, Blaise Compaoré gradually "*naaba*-ified" himself. Crowned Akan Chief by an Ivorian delegation,[56] he started to "Mossi-fy" republican etiquette. At first, he surrounded himself by *naaba* on special occasions: when disembarking an airplane, at national conferences and annual addresses, on provincial trips, and so on. Subsequently, the royal drummers of Koupéla, a Mossi locality, have performed at the inauguration of the president, their musical language translated for the uninitiated by the Samand *Naaba*. The private newspaper *L'Observateur Paalga* described one such occasion as a "truly authentic" event, despite critical opinions expressed elsewhere to the effect that it had a "monarchic odor."[57] More recently, an article in *Journal Afrique Expansion* repeated the rumor that "an image of a hat of a Mossi King . . . was hidden somewhere in the [presidential] palace, like a talisman, to convey the monarchic aspiration of the Head of State."[58] In fact, the private media no longer hesitate, now and then, to evoke the president's *naam* as a way of describing his authoritarian drift; hence the journalist who, indignant about Compaoré's lack of interest in national issues, asked if he "only puts himself out for domestic issues when his *naam* is at stake."[59]

The recommissioning of the myth of Mossi royal power and its associated moral virtues by the president ended up in his rejection by some young Burkinabe. Believing that he had seriously corrupted his office— both the metaphorical office of *naaba* and the official office of president— they took to the streets and overthrew him.

The Aristocratic Ethos Tested by the Chiefs' Partisan Commitment

Throughout his presidency, Compaoré appears to have made the mistake of believing that the mere presence of *naaba* at his side gave historical legitimization to his power—and a guarantee against the risk of losing an election. But not all *naaba* lined up behind him; *vide*, for example, the king of Boussouma, victim in 1996 of an intimidation campaign probably organized by the ruling regime.[60] Those who did support him saw their aristocratic ethos called deeply into question by the ethical stance of the rising mass of protestors who defied his administration. That ethos has its roots in the monarchy's period of uncertainty when Upper Volta moved toward independence. During the 1950s and 1960s, the royals, particularly those around the *Moogo Naaba*, were alarmed to see new elites, largely commoners, reach the highest levels of state. Just like King Prempeh II of the Asante in Nkrumah's Ghana,[61] they played on their ethos, their nobility, to look over the shoulders, so to speak, of the political class. After a disastrous attempt in 1958 by King Kougri (1957–1982) to carry out a coup d'état against the government,[62] the monarchy no longer fought openly against the hostile ruling regime. Instead, it presented itself as the modest *tampuure*, or "refuse," of its subjects, evoking the fact that a *naaba*'s heart must be prepared to suffer in the name of "harmony" (*wumtaaba*), thus turning an idealized disposition into an ideology.[63] This met with some popular success, especially since the first president, Maurice Yaméogo (1960–1966), who was very hostile to the chiefs, was given to corruption, nepotism, cronyism, and the mismanagement of state resources. During the Revolution, by contrast, Thomas Sankara opted for a much more modest lifestyle; nonetheless, while he had no qualms about riding around by bicycle, sometimes in a simple tracksuit, he did not check the abuses carried out by certain members of the CDR. The administration acknowledged as much in 1986 when it denounced the "unacceptable and disgusting acts" carried out by these "exhibitionists."[64]

After the transition of the 1990s, most of the *naaba* were caught up in a dilemma from which they never really extricated themselves: How might they continue to display their aristocratic ethos and their "nonpolitical" stance while supporting a barely democratic regime, which, for the first time since independence, had actually extended its hand to them? That dilemma is to be heard in the words of the chief of the Gourmantche from Fada N'Gourma who, in 1991, declared that "chiefs are above parties" but conceded that circumstances obliged them "to take a stand one way or another."[65] This stand was, of course, in favor of the president. The apolitical posture adopted by the most influential of the royals, starting with Naaba Baongho II, seems to have been more than merely a means to preserve the aura of morality expected to flow from a sacred source of power; it also left open a door in the eventuality of changes of regime. After having to manage the consequences of many coups d'état since independence, the *naaba* appear to be aware not only of the weakness of the political authorities with which they have to live but also the rapidity with which they may be overthrown. The difficulty lies in the necessity of keeping the company of a ruler favorable to them—and from whom they benefit politically and financially—without overly compromising themselves.[66]

In so doing, however, how were they to make citizens believe that their political commitment did not derive from personal ambition? One young *naaba* tried to do so, in 1998, by saying that he had joined the CDP "by chance."[67] Like many self-proclaimed African heads of state who rise from the ranks of the military, the royals most often claim to be obliged to take part in politics in the national interest.[68] But their argument of sacrifice for the collective good did not convince all Burkinabe. Insisted one reader of *L'Observateur*, "the traditional chief should not mix in Western-style politics. The traditional chief must protect society's moral and spiritual values and the people he represents. He reassures, he brings people together. He is the source of comfort for his subjects when all is going badly."[69]

In point of fact, the chiefs were most often reproached not for taking part in politics per se but for the *way* they did it. Their emphasis on the Mossi aristocratic ethos was only credible to the degree that they avoided the impression of engaging in the same practices as their commoner compatriots. Many Burkinabe had no doubt about the motives of those *naaba* who rallied around the ruling party: simply, it was that they gave their support to the hand that fed them most, the CDP, which, being the president's "toy," dominated national public life. Its patronage enabled them to benefit from the state's symbolic, material, and financial largesse. This, in itself, would not have provoked debate had it not been for their ostentatious displays of affluence. The conspicuous decoration and extension of the Larlé and *Moogo Naaba* palaces—which have no official responsibilities—was taken as evidence of the illicit accumulation of personal wealth, evidence that called into question the chiefs' assertions about the disinterested nature of their political activities. Challenges to the sincerity of their moral claims grew ever stronger the more they answered calls from the president to assist in appeasing increasingly violent social and political tensions.

Nobility, Moral Authority, and Mass Protests

The Naaba, *Mediators without Borders*

The cycle of protest against the Compaoré regime started in 1998 following the assassination of independent journalist Norbert Zongo shortly after the national elections.[70] This was followed by a wave of strikes and demonstrations unseen since the mid-1960s. At first, the *naaba* were torn between "neutrality and goodwill"[71] toward the protestors. Their attitude changed substantially following an appeal by the president, who sought their cooperation in order to relegitimize his rule. Without any constitutional recognition, they once again became de facto middlemen between the citizen community and the central authority. Along with representatives of the main religions—Muslim, Catholic, and Protestant—they took on the mantle of "moral authorities," responsible for reestablishing peace in Burkina. This was the logic behind the creation, by the president in 1999, of a "Council of Wise Men" responsible for "promoting social harmony."[72] These men played an important role in the organization, two years later, of a "National Pardon Day."[73] As elsewhere on the continent, from South Africa to Rwanda and Ghana, "pardon," "truth," and "reconciliation" became the watchwords of a regime that, while advocating for peace, made no major political concessions. Indeed, it seemed clear from the outset that the council was unlikely to fulfill the main task assigned to it: a review of unpunished crimes committed since 1960—but particularly since Blaise Compaoré came to power.

This strategy of deescalating social and political tensions translated concretely into an amendment of the constitution and the addition to it of Article 37, which temporarily limited the number of presidential terms[74] and guaranteed press freedom—although that guarantee did not protect overly critical journalists from "accidents."[75] The rhetoric of the ruling party on national harmony, social peace, and the ability of Burkinabe to resolve public conflict quietly and through agreement was spread largely thanks to the symbolic capital of the *naaba*. It was heard most of all in rural areas, where the challenges to the regime were generally weaker, where the influence of chiefs was strongest, and where 80 percent of the population still lived. Thus, for example, *Naaba* Baongho II, a poet in his spare time, regularly invited the nation to partake of "peace," "pardon," and "harmony." He occupied a front seat during the numerous mediations between the CDP and the disenchanted: ordinary protestors, occasional rioters, and, frequently, leaders of opposition parties. His speeches, regularly broadcast on state television and published in progovernment papers, were always vague and consensual, never touching on *actual* politics; ordinarily, those speeches were delivered during anodyne appearances such as at sporting or cultural events. Displaying his "modernity," Baongho II circulated his message/s via his Facebook page, opened in 2010, which bore a motto worthy of a state sovereign: "Solidarity, Work, Peace." He received the title "King of Peace in Africa" from one of the leaders of the Universal Peace Federation (UPF),[76] an association founded by the infamous "Reverend" Moon. One of the UPF's objectives is the "prevention and the resolution of conflicts" in order to achieve "One Family under God."[77] Despite the monarch's carefully phrased communications, few doubted that he was politically involved at the margins of state institutions or that his involvement favored the regime—even though signs of its weakening had been spreading since 2006.

That year saw a prelude to a series of violent incidents with ever-clearer political overtones. In order to counter them, "Blaise the dove"—so nicknamed by a journalist due to his many interventions on the international scene[78]—encouraged the chiefs, starting with the *Moogo Naaba*, to support his calls for "domestic" peace. This was clearly visible in 2010, the year of a presidential election and the celebration of a half-century of independence, when the monarch's media presence grew considerably: Compaoré flattered King Saaga II, who had fought tooth and nail for the reformation of Upper Volta in 1947, by presenting him as a patriot "ahead of his time,"[79] a message widely circulated in the press and the academy.[80] The myth of the Mossi empire hovered, spectrally, over the festivities, albeit not to everyone's taste: many ex-Voltaics, especially in the Bobo-Dioulasso area, did not want to see the colonial territory reformed. The choice of Bobo-Dioulasso, therefore, to host the celebrations was not inconsequential.[81]

The management of collective memory by the ruling regime, abetted by many *naaba*, is evident here. The most influential of those *naaba*, moreover, succeeded in making themselves into "mediators without borders." In so doing, they blurred the distinction between the public and the private: between the formal political space recognized by the constitution, that is, and the informal zones of influence negotiated between themselves and the president. They also rendered murky the line between the Mossi kingdom, over which the *Moogo Naaba* ostensibly reigns, and the national realm in whose name he purports to speak—at the risk of annoying increasingly vocal, dissenting youth.

Fall in Burkina: A Revolution?

The first riots broke out in February following the death of a student in a police station. This event crystallized the frustrations of a young, largely

198 / Benoît Beucher

unemployed generation at the hands of a regime that accorded it almost no political responsibility.[82] The uprising was quickly supported by influential student unions,[83] by opposition parties, and by a mutiny within the army and the police on a scale not seen since 1987. The protestors targeted the symbols of the state—or, rather, of the regime. The CDP headquarters in Ouagadougou were burned down, as was the home of one of the main pillars of its power, General Diendéré. The president's security regiment, headed by Diendéré, mutinied in turn, forcing Compaoré to flee the capital. "The emperor is naked" became the idiom of the day. Some saw all of this as a sign of his weakening *wak*, the dark forces surrounding his person— and, yet worse, of the inability of his "shields" to protect him from invisible forces.[84] In the upshot, speech grew free: ordinary people increasingly, and more openly, criticized Compaoré. He had become a man like any other.

The *Moogo Naaba* did his utmost throughout the crisis to meet the discontented and the victims of the troubles. He was invited to consult with the religious authorities, the judges, and the military in an effort to establish the conditions for a sustainable exit to the crisis, and also took part in "customary authority" talks in 2011 ostensibly to this end as part of the work of the *Conseil consultatif sur les Réformes politiques* (CCRP, Consultative Council on Political Reform). In June, he presented a package of proposals aimed at cleaning up public life, notably by overhauling the *Commission électorale nationale indépendante* (CENI, Independent National Elections Commission), by opening access to public service jobs based on competency, and by "cleansing" the judiciary.[85] The monarch also recommended strengthening open social dialogue, a fanciful proposition given the fact that the creation of the CCRP appears to have been a presidential maneuver to get his bill to amend Article 37 passed on the quiet.

The interventions of the king did not have much impact on the popular protest movement. On the contrary, during 2012 his involvement in the crisis evoked cutting criticism. This was nicely captured in an article that appeared in an independent satirical newspaper. It noted that, while the chiefs had "no institutional status, the republic is not embarrassed to use them to extinguish social fires." What, wondered the writer, did "these men" represent, these men "who, by dint of teaming up with the powerful and the privileged of the day, are now incapable of telling them the truth"?[86] In short, the weakening of the CDP-state also weakened those royals who sought greater compensation for their commitment to the president. Compaoré was aware of this. He tried to charm them by awarding them substantial gratuities: almost US$86,000 for 2011, and the same again for 2012, a sum equal to that allocated to each official religion for its "contribution to the development of the country."[87] Shortly after, the preamble to the constitution was amended to recognize (vaguely) the "customary chieftaincy" as "moral authority custodian of customs and traditions in society,"[88] although it committed no one to anything politically.

In his battle for political survival, in sum, the president invoked a national moral code, supported by the mythology of Mossi royal power, against protestors whom the CDP regularly described as "thugs"—citizens who had their own moral vision of the nation, founded on the "Burkindi" or Burkinabe "way of being."[89] But this only strengthened the opposition, which, for the first time in recent history, joined forces with civil society groups and political parties, starting with the *Union pour le Progrès et le Changement* (UPC, Union for Progress and Change). The royal court was quick to grasp that this was restructuring the Burkinabe political scene. In 2012, one of the King's senior dignitaries, Poé *Naaba*, joined the UPC, enabling the monarchy to have one foot in the presidential circle and the other in the opposition. In 2014, the Larlé *Naaba*, who had been one of Compaoré's most loyal supporters among the nobility, was the only member of parliament to resign from the CDP before joining a new opposition party, the *Mouvement pour le Peuple et le Progrès* (MPP, Movement for People and Progress). Given what was soon to unfold, this strategic reorientation was played out well for the monarchy.

Blaise Compaoré was obliged to cede his presidential seat on 30–31 October 2014, following the biggest popular insurrection in the country since the fall of Yaméogo in 1966. The neutrality staged by King Baongho II, the move into the UPC by his Poé *Naaba*, and the Larlé *Naaba*'s tactical U-turn enabled the monarchy to survive the fall of the CDP without too much damage. The force of royal authority and its mythical foundations remained sufficiently strong for the transition's main stakeholders—including Lieutenant Colonel Isaac Zida, temporary head of state and later prime minister—to visit the *Moogo Naaba* in order to give full moral value to their commitment to hand over power to civilians. This action was widely publicized and even had international impact: France 24, the news channel, described Baongho II as an "essential interlocutor" in the crisis.[90] During his meeting with the king, Zida took advantage of the circumstances to invite the population to "show tolerance, understanding, and patience toward the new authorities."[91] The mere presence of the monarch was meant as a moral guarantee for the new regime, lending legitimacy to a fragile transition process whose legal framework was developed with the support of the *naaba*. There is no doubt that the nobility will continue to be wooed by stakeholders and political parties that understand their influence on the vote of its rural subjects. This is why I remain skeptical about the use of the term "revolution" to describe recent events; unless, that is, the word is taken literally to mean a 360-degree rotation of the political situation, in which everything changes—full circle, so to speak—such that, fundamentally, nothing changes.

Conclusion

The 1990s in Africa saw the reappearance of chieftaincies and royalty on the political scene in tandem with the free-market injunction of good governance. Discussing Benin, Bako-Arifari and Le Meur describe a link between the two phenomena.[92] This seems valid for Burkina too. Structural adjustment, as put in train by President Compaoré from 1991, encouraged the privatization and decentralization of the state and, with it, the delegation of some of its regulatory functions. The *naaba* in Burkina were beneficiaries of this policy. Most Burkinabe trust customary authorities and wish to see them play a more important role in government.[93] The current fashion of finding local economic and social development solutions means that tradition has become a sought-after political resource in the eyes of both political elites and the chiefs themselves. Recourse to it is perceived as a potent source of legitimacy for ruling regimes that seek to advertise their conversion to, or the renewal of their support for, the principles of democracy—especially when multiparty systems have been dented by lack of transparency at the ballot box. Tradition, as Jean-François Bayart has pointed out, is a phenomenon with extremely high political stakes.[94] In Burkina, it was a critical vehicle in the dialogue, and the negotiations, between the Compaoré regime and the more influential royals. Despite appearances, a neotradition was coproduced at the very heart of the state as the CDP appropriated the moral virtues assumed to be intrinsic to Mossi chieftaincy. The capacity of the more powerful *naaba* to make money out of the appeal to their moral universe by the ruler proved to be decisive to his political survival in the face of increasingly widespread and vigorous challenge.

The apolitical stance of the *naaba*, and their presumptive moral superiority with respect to political parties, is also to be found in the disposition and discourse of other African chiefs, notable among them those of the Baoulé in Ivory Coast and the Ifè in Nigeria. It is employed as a means of preserving their aura of authority—often for lack of legitimacy obtained via the ballot box—and an aristocratic ethos that is endlessly mythologized and staged. As we have seen, too, it opens political escape routes in contexts where postcolonial regimes are frequently ephemeral, frequently subject to popular uprisings and/or coups d'état.

While these processes are observable elsewhere, Mossi chieftaincy has played a role in Burkina that cannot be fully grasped without an understanding of its own historical narrative. Nowhere else in former French Africa, I would suggest, have precolonial political institutions seen as great an increase in their influence under bureaucratic centralization as was the case here. This process began before colonial conquest and persisted after it, even as the *naaba* lost their political sovereignty. Throughout the period of French domination, they lived under weak rulers with erratic policies. They also learned much from the antichieftaincy regimen sometimes forcefully applied to them—and were quick to recognize the symbolic, material, and political benefits that came with their "entrance" into modernity and its staging. These were weighty historical trends that continued to structure the postcolonial trajectory of the Burkina state. This is not to argue for simple determinism: it is to interrogate the subtle adjustments necessary between authorities searching constantly for independence from each other while forced to reflect and act on the modalities of their coexistence. Obviously, that coexistence was not always peaceful. It oscillated between mostly fruitless confrontation and strategies of calculated, negotiated adaptation—often marked by misunderstanding.

The only kind of modernization conceivable for the royal court in Ouagadougou has had to be, and is, conservative. Everything—the *naam* or principle of legitimization of divine power—must stay essentially the same in order to change. For the Compaoré regime, all had to appear immobile in the eyes of a rural electorate presumed to be mired in a tradition perceived as ahistorical. Only under these conditions could the fundamentals be transformed: the economy stamped with the seal of neoliberalism, the political scene managed so that the president could remain in office against popular opposition, the constitution amended with the support of the *naaba*. The result is a complex coalition of a republic with a monarchy. It does not quite equal either the restoration of the Ugandan dynasty during the 1990s or the recognition of chiefly authority under Ghanaian law. But Mossi royals continue to keep their kingdoms alive, remaining at the heart of the national political stage, all the while drawing down the capital derived from their historical contribution to the construction of the contemporary state in Burkina. More prosaically, the *naaba* persist in maintaining, sometimes reorganizing, spaces of informal negotiation for themselves with the ruling regime. This indirect rule that never spoke its name—indirect rule that was never really accepted as such—is perhaps the most striking and structuring legacy of colonialism here. It ought not to be seen as a congenital "pathology" or a "dysfunction" of the state in this part of Africa, merely an integral element of its past and its present.

Notes

*   This article is mostly drawn from chapter 7 of my thesis (Beucher 2012), which was published in a revised edition by Karthala (see Beucher 2017). I would like to thank Mary Traynor for the translation of this chapter and Jean Comaroff, John L. Comaroff, and Mariane Ferme for their invaluable suggestions and insights. Of course, all imperfections are my own.

1.   The Mossi (singular, *Moaaga*; plural, *Moose*) make up a society sharing the same language (Moore) and a common ancestor, Naaba Wedraogo. Their political and cultural space is called *Moogo*, or the "World"; see Izard 2003.

2.   Somda 2009.

3.   Burkina Faso, meaning "Land of Incorruptible People," was formerly Upper Volta, a colonial territory created in 1919 and integrated into French West Africa. It became independent in 1960 and was renamed in 1984.

4.   The term *naaba* (plural, *nanamse* or *nanamba*) refers to *naam*, a divine principle legitimizing the ruling of men by its holder. At a customary level, all *naam* and therefore all *naaba* are equivalent. This is how Mossi use the term "chiefs" today, without distinctions of rank. The use of the title, however, which spread widely throughout the colonial period, tends to reduce the complexity of African power. In Mossi country, there are several independent kings called *dima*. Some have the title of *Moogo Naaba* (literally, "Chief of the World"), although that title is most often used for the king of Ouagadougou. These rulers are served by subordinates known under colonialism as "provincial chiefs" (*kug zindba* or *nesomba*), "canton chiefs" (*kombere*), and "village chiefs" (*tengnaaba*). Under French rule, the king of Ouagadougou became the most influential *Moogo* sovereign. During the 1930s, a theory emerged of the existence of a unified Mossi empire under his authority. Originating within the entourage of King Koom II (1905–1942), it became so commonplace that the *Moogo Naaba* of Ouagadougou, currently Naaba Baongho II (1982–), is today regularly referred to as "Emperor of the Mossi" by the media or in official acts, something that does not always go down well with his peers.

5.   The dates between parentheses are those of the reign or mandate of the kings or head of states listed.

6.   I use the term here as defined by Norbert Elias, i.e., a feeling of belonging to an elite crowned with prestige linked to honor; see Elias 1983:chap. 3; and Fusulier 2011:14.

7.   See Hilgers and Mazzocchetti 2010:5–9.

8.   See Hobsbawm and Ranger 1983. For a less mechanical and radical vision of the invention of tradition, see Lentz and Nugent 2000; Ranger 1993; Spear 2003.

9.   Following Max Weber, "discharge" is associated with a model of governance that has recourse to "private" intermediaries, allowing state power to do without a fully-fledged bureaucracy. I share Béatrice Hibou's view that this model of governance does not bespeak the unraveling or absence of the state; in Burkina, in fact, it contributed to its construction. Chiefs are among the actors who blur the lines between private and public, legal and illegal, formal and informal domains, this being a re-

sult of the "quasi-formal power split" that, for Achille Mbembe, is characteristic of "private indirect government." I will not, however, apply this concept in the present analysis as (a) chiefs are not private actors and (b) this type of government by delegation took root well before the introduction of free-market policies in the 1990s. It is actually possible to trace its origins to the colonial period. See Hibou 1999, 2004; Mbembe 2001:chap. 2; Weber 1991:85ff.

10. Given the well-known problems surrounding this term—see the editorial note to this volume—I use it only when it is invoked by relevant stakeholders.

11. *Discours d'Orientation Politique* (DOP), 2 October 1983, Burkinabe Ministry for Information, 8.

12. Balandier 1985:173.

13. The "circle" was an administrative unit corresponding to the British colonial district. The "Mossi circle," administered from Ouagadougou, covered the whole of the *Moogo* as well as some non-Mossi areas.

14. The removal of a sovereign was unimaginable before colonial conquest. A *naaba* obliged to give up his throne usually took his own life, either by strangulation or poisoning. Physical death was generally matched by a symbolic death, which consisted in the erasure of his name from the royal genealogy. During the colonial period, the deposition of chiefs was not unusual; it troubled the institution to the core.

15. Beucher 2012:229–31; Kouanda 2003.

16. Baudu 1956:44–45.

17. Beucher 2010b. See also Jaffré 1989.

18. Billig 1995:6–10.

19. Banégas 1993:95.

20. Interview with Basile L. Guissou, minister on a number of occasions under the RDP, Ouagadougou, 16 December 2008.

21. Conklin 1997.

22. "Résultat des travaux de la première conférence nationale des Comités de Défense de la Révolution du Burkina tenue à Ouagadougou du 31 mars au 4 avril 1986. Thème: Pour le renforcement et l'harmonisation de l'action révolutionnaire au sein des CDR," *Secrétariat général national des CDR* (1986), 140–41.

23. Otayek 1987:119–20.

24. "Tournée de prise de contact et de sensibilisation de plusieurs responsables politiques," *Sidwaya* 401 (21 November 1985), 3.

25. Beucher 2014.

26. "Unité du peuple: Organisation du peuple et du travail," *Sidwaya* 941 (15 January 1988), 2.

27. This was true also of Mende chiefs in Sierra Leone; see Ferme n.d.

28. "Le Naba Karfo de Kaya à Sidwaya," *Sidwaya* 1845 (3 September 1991), 6.

29. Sourwema 1991:6.

30. Grah Mel 2003:354–55; Madiéga 1986:344ff.; Skinner 1989:181.

31. Kiemde 1996:360ff.

32. Loada and Otayek 1995:135.

33. The Fourth Republic was not officially a one-party regime. But, in reality, the CDP had no competition. Opposition parties proliferated without any legal limits but the CDP had substantial resources. In addition, although they were never openly investigated, opposition figures were often eliminated or intimidated without it being possible to identify precise culprits or to establish a link with the president and his entourage—what could be described as "crime by discharge."

34. Interview with HM the Boussouma Naaba Sonre, Ouagadougou, 26 July 2007; Pavanello 2003.
35. Englebert 2002:349.
36. The accumulation of different registers of legitimacy by the princes, especially those obtained from a degree, from a prestigious professional career, as purveyors of significant material and financial resources, and/or from involvement in economic and social development, has contributed greatly to the revival or maintenance of "traditional" authority in contemporary Africa; see, e.g., Argenti 2007; Comaroff and Comaroff 2009:6; Vaughan 1988:45; Warnier 2009:290–302.
37. Beucher 2008; Hubert 2008.
38. Bayart 1993:chap. 5.
39. This controversy was widely discussed in *L'Observateur Paalga* throughout 2003. For an analysis of what was at stake politically, see Beucher 2010a.
40. Izard 2003:62ff.
41. Kambou-Ferrand 1993:138–43.
42. Beucher 2014.
43. Fourchard 2001:130ff.
44. Beucher 2010c.
45. Mossi make up nearly 50 percent of Burkina's total population. Their region is among the most densely populated in the country. While the subjects of the *naaba* do not all vote the same way, few other chiefs can influence the electorate on a national scale. For example, the Ashanti Region in neighboring Ghana accounted for fewer than 18 percent of voters in the national elections of 1996; see Chavagneux 1997:212.
46. The *Kabaka* Mutebi II had his own government and parliament as well as the classic attributes of a sovereign state, namely, a flag, a national anthem, and a motto. Indeed, the Buganda monarchy was seen as semi-autonomous by some Ugandans. See the royal website at http://www.buganda.com and Englebert 2012:346.
47. Sawadogo 2001.
48. Blundo 1998.
49. Lemarchand 1998.
50. Ouédraogo 2006.
51. "Troisième gouvernement révolutionnaire: La différence avec le passé," *Sidwaya* 344 (2 September 1985).
52. "Les groupements Naam: Des efforts de développement à la base," *Sidwaya* 942 (18 January 1988), 12.
53. "Conférence de presse du ministre de l'Action coopérative paysanne," *Sidwaya* 1336 (16 August 1989), 3.
54. "Naam d'hier, Naam d'aujourd'hui," *Carrefour africain* 1075 (21 April 1989), 22.
55. Sawaodogo 2010.
56. Kayorgo 2008.
57. Saint Robespierre 2010.
58. Augustin 2015:85.
59. "Manifs militaires: Ce n'est plus l'armée, c'est un véritable foutoir," *L'Observateur Paalga* 7853 (4 April 2011), 4–5.
60. Meunier 1998:151.
61. Allman 1993:67.
62. Skinner 1989:200–201.
63. Laurent 2010.

64. "Résultat," 13.
65. "Le Yensouangou, chef coutumier du Gourma," *Sidwaya* 1832 (14 August 1991), 2.
66. The *naaba* did not want to suffer the same fate as their counterparts in neighboring Togo, where chiefs have paid a high price for their support of the authoritarian regime of General Eyadema. See Van Rouveroy van Nieuwaal 2000:125–41; Gayibor 2003:105–6.
67. "Naaba Kiba II, chef coutumier de Manga," *Sidwaya* 3451 (16 February 1998), 5.
68. Martin 1993:90–91; Lamizana 1999:77–78; Thiriot 2008:19ff.
69. "Débat: la chefferie traditionnelle est politique," *L'Observateur*, 18 April 2007, http://www.lefaso.net/spip.php?article20278.
70. Harsch 1999; Hagberg 2002; Loada 1999.
71. Hilgers 2009:198–99.
72. Hagberg 2007b.
73. Hagberg 2007a:360ff.
74. This article, added in 2000, introduced a limit of two presidential terms, reducing their length from seven to five years.
75. Carayol 2014.
76. See the king's Facebook page, consulted 2 January 2015, https://www.facebook.com/pages/Mogho-Naaba-Roi-des-Mossé/143732402344065?sk=info.
77. See the UPF presentation brochure, consulted 28 January 2015, http://france.upf.org/images/stories/PDF/upf_fr_v.pdf.
78. "Guinée: Blaise Compaoré: Médiateur sans frontières," *L'Observateur Paalga* 7480 (5 October 2009), http://www.lobservateur.bf/spip.php?page=rubriquearchive&id_rubrique=11417.
79. "Jubilé d'or du Burkina: Blaise Compaoré invite à une introspection nationale," *Fasozine* (11 December 2010), http://www.lefaso.net/spip.php?article39816.
80. Beucher 2010b:7.
81. Haberecht 2013.
82. Hilgers and Loada 2013.
83. On the politicization of the student milieu, see Mazzocchetti 2006.
84. Bieri and Froidevaux 2010; Comaroff and Comaroff 1999; Royer 2002.
85. CSCCT-BF, *Propositions de réflexions pour les réformes politiques* (Ouagadougou, 19 May 2011), 2–3. Thanks to Adrienne Vanvyve from ULB for sharing this document.
86. Quophy 2011.
87. Letter from the Minister of Local Administration and Security, Jérôme Bougouma, to the president of the *Conseil supérieur de la Chefferie coutumière et traditionnelle* on banking information transmission (Ouagadougou, 15 May 2013).
88. Traoré 2012.
89. This expression, popular amongst young protestors, was directed against the administration's stress on national identity based on "civic spirit." Burkinabe national identity has recently been commercialized; hence the marketing, in December 2014, of a range of "Burkindi" clothing. According to its young designer, it was launched so that "the Burkinabe can be a reference point in Africa and everywhere in the world." See Ouédraogo 2014.
90. "Au Burkina Faso, les militaires s'engagent 'à remettre le pouvoir aux civils,'" *France 24*, 5 November 2014, http://www.france24.com/fr/20141104-burkina-faso-militaires-transition-civile-zida-diabre-kabore-campaore-/.
91. Nana 2014.
92. Bako-Arifari and Le Meur 2003:140.

93. A survey was carried out in 2008 by Afrobarometer and the *Centre pour la Gouvernance Démocratique Burkina Faso* (CGD, Centre for the Democratic Governance of Burkina Faso) in the country's thirteen regions. It found that the gap between rural and urban populations on this question is small. A majority (49 percent) said that chiefs should not be affiliated with a political party. See Afrobarometer and CGD 2010.
94. Bayart 2009.

References

Afrobarometer and CGD
    2010   Les opinions des Burkinabè sur la chefferie traditionnelle. *Afrobarometer Briefing Paper* 79 (January), http://afrobarometer.org/publications/bp79-les-opinions-de-burkinabe-sur-la-chefferie-traditionnelle.

Allman, J. M.
    1993   *The Quills of Porcupine: Asante Nationalism in Ghana.* Madison WI: University of Wisconsin Press.

Argenti, N.
    2007   *The Intestines of the State.* Chicago: University of Chicago Press.

Augustin, M.
    2015   La malédiction des jeudis d'octobre. *Journal Afrique Expansion* 398 (January-February).

Bako-Arifari, N., and P.-Y. Le Meur
    2003   La chefferie au Bénin: Une résurgence ambiguë. In *Le Retour des rois: Les autorités traditionnelles et l'État en Afrique contemporaine,* C.-H. Perrot and F.-X. Fauvelle-Aymar, eds. Paris: Karthala.

Balandier, G.
    1985   *Le Détour: Pouvoir et modernité.* Paris: Fayard.

Banégas, R.
    1993   *Insoumissions populaires et révolution au Burkina Faso.* Bordeaux: Institut d'etudes politiques de Bordeaux, Universite de Bordeaux I.

Baudu, P.
    1956   *Vieil Empire, jeune Église.* Paris. La Savane.

Bayart, J.-F.
    1993   *The State in Africa: The Politics of the Belly.* London: Longman.
    2009   La démocratie à l'épreuve de la tradition en Afrique subsaharienne. *Pouvoirs* 2(129): 27–44.

Beucher, Benoît
    2008   Une royauté africaine à l'heure de la mondialisation: Le royaume de Ouagadougou et la question du développement au Burkina Faso. *Sociétés politiques comparées* 6 (June), http://www.fasopo.org/sites/default/files/papier_n6.pdf.
    2010a   Le mythe de l' 'Empire mossi': L'affirmation des royautés comme force d'accompagnement ou de rejet des nouveaux pouvoirs centraux, 1897–1991." In *Révoltes et oppositions dans un régime semi-autoritaire: Le cas du Burkina Faso,* M. Hilgers and J. Mazzocchetti, eds. Paris: Karthala.
    2010b   La naissance de la communauté nationale burkinabè ou comment le Voltaïque devint un 'Homme intègre.' *Politique africaine* 118 (June): 165–86.
    2010c   La reconstitution de la Haute-Volta, enjeu de transactions hégémoniques entre le pouvoir colonial et la royauté moaaga de Ouagadougou? (1919–1947). In *La Reconstitution de la Haute-Volta,* M. W. Bantenga et al., eds. Ouagadougou: L'Harmattan.

2012 Quand les hommes mangent le pouvoir: Dynamiques et pérennité des institutions royales mossi de l'actuel Burkina Faso. PhD dissertation, University of Paris-Sorbonne.

2014 Lendemain de conquête à Ouagadougou: Les officiers de la République française, bâtisseurs d'une royauté africaine (septembre 1896–septembre 1898). In *Sortir de la guerre*, M. Battesti and J. Frémeaux, eds. Paris: PUPS.

2017 *Manger le pouvoir au Burkina Faso: La noblesse mossi à l'épreuve de l'histoire*. Paris: Karthala.

Bieri, A., and S. Froidevaux
2010 Dieu, le président et le wak: À propos de certains phénomènes 'magico-religieux' au Burkina Faso. In *Révoltes et oppositions dans un régime semi-autoritaire: Le cas du Burkina Faso*, M. Hilgers and J. Mazzocchetti, eds. Paris: Karthala.

Billig, M.
1995 *Banal Nationalism*. London: SAGE.

Blundo, G.
1998 Décentralisation et pouvoirs locaux: Registres traditionnels du pouvoir et nouvelles formes locales de légitimité. *Bulletin de l'APAD* 16:147–150, http://apad.revues.org/document543.html.

Carayol, R.
2014 Newton Ahmed Barry, journaliste burkinabè: Je crains pour ma vie. *Jeune Afrique*, 22 August, http://www.jeuneafrique.com/Article/ARTJAWEB20140822175314/.

Chavagneux, C.
1997 *Ghana, une révolution de bon sens*. Paris: Karthala.

Comaroff, J. L., and J. Comaroff
1999 Occult Economies and the Violence of Abstraction: Notes from the South African Postcolony. *American Ethnologist* 26(2): 279–303.

2009 *Ethnicity, Inc.* Chicago: University of Chicago Press.

Conklin, A. L.
1997 *A Mission to Civilize: The Republican Idea of Empire in France and West Africa, 1895–1930*. Stanford: Stanford University Press.

Elias, Norbert
1983 *The Court Society*. Oxford: Blackwell.

Englebert, P.
2002 Born-Again Buganda or the Limits of Traditional Resurgence in Africa. *Journal of Modern African Studies* 40(3):345–68.

Ferme, M.
n.d. Sitting on the Land: The Political and Symbolic Economy of Chieftaincy in Contemporary Sierra Leone. Unpublished manuscript.

Fourchard, L.
2001 *De la ville coloniale à la Cour africaine: Espaces, pouvoirs et sociétés à Ouagadougou et à Bobo-Dioulasso (Haute-Volta), fin XIXe siècle-1960*. Paris: L'Harmattan.

Fusulier, B.
2011 Le concept d'ethos: De ses usages classiques à un usage renouvelé. *Recherches sociologiques et anthropologiques* 42(1):97–109, http://rsa.revues.org/661.

Gayibor, N.
2003 Les rapports entre les autorités politiques et les chefs traditionnels au Togo de 1960 à la fin du XIXe siècle. In *Le Retour des rois: Les autorités traditionnelles et l'État en Afrique contemporaine*, C.-H. Perrot and F.-X. Fauvelle-Aymar, eds. Paris: Karthala.

Grah Mel, F.

2003 *Félix Houphouët-Boigny: Biographie.* Paris: Karthala.

Haberecht, S.

2013 Une ville devient la scène de la nation: Burkina Faso célèbre son Cinquantenaire à Bobo-Dioulasso. In *La Ville de Bobo-Dioulasso au Burkina Faso: Urbanité et appartenances en Afrique de l'Ouest,* K. Werthmann and M. Lamine Sanogo, eds. Paris: Karthala.

Hagberg, S.

2002 'Enough is Enough': An Ethnography of the Struggle against Impunity in Burkina Faso. *Journal of Modern African Studies* 40(2):217–46.

2007a Comprendre sans légitimer: Corruption, impunité et une anthropologie engagée. In *Une Anthropologie entre rigueur et engagement: Essais autour de l'œuvre de Jean-Pierre Olivier de Sardan,* T. Bierschenk, G. Blundo, Y. Jaffré, and M. Tidjani Alou, eds. Paris: Karthala.

2007b Traditional Chieftaincy, Party Politics, and Political Violence in Burkina Faso. In *State Recognition and Democratization in Sub-Saharan Africa: A New Dawn for Traditional Authorities?,* L. Buur and H. Kyed, eds. New York: Palgrave Macmillan.

Harsch, E.

1999 Trop c'est trop! Civil Insurgence in Burkina Faso, 1998–1999. *Review of African Political Economy* 26(81):395–406.

Hibou, B.

1999 La 'décharge,' nouvel interventionnisme. *Politique africaine* 73:6–15.

Hibou, B., ed.

2004 *Privatizing the State.* New York: Columbia University Press.

Hilgers, M.

2009 *Une ethnographie à l'échelle de la ville: Urbanité, histoire et reconnaissance à Koudougou (Burkina Faso).* Paris: Karthala.

Hilgers, M., and A. Loada

2013 Tensions et protestations dans un régime semi-autoritaire: Croissance des révoltes populaires et maintien du pouvoir au Burkina Faso. *Politique africaine* 3(31): 187–208.

Hilgers, M., and J. Mazzocchetti, eds.

2010 *Révoltes et oppositions dans un régime semi-autoritaire: Le cas du Burkina Faso.* Paris: Karthala.

Hobsbawm, E., and T. Ranger, eds.

1983 *The Invention of Tradition.* Cambridge: Cambridge University Press.

Hubert, T.

2008 Larlé Naaba Tigré, King of Jatropha. *France 24,* 16 December, http://www.france24 .com/en/20081216-larle-naaba-tigre-king-jatropha-miracle-plant-ouagadougou -burkina-faso/.

Izard, Michel

2003 *Moogo: L'émergence d'un espace étatique ouest-africain au XVIe siècle.* Paris: Karthala.

Jaffré, B.

1989 *Burkina Faso: Les années Sankara: de la Révolution à la Rectification.* Paris: L'Harmattan.

Kambou-Ferrand, J.-M.

1993 *Peuples voltaïques et conquête coloniale 1885–1914.* Paris: L'Harmattan.

Kayorgo, A.

2008 Blaise Compaoré, chef traditionnel ivoirien intronisé à Kosyam. *L'Observateur Paalga,* 2 May, http://www.lefaso.net/spip.php?article26626.

Kiemde, P.

1996 Réflexions sur le référendum constitutionnel et les élections présidentielles et législatives de 1991 et 1992. In *Le Burkina entre révolution et démocratie (1983–1993)*, R. Otayek, F. M. Sawadogo, and J.-P. Guingané, eds. Paris: Karthala.

Kouanda, A.
2003   La révolte d'Alassane Moumini en 1908. In *Burkina Faso, cent ans d'histoire, 1895–1995*, vol. 1. Y. G. Madiéga and O. Nao, eds. Paris: Karthala.

Lamizana, S.
1999   *Sur la brèche trente années durant: Mémoires*, vol. 2. Paris: Jaguar Conseil.

Laurent, P.-J.
2010   Pouvoirs et contre-pouvoirs dans la société mossi et plus globalement au Burkina Faso. In *Révoltes et oppositions dans un régime semi-autoritaire: Le cas du Burkina Faso*, M. Hilgers and J. Mazzocchetti, eds. Paris: Karthala.

Lemarchand, R.
1998   La face cachée de la décentralisation: Réseaux, clientèles et capital social. *Bulletin de l'APAD* 16 (6 October), http://apad.revues.org/document522.html.

Lentz, C., and P. Nugent, eds.
2000   *Ethnicity in Ghana: The Limits of Invention*. London: Palgrave Macmillan.

Loada, A.
1999   Réflexions sur la société civile en Afrique: Le Burkina de l'après-Zongo. *Politique africaine* 76 (December): 136–51.

Loada, A., and R. Otayek
1995   Les élections municipales du 12 février 1995 au Burkina Faso. *Politique africaine* 58 (June): 135–42.

Madiéga, G. Y.
1986   *Le rôle du RDA dans la reconstitution de la colonie de Haute-Volta (1947)*. Abidjan: Université de Ouagadougou.

Martin, M.-L.
1993   Armées et politique: le 'Cycle de vie' du militarisme en Afrique noire francophone. In *États et sociétés en Afrique francophone*, D. C. Bach and A. A. Kirk-Greene, eds. Paris: Economica.

Mazzocchetti, J.
2006   'Quand les poussins se réunissent, ils font peur à l'épervier . . . .' *Politique africaine* 1(101): 83–101.

Mbembe, A.
2001   *On the Postcolony*. Berkeley: University of California Press.

Meunier, E.
1998   Burkina-Faso: La consolidation du nouvel ordre politique. In *L'Afrique politique 1998*. Paris: Karthala.

Nana, W. A.
2014   Le lieutenant-colonel Isaac Zida chez le Mogho Naaba. *Sidwaya*, 4 November, http://www.sidwaya.bf/m-3016-le-lieutenant-colonel-isaac-zida-chez-le-mogho-naaba.html.

Otayek, R.
1987   Quand le tambour change de rythme, il est indispensable que les danseurs changent de pas. *Politique africaine* 28:116–23.

Ouédraogo, A.
2014   'Burkindi': La nouvelle marque vestimentaire made in Burkina," 29 December, http://faso-actu.net/Burkindi-La-nouvelle-marque (no longer available).

Ouédraogo, H. M. G.
2006   Décentralisation et pouvoirs traditionnels: Le paradoxe des légitimités locales. *Mondes en Développement* 34(133): 9–29.

Pavanello, M.

2003   Le paradoxe de la chefferie constitutionnelle au Ghana. In *Le Retour des rois: Les autorités traditionnelles et l'État en Afrique contemporaine,* C.-H. Perrot and F.-X. Fauvelle-Aymar, eds. Paris: Karthala.

Quophy, F.

2011   Situation nationale: Leçons d'une gouvernance en panne. *Journal du Jeudi,* 13 April, http://www.lefaso.net/spip.php?article41555.

Ranger, T. O.

1993   The Invention of Tradition Revisited: The Case of Colonial Africa. In *Legitimacy and the State in Twentieth-Century Africa,* T. Ranger and O. Vaughan, eds. Basingstoke: Palgrave Macmillan.

Royer, P.

2002   The Spirit of Competition: *Wak* in Burkina Faso. *Africa* 72(3): 464–83.

Saint Robespierre, A.

2010   Prestation de serment de Blaise Compaoré: Entre tradition et modernité. *L'Observateur Paalga* 7782 (20 December), 3–4.

Sawadogo, R.-A.

2001   *L'État africain face à la décentralisation.* Paris: Karthala.

Sawaodogo, S.

2010   Le Kombi-Naam ou le pouvoir des jeunes: Quand la tradition et la démocratie font bon ménage. *Carrefour africain,* 10 February, http://www.lefaso.net/spip.php?article35323.

Skinner, E. P.

1989   *The Mossi of Burkina Faso: Chiefs, Politicians and Soldiers.* Prospect Heights, IL: Waveland Press.

Somda, Y. S.

2009   Il faut un régime constitutionnel monarchique . . . . *Le Pays* 4280 (9–11 January), 10.

Sourwema, I.

1991   Les 82 coutumiers de Zabré soutiennent Blaise Compaoré selon le Naba Tigré. *Sidwaya* 1866 (2 October), 6.

Spear, T.

2003   Neo-Traditionalism and the Limits of Invention in British Colonial Africa. *Journal of African History* 44(1): 3–27.

Thiriot, C.

2008   La place des militaires dans les régimes post-transition d'Afrique subsaharienne: La difficile resectorisation. *Revue internationale de politique comparée* 15(1): 15–34.

Traoré, A.

2012   Révision de la Loi fondamentale burkinabé: Le quitus du Conseil constitutionnel. *Sidwaya,* 10 July, http://www.lefaso.net/spip.php?article49048.

Van Rouveroy van Nieuwaal, E. A. B.

2000   *L'État en Afrique face à la chefferie: Le cas du Togo.* Paris: Karthala.

Vaughan, O.

1988   Les chefs traditionnels face au pouvoir politique. *Politique africaine* 32 (December): 44–56.

Warnier, J.-P.

2009   *Régner au Cameroun: Le Roi-Pot.* Paris: Karthala.

Weber, M.

1991   *Histoire économique: Esquisse d'une histoire universelle de l'économie et de la société.* Paris: Gallimard.

EIGHT

Corporate Kings and South Africa's Traditional-Industrial Complex

SUSAN COOK

Marikana, August 2012

On August 16, 2012, members of the South African Police Service shot and killed thirty-four workers at the Lonmin corporation's Marikana platinum mine in the midst of a wildcat strike. Twenty-eight of the thirty-four slain workers were amaMpondo from Pondoland in the Eastern Cape Province, on the other side of the country. A few days later, *Kumkani* (King) Zano-zuko Sigcau, of Eastern Pondoland, decided to travel to Marikana to meet with the striking miners and to assist the families of the dead in claiming and transporting the bodies home. He also hoped to pay a brief visit to *Kgosi* (King) Leruo Molotlegi, of the Royal Bafokeng Nation, at his capital, Phokeng, just next to Marikana, and itself a site of significant platinum extraction. Paying such a visit on his way to the mine represented a normal, even expected, courtesy for anyone passing through traditionally governed territory. Thus, on August 22, 2012, *Kumkani* Sigcau made the twelve-hour, 1,000-kilometer trip by car with several subchiefs and advisors. They arrived at Phokeng on a warm late winter day wearing formal suits and a somber bearing. The two traditional leaders had never met before.[1]

Their meeting took place in Leruo's formal boardroom, at an oval table surrounded by plush, leather-backed chairs. The amaMpondo visitors sat facing *Kgosi* Leruo's entourage of subchiefs (*dikgosana*), advisors, and staff and were served coffee and tea before he entered the room.

Speaking English, the only language the two leaders share, the Bafokeng king welcomed Sigcau and his delegation, noting that it was very unfortunate that they were meeting for the first time under such tragic circumstances. Expressing condolences for the terrible loss of life at Marikana, he shared his hopes for a peaceful resolution to the ongoing labor crisis and

Figure 3. *Kgosi* Leruo Molotlegi (left) and *Kumkani* Zanozuko Sigcau (right) at Marikana (courtesy of the Royal Bafokeng Administration)

for the smooth return of the deceased miners' bodies to their families in the Eastern Cape. He added,

> I find it strange, actually, that we have never met. I've received representatives from the Kingdom of Lesotho and from the Government of Mozambique, both of whom represent large numbers of migrant laborers living in this area and working in the mines, and yet you, the leader of our fellow South Africans, the Xhosa-speaking Pondos, have never visited before. However tragic the circumstances, I hope this occasion will usher in a new era of friendship and cooperation between us, in the interest of better lives for the ama-Mpondo living in the Royal Bafokeng Nation, as well as their families and communities in Pondoland.

Sigcau responded to Kgosi Leruo's observation by declaring,

> I never wanted to come to this place, and it is my hope and my dream that one day soon, my people will not be forced by poverty and desperation to travel 1,000 kilometers from their homes to find work in your region. We will only achieve this when we develop the economies of our own villages instead of continuing to contribute to the ever-expanding wealth of yours.

He thanked the Bafokeng king for receiving him and his delegation. And for his condolences.

Kumkani Sigcau then requested that *Kgosi* Leruo accompany him to Marikana that day, where he planned to address his people and do what he could to assist the striking workers and the families of the dead. Leruo accepted the invitation. Approximately twelve Bafokeng *dikgosana* and their wives were already waiting patiently outside in two minibuses when the leaders and their attendants emerged from the boardroom. They drove in convoy behind the two sedans conveying the kings and their police escorts.

After traveling for fifteen minutes or so through Bafokeng territory along the N4 highway, the main east-west artery of the North West Province, conversation in the minibuses lapsed as they approached the turnoff to the Marikana mine. Passing through a police checkpoint where scores of armored trucks were parked and razor wire was coiled in huge makeshift barriers, they proceeded to the "koppie" (hill) where, five days earlier, the massacre had taken place.[2] A number of police vehicles stood nearby, and the drivers and bodyguards accompanying the royal entourage alighted to confer with the officials. They were told that, due to the unresolved labor dispute between the unions and the Lonmin mine, and the violence perpetrated by the South African Police Service less than a week before, no company or state personnel were permitted beyond the koppie without the express permission of the striking workers and their union proxies. The only way to travel further was to leave the police behind and be escorted by a union official to the field where the strikers had assembled to hear speeches. The kings agreed to these conditions and were briefed by union and workers' representatives on the protocols they were expected to observe. They and their parties were then led to a makeshift podium erected for the various speakers who had come to address the gathering in what had become an informal theater of public communication across the lines of strife. On one side was open land, where more than two thousand workers sat on the ground, listening intently as one of their comrades recounted the events of August 16. This was mostly for the benefit of President Jacob Zuma, who had also come that day and was waiting to speak. On the other side were shacks where men, women, and children—workers' families— were standing outside or in doorways, watching the proceedings. A few minutes later, someone brought a stack of plastic chairs for the kings and their retinues. Nobody else was offered this courtesy. Not even the state president.

After the strikers' representative sat down to vociferous applause, President Zuma rose to speak. He began in isiXhosa and isiZulu and was imme-

diately heckled, to the extent that one of the workers' leaders felt it necessary to take the microphone from him, to admonish the crowd, and to call
for quiet. Zuma resumed his speech and went on for some twenty minutes
about the tragedy, using the occasion to announce a commission of inquiry to determine what actually happened on August 16. He was quoted,
in translation, as saying, "I hear that . . . you won't leave here until you get
the money you want. I will also send a message to the employer that you
demand 12,500 rand. I haven't met the employer so I don't know his view
on this."[3] The president then declared a week of mourning in honor of the
dead and injured miners.

Zuma's remarks failed to mollify the angry and traumatized workers.
As he sat down, they took to their feet in a defiant upswell of movement
and chanting. The president was quickly escorted to his car and the kings'
bodyguards nervously conferred about what to do. The Bafokeng ruler and
his entourage decided to depart. *Kumkani* Sigcau, in contrast, resolved to
stay on to address his people and offer some consolation. The previous de-
marcations between strikers, visiting officials, and residents dissolved into
a sea of movement with pulsing rivers of people moving in different directions. The air was tense with uncertainty and expectation.

As the Bafokeng delegation piled back into the minivans and left the
scene, some of them remarked on the chaos they had just witnessed. They
spoke knowingly of the "wild" and "uncivilized" Xhosas (*"ba waeld!"*).
They asserted that Xhosa migrant workers living in the area had always
been hotheaded and prone to violence, implying that the tragedy that occurred on August 16 was at least provoked to some extent by the workers,
if not exclusively their fault. The convoy retraced its route past the rocky
outcrop, the makeshift police headquarters at the entrance to the mine,
and back onto the N4. When it arrived in Phokeng, the headmen and their
wives returned to their offices and homes.

Jacob Zuma's visit to Marikana that day was widely covered by national
and international media outlets, but the visit of the traditional leaders received little national attention, except for one article with a photograph
that ran under the headline "Bafokeng King Accompanies Traditional
Leaders to Site of Marikana Tragedy."[4] King Sigcau was not mentioned at
all. And although the two never communicated again after that day, it was
evident to any careful observer that, while they and their constituencies
were bound together in unequal embrace by the political economy of platinum, the mining industry in South Africa was itself inextricably tied to the
institution of traditional leadership.

Traditional Leaders, Corporations, and the State

Although scholars continue to debate the allegedly contradictory persistence, the "resurgence," and the legitimacy of indigenous rulers in Africa—specifically the extent to which hereditary office, customary law, and communal land administration are anathema to modern democracy (Mamdani 1996; Ntsebeza 2005; Oomen 2005)—their rising relevance is hard to ignore in contemporary South Africa. Note, as exemplary evidence, the attendance at the amaXhosa king's coronation in 2015 of the state president, the minister of cooperative governance, and a mining magnate who also happened to be the country's first black billionaire and vice president. In this chapter, I argue that their significance and influence is not only a reflection of political affairs in a context in which policies of decentralization encourage the devolution of authority to local leaders (Crais 2006; Oomen 2005). It is also a key element of the neoliberal economy, especially as it plays out in the mining sector. As the Marikana crisis made clear, the process of extracting the ore that is refined into platinum—which, in turn, is an essential component of catalytic converters in motor vehicles and the electrical components of cell phones across the planet—is deeply embedded in the politics and legalities of land and labor. Kings and chiefs can, and often do, play a crucial role in ensuring stable access to that land and labor, allowing licensed companies to perform their status as good corporate citizens—often a requirement for the renewal of their mining licenses—by helping to prevent conflict or resolve disputes when work relations turn sour. To the extent that Marikana may be seen as a failure of the government to safeguard its citizens, of the company to protect its employees, or of both, it provides a glimpse into the complex ways in which customary sovereigns, as intercalary figures (Gluckman et al. 1949; chapter 1, this volume), interact with the private sector and the state to preserve and perpetuate (neoliberal) "business as usual" in this domain of the economy. A close reading of the Pondo and Bafokeng kings' visit to Marikana on August 22, 2012, also demonstrates that there are vast differences in the capacity of individual rulers to leverage their unique role in these contexts. Before turning to that analysis, though, it is necessary to know more about the key players, present and absent, on that day.

Lonmin

Lonmin plc, a producer of platinum group metals operating in the Bushveld Igneous Complex of South Africa, was formerly the mining division of Lonrho plc, originally incorporated in the United Kingdom on May 13, 1909. It is listed on the London Stock Exchange and is a constituent of the FTSE 250 Index. Its registered office is in London, but its operational headquarters are in Johannesburg. The company and its erstwhile parent, Lonrho, have sustained an unparalleled reputation for ruthless extraction and boundless greed; former British Prime Minister Edward Heath once dubbed it "an unpleasant and unacceptable face of capitalism."[5] The company reported revenue of $965 million in 2014.[6] The labor dispute that gripped its platinum mine at Marikana in August 2012 was neither unprecedented in nature nor exceptional in scale. Eight years earlier, in 2004, 400 rock drill operators (RDOs) had downed tools at Anglo Platinum and were summarily dismissed.[7] In February 2012, 5,000 of them led 12,000 other workers out on strike at the nearby Impala Platinum mine on Bafokeng territory. When the RDOs at Lonmin embarked on the "wildcat" action in August 2012, they were asking for the same wage—R12,500 per month, approximately $1,000 at the time—that RDOs had recently demanded at other mines on the platinum belt. The showdown at Marikana, then, was part of a longer trend in which rock drill operators sought to deal with management outside the received structures of negotiated labor contracts: specifically, those represented by the National Union of Mineworkers (NUM),[8] which had lost membership and grassroots influence here to the more populist Association of Mineworkers and Construction Union (AMCU), which called the strike at Lonmin.

The dispute at Marikana was unprecedented in the scale of violent death that occurred in its wake; even before August 16, a series of confrontations ended with ten workers and mine security personnel brutally murdered. Strike sentiment quickly spread beyond the RDOs, amidst rampant discontent with the ANC-linked NUM. Lonmin, for its part, was unwilling to renegotiate contracts. When, finally, on the day of the massacre, 3,000 angry strikers faced off against some 600–700[9] armed South African police, it was the latter who went on the offensive, killing thirty-four men and wounding seventy-five. Subsequent investigations revealed that most of the dead were shot in the back at close range.[10] None of the officers sustained injuries. As the conflict continued to play out on legal, financial, and political fronts, the broader labor crisis within the platinum sector went on unabated: it continued through mid-2014, resulting in a 0.6 percent contraction of South Africa's GDP—and $900 million in wages lost by workers at Lonmin, Anglo American, and Implats, a large proportion of whom come from Pondoland.[11]

AmaMpondo

Pondoland, formerly known as the Transkei, ethnic "homeland" of the Xhosa-speaking population of South Africa under apartheid, is situated on the Indian Ocean coast in the Eastern Cape Province. AmaMpondo are one of twelve Xhosa-speaking groups and were among the last to be brought under colonial rule in the late nineteenth century (Beinart 1982:55). Unlike other agrarian-based societies in this part of the country, they were slow to respond to the demand for labor in the diamond and gold mines and only began sending men in any significant numbers to the goldfields after the turn of the twentieth century (p. 59). A hundred or so years of labor migration has not brought prosperity to the region, not by any measure. In fact, a long history of underdevelopment and political resistance has made the Eastern Cape into something of an internal colony within South Africa and a forging ground for black nationalist leadership. Taking Port St. John's Municipality as an example of current conditions, unemployment stands at 50 percent, only 3 percent of the population has access to piped water inside their homes, and just over 3 percent has weekly refuse removal. Remittances from migrant laborers working in the mines are one of the most important sources of household income.[12]

Zanozuko Tyelovuyo Sigcau, the amaMpondo ruler who travelled to Marikana in August 2012, was installed as *kumkani* in 2011; he was the ninth paramount chief of the Gcaleka subgroup of the Xhosa Nation. Although he was firmly in power at the time of the massacre, the succession battle that saw him confirmed by the state president, Jacob Zuma,[13] also saw him subsequently dethroned by South Africa's Constitutional Court in 2013, at which point his forebear and rival, Mpondombini Thandizulu Sigcau, was reinstalled (posthumously) as king, with the deceased's widow, Lombekiso Dlamini, serving as regent. At the time of writing, Zanozuko and his allies continue to contest the office, and he is reportedly seeking not only Eastern Pondoland as his rightful jurisdiction but all of Pondoland.

At the time of the Marikana crisis, approximately one third of the Lonmin workforce (8,860 people) came from the Eastern Cape, and most of them were living on land owned by the Bafokeng. Nevertheless, as Keith Breckenridge points out, "These men nurture the dream of returning to live permanently in the countryside. They have in mind a rural world that has few of the resources of the capitalist cities but many of the virtues of the precapitalist commons."[14]

Bafokeng

The Royal Bafokeng Nation is a Setswana-speaking polity in the North West Province, 100 kilometers west of Pretoria. It is one of fifty or so Tswana chiefdoms in Botswana and South Africa that have been intensively studied by historians and anthropologists (Schapera 1943, 1952; Schapera and Comaroff 1991; Breutz 1953, 1989; Coertze 1988; Comaroff and Comaroff 1991, 1997; Legassick 1969). Its population of 150,000 live in twenty-nine villages; about 65 percent of them are ethnic Bafokeng and 35 percent are migrants into the area, some of them recent, many of them there to stay. Approximately 12 percent, in the region of 18,000 persons, identify Xhosa as their home language.[15]

During the apartheid era, the Bafokeng *kgosi*, Lebone I, resisted incorporation into Bophuthatswana, the Tswana ethnic "homeland," and declared his intention to secede from it in 1983. He was eventually accused of sponsoring a coup attempt and was forced into exile in 1988. After the 1994 elections, *Kgosi* Lebone I reclaimed his position as ruler but died soon after returning to Phokeng. His eldest son Mollwane replaced him in 1995. When Mollwane passed away unexpectedly in 2000, his younger brother Leruo ascended to the throne and remains the incumbent today.

The Royal Bafokeng Nation currently owns and occupies 1,400 km^2 of land located within the Bushveld Igneous Complex (above, p. 215), the richest known reserve of platinum group metals in the world (see also chapter 4, this volume). In contrast to other "tribal authorities" that administer territory on behalf of the state, the Bafokeng own theirs by title, having bought it through the offices of the *kgosi*, piece by piece, starting in the 1870s. This was achieved in the second half of the nineteenth century by imposing a tax on men sent to work at the mines in Kimberley. The resulting land acquisition fund was used to buy the farms on which the Bafokeng were living, avoiding the ban on black freehold by making the purchase in the name of their resident German missionary (Mbenga and Manson 2010). While they struggled over the years to retain their right of possession, especially during the apartheid years, the Bafokeng succeeded—if not without recourse to lengthy litigation.

Today in command of mining dividends and a diversified investment portfolio worth $3.5 billion, the Royal Bafokeng Administration (RBA) operates like a small municipality, overseeing infrastructure and basic services. Its other assets include a World Cup stadium, a high-performance sports complex, and a professional soccer team. The Royal Bafokeng Institute was established in 2006 to upgrade the nation's forty-five schools. While unemployment here is estimated at around 35 percent—much less than in Port St. John's in the Eastern Cape—90 percent of those who self-identify as Bafokeng have access to piped water in their houses; only 42 percent of those who do not so identify, including amaMpondo in the area, have such amenities, although they are still a great deal better served than the amaMpondo in Port St. John's. Over 95 percent of people resident on Bafokeng land have access to electricity for lighting and cooking, and 63 percent are served by a weekly trash pickup.[16] In the absence of a "per capita dividend" issued by the RBA, job creation and skills training activities are made widely available. The standard of living in Bafokeng, where many of the community's basic needs are met, thus presents a striking contrast to that in Pondoland, where public services remain meagre.

Bapo-ba-Mogale

For purposes of the discussion below, the Bapo-ba-Mogale "nation" (*morafe*), where the Marikana mine is located, is also a critical constituency. Like the Bafokeng, it is Setswana-speaking and headed by a *kgosi*. Numbering only 35,000, the Bapo-ba-Mogale also reside on platinum-rich land. But, unlike the Bafokeng, they do not own it by title and have thus had to negotiate their access to the territory over the years with Lonmin and other extractive companies through the dubious, arguably corrupt, offices of the state, initially through the Bophuthatswana "homeland" government and, after 1994, through the administration of the North West Province. In 2011, Lonmin announced that it had paid royalties of about R500 million into a "D account" held by the North West Province on behalf of this community and also that monies continued to flow in at a rate of around R40 million per year.[17] Little to none of it has ever been made available to the Bapo-ba-Mogale rulers, however, and has instead been handled by "external administrators." Never audited, despite frequent calls for transparency, this D account receives all revenues owed to the traditionally governed chiefdoms in the province—except the Bafokeng, who are exempt and receive their royalties directly. Succession disputes and power struggles within Bapo royal lineages and councils have been frequent and protracted, but in the wake of the Marikana massacre, the current leader, *Kgosi* Bob Mogale, and his associates formalized a black economic empowerment (BEE) partnership with Lonmin.[18] The projected net share in the mining company for the Bapo Community Local Economic Development Trust is "a miserable 2.85 percent,"[19] compared to the Bafokeng's 13 percent stake in Impala Platinum. But a stake it is, and, as the strikes that began in 2012 dragged on into 2014, *Kgosi* Mogale considered suing Lonmin to force the company and its workers to settle and resume production.[20]

Government of South Africa

While the South African constitution of 1996 recognizes traditional leaders, that recognition is ambiguous at best; various subsequent efforts to pin it down by statute have been complicated and controversial (see Comaroff and Comaroff 2003). The Traditional Leadership and Governance Framework Amendment Act remains the principal legislation laying out the powers and jurisdiction of the country's eight hundred or so kings and chiefs (see chapters 1 and 4, this volume). Under this act, indigenous rulers have a degree of authority over land administration, health care provision, the administration of customary law, economic development, and arts and culture (Crais 2006). The Communal Land Rights Act of 2003, which would have given them additional control over land allocation and administration, was declared unconstitutional and never implemented. In general, district municipalities, the local organs of state, are very weak in the former homeland areas, including Pondoland, the Royal Bafokeng Nation, and Bapo-ba-Mogale. Although those municipalities are obligated to provide basic services, education, policing, and healthcare, delivery is patchy and poor to nonexistent, leaving indigenous sovereigns to do whatever they can to meet the needs of their constituents. In certain areas, they refuse to recognize municipal jurisdiction outright and continue to mete out justice, including corporal punishment.

With regard to the extractive industries, which account for approximately 8 percent of South Africa's GDP, the state has developed, and enforces, a relatively tight regulatory environment—although mining firms make heavy use of private security. The Mineral and Petroleum Resources Development Act of 2002 defines "new order" (as opposed to existing, "old order") rights to minerals and other natural resources, as well as the social and economic responsibilities required of every company with a mining license. Strict rules govern the rehabilitation of the natural environment—soil, water, air, and landscape—during and after extractive operations. They also specify the social responsibility of each corporation, expressed in a five-year Social and Labor Plan. Although these laws are designed to ensure that the adjacent, labor-sending and labor-hosting communities do not suffer the negative consequences of mining, they are constantly skirted. For its part, the state regulator, namely, the Department of Mineral Resources, only enforces them inconsistently.

Corporate Kings and a Seat at the Table

Returning to the events of August 22, 2012, in light of all this raises some interesting questions. How was each of the three traditional leaders—the two present and the one absent on that day—positioned vis-à-vis the tragedy that had taken place at Marikana? Why did *Kumkani* Sigcau pay a courtesy call on the Bafokeng king, whose territory lies adjacent to the mine, and not on *Kgosi* Mogale, who controls the land leased to Lonmin? Why was the interaction between the two monarchs such an uneasy one? Of the more than two thousand people present at Marikana on August 22, is it significant that the kings and their entourages were the only ones offered chairs, taking precedence, in this respect, over the state president?

The Commission of Inquiry, which Jacob Zuma announced to the assembled workers on August 22, was charged with establishing the facts surrounding, and responsibility for, the events that had occurred at Marikana; it was also tasked with examining the underlying conditions, circumstances, and interests that contributed to the violence and loss of life. The starkly unequal flow of resources between the Eastern Cape and other parts of the country noted by *Kumkani* Sigcau in his meeting with *Kgosi* Leruo was confirmed by the evidence. The commission found, at the Lonmin mine, that 36.4 percent of the workers came from the Eastern Cape, more than from any other province, including the North West Province. Living conditions for those workers were unspeakably grim. They received a "living out allowance" that, in contrast to the former hostel system, enabled them to migrate with their families. This was used to rent rooms or build shacks, but most lacked access to sanitation, roads, water, and Xhosa-medium schools for their children. In fact, the situation of the miners is worse, and their living costs are a bigger drain on their earnings, than they had been under apartheid (Breckenridge 2014). Most live on land owned or controlled by "tribal authorities" such as the Bafokeng or Bapo-ba-Mogale that do not wish to provide services such as water reticulation or refuse removal to informal settlements full of people they consider outsiders.[21] The migrants are discriminated against at local clinics, schools, and other government institutions, a fact corroborated by the Royal Bafokeng Administration's own research. On measures such as access to land, dwelling type, knowledge of financial products, education levels, food insecurity, access to water sanitation and electricity, perceptions of safety and security, and HIV infection rates, non-Bafokeng—who, again, are largely workers and their families from elsewhere—fare significantly worse than their Bafokeng neighbors.[22]

In the Eastern Cape, the families of migrants eke out an existence amidst the entrenched poverty, drought, unemployment, and social collapse noted earlier. The remittances sent home to them are never enough to meet basic needs, forcing them to borrow from short-term lenders to make ends meet, which creates a yet deeper cycle of desperation and vulnerability. When the miners eventually return home in their retirement, they are more of a burden than a resource to their communities. *Kumkani* Sigcau's bitterness when meeting the king of "The Richest Tribe in Africa" (Manson and Mbenga 2003) must be read in light of the fact that, in "the poorest areas of the country are where South African migrant labor [is] chiefly sourced, . . . remittances [have] not alleviated poverty."[23] Of course, unemployment and domestic poverty exists in labor-hosting communities as well, including Bafokeng and Bapo-ba-Mogale; the commission's research indicates that, for many local residents in those communities, "the only source of money was mine workers' rent."[24] But the contrast between Pondoland and Bafokeng suggests, at a minimum, that labor-hosting areas fare much better than labor-sending ones—and that, despite the economic symbiosis between locals and migrants, social inequities and enmities remain, are ethnicized, and were the proverbial elephant in the room when the kings met.

These two rulers, I stress, were more than mere embodiments of the structural and material contrasts between the overall circumstances of their subjects. Their respective relationships to the means of mining production were also quite different. As a result of historical circumstances, good fortune, and a fair amount of strategic planning (Mbenga and Manson 2010), *Kgosi* Leruo presides over an administration-cum-business complex that owns, and is therefore empowered to negotiate lease rights to, land containing extremely valuable mineral deposits. The RBN also holds a controlling share in Royal Bafokeng Platinum (57 percent), one of the major extractive companies in the area, and is the largest individual stockholder in Impala Platinum (13.2 percent), among the largest platinum mining firms in the world. The Royal Bafokeng Development Trust stewards all of these resources and determines the allocation of dividends to the investment company, Royal Bafokeng Holdings, and to community development projects costing between $36m to $133m per annum; the RBH investment portfolio was valued at R39bn at the end of 2013.[25] In short, *Kgosi* Leruo is not only a hereditary leader who, in line with the Traditional Leadership Framework Act, presides over a "tribal council" that governs the twenty-nine villages of the nation through a combination of "traditional" and "democratic" structures. He is also an influential corporate executive who has served as an advisor to the South African Department of Mineral Resources, as a member of the Board of Governors for the Mining and Metals Sector at the World Economic Forum, and on numerous other industry bodies at the global level. Although the RBN portfolio does not include Lonmin plc, Bafokeng villages, and in particular informal settlements such as Nkaneng, are key receiving areas for migrant laborers at Marikana and other local mines. The conditions that prevail in those communities, then, are very much under *Kgosi* Leruo's sphere of influence. This explains why, whatever resentment he may have felt, *Kumkani* Sigcau chose to make a "traditional" courtesy call on the Bafokeng ruler. It was, arguably, an attempt to instill a benevolent attitude in him toward the amaMpondo living on his land—and perhaps also an effort to acquire more influence on the platinum belt, where the lives of migrant workers from the Eastern Cape had seemed expendable to both Lonmin and the South African police.

Even though the two men have not spoken since that day, *Kumkani* Sigcau's strategy may have paid off. Three months after the Marikana tragedy, *Kgosi* Leruo summoned the heads of the six major local mining houses to a meeting in Phokeng to discuss immediate and long-term improvements to conditions on the platinum belt for all who live there. Senior officials from the firms, three of them represented by their CEOs, gathered at the RBN's five-star Royal Marang Hotel to hear the king's proposals. His authority, as well as the significant economic stakes for the Bafokeng community, was evident in the meeting. This type of convening power was unparalleled: the senior management of these corporate rivals had never before sat together in this way, let alone to formulate common objectives.

Kgosi Leruo's role as traditional ruler of the villages surrounding the mines is also crucial to the industry. Recall the state regulation that companies prepare and fulfill five-year Social and Labor Plans in order to retain their operating licenses. These plans require various corporate social responsibility initiatives, as well as health and labor practices; the ability of the firms to meet them rests, in large part, on the cooperation and buy-in of local communities. Dealing with this regulatory headache, as the mines regard it, is made infinitely easier by the presence of an organized, literally invested "tribal administration" that might serve both as the legitimate voice of the affected population and as the implementing agency for social development projects that are not within their competency. But a question here: Might customary authority, by enabling the working conditions of the likes of Lonmin and assuring their regulatory compliance, actually conduce to the workers' *dis*interest? The potential for a conflict of interest between profits and people seems all too evident.

When they meet about their common concerns, global mining companies often focus, in discussing the difficulties of obtaining a "social license to mine," on the consent of the local communities affected by their operations. The concept of "community" is crucial here, since it is only vaguely defined in the statutes and regulations; in South Africa, as Kapelus (2002:280) points out, its boundaries are generally presumed to be determined by "the lines of the (*de facto*) authority of the chief" (emphasis added), who is taken, axiomatically, to be its accredited representative. But this may vary according to the grounding of chiefly legitimacy. When, for example, in August 2014, Leruo signed a memorandum with the Rustenburg Municipality promising to participate together in an initiative to improve socioeconomic conditions in the greater Rustenburg area, it was understood that his sovereignty, derived from both his customary and his corporate position, extended well beyond his twenty-nine villages.[26] By contrast, *Kumkani* Sigcau's standing appears to have hinged almost exclusively on his symbolic capital as moral and cultural authority among ama-Mpondo, although, as for all traditional rulers, as Kramer (n.d.) points out, it also depended on his ability to maintain order amongst his subjects—and to protect them from state oppression.

If one were to add "corporate oppression" here, it would make plain how delicately placed are those rulers from key labor reserves between their followers and the mining industry. On the one hand, they are well positioned to advocate for the interests of their people, both the workers and their families back home, with the union, the corporations, and the state. On the other, they tend to be seen as useful "indirect rulers" by employers; recall, again, the classic role of the colonial-era intercalary chief (p. 4). Thus, when Lonmin called a meeting with traditional leaders in the Eastern Cape on February 25, 2014, almost two years into the labor dispute on the platinum belt, they hoped to enlist their moral authority to convince striking employees from their communities to relent in their demands. The kings, including Sigcau, were addressed by public relations executives: "We are by all means trying to avoid the recurrence of the Marikana incident," one is reported to have said. Caught between their subjects' insistence on higher wages and the vague threats of the company representatives, they were reluctant to promise to call for an end to the strike. An AMCU official not present at the meeting was openly critical of Lonmin's motivations: "These are signs of frustration from management. When did they start realizing that there are traditional leaders to be consulted in the Eastern Cape?" In an apparent reference to *Kumkani* Sigcau's visit to Marikana in 2012, he added, "During the 2012 Marikana massacre the same traditional leaders flew to Marikana to reason with management in Lonmin, but management was arrogant towards them."[27]

Which brings us back to the matter of the chairs. This modest gesture of hospitality emanated from the deep respect the amaMpondo workers have for their king as a leader, a moral authority, and an emissary from their families. Recall that President Zuma and his delegation were not given chairs to sit on; nor was anyone else. In affording this singular recognition to *Kumkani* Sigcau, his people made it clear who was sovereign here. And it was not the state, the corporation, or the union. If *Kgosi* Leruo and his followers were also offered seating, it was due to their association with Sigcau. As it happened, neither king took the offer. They stood under the shade of umbrellas held by their bodyguards. But their entourages—several of them elderly men and women—did enjoy the comfort of the chairs in that alien, tense setting. Not quite a seat at the corporate table, but certainly a place of honor, legitimacy, and respect amidst so much public rage, resentment, and confusion.

Chiefs, Kings, and South Africa, Inc.

What then, do these events tell us about the role and relevance of kings and chiefs in contemporary South Africa? Ntsebeza (2005:14) would see the institution(s) banned because of the contradictions inherent in the relationship of "unelected and unaccountable traditional authorities to the country's Bill of Rights." However, those authorities seem clearly destined to survive, even thrive, in these neoliberal times. For one thing, as he observes, their "legitimacy . . . is very much associated with their position in and control of the land allocation process at the local village and tribal authority levels" (but cf. chapter 3, this volume). But it is also buttressed, as we have seen, by the ability to use their authority to broker labor relations, communal consent, and compliance. A good number of them find it possible to avail themselves of novel forms of moral capital in an age of corporate responsibility. As the Marikana case suggests, while the extractive industries need reliable, ethically legitimized access to resources on communally held land, chiefs, and the "communities" they are assumed to represent, will remain relevant and, to a greater or lesser extent, empowered.

But the legitimacy of customary rulers, especially for those whom they purport to represent—often poor rural people, underserved by the state—is not just instrumental. Nor is it limited purely to land management and labor brokerage. Speaking of the northerly reaches of South Africa, Oomen (2005:249) notes that there is "ample evidence of the local adherence to custom, chieftaincy and culture . . . and their centrality to the identity of many South Africans." She distinguishes carefully between the office, and the values it represents, and its incumbents, an issue that Turner (2014) explores with sensitivity in the North West Province (see also chapter 1, this volume). Both conclude that the institution has great purchase among those South Africans in the countryside for whom constitutional entitlements have not translated into direct experience of economic inclusion, recognition, and political respect, this notwithstanding the fact that sentiment toward, and the efficacy of, particular officeholders varies greatly. The Marikana example throws this last point into sharp relief, contrasting the roles of *Kgosi* Leruo of the Bafokeng, *Kumkani* Sigcau of the amaMpondo, and *Kgosi* Mogale of the Bapo-ba-Mogale.

Following Kramer's (n.d.) types of "basic legitimacy" wielded by traditional leaders, the kind derived from cultural affiliation and the capacity to organize their subjects' labor, voting behavior, compliance, and so on characterized the amaMpondo king's performance at Marikana (Williams 2010, in Kramer n.d.:5). Leruo's influence, by contrast, exceeds the cultural or the customary, stretching deep into the world of capital, corporate policy, and the negotiation of contracts. It enables him to take full advantage of the gap between government and the "community," and between public and private sectors, in a decentralized global economy. In short, both rulers exercise a species of authority, ratified by the exigencies of lineage and ritual ascription (see Cook and Hardin 2013), that comes from outside, and extends beyond, the hegemonic, secular state form: authority, that is, that can be deployed in various ways—at a time when the state liberalizes, outsources, and corporatizes—to rule in its stead. And to mediate between it, the customary, capital, and labor. Whether those living under indigenous leaders enjoy the full benefits of citizenship or are relegated, as artifacts of imperial history, to the status of "subjects" (Mamdani 1996), depends, it seems, on political and economic considerations. Where the state is weak and global commerce relatively unfettered, those kings and chiefs who control land with capital value, as do the Bafokeng and Bapo-ba-Mogale monarchs, are well positioned to broker rights, recognition, and resources on behalf of themselves and their constituents. Where their only asset is labor, as in Pondoland, the situation of these subjects and their leaders is much weaker—although arguably more due to the workings of the market than of the law or state power. But, in all cases, the predicament of rural South Africans today appears to be as much a function of the global dynamics of contemporary capital as it is a residue of the colonial past.

The "resurgence" of customary authority in South Africa, in sum, is best viewed not from the provisions of the law but from the balance sheets of global corporations—and from the symbolic behavior of social actors representing a range of political, economic, and sociomoral interests: aggrieved workers, migrant laborers, state presidents, corporate executives, and the kings and chiefs themselves. The "Marikana moment" strongly suggests that the enduring relevance of traditional leadership here is related to a neoliberal business environment in which extractive companies operate within a context in which the state takes a "light touch" approach to the economy, endeavoring to provide a relatively stable currency,[28] basic infrastructure, and a regulatory regime respectful of capital. In this context, there is ample room for indigenous rulers to serve as representatives and brokers of legitimacy, labor, and natural resources, even of competing forms of sovereignty, although these priorities are often incompatible with one another. One might even go so far as to say that customary authorities in South Africa are actually indispensable to the successful management of the neoliberal state, to the extent that they offer major global corporations access to resources, workers, and the "social license to operate" in ways that government alone cannot. Or, at least, some of them do. Reciprocally, moreover, in the absence of state-sponsored development or job creation, their dealings with the corporate world may bring at least some prospect of a livelihood to those who offer them loyalty and support. And who, at a moment of crisis, may offer up a chair for them to sit on.

Notes

1. There is considerable variation in the translation of vernacular terms for high office in South Africa and heated dispute in some quarters over their political connotations; elsewhere, *kgosi* is often rendered as "chief" rather than "king" (see the editorial note to this volume). As Director of Research for the Royal Bafokeng Administration at the time, I was granted permission from Leruo's office to attend this meeting and join the delegation to Marikana.
2. It is beyond the scope of this chapter to offer a detailed account of the Marikana incident. For further reading, see Alexander et al. (2012), Alexander (2013), and Breckenridge (2014).
3. "South African President Visits Mine After Police Shooting," *Deutsche Welle*, 22 August 2012, http://www.dw.de/south-african-president-visits-mine-after-police-shooting/a-16185569, accessed 11 October 2014.
4. "Bafokeng King Accompanies Traditional Leaders to Site of Marikana Tragedy," Martin Creamer, *Mining Weekly*, 24 August 2012.
5. "Mr Heath Calls Lonrho Affair 'The Unpleasant and Unacceptable Face of Capitalism,'" *Times* (London), 15 May 1973, p. 16.
6. See the home page of Lonmin plc at http://www.lonmin.com, accessed 30 November 2014.
7. RDOs are sometimes referred to as the "Kings of the Mine," in recognition of their

critical function in the extractive process. They use jackhammers to loosen the rock in the deepest crawl spaces of shafts that extend 1,000 feet beneath the surface. Undertaking some of the hardest jobs in the mining sector, they are also among the best paid underground workers. See "The 2012 Strike Wave, Marikana and the History of Rock Drillers in South Africa," Paul Stewart, *Global Labour Column*, January 2013, http://connection.ebscohost.com/c/articles/90174420/2012-strike-wave -marikana-history-rock-drillers-south-african-mines, accessed 11 October 2014.

8.   The NUM was founded in 1982, with Cyril Ramaphosa as its first general secretary. It is an affiliate of the Congress of South African Trade Unions, which, along with the African Nationalist Congress and the Communist Party, comprises the tripartite alliance that governs the country. Ramaphosa became deputy president of South Africa in 2014. A businessman with mining interests, he also has a seat on the board of Lonmin plc.

9.   Evidence presented at the Marikana Commission of Inquiry suggests that between 545 and 718 police personnel were deployed to the site from 10–16 August 2012. See Marikana Commission of Inquiry, Phase Two Preliminary Report, 15 August 2014.

10. "The Murder Field of Marikana: The Cold Murder Fields of Marikana," Greg Marinovich, *Daily Maverick*, 8 September 2012, http://www.dailymaverick.co.za/article/ 2012–08–30-the-murder-fields-of-marikana-the-cold-murder-fields-of-marikana# .VusU3qTD8iQ, accessed 30 November 2014.

11. "Mining Strikes Shrink South Africa's Economy," Alice Tidey, *CNBC.com*, 28 May 2014, http://www.cnbc.com/2014/05/28/, accessed 30 November 2014.

12. See St. Johns Municipality, *Statistics South Africa*, 29 April 2015, http://www.statssa .gov.za/?page_id=993&id=port-st-johns-municipality, accessed 30 May 2015.

13. This followed the findings of the Nhlapo Commission, released in 2010, and discussed in chapter 4 of this volume. See "Game of Thrones in Mpondo House," Lulamile Feni, *DispatchLive.co.za*, 28 June 2013, http://www.dispatchlive.co.za/ news/game-of-thrones-in-mpondo-house/, accessed 1 November 2014 (no longer online).

14. "Revenge of the Commons: The Crisis in the South African Mining Industry," Keith Breckenridge, *History Workshop Online*, 5 November 2012, http://www .historyworkshop.org.uk/revenge-of-the-commons-the-crisis-in-the-south-african -mining-industry/, accessed 12 November 2015.

15. See Royal Bafokeng Administration's Population and Use of Land Audit (PULA), Section 1, 2012, http://www.bafokengarchives.com/sites/default/files/publications/ Pula%202011%20A.pdf, accessed 30 November 2014.

16. Ibid.

17. "Platinum Wealth Holds No Shine for People Left in the Dust," Heidi Swart, *Mail & Guardian*, 29 June 2012, http://mg.co.za/article/2012–06–28-platinum-wealth-holds -no-shine-for-people-left-living-in-the-dust, accessed 31 May 2015.

18. See "Lonmin Inks Landmark BEE Deals with Traditional Community," Natalie Greve, *Mining Weekly*, 30 July 2014, http://www.miningweekly.com/article/lonmin -inks-landmark-bee-deals-with-traditional-community-2014-07-30, accessed 30 May 2015.

19. "On the record with Hugh Eiser and Brendan Boyle," Brendan Boyle, *South African Crime Quarterly* 49, September 2014, http://dx.doi.org/10.4314/sacq.v49i1.6, accessed 12 November 2015.

20. "Bapo-ba-Mogale Want Court Action over Mining Strike," *News24*, 8 June 2014,

http://www.news24.com/SouthAfrica/News/Bapo-ba-Mogale-want-court-action -over-mining-strike-20140608, accessed 21 November 2014.

21. See Marikana Commission of Inquiry, Phase Two Preliminary Report, 15 August 2014.
22. Royal Bafokeng Administration's Population and Use of Land Audit (PULA), Section 1, pp. 11–12.
23. Marikana Commission of Inquiry, 2014, p. 44.
24. Ibid., p. 42.
25. See http://www.bafokengholdings.com/, accessed 21 November 2014.
26. "Applause as Bafokeng Leader Inks Pact," Kennedy Mudzuli, *IOL News*, 15 August 2014, http://www.iol.co.za/news/south-africa/north-west/applause-as-bafokeng -leader-inks-pact-1735968, accessed 21 November 2014.
27. "Mines Ask Kings to End Strike," Lulamile Feni, *DispatchLive.co.za*, 26 February 2014, http://www.dispatchlive.co.za/news/mines-ask-kings-to-end-strike/, accessed 31 May 2015 (no longer online).
28. The importance of such regulatory functions is evident in the breach: when, in December 2015, the already-skittish South African rand plummeted in value—due in part to the sudden firing by the president of his finance minister—corporate leaders raised a clamor of objection, threatening to move their capital to a more viable context of operation.

References

Alexander, Peter , Thapelo Lekgowa, Botsang Mmope, Luke Sinwell, and Bongani Xezwi
    2012   *Marikana: A View from the Mountain and a Case to Answer*. Auckland Park, South Africa: Jacana Media.
    2013   *Marikana: Voices from South Africa's Mining Massacre*. Athens, OH: Ohio University Press.
Beinart, William
    1982   *The Political Economy of Pondoland, 1860–1930*. Cambridge: Cambridge University Press.
Breckenridge, Keith
    2014   Marikana and the Limits of Biopolitics: Themes in the Recent Scholarship of South African Mining. *Africa* 84(1):151–61.
Breutz, P. L.
    1953   *The Tribes of Rustenburg and Pilansberg Districts*. Pretoria: Government Printer.
    1989   *A History of the Batswana and Origin of Bophuthatswana: A Handbook of a Survey of the Tribes of the Batswana, S. Ndebele, Qwaqwa and Botswana*. Ramsgate, South Africa: P. L. Breutz [private publication].
Coertze, R. D.
    1988   *Bafokeng Family Law and Law of Succession*. Pretoria: Sabra.
Comaroff, Jean, and John L. Comaroff
    1991   *Of Revelation and Revolution*, vol. 1, *Christianity, Colonialism, and Consciousness in South Africa*. Chicago: University of Chicago Press.
    2003   Reflections on Liberalism, Policulturalism, and ID-ology: Citizenship and Difference in South Africa. *Social Identities* 9(4):445–73.
Comaroff, John L., and Jean Comaroff
    1997   *Of Revelation and Revolution*, vol. 2, *The Dialectics of Modernity on a South African Frontier*. Chicago: University of Chicago Press.
    2009   *Ethnicity, Inc.* Chicago: University of Chicago Press.

Cook, Susan, and Rebecca Hardin
  2013   Performing Royalty in Contemporary Africa. *Cultural Anthropology* 28(2):227–51.
Crais, Clifton
  2006   Custom and the Politics of Sovereignty in South Africa. *Journal of Social History* 39(3):721–40.
Gluckman, Max, J. Clyde Mitchell, and John Barnes
  1949   The Village Headman in British Central Africa. *Africa* 19(2):89–106.
Kapelus, Paul
  2002   Mining, Corporate Social Responsibility, and the 'Community': The Case of Rio Tinto, Richards Bay Minerals, and the Mbonambi. *Journal of Business Ethics* 39:275–96.
Krämer, Mario
  n.d.   Competitive Chieftaincy, the State, and the ANC: Power and Basic Legitimacy of *Ubukhosi* in KwaZulu-Natal, South Africa. Paper presented at the African Studies Workshop, Harvard University, 9 February 2015.
Legassick, Martin
  1969   The Sotho-Tswana Peoples before 1800. In *African Societies in Southern Africa*, Leonard Thompson, ed. New York: Praeger.
Mamdani, Mahmood
  1996   *Citizen and Subject: Contemporary Africa and the Legacy of Late Colonialism*. Princeton, NJ: Princeton University Press.
Manson, Andrew, and Bernard Mbenga
  2003   'The Richest Tribe in Africa': Platinum Mining and the Bafokeng in South Africa's North West Province, 1965–1999. *Journal of Southern African Studies* 29(1):25–47.
Mbenga, Bernard, and Andrew Manson
  2010   *'People of the Dew': A History of the Bafokeng of Phokeng-Rustenburg Region, South Africa, from Early Times to 2000*. Auckland Park, South Africa: Jacana Media.
Ntsebeza, Lungisile
  2005   *Democracy Compromised: Chiefs and the Politics of the Land in South Africa*. Leiden: Brill.
Oomen, Barbara
  2005   *Chiefs in South Africa: Law, Power and Culture in the Post-Apartheid Era*. Oxford: James Currey.
Schapera, Isaac
  1943   *Native Land Tenure in the Bechuanaland Protectorate*. Botswana: Lovedale Press.
  1952   *The Ethnic Composition of Tswana Tribes*. No. 11, London School of Economics and Political Science Monographs on Social Anthropology.
Schapera, Isaac, and John L. Comaroff
  1991   *The Tswana*, rev. ed. London: Kegan Paul International.
Turner, Robin L.
  2014   Traditional, Democratic, Accountable? Navigating Citizen-Subjection in Rural South Africa. *Africa Spectrum* 49(1):27–54.
Williams, J. Michael
  2010   *Chieftaincy, the State, and Democracy: Political Legitimacy in Post-Apartheid South Africa*. Bloomington, IN: Indiana University Press.

NINE

The Currency of Chieftaincy

Corporate Branding and the Commodification
of Political Authority in Ghana

LAUREN ADROVER

On the evening of September 3, 2011, the streets of Cape Coast, Ghana, were abuzz with public jubilation: youth displayed the latest dance moves to music blaring from small shops, families congregated at local outdoor restaurants, and elders sat outside their homes excitedly hailing passersby with the customary festival greeting, *"Afenhyia pa!"* (the year has passed). The crowds, varied in age, gender, and profession, and swelled by visitors from elsewhere in the nation and beyond, had taken to the streets for the town's annual *Fetu Afahye*, a festival observed by Fante-speaking Akan. Its spectacular displays of song, dance, and gunfire celebrated the harvest and paid homage to regional chiefs who presided over the area. A highlight of the day was a well-choreographed procession in which these local leaders were borne through the town in regal palanquins, dressed in their finest ceremonial cloth and royal adornments—gold necklaces, rings, and crowns. This spectacle was a key feature of an annual festivity that permitted chiefs dramatically to perform their authority.

Although the royal procession had concluded at four o'clock in the afternoon, the chiefs were ready to present themselves to the public once more. After retiring to their homes for a while, they appeared again, adorned in another costly ceremonial costume, and headed for the State Dance in the "Town Hall." All chiefs within the Cape Coast jurisdiction were required to attend this official event, intended to offer festivalgoers the opportunity to greet their leaders, acknowledge their authority, and offer good wishes for the coming year. But on this occasion, the chiefs sat in an almost empty banquet room. Less than a dozen visitors had arrived. The chiefs grew increasingly bored, impatient, and annoyed, their frustrations fanned by the sound system blaring from a nearby free concert, where collective cries of adoration were being expressed by the crowd for the latest Accra-based hiplife[1] artist, performing live. The State Dance and the chiefs had been up-staged. The attention of over one thousand festival participants was being drawn by a corporate sponsored event called "Festival Train," rather than by the chiefs who claim ownership over the festival.

Festival Train is a free, nationally televised music concert that is sponsored by Tigo, a multinational telecommunications firm, in collaboration with TV3, one of Ghana's leading broadcasting companies. The corporate event was held during the annual, week-long *Fetu Afahye* festival to benefit from the large crowds it drew. Popular artists with hit singles were brought in from Accra to perform on a professional stage equipped with high amplification and sophisticated lighting. Event coordinators intended the concert to establish a culturally mediated public forum that would draw attention to their brand and promote Tigo's signature services—sending money, making long-distance calls, and so on. Each year, the company selects ten festivals in major towns to launch Festival Train. In that manner, Tigo representatives seek to appropriate the spatiotemporal context of the annual harvest festival—an occasion that recognizes lineage networks, political hierarchies, and cosmological cycles—to promote a set of values centering on commerce, consumption, and the cultivation of brand-consumer relations.

In this chapter, I analyze how a multinational telecommunications firm used the material culture and collective sociality of chiefly celebrations to attach new values to their brands and elaborate their corporate identity.[2] Yet this is not just a case of culture being commodified or traditions being invented. Rather, I suggest, it points to new ways in which global companies operating in Ghana seek to make their brands locally identifiable. In appealing to the political authority of chieftaincy to do this, they go beyond the practices adopted by most marketing professionals to forge a "cultural brand" (Holt 2004). And this created novel tensions. For while both chiefs and sponsors promote the discourse that "chiefs are the custodians of culture," sponsors actually seek to position themselves as analogous to chiefs, displaying symbolic and material references to chiefship alongside corporate logos. I argue that chiefs must thus compete with brand advertisers, who seek to appropriate the forms of cultural production—and the charisma—associated with chieftaincy in order to retain control over a site crucial to the reproduction of their political authority and popular appeal in contemporary Ghana.

While the influence of Akan[3] chiefs in Ghana extends across various domains, they remain synonymous with "culture." Festivals like *Fetu Afahye*, celebrated by Akan communities throughout Ghana, are key sites where chiefs perform their cultural authority. Yet, the increasing presence of corporate sponsors has prompted chiefs to express disapproval of the ways that this threatens to violate "traditional protocol"—described as the rules and norms that govern the production of culture, epitomized in performances that dramatize a community's customs and ideas. Culture, in this sense, is less a "thing" to be preserved than a position in a "field," in Pierre Bourdieu's sense, in which different parties jockey for "ownership" and the political and economic benefits this confers (Bourdieu 1993). In this way, discourses about legitimacy—who really promotes and preserves culture—mask fundamental inequalities that have always been a feature of the field of festivals here (Brown 2003).[4] Bourdieu's notion of a field requires that we understand how ideological statements such as "chiefs are custodians of culture" actively give form to the stakes, dispositions, and values that organize any given field and the ways in which chiefs and sponsors operate within it.

If chiefs participate in festivals to shore up their customary sovereignty, corporate sponsors seek to cultivate emotional and symbolic associations between consumers and their brands (Foster 2007). Recent anthropological approaches to the study of branding practices have given much analytical attention to the symbolic universe constructed by specific brands and their connection to wider local and translocal markets (Manning 2010). Brands have been defined as meta-symbols (Miller 1998), conceptual extensions of products (Arvidsson 2006; Askegard 2006), and privileged semiotic objects (Lury 2004), and so on. I draw upon such semiotic treatments of brands by examining the symbolic fields of cultural difference that they conjure (Coombe 1996), but I go further, by focusing on how branding practices seek actively to transform power relationships and compete for alliances, in this case among chiefs, sponsors, and festival audiences.

I begin with a brief history of the emergence of corporate sponsorship, outlining how multinational firms have become positioned as key economic actors and cultural producers within the field of festivals in Ghana.

Chiefs, Corporate Sponsors, and the Field of Festivals

Festivals have long held both cultural and political-economic significance in Ghana. In the Gold Coast, they were refashioned as colonial spectacles to assert the legitimacy of British authority while incorporating Africans into indirect rule (Cohn 1983; Apter 2005). After Ghana's independence in 1957, President Kwame Nkrumah used them to promote ideologies of nationalism and national culture (Coe 2005; Cole 2001; Collins 2007). With economic liberalization in the 1980s, state-sponsored festivals were re-fashioned as private-sector performances promoting corporate brands and global commodities. Coca-Cola, Guinness, and SAB Miller are among the long list of corporate sponsors who currently underwrite festival produc-tion in Ghana. Increasingly, multinational firms working in telecommuni-cations industries, such as Vodafone, MTN, and Tigo, provide the bulk of the finance that sustains ceremonial events.[5]

Corporate sponsors seek to capitalize upon cultural distinctions by as-sociating festivals with particular forms of commodity consumption (Da-vila 1997; Foster 2002; Guss 2000). Sponsorship is broadly directed toward the creation of *economic* value. Yet a plurality of value forms—material, af-fective, social, and symbolic—must be mobilized to optimize the transac-tions that yield economic gain. New forms of sponsorship and the rise of brand advertising during festivals are key examples of the ways in which global economic changes impact local experience. "Customary" events that are sponsored and, most recently, *invented* by multinationals demonstrate how relations between chiefs and their communities are refashioned via new contexts of consumption that combine corporate branding with pub-lic cultural production (Davila 1997).

Festivals are key sites for the production of culture, that is, performances popularly perceived as representing the sum of a community's customs and ideas. I use the term culture to refer to the way that Ghanaians assess, and make explicit claims to, the cultural, rather than to signal an anthropologi-cal sense of the term. The many senses of culture in play throughout this chapter reflect the usage of those who wield it for their own purposes and the varied essences, attachments, and allegiances they attach to the con-struct (Coe 2005). While some chiefs defined culture as the culmination of customs, ideas, and traditions that they themselves embodied during annual festivals, others broadened their definitions to include the mun-dane practices of everyday life centered around family obligations, food, and greetings. Corporate sponsors, on the other hand, often used culture to imply collective dispositions that could be easily objectified for the mar-ket (Chanock 2000).

Cape Coast residents identify as ethnically Fante, a linguistic subgroup of the Akan, with a unique set of performance traditions. In discussion, many see the contemporary content of culture as vested primarily in chiefs and festivals. During annual harvest festivals, chiefs dress in royal regalia that visually assert their wealth and cultural provenance and display cer-emonial accoutrements—swords, umbrellas, and palanquins—explicitly associated, in Cape Coast communities, with "traditional culture."

Since the late nineteenth and early twentieth centuries, ethnolinguistic groups in the south of Ghana have benefitted from political representation by popular figures who have promoted the prominence of Akan communities and elevated their rituals to the level of national cultural iconography. Well-known nationalists such as Kofi Busia and J. B. Danquah emphasized the organized power and noble traditions of the Akan (Busia 1951). When Ghana became a republic in 1960, Nkrumah marked the event by staging an elaborate parade that mimicked a ceremonial procession of chiefs (Hess 2001:65). The careful orchestration of political regalia and formal Akan music asserted a parallel between the authority of Nkrumah and the power of the Ashanti king (ibid.).

At the time of my research in 2011, the Ghanaian government, which was withdrawing public funding for cultural projects, actively encouraged corporate involvement in festivals. The director of the National Commission of Culture explained: "The government has its role, but the monetary aspect is the problem. Now we have the big companies celebrating with us. Their support goes a long way. We want even more sponsors."[6] With little to no funding available, most chiefs accept corporate support, despite the control that these companies exercise on the material and performative content of festivals. Indeed, it is almost impossible for those who aim to celebrate their festivals and promote their own political positions to do so without corporate financial support. While chiefs are presumed to possess assets in the form of land, much of that land has been sold, acquired by international companies, or is held among a select number of families (Berry 2013). Other sources of chiefly revenue—court fines, levies, etc.— are insufficient to support chiefs and the expenses of maintaining the office. Higher education has become one route to ascension to the stool;[7] some chiefs are professors, architects, attorneys, accountants, and business executives. Many engage in international development initiatives and work to attract investment resources to their areas (Kleist 2011; see chapter 1, this volume). Increasingly, they look to corporate institutions to finance their festivals and entrepreneurial projects.

Yet while chiefs use festivals to publicize their political authority, corporate sponsors challenge their politically distinctive form of authority by overshadowing it with the economic marks of the market. Commodity images and brand-name logos create new forms of social and economic recognition among those who take part in festival celebrations. This is evidenced by the pervasive presence of advertisements during festivals. For example, company logos from the likes of Vodafone, Tigo, and MTN are displayed on T-shirts, large posters on the walls of buildings, and vans covered with colorful advertisements. Now chiefs who used to "own" their local festivals struggle to control sponsors' invasive marketing tactics. More than this: sponsors seek to actually appropriate their authority, to put their logo on its charisma, as it were. When I asked one chief for his view on sponsor advertisements, he responded by reframing my question: "You are asking, are we celebrating a traditional festival or are we advertising for a company? I've presented this same concern to the festival's planning committee. It looks like we are here to promote some sponsor's products, but it is the chiefs who should be the main focus."

Corporate sponsors are also active participants in negotiations over how festivals should be constituted. The brand manager for Star Beer at Guinness Ghana Breweries Ltd. explained their role:

> We were one of the first to go after festivals. . . . Twenty years ago it was nothing. It was just a group of people who came home for their rituals. Star Beer picked it up and made a real thing out of it. For the *durbar* [public ceremony] of chiefs we hired canopies, chairs, transportation, everything. We gave them banners, signboards, branded T-shirts, drinks, and money. We introduced a beauty pageant, football match, live music, all that. Now it's big. We started it. We made that festival.[8]

Sponsors, therefore, do not only reshape the content of existing ritual events. They reconfigure them so as to enhance their marketing potential. A representative from Ghana's largest telecommunications firm explained:

> Each year I send my people to talk to the chiefs and ask: "What day will the festival come up? Have you set up a festival committee? Who is chairing the committee? Can we talk about possible activities so we know how to figure them out?" In these cases, we are in the driving seat.[9]

Sponsors are unanimous as to the potential of these events as generative marketing platforms that can be harnessed to create strategic relations between persons and brands.

Tigo Festival Train, 2011

Tigo Festival Train is a key example of a newly invented corporate event that marks the rise of an emergent trend whereby brand producers expand the "space" of marketing beyond traditional sites for advertising (Moore 2003). Such events aim to establish new ways of engaging with consumers, using chiefly festivals to encourage affective connections with brands. Tigo, as I noted earlier, is a mobile telecommunications service provider. It was introduced in Ghana in 1991 as a subsidiary of Millicom International Cellular, which is based in Luxembourg. Tigo provides mobile phone and Internet services in over thirteen countries across three continents and is the second largest telecom company in Ghana, claiming some four million subscribers. It promotes a brand identity centered on youthfulness, sociality, and leisure. According to its mission statement, the aim of the brand is to "provide services for people who want to be in touch, belong to communities, and to be informed and entertained, enabling them to express their emotions and enhance their lives."[10]

Tigo's marketing and brand management personnel with whom I consulted tended to belong to Ghana's burgeoning urban elite—men and women between the ages of twenty-eight and forty-two, who were university educated at home and abroad. These characteristics contrasted with the socioeconomically diverse audiences who attended festivals at Cape Coast, about whose tastes the brand producers probably knew relatively little. Above all, it was presumed that a diverse audience would be attracted by the offer of free entertainment. Tigo representatives explained that they hoped that, with a focus on live music by popular artists, they would draw the youth. Yet the actual participants I observed varied widely in age and economic status, ranging from secondary school and university students to shopkeepers and informal vendors.

The event organizers literally set the stage for creating strategic associations between the Tigo brand and Festival Train participants, this through the medium of material culture and performative and discursive references that elaborated a brand identity in explicitly customary terms. The concert was performed in the central square, where chiefs had gathered the night before to ritually slaughter a bull for the collective purification of the town and its residents.[11] In preparation for Festival Train, a professional-quality stage transformed the square into a site for a well-appointed corporate event. A huge banner, in the company's trademark blue, created the backdrop for the stage. The Tigo logo was featured in the center, large white lower-case letters spelling "Tigo" in a soft and playful font; an opened letter "u" underscored the "g" and "o," creating the image of a smile. An upside down letter "u" rested above the "o," forming an eyebrow, the added characters transforming the right side of the logo into an emoticon representing a smiley face and the wink of an eye. The banner evoked the youthfulness and sociality the brand sought to promote, with its laughing eyes peering into the crowd and the wink begging recognition from audience members.

Concert hosts advertised Tigo services in between performances by each artist. A main promotional focus was "Tigo Cash," a financial product that allows subscribers to use their mobile phones as a bank account. As the program hosts reminded patrons, "now you can use your mobile phone to send money from anywhere and to anyone in Ghana—for free!" When the stage was clear, the sound technician played prerecorded audio commercials advertising Tigo. Company representatives made their way through the dense crowds throughout the event, distributing promotional gift items such as pins and key rings and advertisements about product offers or new services. In sum, the audience at Festival Train took part in a festival event that focused on the promotion of the Tigo brand and the production of consumers, rather than the recognition of Cape Coast chiefs and the reproduction of their subjects.

Local cultural artifacts were carefully positioned on the stage against the corporate backdrop: a royal chieftaincy throne, a ceremonial sword, and *fontomfrom* drums among them. Hand-woven *kente* cloth was draped over large speakers. Each object made reference to the beliefs and practices of Akan chieftaincy: the wooden throne is associated with state power and royalty; the ceremonial sword and *kente* cloth are both forms of regalia that identify rulers, enhance their social status, and demonstrate their link to ancestral power; and the *fontomfrom* are ritual drums used to praise royals and communicate their presence. Tigo event coordinators used these ceremonial objects to acknowledge, through the practice of appropriation, chieftaincy and the ritual authority marked by the festival. But these objects were also profoundly out of place on the corporate stage, their meanings abstracted and redirected toward the ends of corporate branding. Tigo's special events coordinator explained that these "props," as he called them, were used to cultivate a brand identity that resonates with cultural registers recognized by the Fante-speaking Akan who celebrate the *Fetu Afahye* festival:

> We use props on stage to show that the festival is on and that it's not just about music but about the celebration of the culture of the people. We put traditional *fontomfrom* drums on stage with chieftaincy stools and swords. We even had some drummers come out wearing *kente* cloth. It creates a key connecting moment with the brand. These are key things that people love to see, so we create a platform to make that happen. This is where brand loyalty and brand affinity comes into play.[12]

For Tigo representatives, as well as numerous other sponsors with whom I spoke, the meaning—and power—of culture had much to do with performing arts and public display; consequently, these local performance moments were key to creating a "connecting moment" with their brand. Sponsors' definitions of culture echoed a popular phrase often used as a synonym for the same thing in Ghana in the 1960s and 1970s: "drumming and dancing" (Coe 2005). Indeed, as I have noted, the strategic redeployment of these ritual performances, especially those associated with chiefly authority, are by no means new in Ghanaian history.

Yet there are differences between these earlier deployments and corporate methods of representation that, being more explicitly geared towards economic profit, point to the ways in which the logic of commodification establishes exchange relations between economic and cultural capital. The corporate spectacle co-opted specific local performances and material forms, recasting them as objectified cultural types and features of a corporate identity. The staging of Tigo's corporate identity echoes Jean and John Comaroff's (2009) notion of an identity economy whereby the ceremonial aspects of chieftaincy are both commodified, "made into the basis of *value-added* corporate collectivity, and claimed as the basis of shared emotion, shared lifestyle. . ." (p. 2). Moreover, it is not just that culture is being commodified but that the corporate brand is rendered explicitly cultural in ways that have real economic and political consequences (Comaroff and Comaroff 2009).

Sponsors engaged in cultural appropriation by aligning the content of local cultural practices with corporate brands. Beyond adorning the Tigo branded stage with ethnically Akan material forms, sponsors adapted other locally resonant practices to establish emotional connections between consumers and brands. Musicians from Cape Coast were invited to perform songs in Fante that incorporated regional influences and dance styles. The rhythms of the *fontomfrom* and side drums were prominent in the performances of local musicians. In advance of their performances, musicians were encouraged to reference Tigo in their lyrics. Those who obliged helped to advance Tigo's mission to fuse the content of popular cultural practices with corporate brands. Moreover, patrons were also active participants. They danced in sync with the beats of Akan drums and both initiated and replied to lyrical exchanges of call and response. Performers used other local references to excite crowds and signal regional affiliation. Some shouted out the customary festival greeting, "*afenhyia pa.*" Situated practices marked with concrete local references were not limited to local artists. The headliner for the 2011 Festival Train event was the popular Accra-based hiplife musician Eduwoji. He wore several colorful strands of glass beads around his neck and wrists, which is a common mode of adornment among chiefs.

He also wrapped *kente* cloth around his waist in lieu of trousers.[13] In these ways, Tigo sought to cultivate its corporate identity by creating a venue in which it could be associated, via the transformative power of cultural performance, with the cultural signifiers associated with chieftaincy.

Corporate Culture and Its Discontents

Many patrons of Festival Train donned the company's branded garments during the concert and spoke approvingly of the company as a socially responsible brand that fostered local culture. A member of the audience expressed approval of the presence of "drums, canoes, and chiefly symbols" on stage, and commended the corporation for allowing "us, the youth, to get to know parts of our culture" and "help spread the word, even outside this area." There is evidence, here, not merely of how the corporate brand becomes explicitly cultural (above) but of the fact that the company assumes the role of revaluing and reproducing that culture in its own name—not merely for its original producers, but for a wider market (Comaroff and Comaroff 2009).

For their part, the chiefs claimed that Festival Train exemplified how sponsors exploit festivals by transforming sites intended for political ritual into spaces for brand advertising. Nana Kwabena, a chief who has played a central role in organizing the festival for the past thirty years, put it thus:

> I am not against Tigo! I am not against Tigo as I am not against Guinness or Vodafone or MTN or any corporate bodies. My job is the planning and execution of the festival. By telling us you have supported us does not mean that Cape Coast is yours! At the end of the day it is about being able to sustain the life of the festival.[14]

A queen mother shared a similar view: "The brands are in focus more than the chiefs. Soon the essence of the festival and our traditions will be lost, lost to corporate sponsors."

In fact, almost all Cape Coast chiefs questioned were critical of Tigo and the production of Festival Train. Their dismay opened up a space for critique, not simply about Festival Train but about the activities of other corporations as well. While some concert patrons certainly approved of Tigo and their stated commitment to promote the cultural values of the community, the royals viewed the sponsors' interventions as having the opposite impact: not as promoting cultural values but rather as degrading them by drawing attention toward brand advertising and away from the intended focus of the festival, namely themselves and their office.

Herein lies a key contradiction linked to Tigo's brand marketing: by appealing to culture, by associating with symbols of chieftaincy, and by refashioning the very context in which that "culture" is perceived to be embodied, corporations transform the field that they aim to appropriate by insinuating themselves into it. Tigo's staged affiliation with chieftaincy through the use of *kente*, drums, and other material and embodied significata epitomizes this contradiction. On the one hand, the sponsored performance explicitly invoked symbols of local political authority to elaborate a brand identity in a way that underscores local cultural sensibilities. Yet, on the other, the representatives of the corporation disregarded that royal authority by scheduling the Festival Train at the same time as the State Dance, the event hosted by chiefs, an event intended to publically assert their sovereignty.

For their part, corporate sponsors claimed that their participation in festivals set up a mutually beneficial relation between cultural and commercial enterprise. True, the company was motivated by economics: festivals were venues for marketing that aimed at establishing relationships between consumers and brands. But their sponsorship also had to do with establishing social connections with chiefs and communities and with publicizing their support for "local culture." A marketing associate at Tigo explained:

> From our perspective, *festivals are not a purely commercial venture.* We identify with the traditional area as well as the authorities [chiefs]. Relationships are built. In the case of sponsorship, it is not something where you always get immediate returns. Even though we generate a lot of money, at the end of the day, you realize *it is more a social intervention.* One lasting effect we aim for is getting people to feel the brand and later request it when the festival is long over (emphasis added).[15]

Festivals, in sum, are sites that demonstrate the inseparability of cultural and economic values. Sponsors defined "social interventions" as moments when they could demonstrate, via financial donations, their commitment to Ghanaian culture; because Ghanaians loved their culture, they believed, it followed that corporations should be presented as sharing that love, concern, and emotional attachment. Here the underlying connection between culture and visions of corporate branding becomes clear: "culture" is perceived and framed as an animating force with affective dimensions that might resonate with the sensibilities of brands and, by extension, person-brand relations. Marketers repeatedly emphasized that branding activities must create "strategic links" between consumers and commodities, links that foster "emotional connections," allowing people to "get a feeling for the brand" and ultimately "trigger desires for brand-name goods." It was precisely because the sponsoring corporations were aware of the popular, affectively laden association between chiefs and culture that they sought to establish an identity within local cultural registers. The sovereignty of chiefs was manifested in the reciprocal relations of beneficence and recognition that exist between them and their subjects, and it is this relationship in essence that corporate sponsors seek to establish between would-be consumers and their brand. At the same time, by upstaging royal authority, and their role as the custodians of culture, do these sponsors not risk undermining the very charisma from which they seek to draw strength?

Conclusion

All the chiefs I spoke with, to reiterate, were highly critical of the Tigo Festival Train and its place in the annual *Fetu Afahye* in contemporary Cape Coast. For present purposes, what is important about their agitation over it—and, in particular, their distress over the scheduling conflict it occasioned—was that it opened a space for critique about corporate sponsorship at large. Unlike some patrons, chiefs viewed sponsors not as promoting cultural values but as degrading them by drawing the ethos of festivals toward brand advertising and away from traditional authority. Both the chiefs and the corporations agreed that the local rulers are the custodians of culture. But the royal rulers complained that the latter only promoted that culture to further their economic interests. At the same time, because of a lack of other means of support, these rulers have become ever more dependent on cooperate support to sustain the elaborate rituals central to the reproduction of their authority. And herein lies the irony: the chiefs were disgruntled because they claimed that festivals and related forms of cultural production had always been their sovereign domains, vehicles *they* used to promote their own interests; now they were forced to compete with corporate sponsors to exercise control over these same events. As one of them explained: "Sponsors make their cash donations and think they can take the event for themselves. It is not correct. It is the chiefs who own the festival." In this way, discourses about who really promoted and preserved "culture" index fundamental inequalities, and struggles, that have always been a feature of festivals and the various actors who exploit them toward their own divergent ends (Brown 2003). Most recently, the challenge to chiefly authority comes from assertive corporate marketers who seek, by taking full charge of the material and symbolic markers of that authority, to appropriate it so as to animate their branded goods with the attachment and loyalty it customarily imbues.

Chiefs, by contrast and in opposition, struggle to retain control over the form and execution of the spectacular ritual complex that is central to the public affirmation of their authority and supreme legitimacy as "custodians of culture." But their ownership of such cultural capital is increasingly challenged by their reliance on corporate economic support to stage the rituals that give it life. Meanwhile, their corporate sponsors face their own contradictions. In seeking to take hold of the authority of the chiefs, and assume their role as animators and perpetuators of culture, the companies might indeed produce new loyalties and allegiances, propelled by the effort to fix their identity to royal signs and objects. But, just as Tigo's Festival Train sported the simulacra of chiefly authority without chiefs and produced a "nontraditional" kind of local culture, so companies risk banalizing the very charisma they seek to draw upon. The invention of corporate-sponsored festival events, then, has both short- and long-term implications for the sovereignty of chiefs. In the short term, chiefs, who have limited venues in which to perform their authority and secure the allegiance of diverse constituents, must devise new ways to attract popular attention, while simultaneously putting restrictions on sponsors who disregard their claims to ownership over festival events. In the long term, the very nature of chiefly authority itself is at stake. If corporate sponsorship continues at the rapid pace established over the past several years, the allegiance of many festival patrons is likely to weigh in favor of corporate institutions. But this, as I have suggested, might turn out to be a pyrrhic victory, for in their eagerness to possess the animating power of the chiefship, and all that it bequeaths, the corporations risk killing the very ineffable force they hope will give vital lifeblood to their own enterprise.

Acknowledgments

I am grateful to the many Cape Coast chiefs, festival patrons, and corporate representatives who graciously offered me their time and insights. I am also grateful to Karen Tranberg Hansen, Robert Launay, Jessica Winegar, and Brooke Bocast for their thoughtful feedback. The fieldwork on which this chapter is based was supported by the Fulbright Foundation and Northwestern University, and preliminary research was supported by the University of California, Los Angeles. Earlier versions of this chapter were presented the 2014 African Studies Conference at Harvard University and the 2012 American Anthropological Association annual meeting in San Francisco. I thank those audiences for stimulating comments and questions that contributed to the present version.

Notes

1. Hiplife is a popular music genre that emerged in Accra during the 1990s. Hiplife music combines American hiphop and Ghanaian highlife (see also Collins 2007; Shipley 2009).

2. This chapter draws on extensive multisited fieldwork conducted in Ghana (2006, 2009, 2011, 2013) focusing on festivals and the political economy of cultural production. Over the course of my research, I collected over 100 ethnographic interviews with a variety of persons related to festival performances including chiefs, audiences, members of festival planning committees, and corporate sponsors, among others. Other methods included archival research, collection of oral histories, and participant observation.

3. The Akan are the largest ethnolinguistic group in Ghana, residing in the southern regions of the country. Their languages include Twi and Fante and various regional dialects such as Asante Twi and Akwapim Twi. The Akan subgroups share several attributes such as tracing of descent, inheritance of property, and succession to political office.

4. I thank Robert Launay for drawing my attention to this useful insight.

5. A number of national companies, such as Protector Condoms and Paramount Distilleries Ltd., also contribute funds. Local business owners living in towns in which festivals are celebrated often make small monetary donations as well.

6. Interview, January 9, 2011.

7. "Stool" refers to the chiefly seat, its symbolic embodiment of chiefly sovereignty, and the political organization of which it is the apex. For more on the history and development of Akan political organizations, see Arhin (2002), McCaskie (1995), and Wilks (1993).

8. Interview, April 26, 2011.

9. Corporate agents hire persons to conduct "fieldwork" at festival sites months before events are celebrated in order to learn about chieftaincy disputes, when the festival will be held, and other relevant social and political dynamics. Branding activities are thus well researched.

10. See http://www.millicom.com/where-we-operate/ghana.

11. For more on the symbolism of the bull sacrifice and the history of *Fetu Afahye*, see Apter (n.d.).

12. Interview, November 5, 2011.

13. Beads and *kente* are linked to Akan chieftaincy and have been appropriated and redeployed in various national and commercial contexts.

14. Interview, August 31, 2011.

15. Interview, March 3, 2011.

References

Apter, Andrew

    2005   *The Pan-African Nation: Oil and the Spectacle of Culture in Nigeria.* Chicago: University of Chicago Press.

    n.d.   History in the Dungeon: Atlantic History and the Spirit of Capitalism in Cape Coast Castle, Ghana. Paper presented at the African Studies Workshop, Harvard University, 2 February 2014.

Arhin, Kwame

    2002   *The Political Systems of Ghana: Background to Transformations in Traditional Authority in the Colonial and Post-Colonial Periods.* Accra: Historical Society of Ghana.

Arvidsson, Adam

    2006   *Brands: Meaning and Value in Media Culture.* London: Routledge.

Askegard, Soren

    2006   Brands as a Global Ideoscape. In *Brand Culture,* Jonathan E Schroeder and Miriam Salzer-Morling, eds. London: Routledge.

Berry, Sara

    2013   Questions of Ownership: Proprietorship and Control in a Changing Rural Terrain—A Case Study from Ghana. *Africa* 83(1):36–56.

Bourdieu, Pierre

    1993   *The Field of Cultural Production.* Oxford: Blackwell.

Brown, Michael

    2003   *Who Owns Native Culture?* Cambridge, MA: Harvard University Press.

Busia, Kofi A.

    1951   *The Position of the Chief in the Modern Political System of Ashanti.* London: Oxford University Press.

Chanock, Martin

    2000   'Culture' and Human Rights: Orientalising, Occidentalising, and Authenticity. In *Beyond Rights Talk and Culture Talk: Comparative Essays on the Politics of Rights and Culture,* Mahmood Mamdani, ed. New York: St. Martin's Press.

Coe, Cati

    2005   *Dilemmas of Culture in African Schools: Youth, Nationalism, and the Transformation of Knowledge.* Chicago: University of Chicago Press.

Cohn, Bernard

    1983   Representing Authority in Victorian India. In *The Invention of Tradition,* E. Hobsbawm and T. O. Ranger, eds. Cambridge: Cambridge University Press.

Cole, Catherine

    2001   *Ghana's Concert Party Theatre.* Bloomington, IN: Indiana University Press.

Collins, John

    2007   Popular Performance and Culture in Ghana: The Past 50 Years. *Ghana Studies* 10:9–64.

Comaroff, Jean, and John Comaroff

    2009   *Ethnicity, Inc.* Chicago: University of Chicago Press.

Coombe, Rosemary

    1996   Embodied Trademarks: Mimesis and Alterity on American Commercial Frontiers. *Cultural Anthropology* 11(2):202–24.

Dávila, Arlene

    1997   *Sponsored Identities: Cultural Politics in Puerto Rico.* Philadelphia, PA: Temple University Press.

Foster, Robert
  2002 *Materializing the Nation: Commodities, Consumption, and Media in Papua New Guinea.* Bloomington, IN: Indiana University Press.
  2007 The Work of the New Economy: Consumers, Brands, and Value-Creation. *Cultural Anthropology* 22(4):707–31.
Guss, David
  2000 *The Festive State: Race, Ethnicity, and Nationalism as Cultural Performance.* Berkeley, CA: University of California Press.
Hess, Janet
  2001 Exhibiting Ghana: Display, Documentary, and "National" Art in the Nkrumah Era. *African Studies Review* 44(1):59–77.
Holt, Douglas
  2004 *How Brands Become Icons: The Principles of Cultural Branding.* Boston, MA: Harvard Business School Press.
Kleist, Nauja
  2011 Modern Chiefs: Tradition, Development, and Return among Traditional Authorities in Ghana. *African Affairs* 110(441):629–47.
Lury, Celia
  2004 *Brands: The Logos of the Global Economy.* London: Routledge.
Manning, Paul
  2010 The Semiotics of Brand. *Annual Review Anthropology* 39:33–49.
McCaskie, Tom C
  1995 *State and Society in Pre-Colonial Asante.* New York: Cambridge University Press.
Miller, Daniel, ed.
  1998 *Material Cultures: Why Some Things Matter.* Chicago: University of Chicago Press.
Moore, Robert
  2003 From Genericide to Viral Marketing: On 'Brand.' *Language and Communication* 23(3):331–57.
Shipley, Jesse
  2009 Aesthetic of the Entreprenuer: Afro-Cosmopolitan Rap and Moral Circulation in Accra, Ghana. *Anthropological Quarterly* 82(3):631–68.
Wilks, Ivor
  1993 *Forests of Gold: Essays on the Akan and Kingdom of Asante.* Athens, OH: Ohio University Press.

TEN

Fallen Chiefs and Sacrificial Mining in Ghana

LAUREN COYLE

In December 2011, an imperiled chief attempted to return to his home village, Sansu, on the outskirts of Obuasi, a legendary gold mining town in the heart of Ghana's Ashanti Region. He was there for the Christmas holiday, he announced, his muffled voice projected through a battery of armed bodyguards. A band of irate youth met him upon his arrival. Many of them were local, small-scale miners called "galamseys," who often operate illegally on the large mining concession licensed to transnational mining giant AngloGold Ashanti (AGA).

The chief's mere physical appearance was an affront: many in the community had vowed to kill him should he dare return in person. Any time he tries to do so, he comes in a convoy of armored cars, surrounded by guards. On this occasion, livid youth rushed at him, attempting to remove his sandals, a performative act that would execute his destooling, or formal overthrow. As on previous occasions, violence erupted and ricocheted throughout the village. A small group of those still loyal to the chief went after those who sought his overthrow, brandishing guns, knives, and machetes. As one villager recounted shortly afterward, "Brother was slashing brother, sister slashing sister. Blood was everywhere, running and running. All because this man had the nerve to try to come."

The sandals remained on the chief's feet, by the sheer force of his heavily armed guards. Nevertheless, he cannot rule the town. He no longer stays in the community, rarely visits, and does not preside over court cases, festivals, funerals, and the like. He rarely even tries any more. Effectively, he has surrendered his reign, although he remains formally installed and continues to cultivate relations with a number of "loyal" youth in the community, many of them kin or affines. Some of his subjects are less negative than ambivalent about him, recalling the days of his beneficent provisioning and protection of the village. They also point out that he maintains ties, however fraught or compromised, to the ancestors, on whose authority he was enstooled. As such, he continues to be a pivotal link to the vitality, fertility, and productivity of his people and their customary lands.

This village, Sansu, is the site of one of the most dramatic cases of fallen chiefs in Obuasi. Many of its residents allege that their ruler had enjoyed close ties to AGA and had allowed for the dispossession and destruction that followed from its use of surface mining, or open-pit blasting, from the early 1990s. They had also charged his predecessor with much of the same—overthrowing him violently, burning his palace to the ground, and afflicting him with restlessness, insomnia, and other unpleasant maladies for the rest of his life. Nor is this surprising: Sansu had been forced to forfeit much of its farmland to AGA and had lost twenty-three sacred streams, which housed tutelary deities and spirits. Those streams also furnished fish and, critically, drinking water. In the power vacuum and amidst the devastation left behind by the absentee chief, it is the galamsey operators, artisanal miners, who often perform the customary functions of governance (see also chapter 11, this volume). As this suggests, Sansu is, in many ways, a paradigmatic hyperfiguration of the acute social tensions, and the contradictions, that afflict Obuasi. The case of its fallen chiefs is indexical of broader political, social, and spiritual transformations here.[1]

A dramatic shift in customary rule has recently swept Obuasi and its surrounds, this in consonance with many of the counterintuitive transformations and resurgences of chiefly politics that John and Jean Comaroff trace in chapter 1 of this volume. Far from vanishing from view with "modernization," chiefs around Obuasi have opened up novel avenues, novel means and ends, of rule. Although their positions are imperiled in many ways, changing circumstances have generated the conditions for new channels of patrimony, modes of dispossession, and mechanisms of capital accumulation.

In many ways, the town itself, dubbed Ghana's "Golden City," is iconic of development dreams dashed for the postcolonial nation. Neoliberal reformers sold the privatization of its mine as a panacea for the new era, inaugurating the liberalization of the industry in the first structural adjustment reforms, enacted in 1986. The industry was also to serve as a beacon and a blueprint for similar programs that would subsequently be implemented across Africa. Yet dark realities betrayed glittering visions. The violence, destruction, and unemployment that followed upon structural adjustment rendered the mine a "poisoned chalice"—and a blatant blot on the country's celebrated reputation as a model "rule of law" democracy for sub-Saharan Africa.

Obuasi boasts the third most plentiful gold mine in Africa. Its riches have been tapped for centuries. Industrial underground operations began in 1897, shortly before the British formally colonized Asante to the north of the original Gold Coast colony. In fact, securing access to its bounty was a major enticement for imperial incursions into the region (Hopkins 2000; Dumett 1998; Crisp 1984; Austin 2005). AGA, among the largest gold mining companies in the world, holds the concession to working it under a lately renewed ninety-nine-year lease. Recent times have seen much violence and social turmoil in the town, owing in particular to the effects of surface mining, as well as to the retrenchment of many laborers and the heavy-handed policing of the galamseys. Neoliberal reforms ushered in this new era of highly lucrative, capital-intensive open-pit blasting, bringing with it the aforementioned destruction of local farmlands and streams—which, in turn, has resulted in much grassroots advocacy, especially by Wacam, an Oxfam-funded Ghanaian mining-activist NGO. Together with civil society groups from around the world, Wacam succeeded in garnering the inglorious "Public Eye Award" for AGA, which named it "the most socially and environmentally irresponsible company in the world" for 2010; in winning the award, AGA "triumphed" over British Petroleum, a fellow nominee, in the same year as its notorious oil spill in the Gulf of Mexico (Coyle 2015).[2]

These reforms, I will argue, have furnished the conditions for a new incarnation of rentier capitalist chiefs, chiefs well positioned to bargain with the mining company in ambiguous legal circumstances, often trading land, water, and livelihoods for personal enrichment. Most of the fields and streams in the areas surrounding Obuasi remain under customary tenure. In many of the dispossessed communities, subjects have castigated chiefs for having allowed their expropriation, at times profiting greatly from it. These subjects allege that their rulers have made unofficial, illicit deals with AGA personnel.[3] Even where this has not in fact happened, accusations persist regardless, undermining the integrity of customary authority.

In the upshot, a number of chiefs have lost legitimacy, although customary legal *authority* remains respected and, in many ways, upheld. Incensed subjects continue to make claims *against* their rulers *in the terms of* customary legal orders—and simultaneously in registers alike pragmatic, spiritual, and institutional—thereby attesting to the enduring cultural power and ideological integrity of those orders. As I have already intimated, some of the rulers who have been most compromised have been formally destooled, removed from the throne of customary Akan power. While this has been more the exception than the rule, even ones who have not been, de jure, have lost much of their de facto authority. They are seen to have betrayed their sacred duties to hold the stool in trust both for the ancestors and for subjects living, unborn, and yet to be reborn.

To the degree that it violates the customary laws of the stool, the extraction by chiefs of rents from both formal and informal mining inflicts sacred harm not only on themselves; it also visits violence upon the collective social spirit, including the health and vitality of subjects, ancestors, and local gods. For these chiefs, the lure of riches appears to be *so* strong that gold's auratic, numinous status—as well as the divine status of customary rule—seems eclipsed by the seductions of private gain.[4]

Gold occupies a pivotal place in Akan cosmology. It is held to be both a sacred symbol and a manifestation of *Nyame*, the ultimate creator god (Meyerowitz 1951a:197–206; Ofosu-Mensah 2011a, 2011b);[5] note that the pinnacle throne of Asante is the Golden Stool (*Sika 'Gua*), venerated as the seat of the collective soul or spirit (*sunsum*) of the people (see, e.g., Sarpong 1971, 1996; Brempong 2006; Rathbone 2006; Danquah 1944).[6] In everyday conversation, one often hears "*sika*," the word for gold; it is also used for wealth or money. One also hears "*sika kra*" (or, at times, "*kra sika*"), meaning "soul's gold." This latter usage indexes the precious metal's sacred status as an aspect of the supreme *Nyame*.[7] Accordingly, gold occupies a prime place in the signification of rank, sacred gifting, and general valuation. As Thomas McCaskie (1983:26) argues, it "is located conceptually and materially at the very core of the historical experience of [Asante] society and culture."[8] Its centrality is at once economic and sacred, substantive and metaphysical. This remains true today.

The circulation, accumulation, and generalized economic deployment of gold played a significant role in the formation and transformation of Asante society; from the late fifteenth to the late seventeenth centuries, especially, its trade was critical to the emergence and consolidation of this polity. The predecessors of the Asante, and of the Akan peoples at large, mined and exported the precious metal in abundance, thereby integrating them into the translocal economy of the time. This conferred on them a considerable measure of political power and economic purchase despite their position at the margins of the capitalist world (McCaskie 1983:26; Austen 1987; Austin 2005). It also expedited the rise of the Asante state and the extension of the Asante Empire. The forbears of the Asante had bartered gold for slaves, which, many scholars argue, drove their society from a pre-

dominantly hunting and gathering to an agricultural one. Later, the imperial Asante conquered neighboring groups and forcefully subjugated them.
At times, they enslaved the vanquished, bringing them to mine in Obuasi,
as well as to serve in many other bonded roles. The accumulation of gold
also facilitated the amassing of wealth in other convertible forms, such as
nonslave labor and agricultural goods. Arguably, it also initiated and deepened patterns of stratification in their world. First emerged the category of
the "big man" with surplus (ɔbirɛmpɔn; pl. abirɛmpɔn). Next came territorial
chiefships, which ritually consecrated successful abirɛmpɔn. Lastly, the unified state of Asante congealed, with the Asantehene as its paramount sovereign and the ultimate human-divine guardian of the soul of the nation.
His office and his powers rested upon the divine Golden Stool, which had
fallen from the sky, summoned by a powerful high priest, Okomfo Anokye,
and bequeathed by the gods. According to Asante oral histories, the stool
fell into the lap of Osei Tutu, the first Asante king (McCaskie 1983:26–27;
Wilks 1979; Sarpong 1971).[9]

Much has been written about the economic significance of gold in histories of the Asante. Much has also been penned about its political and
economic dimensions in present-day conflict in Ghana. Yet a great deal
has yet to be understood about its symbolic and spiritual significance, including its intricate imbrications in chiefly rule and customary law. As Mc-
Caskie (1983:27) has noted: "At the most fundamental ethical and intel-
lectualist levels, we simply do not comprehend the 'meaning' of gold in
historic Asante society." This is still the case. It also holds for knowledge
about the cosmological and symbolic dimensions of gold and customary
rule in contemporary Ghana.

According to cosmological histories of the Akan, gold is a kindred symbol with the king and the sun, all properly read as keys to unseen, underlying dimensions of divine consciousness and cosmic order.[10] The originary,
bisexual god, Nyame Amowia, incarnate in the moon, begot the god of the
sun, conferring on him her kra, her eternal life force and life-giving capacity. This transfer rendered the sun god "the Only Great Nyame (Nyame;
ko, only; pɔn, great), generally drawn together as Nyankopɔn" (Meyerowitz
1951b:24). The kra is considered bisexual, with the female aspect manifest
in the bodies or substance of the moon and sun—standing, metonymi-
cally, for fire—and the male aspect as "the spirit, the essence . . . or that
which is truly divine" (ibid.). The king personifies the sun (traditionally,
symbolized in gold) and the queen mother, the moon (traditionally, symbolized in silver). Each receives the kra of his or her spiritual predecessor in
the royal line as he or she is enstooled.

In its numinous connections, gold can be interpreted as a "transferential agent—something that readily transgresses and conquers the vitally important Asante boundaries between 'nature' and 'culture'" (McCaskie 1983:27). It occupies a liminal symbolic space of the first order, constantly redrawing lines and recalibrating axes that concern "matter out of place." It also has the capacity to purify or pollute persons, actions, and objects within its realm (Douglas 2002). In this fundamental transgressive capacity, gold may be likened to excrement (McCaskie 1983). Indeed, the two are intertwined in many rituals pertaining to wealth creation, acquisition, and dissolution. The divine nature of gold confers, on those who can communicate with it, the ability to foster the creation of wealth, not least by being able to discern its location in the womb of the earth. This also allows adepts to participate in the appearance, accumulation, diminishing, or vanishing of wealth. Gold governs a whole suite of ritual protocols and taboos for those who seek to address it spiritually, to mine it, to adorn themselves with it, or to otherwise approach or handle it.

How can these sacred, dangerous, and enigmatic dimensions of gold help to illuminate the symbolic valence of fallen chiefs, the destructiveness of mining, and communal ruin? How have extractive technologies and shadow dealings led to the decline of chiefly authority in some of the most severely affected communities? To what extent has bodily and environmental assault at the hands of AGA provoked political and spiritual repercussions for indigenous governance and other realms of social life? More broadly, what do mining violence and discredited sovereigns in Obuasi reveal about global forms of accumulation by dispossession under "neotribal capitalism" (Rata 1999, 2011; Li 2010; Kirsch 2014; Harvey 2004)? Or about the commodification of ethnicity surrounding contested claims to "traditional" wealth (Comaroff and Comaroff 2009; Cook 2011; Manson and Mbenga 2003; Hardin 2011)? Lastly, what does this case tell us about the vaunted vitality of "customary" rule in Ghana's constitutional democracy, one often lauded, as mentioned above, as a model of the "rule of law"? It is to these questions that this essay is addressed. As it turns out, an analysis of the sacred dimensions of gold and the violence of extraction renders legible otherwise obscure forms of emergent politics—and much else besides.

In interrogating the interests of these rentier capitalist chiefs and the tensions inherent in neotraditionalist claims lodged under the purview of Ghana's plural property regimes, I draw upon Elizabeth Rata's (1999, 2011) theory of neotribal capitalism. Rata argues that the consolidation of the economic interests of newly emergent elites often drive revivalist, neotraditionalist movements and resource claims. She shows that, when such movements arose among Maori in the post-1960s era, they resulted *not* in the resuscitation of communal social relations or modes of production. Rather, elites banded together under the sign of ethnicity to acquire "traditional" land and water as newly commodified resources, manned by newly commodified forms of labor, and embedded in newly capitalized relations of production, distribution, and alienation.

Here, I also draw upon the related, broader arguments that Jean and John Comaroff (2009) advance in *Ethnicity, Inc.* They argue that transformations in neoliberal capitalism have generated fertile conditions for the refashioning—and, at times, reinvention—of ethnicity, eventuating often in ethnic incorporation and commodified ethnic identities. The lucrative stakes involved have tended to create newly charged principles of exclusion, stratification, and historically sedimented lines of difference. In the process, ethnic groups have increasingly come to take on corporate forms, while corporations forge new markets for ethnicity and the consumption of cultural property.

The Obuasi case does not involve a neotraditionalist or revivalist political movement, or the creation of the Asante as a newly fashioned economic entity—although the kingdom *is*, in fact, now incorporated. Yet ethnic commodification and neotribal capitalism have borne heavy consequences for the local cultural worlds and for political authority in the penumbra of the Ghanaian mining industry. They have brought new opportunities for a number of chiefs, kings, and queen mothers to voice claims to customary lands in ways that, in effect, commodify them and disinherit their subjects under the ersatz sign of traditional sovereignty. Often, this has had the effect of eviscerating the same customary laws whose sacred authority they purport to invoke. Chiefs effect these forms of dispossession and alienation either through the formal legal system and its land negotiation processes or in the shadows of the legal system, through undisclosed deals with mine management or agents of the state.

I argue that the emergence of rentier chiefship, with its political, economic, and spiritual consequences, has been facilitated by the most recent incarnation of Ghana's neoliberal democracy, which emphasizes political devolution and the formalization of land markets—which, in turn, encourage alienation rather than continuous allodial title. The same processes that have emboldened chiefs, however, also have weakened them, by leaving them *no option* to refuse to negotiate with mining companies and their demands for access to land once the state ministry has licensed their concessions. This is to say that what may appear as callous disinheritance on the part of profit-mongering rulers, in cahoots with a rapacious extractive sector, is facilitated, even perversely *incentivized*, by the broader economic and legal regimes at play.[11]

Dispossessions of the Golden Town

The Obuasi mine was owned and operated by Ashanti Goldfields Corporation (AGC) from the start of its industrial operations in 1897 until 2004, when AGC merged with the global parent company, AngloGold, to form AGA. The town rests forty miles southwest of Kumasi, the capital of the Ashanti Region. Although there is no definitive census data, the most recent governmental sources indicate a population of around 175,000 for the municipality. Obuasi sits entirely within the hundred-square-mile concession of AGA.

Surface mining arrived in town not long after it was legalized in 1986. Before that, underground operations caused limited damage—some poisoning of orange trees and intermittent leakages of toxins into the water supply—but most cultivation and fishing continued undisturbed. Once open-pit mining began, however, giant holes were blasted into the earth. This obliterated the farms directly in its path and destroyed much of the surrounding ecology through cyanide spillage, unregulated waste disposal, rain drainage problems, and the deposit of towering heaps of rock and other industrial detritus. Amidst all this devastation, as I have already noted, "traditional" authority has retained its significance, all the more so since, while some land has been sold into family or individual freehold, much of it is still under customary tenure, as is the case with an estimated 80 percent of the ground surface of Ghana (Nugent 2010; see also chapter 3, this volume).

The British colonial administration, in collaboration with indigenous sovereigns, established a system of dual legal domains—"customary" and "state," each with its own authorities—as separate, interacting spheres of government under indirect rule (Rathbone 2000, 2006; Odotei and Awedoba 2006; Busia 1951; Nugent 2010; Berry 2001); it remains largely intact to this day, albeit in modified form. As elsewhere in Africa, some features of the customary order were invented (e.g., Ranger 1983; Chanock 1985; Snyder 1982; Cohn 1996; Lentz and Nugent 2000; Mann and Roberts 1991). In Ghana, one of the most pronounced inventions concerned land tenure.[12] Under colonialism, a prohibition against alienating stool territory was promulgated and then projected back onto Akan history as though it had been there since time immemorial. In fact, throughout much of the nineteenth century, paramount chiefs gave away stool holdings, and also subjects, to settle public and personal debts. This grew increasingly common with the rise of the cash economy and the emergence of an autochthonous class of merchants and bourgeois proprietors (Amanor 2008; Hopkins 2000; Von Laue 1976).

The Gold Coast was exceptional in colonial history in that its authorities never imposed direct taxation on the population. In the early 1850s, the British administration attempted to introduce a poll tax to cover bureaucratic expenses, but popular resistance swiftly laid to rest any possibility of its implementation. Later, it sought to take possession of the land under an act passed in 1897, but southern chiefs and intellectuals sent an envoy to London to protest it and were successful (Nugent 2010; Kimble 1963). Although the state could not impose taxation or control land, it *was* able to levy mining royalties. However, the economic significance of these was greatly eclipsed by revenue from import/export duties, particularly following the rise of cocoa exportation and consumer-good importation in the 1920s (Austin 2005; Chalfin 2010; Beckman 1976; Hill 1963). This indirect taxation supported a concerted development initiative, as a result of which the southern part of the country had decent healthcare facilities, schools, and roads—much better than those in similarly situated colonial contexts (Nugent 2010:46).

As for the mining sector, the British administration was able to grant concessions to corporations, but only in consultation with chiefs, who retained, as they still do, jurisdiction over the surface rights of stool land. The AGA concession itself spans five traditional stool territories, which are administered by their respective traditional councils and paramount chiefs. The most prominent of these, for Obuasi, is the Adansi Traditional Council. It is made up of seven divisional councils, four of which cover areas in Obuasi Municipality: Edubiase, Akrokerri, Ayease, and Dompoase. The *ohemaa* (queen mother) of Akrokerri presides over the vast majority of the customary surface land within which much of Obuasi sits. She is the most powerful traditional ruler in the town, answerable to paramount chiefs and, ultimately, to the Asantehene, the king of Asante.[13] Chiefly rule is territorial rather than descent-based. However, descent may come into play, and often does, through preferential selection when the queen mother, elders, and ancestors select a successor for a deceased, overthrown, or otherwise indisposed chief. Lower-level chiefs and subchiefs need not necessarily come from Adanse or Asante matrilineages. They may hail from other groups within the larger Akan world. However, the higher-order paramount chiefs, who report directly to the Asantehene, must be Asante. Many of the local chiefs, whether seen as legitimate or not, no longer live in their "traditional" villages, having taken up private residence in various parts of the town. Some live very near AGA's management bungalows or the estates built to provide subsidized housing for its laborers. Some of the wealthier ones even have their primary homes outside of the country.

Obuasi has effectively been a company town since the early days of British colonial incursion and the onset of industrial extraction in Ghana. It is dominated by AGA in ways not seen elsewhere in the country, including in the other major deep-pit town, Tarkwa, in the Western Region. Common parlance has it that "Obuasi is the mine, and the mine is Obuasi," also that "the company is like a god" and "a law unto itself." Because it is the principal provider of resources, its informal "social contracts" with town residents and with local chiefs are of great consequence. Not only does it employ a large number of people—both on its own account and through its various independent contractors—but it also participates in the construction and maintenance of roads, schools, hospitals, civic venues, recreational centers, electrical grids, and so forth. Much of the local police force is drawn from AGA's private security ranks.[14] For all the centrality of the mine, however, chiefship—precisely because it has sustained its significance—lives alongside it in an uneasy parallel world.

In Ghana, indigenous rulers have never been formally incorporated into the state, and thus, in many ways, have never been subject to its direct orders or authorization. Outside of district capitals, their dealings with subjects and with state officials tend to be conducted at "traditional" palaces. Even where their sovereign prerogatives are circumscribed de jure, they remain in force de facto throughout much of rural Ghana, where the political economy of land use and local governance are central to the lives and reproduction of kin groups (Nugent 2010; Berry 2001; Odotei and Awedoba 2006; Ray 1996; Herbst 1993). This is true in Obuasi peasant communities, for which chiefs, until recently at least, remained the primary and most accessible adjudicating and provisioning authority.

Today, in Obuasi and throughout the nation, chiefs control the mobilization of resources, to the extent that they can, through levies or communal labor. They do so either to accumulate wealth in their office, to redistribute it through traditional channels, or to fund infrastructure (Whitfield 2005; Abotchie 2006; Abdulai 2006). They also lobby local, regional, and central governmental bodies, as well as NGOs, for financial support. The more enterprising among them attempt, in addition, to secure venture capital for income-generating projects (Brempong and Pavanello 2006:9–10; Owusu-Mensah 2013); some even commit their own personal wealth to these ends. Often, too, they seek investment from development agencies or companies, national and/or foreign (see also chapter 6, this volume).

The formal division between traditional and state authority is enshrined in the constitution: under Article 22, chiefs exist as *nonstate* sovereigns, holding stools and skins in trust for their subjects. As we saw in chapter 3, the law forbids their involvement in politics, executive activities, or administrative affairs outside of their domains. Conversely, the encroachment of the government into their affairs is forbidden. Although this line is not always clear in practice, there is a popular sense that there *is* one—with very real political and distributive effects for the vast majority of Ghanaians who either live on, or remain tied to, traditional lands (Nugent 2010 Arhin 2002; Odotei and Awedoba 2006; Adjaye 1999). This zone of ambiguity bedevils the efforts both of chiefly subjects affected by mining and of government officials to determine jurisdiction, standing, and regulatory responsibility.

Many of the rulers in Obuasi lament that this dual legacy has sidelined them from participation in the neoliberal economy, especially with respect to land negotiations. How so? In part, because *subsurface* rights have been nationalized since structural adjustment, leaving transnational companies to sign concessionary contracts with the state *without* needing first to consult them, elected regional government officials (known as district assembly members), or indigenous communities. When corporations do negotiate with local authorities for surface rights, *after* a subsurface concession is already in hand, they tend to deal more with district assemblies than with chiefs. Further, under prevailing statutory provisions, those who inhabit surface land have no right to debar industrial extraction and its forms of destruction. The law only requires that the mine offer them "fair, prompt, and adequate" compensation, the precise terms of which are left ambiguous, often with tragic consequences for the most vulnerable of the displaced and dispossessed (Ghana Minerals and Mining Act 1986; Ghana Minerals and Mining Act 2006).

The most heated arguments in Obuasi today revolve around what has been "negotiated, agreed upon, and laid to rest," with respect to community displacement and resettlement, claims to land rights, recompense for loss, and the provision of alternative livelihoods (Akabzaa et al. 2008; Commission on Human Rights and Administrative Justice 2008; Akabzaa 2000). The exact character of early compensation negotiations in the 1990s is contested by various parties, although many people tell a similar basic story. AGA, they say, announced that it had to take over the surface ground so that it could mine; often the company would constitute a committee of local opinion leaders, in consultation with the chief, to preside over the deliberations on behalf of all concerned, but these committees became yet another object of unrest, as many felt unfairly represented. Nonetheless, once an agreement was reached, AGA personnel went about doing the requisite rites with chiefs and ritual experts to pacify local deities and to placate the gold spirit. Thereafter, the company would come before blasting to deal with the peasant farmers who were about to be dispossessed. Many allege that, committee consultations notwithstanding, in the final analysis the mine dealt primarily with the chiefs, who would walk away "with large brown envelopes." Several of the evicted landholders also told me that they did not understand AGA's compensation offers—rather paltry, by their lights—to be negotiable.[15]

Many emphasized, too, that they had viewed the mine as a national enterprise under the previous Rawlings regime. What it decreed was law, backed by the army. Longtime residents of Obuasi often recalled, when I asked about the mine, that soldiers intermittently arrived to "sweep" the town during the days of military rule, especially in the 1980s. As one local politician put it, in casual conversation over lunch with me, alluding to Kwame Nkrumah's mordant text *Dark Days in Ghana* (1968):

> These were the true dark days of Ghana, when the Rawlings military regime would come through. Anyone suspected of stealing from the mine—which often meant anyone that was rich and not a known loyal of the regime— easily could have the house searched and ransacked. The military would take so many things. And the penalties for theft were brutal. The soldiers would take people out in public, in town, and beat them. And I'm not talking normal beatings. They would strap them to wooden planks or platforms and beat them with the ends of their guns. There also were rapes. The military even would rape women in public view, for people to see and witness.

This history of spectacular policing and grotesque violence weighed heavily on the collective memory of many in town, amounting to a "standardized nightmare" (Wilson 1951), a nightmare rife with spiritual inflections, to be sure: military personnel were widely viewed as almost inhuman, often possessed by nefarious spirits, malicious powers, or vengeful deities. Such was the legacy of the might of the mine.

These chilling specters were also etched into the psyches of those dispossessed by AGA in the early days of the transition to democracy. One woman from a community that lost all of its farmland—and, ultimately, its chief—to surface mining in the early 1990s told me that, when the company arrived to announce compensation:

> The ghost of the military regime was still heavily with us, hanging over us, somehow controlling our actions. . . . The amounts were very, very inadequate. It wasn't an amount that we all consented to. It was something that the company devised themselves. "We are going to give you this. And it ends there." . . . I was a farmer, and I was depending heavily on the farm. And the farm was the major source of livelihood, so when the farm was bulldozed away, my livelihood was also bulldozed away. . . . Because I was getting money from the produce, and that's what I was using to maintain the family. And when I lost the farm, that source of income also cut off.

This particular community was first affected by violent blasts that left cracks in homes—made mostly of mud and thatch, and sometimes cement—caused by trembling ground or loose flying boulders. Its farmlands also were destroyed by toxic waste leaching from surface mine operations.

In Sansu, the village featured at the start of this chapter, tensions have recently continued to mount. AGA has been constructing a new royal palace at its center, said to cost an ungodly sum. It is unclear how the chief plans ever to inhabit it without its being destroyed. Recall that his predecessor, at the time of his destooling, had his palace burned to the ground. The youth—mostly men, some women—had marched with their heads wrapped in red cloth, like warriors, and encircled the palace, chanting war songs and demanding that he emerge. "He was not there at the time, but if he would have been home, the youth would have burned him alive," said one man, who had been part of the group. "I'm telling you. The youth. You know, this community is very calm, but when these people start their own thing, you will clap for them. When they decide to do something, nothing stops them." A local chief insisted to me that the previous ruler of Sansu had *not* actually been removed: in order to avoid the terror and ignominy that attend a destooling, he had elected to abdicate. But his former subjects maintained otherwise, that, under threat of death were he to return, he was destooled. As one explained to me, "We were looking for his life, and he decided not to visit the community again. If he had visited, or if he had insisted that, no, he will continue [as] chief, we would have killed him. By all means, we would have done that."

Many people in Sansu told me that neither the state nor AGA police patrol the area anymore; I never saw a police car in the village. Its residents do not pay for their electricity, and armed youth threaten to deal with anyone who would force them to do so. They say that being hooked up to the company's grid is the only tangible benefit they have seen from mining activity, amidst so much devastation, and refuse to have it taken from them. The local armed galamseys, in particular, guard the electrical hook-ups. Townspeople view such formally illegal activity as completely justified, a form of what Janet Roitman has called, in another context, "the ethics of illegality" (2006). Perhaps the most intriguing thing about Sansu is the emergence of informal governance at the hands of these galamseys, who offer considerable financial support to a community stripped of any reliable livelihood. In filling the power vacuum left by the chief, their leaders, who reside in Sansu, rule alongside the elected district assemblyman and the local council. Together, these authorities occupy the void left by the abdication of customary rule, acting as effective sources of policing, provisioning, and adjudicating.

To add to the tension, the absentee Sansu chief had been asking AGA for jobs for his subjects, this being part of a pitch for the company's "social responsibility" initiative to hire unemployed youth from communities affected by surface mining. But the ruler has been accused of selling those jobs to the highest bidders in an impoverished nearby community. The Sansu assemblyman told me, "He knows better than to try that here, in our community. So he goes [there, to the other community]. And helps his family. That's all he usually cares to do." Others added that the jobs would last just six months, leaving the laborers "casual," without severance rights or other legal entitlements that attach to permanent employment. Needless to say, these rentier practices have outraged the subjects in whose "trust" the chief is supposed to hold the land and other resources under customary and state law.

Another, more recent source of rents is informal mining: rulers extract payments from those seeking access to stool lands—and often to individual and family holdings misrepresented as stool lands—for their own financial gain. Increasingly, galamseys and small foreign companies, many of them run by Chinese managers, now mine on fields at the outskirts of Obuasi, citing royal permission to do so. Ordinarily, the rulers, for their part, deny granting concessions to the galamseys or collecting rents from them. Few believe them. They point out that the chiefs do nothing to stop the destructive activities of these interlopers, who, it appears, hire some of their subjects as poorly paid, poorly treated laborers—all of which has further exacerbated the fraught relations between communities and their traditional authorities.

Repercussions of the Numinous Realm

The spiritual realm has registered profound turmoil following the destruction of streams, farms, trees, and livelihoods. As one would expect in the circumstances, accusations of witchcraft, sorcery, and other cursing activity abound. They have become rampant in the wake of all the devastation as people seek to reckon with, and find proximate causes for, it.

The disruptions run deep. The deities and spirits that inhabit this ecology are said to have grown angry and vengeful. Some of the rivers, in particular the legendary River Fena, no longer can be inhabited by them. One prominent priest informed me that it has been so polluted that, when he ritually calls the gods, they often do not respond or accept his offerings. He now gathers cleaner water from a borehole near his home village and carries it, in a sacred calabash, to the side of the river, using it to call the deities. When I asked why they cannot live in the river any more, he replied, "Can you live in a filthy, polluted place—in toxic things? This is certainly not fit for the gods."

Another prominent priestess of a similarly afflicted community told me that the gods with whom she works have also become incensed at the destruction. Some local deities and spirits, she added, have even left the area. Although she does not speak directly with those of River Fena, she communes with the deities of five local rivers, all of which had been adversely affected by surface mining. "It is true," she confirmed, "that, once a river gets polluted, it is hard for the god to stay in there. So, what happens is that they start moving about. The gods will come out of the water." She was quick to clarify, however, that the pollution of a river does not necessarily spell the wholesale stripping of its sacred force and spiritual power: "Once a river or stream gets polluted, it is not that it loses all of its power. If you go there, and it's not the time to go there, something may still happen to you. However, there are streams here that we worshipped that have been destroyed as a result of the [surface] mining. We have incurred some wrath as a result."

The priestess, echoing other ritual authorities, stressed the ways in which local gods register their wrath on the bodies of community members, especially those of infants, whose fragility leaves them most open to spiritual incursion. This heaping of spiritual wrath upon the most vulnerable—at times, in fatal script—tends to induce moral panic. The fate of children renders particularly visible the horrors of the violence and destruction wrought on their world. This is not only because elders, chiefs, and parents are seen to have failed to protect the youngest and most vulnerable, itself disgrace enough. It is also because their failure debars them from becoming ancestors in the afterlife, thus also erasing any prospect of reincarnation. In these circumstances, death becomes simple and finite. And, therefore, terrifying.

At times, the local gods have taken it upon themselves to punish those who have destroyed farmlands, either through AGA's surface mining operations or through galamsey activity. As one priestess interpreted these occurrences:

> The gods attack the destroyers. There are cases abounding that indicate that the gods attack those who are destroying the farmlands, especially those who work on the excavators and the bulldozers. Sometimes, they will be working, and the machine will cease for no apparent reason. You will check, and there is nothing wrong with the machine, but it won't be working. Sometimes, too, those who are working, something will just pierce them from nowhere. There is a case where somebody was sitting on an excavator, working, and something, a tree from nowhere just pierced the ears, and he died as a result. There are so many cases. . . . When it happens like that, some of the Ghanaian workers will tell the white guys that it is as a result of this, and so they will go and see the chief, and they will pacify the gods before they will continue the work. . . . Sometimes, the guys will experience slaps. . . . The operator won't see, but if somebody has a spiritual eye, they will see that that is what is happening. Sometimes, when it happens like that, and they [the persons attacked] go to the god of that respective area, the god will tell them [through a medium], "Yes, I came there to do that."

Despite these spiritual reprisals, many feel that their gods (*abosom*, or lesser deities) and ancestors have abandoned them. This sense is amplified where the chief has fallen and there is no legitimate custodian of the stool, the sacred conduit for exchanges between the living and the dead. A common formulation is that "the ancestors themselves have changed." People seem to mean this in a broader sense: that ancestors and living elders have not protected the land or prepared the younger generations to navigate the dramatically shifting terrain of the day. Talk of change on the part of the ancestors also seems to index *their* declining capacity to deal with social, moral, and environmental transgressions by means of traditional curses, spiritual arrests, or other penalties. For example, chiefly violations of stool protocols seem not to be cursed as much as they once were; similarly, those who mine or farm on taboo days do not incur the same spiritual sanctions that they are said to have done in times past.[16]

But ancestral wrath, and growing impotence, also has other sources. To this day, those working stool lands are obliged to render a portion of their proceeds to the local ruler, who receives it on behalf of the stool.[17] This remains inscribed in customary law, although it also partakes of the duty and sensibility inherent in an Asante proverb: *Sika pereguan da kurom' a, ewo amansan*, or "If there is a *pereguan* [a very large amount in the traditional Akan monetary system] worth of gold dust in a town, it is for the whole people" (Rattray 1916:163; see also Christaller 1879; Gyekye 1997:154–55). In practice, the negotiated shares vary widely and, increasingly, are not paid at all. The queen mother of Akrokerri—who, as noted earlier, rules the territory beneath which most Obuasi gold is found—complained to me that those who mine on traditional terrain tend only to give initial payments, and perform the requisite sacrificial rituals, to pacify the local gods and call the gold spirit. "They come, we perform the rituals, and they say they will come back and pay their share when they hit rock, but then we mostly never hear from them again," she explained. When I asked about physical or spiritual policing, she replied,

> We don't have the resources to maintain our own physical police force. We can issue spiritual punishments, and we can send spirits to see what is going on. But usually, the heads of these galamsey groups have hired some of the local youth. These local boys are all my own sons. I cannot be too harsh on them.

The chief linguist (or "mouthpiece," the *okyeame*), sitting to the side of the queen mother, readily agreed. The flagrant disregard for customary protocols and rituals, they added, had fostered moral decay and resulted in many forms of spiritual disruption. "It is clear that the ancestors, in particular, are angry. Things cannot continue this way," the queen mother said.

Many traditional authorities invoke what remains of the continued power of the spiritual realm to argue for the sheer impossibility of chiefly corruption. They maintain that, while their subjects blame them for misfortunes caused by others or by their own actions, rulers would never misuse funds for private gain for fear of ancestral punishment—especially from the spirit of the stool. This is all the more so since, they point out, the chiefs themselves are possessed by these stool spirits, whose personalities they take on. One prominent ruler, heavily involved in the politics of dispossession, told me how he took on the disposition of a warrior once he was enstooled; this, he said, had been the occupation of the ancestral spirit of his stool during a human incarnation many generations before.

In other words, the actions of the chief may be, often are, those of the ancestral spirit who guards the stool in trust for his subjects.[18] Even when his actions are his own, however, he remains under the regulatory gaze of that deity and of other concerned spirits who inhabit the area. If, then, he transgresses the laws of his office—for example, by misappropriating sovereign wealth—the consequences are likely to be serious. As this same ruler put it, "The ancestors will disgrace you [if you misuse stool wealth]. You might fall sick suddenly, or you might appear in public and start talking nonsense, like a madman. You might be naked. This can happen. They might even ruin your entire life. You might go mad or even die." I asked him if it were possible to evade ancestral surveillance and control. Absolutely not, he said. "They will know, certainly, and you will be punished. Chiefs just can't do it."

Particularly with respect to ill-gotten gains, spiritual empowerment becomes ever more crucial the more affluent a person becomes. This is not only on account of rampant envy and possible spiritual attacks. It is also because the wealth itself may ultimately consume the holder if his or her spirit is not strong. Given the whims and appetites of wealth—or "hot money," so to speak—there is an inbuilt danger to every get-rich-quick scheme. Herein lies a structural interplay between what Victor Turner theorized as the two modes of antitemporality: namely, the eternal, continuous divine with its own transcendent justice *and* the iconoclastic, individualistic "cheating" of culturally proper sequencing (Turner 1982; see also Puett 2013). The cheating of transcendent time can yield powerful yet also grievous and short-lived results for those who engage it—be they chiefs, miners, or anyone else. Quick-money riches and other ill-gotten gains may swiftly reverse fortunes and may ultimately "eat" the initial beneficiary through death, madness, destitution—or, at the very least, by eliminating any erstwhile gains. Chiefs will invoke this sequence of moral repercussions as the severe spiritual consequences of unjust gains collected under the purview of the stool.[19]

Unfortunately, according to their subjects, many chiefs *are* misappropriating stool funds, all the more so, it appears, over the past couple of decades; *vide*, for example, the Sansu ruler who can no longer return to meet his customary obligations. The current Sansu assemblyman—who, with some galamsey leaders and church elders, now hears cases in his place— explained that "[t]he chief cannot even invite anyone into his house [to hear their disputes] . . . People take disagreements to us instead. With those things we cannot solve, we push them to the police station." For matters of a spiritual nature, the leaders refer them to a local priest not closely connected to the exiled chief. The misfortunes of his overthrown predecessor, in his later life, are also commonly thought to have been the just result of spiritual punishment, prompted by the betrayal of his subjects, whose lands he alienated to AGA. As one of those subjects recalled, approvingly:

> [This chief] was creating problems for people in the community, tormenting them, and people started crying, "Oh, dear god, when are you going to listen to us?" Then, they started calling the gods, "When are you going to hear what we say?" Later, when he was destooled, before he died, there was this boil in the ear for one year. This man couldn't sleep for one year before he died. And he couldn't hear properly.

Other rulers have found themselves in similarly compromised circumstances, with practical, spiritual, and psychic consequences for their subjects. Among the disrupted ritual occasions are *Adae* festivals, which take place in six-week cycles, each with two component ceremonies: an *Akwasidae*, held on a Sunday, and *Awukudae*, held on a Wednesday. There are nine cycles of the *Adae* in the Akan calendar, of which the ninth marks the new year; these festivals are thought to be critically important for strengthening, renewing, and honoring ties among the living and between them and the ancestors. The latter are fed in the rooms housing the blackened stools that serve as the seats for their spirits. The chief figures prominently in the rite, representing his subjects in the collective communion with the ancestors.[20] Observes Emmanuel Akyeampong (1999:295), "The *adae* celebrates one's genealogy. To abrogate it is the equivalent of genealogical erasure or social death." The failure of a ruler to preside, therefore, renders tenuous and uncertain the crucial premonitions, revelations, protections, fortunes, and other benefits that the living enjoy at the pleasures of their ancestors and other spirits. It also threatens their prospects of ascending into the ancestral realm once they die. Such are the complex repercussions of the trauma and violence wrought by the declining legitimacy of chiefship in Obuasi.

Conclusion

What remains of the legitimate reign of the customary in this theater of destruction? Rentier chiefs, violent dispossession, and spiritual disruption abound, largely unabated, in the crucible of neoliberal mining in Obuasi. To be sure, chiefly authority and disputes concerning it continue to revolve, in many ways, around claims to traditional lands (Berry 1998, 2001; Amanor and Ubink 2008). But these conflicts also throw into relief

other facets of contemporary chiefship that likewise are foci of contestation and transformation: mining rents, political overthrow, spiritual terror, and the social repercussions of ill-gotten wealth notably among them.
Chiefship is still very much about land and boundaries, but, especially in
extractive theaters, it is about much else as well. The Obuasi world is re-
fashioned by broader cultures of neotribal capitalism, the statecraft of political devolution, and the commodification of ethnic claims and resources
(e.g., Comaroff and Comaroff 2009; Rata 1999, 2011; Li 2010; Kirsch 2014;
Rouse 2017; West and Kloeck-Jensen 1999). The confluence of these things
has begotten a universe of dissatisfied subjects and ruptured social contracts. Those subjects have seized the terms of customary law to unseat or
disempower some of their chiefs. In so doing, they have sought to resignify
and revitalize, rather than abandon or efface, "traditional" forms of political authority—centered on the traumatic-yet-productive "vacant stool"—by
drawing upon spiritual sanction and the symbolic power of the ancestral
realm. People here continue to make appeals to the numinous force that
lies behind customary authority, despite earthly betrayals on the part of
its living incumbents. Perhaps we might understand these appeals, along
with the divine policing of transgressions of the law, as partaking of Benjamin's (1978:300) dictum that "all the eternal forms are open to pure divine
violence, which myth bastardized with law." Law, in this instance, refers to
manifest earthly laws drawn, in Ghana, from both the jurisdiction of the
customary and the jurisdiction of the state.

These new constellations of political life, those that arise in the shadow
of compromised chiefs and from the ashes of divine orders, draw upon received sources of sociality and spiritual power. In this way, violated subjects
evince their ambivalent fealty to "traditional" offices, to their transcendent
grounding, and, in complex ways, to earthly authority. Through their resistance and their everyday practices, they have begun to forge new futures for
customary law, sovereign power, and constitutional democracy in Ghana.
They draw strength from demands anchored in enduring moral economies
of wealth and in emerging forms of collective action. Here, again, Benjamin's admonition, at once retrospectively insightful and prescient: "Divine
violence, which is the sign and seal but never the means of sacred execution, may be called sovereign violence" (ibid.).[21] By revealing the poverty
and injustice of so much sovereign violence, wielded by both chiefs and
the state, these subjects give voice to a deep-seated sense of entitlement
to labor, to livelihood, to a viable future, and to a just share in "sovereign
wealth"—whether they be gained through or in spite of customary rulers.
Herein lies a freshly charted pursuit of justice on the part of the dispos-

sessed, thus to address the precarity of their existence. Theirs is a slow insurgency, conducted, in a theater of shadows, at once in the goldfields, at the ruler's palace, in the realm of the transcendental, and at the edges of the sovereign polis by means of simulacra of the law. In so doing, they fashion a new cultural politics of land, labor, and citizenship at the heart of a "rising" African economy, one that, on pain of their flesh and blood and spirit, asserts a forceful claim on the future.

Notes

1. This chapter is based on ethnographic fieldwork conducted in Obuasi during several extensive trips between 2010 and 2012.
2. This case resonates with other findings across a flourishing critical literature on anthropologies of social conflict and corporate social responsibility in extractive theaters and elsewhere. See, e.g., Kirsch (2007, 2014); Rajak (2011); Golub (2014); Jacka (2015); Li (2015); Dolan and Rajak (2016); Welker (2009, 2014); Turner (1995); Ballard and Banks (2003); Tubb (n.d.); Bridge (2004); Coumans (2011).
3. Increasingly, galamseys also are said to enter shadow deals with chiefs, displacing farmers and destroying water sources. See, e.g., Coyle (2015, n.d.); Hilson (2006).
4. Also at play is the rising prominence of Pentecostal and charismatic Christianity in Obuasi—and, of course, across Africa, more generally. These churches have assumed a prominent presence here since the late 1990s. This has led to ambivalent declines in adherence to "traditional" ritual codes and beliefs among some chiefs *and* subjects. These newly flourishing brands of Christianity tend to denounce many customary practices as demonic, idolatrous, or otherwise sacrilegious. See, e.g., Coyle (2015, n.d.); Meyer (1999); Shipley (2009); Goldstone (2011); Piot (2010); Marshall (2009).
5. For extensive discussion of Akan ideas of the soul, of the sacrality of gold, and of relations among chieftancy, ancestors, and deities, see Busia (1954); Meyerowitz (1951a, 1951b); Wilks (1979, 1993); McCaskie (1983, 1992).
6. All italicized foreign words in this essay are Akan or Twi, in the Asante dialect, unless otherwise noted.
7. The spiritual properties of gold and other metals and minerals weave their way through landmark studies of mine labor and consciousness; see, e.g., Taussig (1980); Nash (1993); Worger (1987); Ferry (2005); Golub (2014); Kirsch (2014); Morris (2008); Smith (2011); Jacka (2015); Povinelli (1995); Walsh (2003). Gold's sacred dimensions as spirit and body (matter) also bespeak its integrative alchemical capacity "to make of the spirit a body and of the body a spirit"; see, e.g., Burckhardt (1987, 1997); Eliade (1978).
8. See also Garrard (1980); McLeod (1981); Arhin (1978); Ayensu (1997). Pietz (1985:16) analyzed the ways in which the Akan goldweights rendered commensurable economic and metaphysical values among the Akan and those European and Arab traders who arrived to seek gold and other objects: "The goldweights, then, functioned precisely to relate incommensurable social values, those from traditional Akan culture as expressed in proverbs or traditional healing, with the newer market values introduced from outside. The brass figures constituted a new cultural territory embodying the possibility of movement across diverse value codes: the

weights were singular productions of Akan artists (students of these objects often remark on the seeming infinity of different forms given to these figures) that could function in the market activity of gold weighing, communicate the traditional wisdom of some native proverb, or be endowed with power to protect or to heal sick individuals when worn upon the body."

9. This origins story regarding divine provenance of foundational rule, of course, has many resonances across the literature on divine sovereigns and transcendent derivations of legitimacy, authority, and power; see, e.g., Kantorowicz (1957); Sahlins (1985); Schmitt (2005); Valeri (1985); Taussig (1997); Agamben (1998); Mbembe (2003); de Heusch (1982, 1986); Hansen and Stepputat (2006); Santner (2011); Hocart (1927); Frazer (2002).

10. This conception partakes of Evans-Pritchard's intricate discussion of symbols, referents, and cosmology in *Witchcraft, Oracles, and Magic among the Azande* (1937); see also Turner (1967, 1975); Bourdieu (1991). For cognate discussions of symbolization, referents, and unconscious dynamics, see, e.g., Butler (1997); Aretxaga (2003); Bataille (1991); Freud (2001); Eliade (1960); Stewart (2003).

11. This argument aligns with a central contention in critical legal studies. Legal regimes create the contours of economic life through ways both prohibitive *and* permissive. The permissive forms of legal systems—particularly, the often-tacit privilege to injure (for example, through exclusion, displacement, or dispossession of property or claims to it)—often remain hidden beneath the surface of legal consciousness. This serves to naturalize the economic and social processes that legal constellations help to produce, though always through dialectical interplays. Such interpretive sleights of hand also tend to localize violence in particular actors or in "economic winds," rather than analyzing the ways in which the violence is generated and incentivized by legal rules at play. Law permits, performs, and produces certain versions of the world at the same time as it disallows, prohibits, and represses others. See, e.g., Kennedy (1997, 2006); Brown and Halley (2002); Desan (2015); Harcourt (2011); Hale (1923); Hohfeld (1964).

12. The effects of the "invention of tradition" in the parts of the colony that lacked centralized political authority differed markedly from those with more kingdoms, of which Akan groups were a part. In the resource-scarce savannah regions (present-day Upper East and Upper West Regions) and also in the present-day Volta Region, there had been no continuous centralized authority, and social order was maintained generally by communal consensus. The British, however, created administrative offices in which they installed "chiefs." The authorities bestowed these chiefs with the authority enjoyed by rulers in the other regions of Ghana, present-day Northern, Brong-Ahafo, Ashanti, Western, Central, Eastern, and Southern Volta Regions; see, e.g., Goody (1975); Arhin (2002); Allman and Parker (2005); Lund (2008); Lentz (2007); Lentz and Nugent (2000); Ray (1996).

13. The other traditional councils that cover areas of AGA's concession, each with their own divisions, are the Bekwai, Adankraja, Manso Nkwanta, and Manso Mem councils.

14. These facets of a virtual company town echo those of similar extractive sites throughout colonial and postcolonial Africa—and elsewhere. See, e.g., Ferguson (1999, 2005); Watts (2004); Robotham (1989); Worger (1987); Crush (1992); Godoy (1985); Frynas (1998); Morris (2008); Powdermaker (1962); Nash (1979).

15. AGA officials claim that, after the initial upheaval following the dispossession

of Sansu, AGC (AGA's predecessor) enlisted the aid of the state's Land Valuation Board to determine rates of compensation for the various pieces of land and for the houses and crops that sat atop it. Mine officials told me that the board arrived in 1994 to determine payment for subsequent dispossessions and displacements. AGA officials maintain that the board, then, is to blame for the levels of compensation, which many subjects viewed as inadequate. Mine officials and subjects also alleged that certain chiefs were involved in the valuation process and in the adjudication of contested claims. These dimensions of the controversy are discussed at greater length in Coyle (2015, n.d.).

16. In contrast to AGA operations, galamseys *do* routinely observe chiefly labor mandates and customary law in refusing to work during *Adae* festivals and on Tuesdays, a day (*Dabone*) tabooed for labor by the river gods, Bono (the most powerful local deity, an earth god), the ancestors, and others. As galamseys often work near rivers, this prohibition is crucial. Farmers observing traditional labor taboos also do not work on these days. As Ofosu-Mensah (2010:132) explains, regarding the taboo of working during *Adae*, "It was believed that the ancestors would punish a miner who flouted this custom by causing him to be buried alive by the earth."

17. Traditionally, the spiritual nature of gold was held to wield an omnioptical gaze and to compel honesty in its finder. As Meyerowitz (1951a:199) documented, "it was rare for anybody to pick up a nugget on land to which he had no claim, and all gold found was brought to the *Omanhene* and the clan chief for the two-third deduction." Each nugget was considered to fall under the sovereign purview of the royals and the spirits who governed the land under which it was found. Land in Akan territories is, in the first instance, owned or ruled by a deity. This was typically Asaase Afua (a supreme deity), Asaase Yaa (another supreme deity), or a local Earth God/ess. When a nugget was found, it was presented, by customary protocol, to the state treasurer (*Sannaahene*), who divided it into three shares. The *Omanhene* would then present the blindfolded finder with those three shares in an outstretched hand. The finder selected one, deemed his "soul's share," which he was allowed to keep (Meyerowitz 1951a:197).

18. In previous times of crisis, living rulers would sometimes intentionally stand atop stools, thus demeaning or disgracing them. They would do this to rouse the ancestors into action, to cause them to "wake up" to the this-worldly realm in order to help their subjects (Obeng 1996:24; McLeod 1981:117).

19. Miners and others will often consult spirit mediums for access to quick-money ritual power, as they ordinarily cannot generate it of their own accord. The prevailing sense is that, by entering such agreements, the spiritual clients "bind" themselves to deities or spirits and their channels. The sacrificial demands in these regimes are said to ascend, almost systematically, until one will not or cannot "satisfy" or "pacify" the spiritual force any longer. At that point, the spirit "consumes" the person, her possessions, her freedom of will and consciousness, her life force, her vitality.

20. The *Akwasidae* celebrations generally involve a large public feast, though the central ritual feast in the Stool-house—where the ancestral stools are kept and venerated—is closed to all but authorized participants (Ofosu-Mensah 2010:131n38).

21. Benjamin distinguished between mythical and divine violence, equating the former with lawmaking violence. He specifies the mythical nature of lawmaking violence in both the executive and administrative domains (Benjamin 1978:295, 300).

References

Abdulai, A. I.
2006   The Ghanaian Chief as a Manager: Between Tradition and Modernity. In *Chieftaincy in Ghana: Culture, Governance and Development*, I. K. Odotei and A. K. Awedoba, eds. Accra: Sub-Saharan Publishers.

Abotchie, Chris
2006   Has the Position of the Chief Become Anachronistic in Contemporary Ghanaian Politics? In *Chieftaincy in Ghana: Culture, Governance and Development*, I. K. Odotei and A. K. Awedoba, eds. Accra: Sub-Saharan Publishers.

Adjaye, III, Awulae Annor
1999   Local Government vis-à-vis Chieftaincy in Ghana: Interplay of Authority, Power and Responsibilities. In *Akan Worlds: Identity and Power in West Africa*, P. Valsecchi and F. Viti, eds. Paris: L'Harmattan.

Agamben, Giorgio
1998   *Homo Sacer: Sovereign Power and Bare Life*. Stanford, CA: Stanford University Press.

Akabzaa, Thomas
2000   *Boom and Dislocation: The Environmental and Social Impacts of Mining in the Wassa West District of Ghana*. Accra: Third World Network-Africa.

Akabzaa, Thomas M., J. S. Seyire, and K. Afriyie
2008   *The Glittering Façade: Effects of Mining Activities on Obuasi and Its Surrounding Communities*. Accra: Third World Network-Africa.

Akyeampong, Emmanuel
1999   Christianity, Modernity, and the Weight of Tradition in the Life of Asantehene Agyeman Prempeh I., c. 1888–1931. *Africa* 69(2):279–311.

Allman, Jean, and John Parker
2005   *Tongnaab: The History of a West African God*. Bloomington, IN.: Indiana University Press.

Amanor, Kojo Sebastian
2008   Sustainable Development, Corporate Accumulation and Community Expropriation: Land and Natural Resources in West Africa. In *Land and Sustainable Development in Africa*, K. S. Amanor and S. Moyo, eds. London: Zed Books.

Amanor, Kojo Sebastian, and Janine Ubink
2008   Contesting Land and Custom in Ghana: Introduction. In *Contesting Land and Custom in Ghana*, J. M. Ubink and K. S. Amanor, eds. Leiden: Leiden University Press.

Aretxaga, Begoña
2003   Maddening States. *Annual Review of Anthropology* 32:393–410.

Arhin, Kwame
1978   Gold-Mining and Trading among the Ashanti of Ghana. *Journal des Africanistes* 48(1):89–100.
2002   *Political Systems of Ghana: Background to Transformations in Traditional Authority in the Colonial and Post-Colonial Periods*. Accra: Historical Society of Ghana.

Austen, Ralph
1987   *African Economic History: Internal Development and External Dependency*. Oxford: James Currey.

Austin, Gareth
2005   *Labour, Land and Capital in Ghana: From Slavery to Free Labour in Asante, 1807–1956*. Rochester, NY: University of Rochester Press.

Ayensu, Edward S.
1997   *Ashanti Gold: The African Legacy of the World's Most Precious Metal.* London: Marshall.
Ballard, Chris, and Glenn Banks
2003   Resource Wars: The Anthropology of Mining. *Annual Review of Anthropology* 32: 287–313.
Bataille, Georges
1991[1949]   *The Accursed Share: An Essay on General Economy*, vol. 1. R. Hurley, trans. New York: Zone Books.
Beckman, Björn
1976   *Organising the Farmers: Cocoa Politics and National Development in Ghana.* Uppsala: Scandinavian Institute of African Studies.
Benjamin, Walter
1978[1921]   Critique of Violence. In *Reflections: Essays, Aphorisms, Autobiographical Writings.* E. Jephcott, trans. New York: Schocken Books.
Berry, Sara
1998   Unsettled Accounts: Stool Debts, Chieftaincy Disputes, and the Question of Asante Constitutionalism. *Journal of African History* 39(1):39–62.
2001   *Chiefs Know Their Boundaries: Essays on Property, Power and the Past in Asante, 1896–1996.* Oxford: James Currey.
Bourdieu, Pierre
1991   *Language and Symbolic Power.* G. Raymond and M. Adamson, eds. Cambridge: Polity Press.
Brempong, Nana Arhin, and Mariano Pavanello
2006   *Chiefs in Development in Ghana: Interviews with Four Paramount Chiefs in Ghana.* Legon: Institute of African Studies, University of Ghana.
Brempong, Owusu
2006   Chieftancy and Traditional Taboos: An Empirical Approach. In *Chieftaincy in Ghana: Culture, Governance and Development*, I. K. Odotei and A. K. Awedoba, eds. Accra: Sub-Saharan Publishers.
Bridge, Gavin
2004   Contested Terrain: Mining and the Environment. *Annual Review of Environment and Resources* 29:205–59.
Brown, Wendy, and Janet Halley
2002   Introduction. In *Left Legalism/Left Critique*, W. Brown and J. Halley, eds. Durham, NC: Duke University Press.
Burckhardt, Titus
1987   *Mirror of the Intellect: Essays on Traditional Science and Sacred Art.* New York: SUNY Press.
1997   *Alchemy: Science of the Cosmos, Science of the Soul.* Louisville, KY: Fons Vitae.
Busia, Kofi A.
1951   *The Position of the Chief in the Modern Political System of Ashanti.* London: Oxford University Press.
1954   The Ashanti of the Gold Coast. In *African Worlds: Studies in the Cosmological Ideas and Social Values of African Peoples*, D. Forde, ed. London: Oxford University Press.
Butler, Judith
1997   *The Psychic Life of Power: Theories in Subjection.* Stanford, CA: Stanford University Press.

Chalfin, Brenda
    2010   *Neoliberal Frontiers: An Ethnography of Sovereignty in West Africa.* Chicago: University of Chicago Press.
Chanock, Martin
    1985   *Law, Custom, and Social Order: The Colonial Experience in Malawi and Zambia.* Cambridge: Cambridge University Press.
Christaller, Johann Gottlieb
    1879   *A Collection of Three Thousand and Six Hundred Tshi Proverbs.* Basel: Basel Missionary Society.
Cohn, Bernard
    1996   *Colonialism and Its Forms of Knowledge.* Princeton, NJ: Princeton University Press.
Comaroff, John L., and Jean Comaroff
    2009   *Ethnicity, Inc.* Chicago: University of Chicago Press.
Commission on Human Rights and Administrative Justice (CHRAJ, Ghana)
    2008   *The State of Human Rights in Mining Communities in Ghana.* Accra: CHRAJ.
Cook, Susan E.
    2011   The Business of Being Bafokeng: The Corporatization of Tribal Authority in South Africa. *Current Anthropology* 52:S151–S159.
Coumans, Catherine
    2011   Occupying Spaces Created by Conflict: Anthropologists, Development NGOs, Responsible Investment, and Mining. *Current Anthropology* 52:S29–S43.
Coyle, Lauren
    2015   Tender Is the Mine: Law, Shadow Rule, and the Public Gaze in Ghana. In *Corporate Social Responsibility? Human Rights in the New Global Economy,* J. Kelly and C. Walker-Said, eds. Chicago: University of Chicago Press.
    n.d.   *Fires of Gold: Law, Land, and Sacrificial Labor in Ghana.* Book manuscript.
Crisp, Jeff
    1984   *The Story of an African Working Class: Ghanaian Miners' Struggles, 1870–1980.* London: Zed Books.
Crush, Jonathan
    1992   Power and Surveillance on the South African Gold Mines. *Journal of Southern African Studies* 18(4):825–44.
Danquah, J. B.
    1944   *The Akan Doctrine of God: A Fragment of Gold Coast Ethics and Religion.* London: Lutterworth Press.
de Heusch, Luc
    1982   *The Drunken King, or, The Origin of the State.* R. Willis, trans. Bloomington, IN: Indiana University Press.
    1986   *Sacrifice in Africa: A Structuralist Approach.* Manchester: Manchester University Press.
Desan, Christine
    2015   *Making Money: Coin, Currency, and the Coming of Capitalism.* London: Oxford University Press.
Dolan, Catherine, and Dinah Rajak, eds.
    2016   *The Anthropology of Corporate Social Responsibility.* New York: Berghahn.
Douglas, Mary
    2002[1966]   *Purity and Danger: An Analysis of Concepts of Pollution and Taboo.* London: Routledge.

Dumett, Raymond E.
 1998 *El Dorado in West Africa: The Gold-Mining Frontier, African Labor, and Colonial Capitalism in the Gold Coast, 1875–1900.* Athens, OH: Ohio University Press.
Eliade, Mircea
 1960 *Myths, Dreams, and Mysteries.* Philip Mairet, trans. New York: Harper & Row.
 1978 *The Forge and the Crucible: The Origins and Structures of Alchemy.* Stephen Corrin, trans. Chicago: University of Chicago Press.
Evans-Pritchard, Edward E.
 1937 *Witchcraft, Oracles, and Magic Among the Azande.* Oxford: Clarendon Press.
Ferguson, James
 1999 *Expectations of Modernity: Myths and Meanings of Urban Life on the Zambian Copperbelt.* Berkeley: University of California Press.
 2005 Seeing Like an Oil Company: Space, Security, and Global Capital in Neoliberal Africa. *American Anthropologist* 107(3):377–82.
Ferry, Elizabeth
 2005 Geologies of Power: Value Transformations of Mineral Specimens from Guanajuato, Mexico. *American Ethnologist* 32(3):420–36.
Frazer, Sir James George
 2002[1890] *The Golden Bough.* New York: Dover.
Freud, Sigmund
 2001[1914] *On Dreams.* M. D. Eder, trans. London: William Heinemann.
Frynas, J. G.
 1998 Political Instability and Business: Focus on Shell in Nigeria. *Third World Quarterly* 19(3):457–78.
Garrard, Timothy F.
 1980 *Akan Weights and the Gold Trade.* New York: Longman.
Ghana, Government of
 1986 Minerals and Mining Act of 1986.
 2006 Minerals and Mining Act of 2006.
Godoy, Ricardo
 1985 Mining: Anthropological Perspectives. *Annual Review of Anthropology* 14:199–217.
Goldstone, Brian
 2011 The Miraculous Life. *Johannesburg Salon* 4:81–96.
Golub, Alex
 2014 *Leviathans at the Gold Mine: Creating Indigenous and Corporate Actors in Papua New Guinea.* Durham, NC: Duke University Press.
Goody, Jack, ed.
 1975 *Changing Social Structure in Ghana: Essays in the Comparative Sociology of a New State and an Old Tradition.* London: International African Institute.
Gyekye, Kwame
 1997 *Tradition and Modernity: Philosophical Reflections on the African Experience.* New York: Oxford University Press.
Hale, Robert
 1923 Coercion and Distribution in a Supposedly Non-Coercive State. *Political Science Quarterly* 38(3):470–94.
Hansen, Thomas Blom, and Finn Stepputat
 2006 Sovereignty Revisited. *Annual Review of Anthropology* 35:295–315.

Harcourt, Bernard E.
2011   *The Illusion of Free Markets: Punishment and the Myth of Natural Order*. Cambridge, MA: Harvard University Press.

Hardin, Rebecca
2011   Concessionary Politics: Property, Patronage, and Political Rivalry in Central African Forest Management. *Current Anthropology* 52(S3):S113–25.

Harvey, David
2004   The 'New' Imperialism: Accumulation by Dispossession. *Socialist Register* 40:63–87.

Herbst, Jeffrey
1993   *The Politics of Reform in Ghana, 1982–1991*. Berkeley, CA: University of California Press.

Hill, Polly
1963   *The Migrant Cocoa-Farmers of Southern Ghana: A Study in Rural Capitalism*. Cambridge: Cambridge University Press.

Hilson, Gavin
2006   *Small-Scale Mining, Rural Subsistence and Poverty in West Africa*. Rugby, UK: Practical Action Publishing.

Hocart, A. M.
1927   *Kingship*. London: Oxford University Press.

Hohfeld, Wesley Newcomb
1964[1919]   *Fundamental Legal Conceptions as Applied in Judicial Reasoning*. W.W. Cook, ed. New Haven, CT: Yale University Press.

Hopkins, Anthony
2000   Asante and the Victorians: Transition and Partition on the Gold Coast. In *Imperialism, Decolonization, and Africa: Studies Presented to John Hargreaves*, R. Bridges, ed. New York: St. Martin's Press.

Jacka, Jeremy
2015   *Alchemy in the Rain Forest: Politics, Ecology, and Resilience in a New Guinea Mining Area*. Durham, NC: Duke University Press.

Kantorowicz, Ernst
1957   *The King's Two Bodies: A Study in Medieval Political Theology*. Princeton, NJ: Princeton University Press.

Kennedy, Duncan
1997   *A Critique of Adjudication: fin de siècle*. Cambridge, MA: Harvard University Press.
2006   Three Globalizations of Law and Legal Thought: 1850–2000. In *The New Law and Economic Development: A Critical Appraisal*, D. M. Trubek and A. Santos, eds. New York: Cambridge University Press.

Kimble, David
1963   *A Political History of Ghana: The Rise of Gold Coast Nationalism, 1850–1928*. Oxford: Clarendon Press.

Kirsch, Stuart
2007   Indigenous Movements and the Risks of Counterglobalization: Tracking the Campaign against Papua New Guinea's Ok Tedi Mine. *American Ethnologist* 34(2):303–21.
2014   *Mining Capitalism: The Relationship between Corporations and Their Critics*. Berkeley, CA: University of California Press.

Lentz, Carola
2007   Decentralization, the State, and Conflicts over Local Boundaries in Northern Ghana.

In *Twilight Institutions: Public Authority and Local Politics in Africa*, C. Lund, ed. London: Wiley-Blackwell.

Lentz, Carola, and Paul Nugent
2000 *Ethnicity in Ghana: The Limits of Invention*. New York: St. Martin's Press.

Li, Fabiana
2015 *Unearthing Conflict: Corporate Mining, Activism, and Expertise in Peru*. Durham, NC: Duke University Press.

Li, Tania
2010 Indigeneity, Capitalism, and the Management of Dispossession. *Current Anthropology* 51(3):385–414.

Lund, Christian
2008 *Local Politics and the Dynamics of Property in Africa*. Cambridge: Cambridge University Press.

Mann, Kristin, and Richard Roberts
1991 *Law in Colonial Africa*. London: James Currey.

Manson, Andrew, and Bernard Mbenga
2003 'The Richest Tribe in Africa': Platinum-Mining and the Bafokeng in South Africa's North West Province, 1965–1999. *Journal of Southern African Studies* 29(1):25–47.

Marshall, Ruth
2009 *Political Spiritualities: The Pentecostal Revolution in Nigeria*. Chicago: University of Chicago Press.

Mbembe, Achille
2003 Necropolitics. *Public Culture* 15(1):11–40.

McCaskie, Thomas C.
1983 Accumulation, Wealth, and Belief in Asante History. I. To the Close of the Nineteenth Century. *Africa* 53:23–43, 79.
1992 People and Animals: Constru(ct)ing the Asante Experience. *Africa* 62(2):221–47.

McLeod, M. D.
1981 *The Asante*. London: British Museum Publications.

Meyer, Birgit
1999 *Translating the Devil: Religion and Modernity among the Ewe of Ghana*. Trenton, NJ: Africa World Press.

Meyerowitz, Eva L. R.
1951a *The Sacred State of the Akan*. London: Faber and Faber.
1951b Concepts of the Soul among the Akan of the Gold Coast. *Africa* 21(1):24–31.

Morris, Rosalind
2008 The Miner's Ear. *Transition* 98:96–115.

Nash, June
1979 *We Eat the Mines and the Mines Eat Us: Dependency and Exploitation in Bolivian Tin Mines*. New York: Columbia University Press.

Nkrumah, Kwame
1968 *Dark Days in Ghana*. London: Lawrence & Wishart.

Nugent, Paul
2010 States and Social Contracts in Africa. *New Left Review* 63:35–68.

Obeng, J. Pashington
1996 *Asante Catholicism: Religious and Cultural Reproduction among the Akan of Ghana*. New York: E. J. Brill.

Odotei, Irene K., and Albert K. Awedoba, eds.
  2006 *Chieftancy in Ghana: Culture, Governance, and Development*. Legon: Sub-Saharan Publishers.
Ofosu-Mensah, Emmanuel Ababio
  2010 Traditional Gold Mining in Adanse. *Nordic Journal of African Studies* 19:124–47.
  2011a Gold Mining and the Socio-Economic Development of Obuasi in Adanse. *African Journal of History and Culture* 3(4):54–64.
  2011b Historical Overview of Traditional and Modern Gold Mining in Ghana. *International Research Journal of Library, Information, and Archival Studies* 1(1):6–22.
Owusu-Mensah, Isaac
  2013 Politics, Chieftancy, and Customary Law in Ghana. *KAS International Reports* 9:31–48.
Pietz, William
  1985 The Problem of the Fetish, I. *RES: Journal of Anthropology and Aesthetics* 9:5–17.
Piot, Charles
  2010 *Nostalgia for the Future: West Africa after the Cold War*. Chicago: University of Chicago Press.
Povinelli, Elizabeth
  1995 Do Rocks Listen? The Cultural Politics of Apprehending Australian Aboriginal Labor. *American Anthropologist* 97(3):505–18.
Powdermaker, Hortense
  1962 *Copper Town: Changing Africa; the Human Situation on the Rhodesian Copperbelt*. New York: Harper & Row.
Puett, Michael
  2013 Economies of Ghosts, Gods, and Goods: The History and Anthropology of Chinese Temple Networks. In *Radical Egalitarianism: Local Realities, Global Relations*, M. M. J. Fischer, F. Aulino, M. Goheen, and S. J. Tambiah, eds. New York: Fordham University Press.
Rajak, Dinah
  2011 *In Good Company: An Anatomy of Corporate Social Responsibility*. Stanford, CA: Stanford University Press.
Ranger, Terence
  1983 Invention of Tradition in Colonial Africa. In *The Invention of Tradition*, E. Hobsbawm and T. Ranger, eds. New York: Cambridge University Press.
Rata, Elizabeth
  1999 The Theory of Neotribal Capitalism. *Review (Fernand Braudel Center)* 22(3):231–88.
  2011 Encircling the Commons: Neotribal Capitalism in New Zealand since 2000. *Anthropological Theory* 11(3):327–53.
Rathbone, Richard
  2000 *Nkrumah and the Chiefs: The Politics of Chieftaincy in Ghana, 1951–1960*. Athens, OH: Ohio University Press.
  2006 From Kingdom to Nation: Changing African Constructions of Identity. In *Chieftaincy in Ghana: Culture, Governance and Development*, I. K. Odotei and A. K. Awedoba, eds. Accra: Sub-Saharan Publishers.
Rattray, R. Sutherland
  1916 *Ashanti Proverbs: The Primitive Ethics of a Savage People*. R. Sutherland Rattray, trans. Oxford: Clarendon Press.

Ray, Donald I.
    1996   Divided Sovereignty: Traditional Authorities and the State in Ghana. *Journal of Legal Pluralism and Unofficial Law* 37/38:181–202.
Robotham, Donald
    1989   *Militants or Proletarians? The Economic Culture of Underground Gold Miners in Southern Ghana, 1906–1976*. Cambridge: African Studies Centre.
Roitman, Janet
    2006   The Ethics of Illegality in the Chad Basin. In *Law and Disorder in the Postcolony*, J. Comaroff and J. L. Comaroff, eds. Chicago: University of Chicago Press.
Rouse, Carolyn
    2017   *Development Hubris: Adventures Trying to Save the World*. Princeton, NJ: Princeton University Press.
Sahlins, Marshall
    1985   *Islands of History*. Chicago: University of Chicago Press.
Santner, Eric
    2011   *The Royal Remains: The People's Two Bodies and the Endgames of Sovereignty*. Chicago: University of Chicago Press.
Sarpong, Peter Kwasi
    1971   *The Sacred Stools of the Akan*. Accra: Ghana Publishing Corporation.
    1996   *Libation*. Accra: Anansesem Publications.
Schmitt, Carl
    2005[1922]   *Political Theology: Four Chapters on the Concept of Sovereignty*. Chicago: University of Chicago Press.
Shipley, Jesse Weaver
    2009   Comedians, Pastors, and the Miraculous Agency of Charisma in Ghana. *Cultural Anthropology* 24(3):523–52.
Smith, James H.
    2011   Tantalus in the Digital Age: Coltan Ore, Temporal Dispossession, and 'Movement' in the Eastern Democratic Republic of the Congo. *American Ethnologist* 38(1):17–35.
Snyder, Francis G.
    1982   Colonialism and Legal Form: The Creation of 'Customary Law' in Senegal. In *Crime, Justice, and Underdevelopment*, C. Sumner, ed. London: Heinemann.
Stewart, Charles
    2003   Dreams of Treasure: Temporality, Historicization, and the Unconscious. *Anthropological Theory* 3(4):481–500.
Taussig, Michael
    1980   *The Devil and Commodity Fetishism in South America*. Chapel Hill, NC: University of North Carolina Press.
    1997   *The Magic of the State*. New York: Routledge.
Tubb, Daniel
    n.d.   *Washing Gold and Cocaine: Gold-Based Money Laundering in Colombia*. Manuscript.
Turner, Terence S.
    1995   An Indigenous People's Struggle for Socially Equitable and Ecologically Sustainable Production: The Kayapo Revolt Against Extractivism. *Journal of Latin American and Caribbean Anthropology* 1(1):98–121.
Turner, Victor
    1967   *The Forest of Symbols: Aspects of Ndembu Ritual*. Ithaca, NY: Cornell University Press.

1975   Symbolic Studies. *Annual Review of Anthropology* 4(1):145–61.

1982   Images of Anti-Temporality: An Essay in the Anthropology of Experience. *Harvard Theological Review* 75(2):243–65.

Valeri, Valerio

1985   *Kingship and Sacrifice: Ritual and Society in Ancient Hawaii.* P. Wissing, trans. Chicago: University of Chicago Press.

Von Laue, Theodore H.

1976   Anthropology and Power: R. S. Rattray among the Ashanti. *African Affairs* 75(298): 33–54.

Walsh, Andrew

2003   'Hot Money' and Daring Consumption in a Northern Malagasy Sapphire-Mining Town. *American Ethnologist* 30(2):290–305.

Watts, Michael J.

2004   Resource Curse? Governmentality, Oil, and Power in the Niger Delta, Nigeria. *Geopolitics* 9(1):50–80.

Welker, Marina

2009   'Corporate Security Begins in the Community': Mining, the Corporate Social Responsibility Industry, and Environmental Advocacy in Indonesia. *Cultural Anthropology* 24(1):142–79.

2014   *Enacting the Corporation: An American Mining Firm in Post-Authoritarian Indonesia.* Berkeley, CA: University of California Press.

West, Harry, and Scott Kloeck-Jensen

1999   Betwixt and Between: 'Traditional Authority' and Democratic Decentralization in Post-War Mozambique. *African Affairs* 98(393):455–84.

Whitfield, Lindsay

2005   Trustees of Development from Conditionality to Governance: Poverty Reduction Strategy Papers in Ghana. *Journal of Modern African Studies* 43(4):641–64.

Wilks, Ivor

1979   The Golden Stool and the Elephant Tail: An Essay on Wealth in Asante. *Research in Economic Anthropology* 2:1–36.

1993   *Forests of Gold: Essays on the Akan and the Kingdom of Asante.* Athens, OH: Ohio University Press.

Wilson, Monica

1951   Witch Beliefs and Social Structure. *American Journal of Sociology* 56(4):307–13.

Worger, William

1987   *South Africa's City of Diamonds: Mine Workers and Monopoly Capitalism in Kimberley, 1867–1895.* New Haven, CT: Yale University Press.

ELEVEN

Colonizing Banro

*Kingship, Temporality, and Mining of Futures
in the Goldfields of South Kivu, DRC*

JAMES SMITH

In 2006, residents of the Shi *chefferie*, or chiefdom, of Luhwindja, South Kivu, came back down from the hills after a battle remembered with horror as *Le Onze*. During this dramatic, deadly confrontation on 11 June 2005, government troops chased away both the local defense force comprised of civilians and the Forces for the Democratic Liberation of Rwanda (FDLR), the Hutu rebel militia. They had been living in Luhwindja, "protecting" the community as well as the acting *mwami* (chief/king; plural, *wami*), Justin Karhibahaza Mukuba, younger brother of the then recently murdered *Mwami* Philemon Kashema Mukuba. When the Luhwindjans returned home, they were surprised to see UN trucks, which they later learned were carrying personnel of the Canadian gold mining company Banro, who went about setting up tents at Twangiza, where they would soon build a factory.

People in Luhwindja knew that they were witnessing the culmination of a long, complicated history involving the control of their goldfields by international companies—with direct effects on their way of life, which had long been dependent on artisanal mining. In 1996, Banro had purchased the rights to the state-owned company Sominki's Congolese concessions. But when Laurent Kabila and his supporters ousted President Mobutu in the First Congolese War, the new president refused to accept this agreement. He argued, on the radio and in other public forums, that Banro was not interested in the "development" of the country and even insinuated that the company was angry with him and might try to do him harm. During his three years in office, he created a new public corporation, Somico (Societe Miniere du Congo), and made *Mwami* Philemon, from Luhwindja, its director. It is not entirely clear why he did this, but it seems related to the fact that Philemon had long asserted his customary rights to all the products of the town, including its gold, and had resisted incursions from foreign firms.

After Laurent Kabila had become president, he ordered the Rwandan and Ugandan troops who had put him in power to return home. To make a long story short, they refused, instead inciting a rebellion of Congolese with putative Rwandan ancestry. The sustained presence in the Eastern Congo of the FDLR, the Hutu militia, was the main reason for their unwillingness to leave. The intervention of the Rally for Congolese Democracy (RCD), backed by the Rwandan government, culminated in the Second Congolese War, which began in 1998 and formally ended in 2003 but continued in some areas for a few more years. Conflict persists in some places to this day. Laurent Kabila was assassinated during the middle of the war, in late 2001, and his son Joseph became president. While Laurent had rejected Banro's claims to Sominki's properties, Joseph supported them.

Mwami Philemon was murdered in Paris a few weeks before the assassination of Laurent Kabila, leading many people in Luhwindja to connect the two deaths (see more on this below). While some blame supporters of Mobutu, or point to debts that the *mwami* is said to have had, others believe Banro was involved. Some even argue that its desire to regain access to the land it had purchased from Sominki was among the chief reasons for the Second Congolese War.

I have conducted fieldwork in two different towns in which Banro has mining operations—Luhwindja (South Kivu) and Salamabila (Maniema). The first is a Shi chiefdom—although Shi are more likely to translate *mwami* as "king" than as "chief"—while the second is populated mainly by Bangubangu, who have no history of hereditary rulers; among them, *mwami* refers to a lineage head or to a senior with ritual knowledge, which includes the ability to communicate with ancestors. A major contrast between them is that, in Luhwindja, the *mwami* and *mwami kazi* (female ruler; see below), the regent who currently rules the *chefferie*, have absorbed much of the public discontent regarding Banro; in Salamabila the antagonism is directly between corporation and populace. In early 2016, one of company's security personnel fired on peaceful protestors in the town, killing one. The protestors were demonstrating against their expulsion from the goldfields they had been mining since the liberalization of artisanal extraction under Mobutu. In Salamabila, there was little disagreement about who was to blame. But in Luhwindja, that is not so: *wami* are seen to be, at least potentially, even more selfish and exploitative than Banro. As we have already seen, they do more than merely collaborate with, or absorb the blame for, foreign companies: Philemon and his brother, the acting *Mwami* Justin, might have offered a measure of resistance to foreign capital, but they also sought, by drawing upon their customary authority, to profit from the corporatization of gold mining.

In this chapter, I describe some of the historic and current conflicts and collaborations among *wami*, ordinary people, and companies in Luhwindja, focusing on their temporal dimensions. My reasons for dwelling on temporality are multiple. For the most part, the study of chiefs in Africa has had a surprisingly strong spatial bias: these rulers are described as having governed rural territories, controlling labor in them despotically, with a more or less disingenuous nod to the past (Mamdani 1996). According to this logic, chiefly subjection is to national citizenship as country is to city, peasant to wage laborer. All exist along a spatial-geographic axis in which temporality is suspended because everyone exists in the same time, the time of capitalism, this being a point that Raymond Williams argued long ago in *The Country and the City* (1975). Given this perspective, it is all too easy to see chiefs as agents of parochial conservatism, of local belonging, in contrast to cosmopolitan global citizenship. They play a purely reactive part in a rather mechanistic story of globalization, in which capital flows trigger reactionary outbursts of local autochthony (Geschiere 2000). In this story, customary authorities are either barriers to global flows or their unwitting agents. A focus on temporality, by contrast, opens up new imaginative possibilities. It also brings us closer to what people on the ground actually think about their sovereigns, and how they try to use them to change their situations—not least by the channeling of invisible forces, including the world of ancestors.

The temporality of chiefs is complex, especially in this last respect. They do not simply represent or speak for the historic past, either precolonial or colonial. They also are typically thought to have a collaborative relationship with ancestors and so are supposed to have access to an alternative ontological realm on which their descendants depend. Those ancestors embody the ways, habits, and values of time immemorial, but they do not exist in the past perfect; they reside alongside us, "living" proof that the past is never really past. In Luhwindja, this temporality is still more complex, because the relationship of kings to the ancestral realm is not unchallenged—particularly, but not only, in the case of the reigning regent, the *mwami kazi*. Some see their role as agents of modernity to be more important than their role as agents of the past. Moreover, Luhwindjans' understandings of the temporality of *bwami* ("kingship") are not easily distinguished from Euromodern ideas about sovereignty, past and present, including the Euromodern preoccupation with the category of the medieval.

Some Preliminary Thoughts on Feudalism

I remember a conversation I had a few years back with a man I will call Gilbert, a white South African engineer and on-site managing director of Banro in Luhwindja, who proudly proclaimed that his expertise was limited mainly to blowing up holes in the ground. I suspect that his humility reflected the powerful simplicity of his work: he knew that mines could unleash unpredictable events and forces and that Banro's work would shake up a social world that, in his mind, belonged to an outmoded time. At that point, white Banro employees still felt comfortable driving around Luhwindja, and so Gilbert escorted me in his Land Cruiser from the factory to the house where I was staying. As he talked, he gradually moved away from his area of expertise to his vision for the future of Luhwindja. He began by stating that its people were feudal, living under an oppressive aristocracy. Banro and the gold mine would upend all anachronisms and drag them, against their will, into World History:

> Banro will revolutionize this society. We will force these feudal people to completely change the way they live. They are going to get money and buy businesses, and that will weaken the hold of the aristocracy and the *mwami*, and then people will have to decide for themselves for the first time what the future will look like.

Gilbert's comment was conventional in many ways. For him, Luhwindja existed in a different time from the rest of the world; its present was analogous to Europe's medieval past. His denial of its coevality had the added benefit of allowing him to downplay Banro's dispossession of its people from their homes, land, and goldfields. From this linear understanding of history, and of the birth of European modernity out of feudalism, Gilbert also generated the hopeful expectation of a positive future for Luhwindja based on the capacity of money and markets to liberate it from tyrannical custom. His claim was permeated by dubious assumptions. Perhaps the most consequential was the notion that Luhwindjans believed that the *mwami kazi* represented their interests because she, or her office, was sacred and traditional—and because "her" people accepted her sacrality without question. After all, Banro had paid her an unknown amount of money as compensation for the revenue she would be losing from artisanal miners. They also relied on her to determine the best distribution for the "development funds" the company promised to contribute to the community for projects, infrastructure, and services.

Gilbert's views on feudalism would not have been completely alien in Luhwindja. After all, chiefship here is partially mediated by the European understanding of feudalism as it is imagined to have existed in the West. Colonialism instrumentalized the medieval in the form of what is often glossed as "indirect governance." It bolstered kingly authority while associating kings with the customary past in opposition to the "modern," secular authority of emerging educated elites, called, in the DRC, the *evolue*, or evolved. And so it is inevitable that many Africans, especially the mission educated, would come to see indigenous rulers in much the same way as Enlightenment thinkers saw those of the Middle Ages. Thus, for example, a good number of them questioned whether the *mwami* and *mwami kazi* ought to have been compensated for their loss of revenue when Banro had artisanal miners expelled from their concession: Why, they asked, should the company give money to a traditional authority representing a parochial past rather than contribute to the future development of Luhwindja as a whole?

But those who knew more about the history of the office might have pointed out the vanguard role that *wami* have actually played in the past. This is especially so with respect to the democratization of mining, from which both royalty and nonroyalty were excluded in colonial times—partly because gold and money were thought to undermine traditional authority by commercializing it, so to pollute it with the present.

Bwami's Multiple Temporalities: The Old Testament, Ancestors, and Literary Bureaucracy

Luhwindjans' narratives of the history of *bwami* convey the multiple temporalities that emerge in and through the institution—including the temporalities of other places. At the very least, these narratives suggest that *wami* have long tried to carve out larger roles for themselves than the label "custom" would imply. Tellingly, for many, this history is permeated by their understanding of other histories, in particular, Old Testament stories of kings such as David, as well, vaguely, as those of France's "medieval" past prior to the French Revolution. It is common for people to range freely between Bible stories, colonial history, and anecdotes about the Sun King when chronicling "traditional" Luhwindja kingship. But there *are* certain things that can be inferred about the present from their accounts of the past.

The first *wami* are said to have come from Rwanda. In these stories they are cast as potentially dangerous aliens who had to be domesticated by the true autochthons through exchange. According to their telling, people from Rwanda were wandering around looking for places to herd their cattle and saw a fire burning near Twangiza, where Banro currently has its factory. That fire was a product of the ingenuity of the first family of Luhwindja, a lineage now closely connected to, but distinct from, the lineage of *wami*. In most versions, that family fled these potential enemies but were called back later by the Rwandans and told not to be afraid. On their return, they sat with the interlopers, with whom they came to an agreement about settlement. Over time, the once dangerous foreigners constituted a royal clan that extended its convivial dominion over locals by indebting them through the loan of livestock. They became owners of the land through their cattle; even today one acquires a holding by giving cattle, or a monetary substitute, "back" to its rightful owner, the *mwami*. Today, Sara Geenen (2015) points out, miners assert their customary claims to their sites by virtue of their payments to the king's tax collectors. These recorded historical payments mean that residents' land claims are valid—and that Banro is expected to acknowledge them when compensating people for revenue lost.

If livestock allowed these interlopers to rule, it was not as if the Rwandans had all the power. Whereas that power is portrayed as being rooted in animals—and in the obligations and relations they produced—Luhwindja's indigenes possessed the ability to manage nature and the world of ancestors. Over time, as they became more closely connected through exchange and marriage, the separateness between the Rwandan Others and the original inhabitants, and between their respective powers, dissipated. It was the inherited potency of that first Luhwindja family that *Mwami* Philemon would later use to make the Tutsi invaders sick and unable to continue during the First Congolese War of 1996. Philemon escaped to Belgium after that, which is said partly to account for why Luhwindja, deprived of his relationship to the ancestors, was invaded by different occupying armies.

At another level, the origin narrative suggests a strong ambivalence in contemporary attitudes toward *wami*, projected onto the past: the birth of *bwami* consisted in a sacrifice of autonomy for the promise of wealth in livestock, which ended up actually yielding debt and social stratification. Once the new hierarchical social order established itself, it became almost impossible to stop the rapaciousness of particular kings. But, as the story suggests, *bwami* consisted in the marriage of two different kinds of power that could, theoretically, be separated once more if an officeholder ceased to be the protector of Luhwindja. Today, for example, the *mwami*'s totems, including a dog and a leopard, are said to have abandoned his home, indicating that the boy ruler and his regent, the *mwami kazi*, have lost their moral legitimacy in the wake of Banro's invasion. By benefiting financially from their involvement with the company at the cost of their subjects, they are no longer recognized as the guardians of "nature" or "custom" by these animals themselves. In similar vein, many remember that *Mwami* Philemon's leopard howled continually when the Canadian firm first arrived; in so doing, it communicated the concerns of the ancestors.

The transformation of *wamis*' powers during the colonial period is told through a series of stories, many of which have to do with literacy and colonial bureaucracy. The initial contact between the first *mwami* and Belgians is described as tragic for the former: he left Luhwindja to meet the colonizers as they were coming from Maniema Province in the east and died of malaria during the trip. His son, *Mwami* Cibwire, ruled after that, from roughly 1900 until the early 1930s, and was the first king to act as a colonial functionary, collecting tax for the authorities, who, it seems, were often dissatisfied with him. Luhwindjans say that the *wazungu* (Europeans) went to Cibwire, asking for one of his sons to be educated at the mission school so that he might help the ruler with writing and administration. Fearing that the Belgians would eat that son, he refused, but the *wazungu* were persistent. Cibwire knew that one of his offspring, Mulinda Babisha, was a *bandiya*, a criminal with "bad habits" who was hated by everyone, even his own family. So the ruler gave him to the Europeans, thinking they would kill and eat him. Instead they sent him to school, as promised. When he returned, he not only came with great knowledge. He was also close to the *wazungu*. Cibwire's firstborn, Rusagara, was the rightful heir, but the authorities forced Mulinda Babisha onto Luhwindja and the ruling descent group because he could keep records and accounts. Everyone protested, explaining that Babisha was incapable of "living well with people." To no avail.

As the residents of the *chefferie* had anticipated, *Mwami* Mulinda Babisha, backed by the Belgians, used his position both to appropriate his subjects' fields and cows and to imprison his enemies. In 1932, he is said to have written a letter to the colonial government, informing them that his brother, Ntama, was growing marijuana at Twangiza. Babisha called on the authorities to chase Ntama out because he wanted the land. When the police came, there was a battle. People were killed and Ntama was imprisoned. In Luhwindja, the story goes that, when the local Belgian administrator made his written report to the provincial administration, his superiors asked him why he had ordered this violent attack. According to older informants, the white administrator said that it was not he who had killed those people. It was the letter that the *mwami* had written to him. In other words, the ruler's incendiary, perhaps disingenuous communication had provoked a response way out of proportion with the crime, if there had been one. The police followed up by arresting Babisha and imprisoning him in Lubutu, some distance away. The capacity to write letters, the narrative suggests, was a source of colonial potency that the *mwami* tried but failed to control for his own advantage. Ironically, he ended up in prison because of that letter. In the upshot, Cibwire's firstborn, Rusagara, became *mwami* and governed until 1939. But the conflict continues. For example, in the spring of 2015, some of the descendants of Mulinda Babisha, abetted by local armed groups, attacked the *mwami*'s house with AK-47s and grenades, apparently in an effort to murder the *mwami* and *mwami kazi*. They were ultimately repelled by the army.

These events point to the ambivalent nature of customary authority during the colonial period. On the one hand, overrule diminished the power of *wami*: they often clashed with the authorities and found themselves imprisoned, as in the case of Mulinda Babisha and the brothers Mukuba and Ruvura, discussed below. On the other hand, the Belgian presence greatly enhanced their standing: not only did it elevate them into bureaucrats with the ability to write letters and summon government forces at will, but state-sanctioned violence gave them a new kind of legitimacy, enabling them to mediate between ordinary Congolese and the Europeans. There was a downside, however: their authority was now nested within an even larger and more encompassing suzerainty, in which Luhwindja's emerging mission-educated elites were even more fluent.

After Rusagara, *Mwami* Mukuba (1939–1986) took over but was soon imprisoned for failing to hand over taxes that he had collected to the government, keeping them instead for himself and his kin. While he was incarcerated, a Belgian functionary acted in his stead for about a year but decided that this was "not work for Belgians": someone from the *mwami*'s family should be governing as "regent." According to my interlocutors, this is the first time that the concept of regency was explicitly deployed here; a regent mother had been installed during the colonial period in neighboring Shi chiefdoms, but not in Luhwindja. The authorities visited Mukuba in jail to ask him who the interim *mwami* should be. He named his brother, Ruvura, because he was clever. But Ruvura is said to have thought the job of mediating between the colonial state and his people too dif-

ficult, so he fled. The police picked him up and threw him in jail along
with his brother, after which he was forced to rule, which he did between
1942 and 1946. Eventually he grew into the task, realizing the "virtues" of
leadership—and the opportunities for enrichment that the position conferred. Some speculated that artisanal gold mining, which began in earnest
during this time, might have had something to do with it. When Mukuba
was released from prison, Ruvura refused to forfeit his position, but the
police forced him to abdicate, thus demonstrating that kingship was subordinate to the larger colonial administrative system in which it was nested.

By the end of the colonial period, many in Luhwindja appear to have
thought about *wami* in much the same way as did Enlightenment Europeans of their monarchs: at worst parasites, at best necessary evils. As one
older man put it, reflecting on the colonial period: "Kings were always
lazy . . . They could take your land, your cows, and your wives, and you
could do nothing to stop them." But, he went on, they protected Luhwindja
from enemies, established laws, and settled disputes. They also adjudicated
land rights, the flow of water through agricultural plots, and, later, mining
claims. Moreover, while a new generation of mission educated elites came
into open conflict with *wami*—seeing them as the embodiment of a ret-
rograde past—these indigenous authorities developed a new alliance with
the poor: "The poor loved the rulers because they helped with school fees,
provided homes for orphans, and even found jobs for some people." And
they opened the door to artisanal gold mining, which changed everything
for them and their subjects alike.

Democratizing Gold Mining, or How the *Mwami* Went from Being Ignorant of Gold to Being the Owner of All Gold

The discovery of gold in Luhwindja during the 1940s had an ambivalent
impact on *wami*: it circumscribed and undermined their authority over the
land but gave them a new source of wealth and a different kind of popular legitimacy. In the late colonial period, neither ruler nor residents could
legally dig or lay claim to the metal. Older people recall how the Belgians
told them that it was poisonous, that merely touching it required inces-
sant hand washing for months on end. Even the *mwami*, the guardian and
"owner" of the soil, was not involved in extraction. Nor was he given any
compensation for what was mined.

But a new relationship emerged between artisanal miners and *wami*
during this period: these men, who referred to themselves as "geologues"
(see below), mined the MGL concession at night—MGL was the company

then licensed to operate in Luhwindja—and paid a certain quantity of gold to the ruler as tribute. In exchange, he worked to ensure that the police did not go after them and provided protection for those who were prosecuted. The wealth brought to the *mwami* was relatively limited, but the operations of that first generation of geologues gave fresh life to the notion that he was the owner of the soil, or *udongo*, and to the claim that the "soil" extended beneath the ground, encompassing the minerals in it. This also meant that ordinary people could acquire customary rights to mining land. Moreover, the new relationship between the artisans and the ruler gave material substance to the perception that the *Mwami* was a patron of the poor, since only those without other meaningful livelihoods engaged in this kind of work.

On the surface, Mobutu Sese Seko's postcolonial government diminished the authority of chiefs, but in reality the liberalization of gold mining gave a new life to *wami* in Luhwindja. While the "general property law" of 1973 rendered all land and subsoil the possession of the government, it also made ambiguous provisions for customary authority (Geenen and Claessens 2013). Mobutu nationalized the main mining companies during the same period; MGL was taken over by Sominki, Societe Miniere et Industrielle du Kivu, a semi-public company, in 1976. But, as Sara Geenen (2011:13) explains, "due to bad management, and combined with a more general economic crisis, the nationalization and 'Zairianization' measures had a disastrous effect on Congo's mineral production." When Sominki abandoned its claims, miners settled into the shafts and dug. One of them reflected the general sense that extraction was opened up to everyone by the nationalization of land when he said, "Before 1973 there were artisanal miners, but it wasn't legal. Mining was a form of theft. But after 1973 everyone did as they wanted." In 1982, Mobutu officially legalized artisanal gold mining in an act seen as one element of a larger policy of *debrouilliez vous*, or "take care of yourself"—also referred to as "Article 15," although no such article seems to exist—meaning that one should use the official position or resources at one's disposal to make a living.

Even when they are supportive of the claims of artisanal miners, most published accounts of this period describe them like a plague of parasites, or an infectious disease, taking over the decaying body of the state-corporate nexus. They tell how, for example, the miners began to "infiltrate shafts," notwithstanding "repressive policies." But these geologues understood what was happening in very different terms. As in the colonial period, in paying tax to the *mwami*, they believed themselves to be acquiring customary rights to prospect and even to own specific holes (see Geenen

2015; Geenen and Claessens 2013), all the more so since their tribute bolstered the wealth of these local rulers. While the authority of *wami* was formally curtailed under Mobutu, at least one man remembered that the president had recognized their sacred powers over the earth to include gold.

> The *mwami*'s power doesn't come from law, but from God. . . . These powers brought rain and crops, and gold is one aspect of this, passing from God through the *mwami*. But *wami* didn't know about gold until the Belgian mining company opened operations in the 1950s, and then people were not allowed to touch it. The only way to get money was to sell our milk to a Belgian dairy operation. But then Mobutu opened up mining and that meant it was also opened up for the *mwami*, who became rich from the gold that was dug. And so the town of Luhwindja was built.

Mwami Philemon (1988–2000), who would later contest Banro's claims to Luhwindja, was among the rulers enriched and empowered by the liberalization of gold mining, benefitting from a reciprocal relationship with the uneducated, comparatively poor artisanal miners.

Mwami *Philemon and Somico*

Philemon is remembered for joining the historical legacy of *wami* with a project of future-oriented modernization, underwriting an alternative teleology of modernity rooted in the remembered past. For example, he is lauded for redistributing his wealth in line with traditional values: he gave money to those who needed it, paid children's schooling, and brought machines to build roads. At the same time, he also developed a system of taxation known as the *facture*, or receipt. His administration maintained records of how much miners produced; the percentage that they now paid in tax turned out to be greater than anything ever collected before. By employing the power of writing, numbers, and bureaucracy in new ways, Philemon became one of the wealthiest of all Luhwindja rulers. He also joined with university students and local elites to institutionalize the CODELU, Community for the Development of Luhwindja, because he knew that, in the era of *debrouillez vous*, his subjects had to look out for each other.

When people talk about how attitudes toward the *mwami* have changed since Philemon, they recall the time that his followers saved his life from his creditors: one day he called together the elders of all the lineages and admitted that he had misused the money of army generals to whom he had promised gold. He beseeched them, "You are my security, and if you don't do anything I'll die." The old men went to every village in the *chef-ferie* saying, "If the *mwami* dies, Luhwindja will die and we will all die, and this land will be taken away from us." Believing that their territorial claims rested on the tribute they had been paying to *wami*, his subjects brought goats, gold, bananas, cassavas, and chickens to the ruler, who sat emaciated at the back of his compound. A refugee in his sacred house, and in the village he was supposed to rule over like a god, he was still only able to pay back half the cash. He is said to have used some of it to get protection from Mobutu, who sent the police to guard over him. He was still in trouble when the First Congolese War began in 1996.

As I have already noted, Philemon also challenged foreign capital head-on. Toward the end of Mobutu's reign, Banro negotiated a contract with the government, forming a new company, Sakima, Société Aurifère du Kivu-Maniema, with "93 percent of the shares belonging to Banro and 7 percent to the Zairian state" (Geenen and Honke 2014:13). This was just before the First Congolese War, in which the Allied Forces for the Democratic Liberation of Congo (AFDL), headed by Laurent Kabila, swept through Congo, expelling Mobutu. Around that time, *Mwami* Philemon jailed a group of white men who had arrived by helicopter. These men claimed to be from Sakima, which people in Luhwindja today understand to have been Banro. A couple years later, in 1998, Laurent Kabila revoked Banro's mining titles, citing "irregularities in the liquidation of Sominki and the creation of Sakima" (cited in Geenen and Claessens 2013:93). He created Somico, a state-owned company, with *Mwami* Philemon as director. Not only did this represent a rejection of the claims of outside investors, but it also implied that the president backed the customary authority of the ruler against the corporation. In Luhwindja, moreover, it bespoke a new alliance between their *mwami* and the national leader, united against the foreign company.

The Rally for Congolese Democracy (RCD) rebellion broke out in South Kivu in 1998 (above, p. 280), just a few days after the creation of Somico. While Banro is alleged to have allied itself with the RCD, Philemon and his brother, Justin, were supported by Somico and, as noted earlier, the Hutu FDLR (Geenen et al. 2013). Over the next several years, Luhwindja was invaded by several militarized groups. During this period there was no industrialized extraction, but artisanal mining continued, with Philemon, and later Justin, collecting rents from the geologues. Indeed, it would not be until 2005, right after *Le Onze*—the deadly confrontation with which I began, when Congolese government troops chased out the FDLR, along with acting *Mwami* Justin—that Banro would finally arrive to build a future out of the ashes. Throughout the hostilities, Philemon and Justin had argued that Somico belonged to the people of Luhwindja, who should resist expropriation by foreign companies like Banro (see also Geenen and Claessens 2013). In other words, they used the troubled situation to further cement a link between mining and kingship. And to do so in a way that seemed to include a future for artisanal gold miners.

It was in December 2000 that Philemon was murdered in Paris, allegedly on the way to the party of a friend of Mobutu. His charred corpse was found by the road side; when it was returned to Luhwindja, nobody was allowed to see it. President Laurent-Desire Kabila was assassinated a few weeks later, on January 16, 2001. Their near-simultaneous murders challenged Somico's claims to the mining concession and opened the way for Banro to follow through on its purchase of Sominki, thence to begin mining in Luhwindja and elsewhere in the Eastern Congo. But, while Philemon was out of the picture, Banro still had to contend with his angry and courageous brother, the acting *Mwami* Justin, who had now allied himself fully with the FDLR, some of whose cadres, recall, had remained in or returned to Luhwindja.

The Democratic Militarization of Luhwindja and the Coming of the *Mwami Kazi*

After Philemon died, Luhwindja was governed by a council of five, of whom Justin was one. When the Rwandan-backed RCD entered the Second Congolese War and established its dominance, those who were able fled to the forest, Justin among them. After a short while, however, he "returned to die in the village," thereby becoming a local hero. It is said that, at this time, he was "made *mwami*" by the people, his relationship to them being consolidated by the conflict. Unlike other rulers, he did not depend on the *baganda*, senior advisors, but drew support from artisanal miners, from whom he also collected tax. Later, in the middle of the upheaval, the governor recognized Justin as the *mwami*'s official representative, giving him the authority to "sign papers and write letters."

In due course, Justin appears to have "tired" of Luhwindja being harassed by armed groups and of the ongoing theft of cows. He wrote to the RCD governor in South Kivu, requesting that his subjects be allowed to arm themselves against the Hutu FDLR. The provincial government, very unusually, agreed. And so his subjects used their earnings from gold to purchase weapons. In the years that followed, women would go to the fields with AK-47s strapped to their backs; nearly everyone, by all accounts, was armed. Even today, many still have weapons hidden in their homes, a fact of which Banro is well aware.

But Justin probably went too far when he turned around and allied himself with the FDLR, or, rather, when, under his authority, Luhwindja domesticated the Hutu militia. According to a popular story, its cadres grew weary of "being licked" by the locals and eventually asked Justin if they could just live in the town—whose residents, for their part, wanted to trade with the soldiers. Soon the ruler was flanked by a retinue of FDLR personnel everywhere he went. Some of them had a camp in the center of Luhwindja and stayed there for a year or so between 2004 and 2005. Banro, it is alleged, continued to visit and prospect during the occupation under the disguise of the UN. As one man remembered,

> Banro was having a hard time entering Luhwindja because Justin wouldn't allow it, so they came up with the strategy of coming with MONUC [the military wing of the United Nations, later renamed MONESCO], and they didn't even stop in to see Justin. They used MONUC trucks, and people thought it was MONUC when it was Banro. This was Banro's way of entering [their concession at] Twangiza to understand what was there and what "the politics" were like.

Some time after this, in 2005, Esperance, Philemon's widow from the district of Kalehe and later the *mwami kazi*, came to Luhwindja to convince the population to accept both Banro's claims to its concession and her regency. One of my informants explained that "the *mwami kazi* came to talk to Justin to figure out a way for Banro to come here. Banro couldn't enter while the FDLR was living in Luhwindja, so she came to figure out how to make that happen." The pretense was that Justin was not a good bureaucrat and had failed to keep Esperance's young son, Tony, apprised of production yields at Twangiza. Another added, "Esperance accused Justin of not sending reports to her son, the *Mwami* Tony, on a regular basis while he was in Belgium. So they talked about bringing reports for the *mwami*, the FDLR leaving, and Banro entering." And then, suddenly, people surrounded Esperance's car, yelling, "We don't want Banro because we have Somico!," the company associated with Philemon and Laurent Kabila. Luhwindja's "local defense," joined by a small group of FDLR, fired their guns into the air. The *mwami kazi* fled. Another man continued the story, again drawing attention to the efficacy of letter writing and the governor's office: "After that, all of . . . those who were close to her got trouble from Justin, and were beaten

on the street, and most of them went to Kaziba [a nearby town] and Bukavu. This allowed the *mwami kazi* to write the governor and order a war."

Throughout the Eastern DR Congo, it is commonly thought that "war
comes from weakness," that the strong do not attack others. The point is
usually made with reference to militias comprised of impoverished youth
who join only because they lack other opportunities. Sometimes the phrase
is used to explain Rwanda's invasion in the Second Congolese War and in
subsequent "insurrections." In this case, it referred to Esperance's outsider
status in Luhwindja. She had no kinship ties there, "no uncle . . . no one
to stand for her," making her a lone, jealous widow and a potential witch.
The rumor of her letter to the governor about the Machiavellian Justin was
ostensibly about the enemy FDLR. But, in hindsight, its true purpose was
taken to be to encourage the entry of Banro, thus to consolidate her position. During the day-long firefight, *Le Onze* (above, p. 279), that followed
her alleged request "to order a war," the national army (FARDC) came with
"big guns on turrets on top of their cars" and Justin ran away. Soon thereafter, people from neighboring villages—including Kaziba, whence the governor of South Kivu hails—came to pillage homes in Luhwindja:

> Then, after a couple more days, Land Cruisers started coming, and it was
> Banro, and we knew they had finally entered. On the day of the war, Banro
> was close by in Kaziba [at the governor's home], listening to how the war was
> going. We knew that because people were running back and forth on that
> day, and some went to Kaziba because they had relatives there, and that's
> how they knew Banro was there waiting. And then the *mwami kazi* came and
> ruled Luhwindja.

With Justin out of the picture, Esperance returned to Luhwindja to govern as regent for the young *mwami*, Tony. It was then that she invented the
title *mwami kazi*, "woman king," throwing it out here and there to see if
it would stick. At times it did, at others it was met with resistance. As for
Justin, he fled to Nairobi and, in 2006, was elected to parliament. One day
he received a call from residents of Luhwindja, who had heard on the radio
and TV that he was no longer a parliamentarian. He could not believe it,
repeating over and over, "but I am in parliament right now." A court had
alleged that he was guilty of election fraud. Some of his former subjects
were convinced that Esperance was behind the accusation. He died a few
years later.

While the *mwami kazi* was not welcome when she first arrived, having
been blamed for *Le Onze* and the presence of Banro, the educated leaders

of the civil society organization CODELU interceded on her behalf. They hoped she would defend their interests in dealing with the mining company, which, they thought, could bring development to Luhwindja, in particular by allowing the town to exchange its gold reserves for a future that no longer depended on limited and ephemeral mineral resources. They wanted Banro to build schools, roads, and hospitals, and to contribute to community projects, like a new market. They even went so far as to ensure that Esperance was selected as one of three MPs representing "custom" in the provincial parliament.[1] The company and the *mwami kazi* also worked together to get the artisanal miners to leave their sites, ostensibly on condition that they would be compensated with money, jobs, or an alternative site at which to mine. According to one member of the CODELU, however, this only applied to those who "were known," those who had paid tax to the *mwami* in the past. In other words, the ruler's financial records formed the moral and contractual basis for compensation to the geologues. For her part, the *mwami kazi* appeared uninterested in ensuring that even those who had paid tribute received their fair share. As an informant recalled:

> People never wanted that woman because she brought war here, but eventually we began to agree with her slowly, even to bring her goats and chickens, but then we eventually realized that we can't work with Banro without also having someone to help us stand up to Banro.

The *mwami kazi* and Banro were soon perceived to be inseparable. This was brought home by the fact that Esperance would regularly fly between Bukavu and Luhwindja on the company helicopter. Eventually, she was seen as the more dangerous of the two: a greedy foreigner, totally removed from the community, who wanted to retain power at all costs and refused to give up her office. This, it was said, was why she made her son, the *mwami*, stay abroad, perhaps bewitching him into doing so. Local people who returned home from London claimed that the young man, now well over eighteen, regularly missed appointments they had with him; even worse, he "ran away" from them at the last minute. What well-adjusted person would do this? When some Luhwindjans wrote to the president and the governor contesting Esperance's legitimacy, they were jailed: in 2010 about thirty people were incarcerated by the governor for more than six months for signing a petition to dismiss her. They were later freed, perhaps by order of the president, since both the governor and the *mwami kazi* expressed surprise when they returned to the town amidst great fanfare. Rumor had it that the two of them were sleeping together, that this explained why the petitioners had been imprisoned when they had not broken the law. Rather than being married in Luhwindja and being domesticated by her kin there, it was widely insinuated, Esperance was effectively wed to the provincial government, whose loyalties lay with Banro.

For the CODELU, the *mwami kazi* was an affront to the traditional past *and* to modern state law. Her reign provoked these educated elites to re-imagine a moral foundation for *bwami* rooted in custom *and* contract. One of them posited a future based on a hard won rapprochement between the customary and bureaucratic literacy:

> If someone is to be *mwami*, they're supposed to have a letter from the Minis-try of Interior, even if it is an interim position. The state writes a letter recog-nizing this authority after discussing with the seniors, and in this [instance] there's no time that this ever happened. The seniors never sat down and said, "Okay, this *mwami* has authority." Instead, she insulted the seniors at every turn! But the *mwami* is supposed to get all the secrets of everyone from the *baganda*, the secrets of every place and its history. Instead, the main sup-porter she has is the governor. But the governor has no authority to place the *mwami*. He just makes it official.

According to this interpretation, it was the Ministry of Interior that ought to have legalized her reign. But the bureaucracy had failed because of the collapse of government during the war. As a result, Esperance was propelled into office purely by virtue of her motherhood. Her legitimacy hinged on the whereabouts of a missing "letter of introduction":

> Justin had left suddenly, and there was no one administering in Luhwindja, and so in this chaos, she didn't go through the whole process. . . . At first, it was only educated people talking about this, but now even lowly people talk about this. Everyone agrees she shouldn't be the authority here because she doesn't have a letter. *Where is her letter* [from the Ministry of Interior], every-one wants to know!

But more than a missive from a remote authority was at issue. That letter should have been an expression, and the realization, of the *mwami kazi's* genuine customary authority, an authority that depends on "living well" with the *baganda*. Had she done so, engaging in acts of reciprocity and the circulation of knowledge, this letter from the government would have been forthcoming. Esperance, however, had acted too independently: "*People are the* mwami *and the* mwami *is the people*. But the *mwami kazi* brought the ways of Europe with her, and tried to make Luhwindja like Europe, where everyone is on their own."

If the *mwami kazi* had brought the "ways of Europe" to Luhwindja, the geologues would bring the world to the town—and the town to the world—via the instrument of the strike.

The Strike of 2011 and the Rise of Kadumwa

Fast forward to 2011, when the artisanal miners and the CODELU joined forces to protest both Banro's evacuation of people from their sites of extraction and its failure to make good on its promise of jobs or land in compensation. Together they organized a strike, paralyzing operations for three days. On the first day, the geologues took up a position between the laborers' camp and the factory, preventing employees from getting to work. They set fire to tires and felled trees to block the roads. Some hours later, Banro found another access route; the miners rushed to block that one too. By the second day, company workers had insufficient gas to run their generator and were short of food. They sent for the army and the police, who showed up and threatened to kill people. Realizing that they could leverage the weight of international opinion and the NGO world against Banro, some CODELU representatives insisted that the protesters not fight back or be in possession of rocks and other weapons. As one reminded the crowd, "international law says police cannot inflict violence on people who don't have rocks or knives, or weapons."

Finally, Colonel Kovo, of *Le Onze* fame, arrived. After first trying to intimidate the crowd, he ended up drinking beer with the miners, along with the state mining police and Banro's unarmed security forces from South Africa. Gilbert, the company's on-site director, came down from the factory and listened to a young man who spoke a little English give a speech about how they had been promised work, a better life, roads, water, electricity, and nice homes. Why, he asked, was Banro bringing people from foreign countries to do such menial tasks as tending the flowers when the village was hungry? Why wouldn't they at least buy food from Luhwindja? Ultimately, Gilbert ordered the police and the army to withdraw but asked the artisanal miners, who now numbered in the thousands, to allow his employees to bring in gas for the generators. Initially they said no, but relented. For his part, Gilbert brought 50 kilograms of meat and rice to "open the road." But the protestors remained.

Over the next couple days, to the surprise of everyone, some Banro workers, who hailed from all over the world, stopped by to applaud the protestors, urging them to continue in the interests of their community.[2] On the third day, every single road into Luhwindja was closed. Its residents only allowed the hospital truck to pass. The whole place, it seemed, was now on strike:

> You can't know who decided this. It's like the whole village woke up and closed the roads. Even women and children and old people brought stones and wood. There's one small path that you can enter Banro from. Well, some eighty-year-old guy woke up in the morning and closed that road. He put rocks by the road, and a rope, and said, "I don't want anyone to cross the road." And people asked themselves, what does this old man know about Banro, and why did he do it? Who told him to do it? He just did it.

Taking advantage of the deployment of company security forces to the roads, the strikers seized Kadumwa, located on the land of a small descent group within the Banro concession. They dug gold there, sold it, and used some of the income to buy food and beer for the protestors up on the road. It was then that Kadumwa came to be seen as a place where people might raise small amounts of money in hard times, a place of reciprocity.

The Sun Rises and Sets on Kadumwa

In 2013, representatives from the CODELU went to the Banro office bearing a picture of a cow with many people sucking from its teats. They said that the beast was the community of Luhwindja, whose milk was the gold that came from the earth. This milk, they insisted, was not the property of the *mwami* or *mwami kazi*. Nor did it spring forth from under ground belonging to the state. Rather, it was the perpetual gift of their elders, those who had died; the whole community ought to suck from that teat. But Banro had poisoned the cow, and the grass on which it grazes, with its cyanide waste—which *was* killing cattle. After a few days, representatives of the company from Toronto showed up to discuss the painting. They thanked the CODELU for it but said that the animal was actually sickened by parasites, which had stopped its milk. The artisanal miners were an infection that would eventually kill it. Banro asked the local community and the CODELU to help them eradicate that infection.

In fairness, the artisanal miners in Kadumwa *do* sometimes say that they had colonized Banro: "We are on Banro property and so Banro is compelled to speak with ordinary people, and not just the *mwami kazi*." And, like effective parasites, they moved to other company sites, surrounding its machines and digging alongside them. The geologues also appeared to have domesticated the local police and military, which refused to act against them.[3] For their part, the armed forces insisted that they were the friends of the artisanal miners, from whom they received gifts of gold dust—which, everyone claimed, was not compulsory but a sign of friendship. "I have never received anything from Banro," they routinely said, implying that their moral obligation to the geologues exceeded their obligation to Banro, the governor, and the *mwami kazi.*

Although many had been displaced by Banro and were angry about it, the artisanals also learned a great deal from the company. For example, while there had been miners at Kadumwa before, they had worked mainly at the topsoil. As the diggers watched machines break up rocks on the surface to get to the motherlode below, they began to follow suit. More substantially, Banro's visible depletion of their wealth had taught local people a lesson: they could not count on gold being there forever. As one observed, "Before, artisanal miners just spent their money on beer and women. Now all the miners want to build something. Even a small kid—all he thinks about is building a building." One student caught the zeitgeist well in a school essay on whether Kadumwa was a blessing or a curse: "The sun rises and sets over Kadumwa," she wrote, envisaging a secure future. Banro, by contrast, ate that future one kilo of gold at a time.

But gold is not the only thing that miners at Kadumwa produced. They also made a social world. The geologues see themselves as creative entrepreneurs with a countercultural, even revolutionary, mindset. Said one, "The time to help the *mwami* and the pockets of the *mwami* has ended. There is the law of custom and the law of government. The law of custom is passé." As Kadumwa grew, the artisanals expressed pride in its organization, contrasting it positively to the rest of Luhwindja: Kadumwa was lit up with generators, and there was genuine "law" there, unlike places living under the "false government" of custom. They were proud of the ingenuity of their homegrown organization, of the diggers' committees, of their "fierce" police brigade, of the council that oversees disputes, and of the sanitation committee that goes from door to door to ensure that all the hotels, restaurants, and brothels are clean. Their director-generals kept records of everyone and their movements. They knew who was married and who was not, thus to discourage adultery cases and the ensuing conflict. Meanwhile, government police were reluctant to go into Kadumwa, partly out of fear for their safety, partly because they were uncertain about the law. In response to international pressure surrounding "conflict minerals," President Kabila had forbidden soldiers and police from being present at the mines: arresting miners could turn out to be illegal, as they could have acquired their rights from the *mwami*, a legally recognized customary authority. The artisanal miners were fully aware of this.

At one point, Ministry of Mines officials, accompanied by police, came to Kadumwa to count people, but the miners did not want them there. They worried that the ministry might try to remove them on the ground that they had dug poorly; also, in order to avoid a census, the local administration of Kadumwa had already completed its own. They gave the visitors beer and told them to wait while they brought the information sought by the ministry. Later, the *mwami kazi* phoned the president director-general of Kadumwa, its leading administrator, to ask why the visitors had been "chased" away. But there was little she could do. One miner at Kadumwa put it like this:

> If people see there is no government, then better for us to create our own state. The government of Congo now comes in conflict with people who have organized their own government. The people from the brigade have the same job as the mining police, so of course there is conflict.

A bottom-up argument about development was also being expressed here, centered on the opposed figures of Kadumwa and the Banro factory at Twangiza. Which, in the end, was more generative of progress, which was more criminal? Clearly, went the claim, the geologues had done more for Luhwindja than had the mine. They had "built up" the town, while company employees, who refused to buy produce from locals, poured all their money into the city of Bukavu. The government might say that the artisanals' unregulated use of mercury was toxic, but what of the toxins Banro spewed into the groundwater? Cash was also "disappearing" at Twangiza through the corruption of its officers and the "manipulation of paper." By contrast, the geologues of Kadumwa were creating something enduring. They had brought a measure of stability to people long afflicted by war and fluctuating mineral prices. What is more, Banro was bound eventually to withdraw, leaving Luhwindja like all the other colonial mining towns that were now impoverished, violated shells of their former selves. If Kadumwa was bringing the community together, the company was tearing it apart. Most of all, the artisanal miners had established productive social networks with local people, including state officials and army personnel, even employees of Banro. It became common for their "friends" from the army and the company to stop by, get a tomato can filled with dirt, and then pay a child a small amount to sift through it for gold—thus helping them to get through the week. Kadumwa, in short, was the alternative future that Banro laborers could not ignore: they were forced to confront it every morning en route to work and saw it growing larger day by day.

The so-called colonization, or recolonization, of Kadumwa had a serious impact on the power of the *mwami* and *mwami kazi*. Soon after the seizure of the site, Banro officers declared that they would no longer meet with the *mwami kazi* alone. Increasingly, they appealed to the CODELU, whose leaders joked about the company's complaints against Esperance: "Please save us from this woman and her demands—we are tired of her. She has annoyed us so much." They also called again on the CODELU to help them expunge the geologues from Luhwindja. Soon it was its head, not the *mwami kazi*, who rode in that helicopter.

As the company distanced itself from Esperance, she tried to demonstrate her authority over the artisanals by collecting levies from them. When a new site of extraction opened up near Kadumwa in 2013, she sent her tax collectors. But the geologues chased them away, asserting that "the *mwami* doesn't have the right to collect tax from here." A sense of ownership was also emerging from the troubles they had endured. "We fought for this space with the price of blood. Who is going to pay *me* tax?" one man joked. Another continued,

> The *mwami* worked with Banro to kick us off the places we were previously, and she has repeatedly denounced Kadumwa. We are the enemies of the *mwami*. We are the enemies of custom. . . . How now can you collect tax for something that isn't yours, and you have no part in it?

By demanding tax, Esperance might conceivably have been trying to align with the geologues against Banro. Tax, historically, *has* implied a recognition that the miners have a right to be, and to work, where they are; it bespeaks the kind of reciprocal exchange that *wami* are supposed to share with their subjects. But that is not at all how the latter interpreted it. As they put it, "If you see small ants coming in a line, it means big ones will follow behind them." The big ants here were Banro, which, the artisanals believed, could not remove them without the support of the *mwami kazi*. In the event, payments to her would *not* ensure their customary entitlement to the land: because she owed a debt to the company—which had given her money and owned the terrain on which she was trying to collect tax—any cash paid to her would indebt her even more and, eventually, oblige her to evict them. Their expulsion, in short, would be the price of Esperance's debt.

For now, to bring an ongoing story to a pause, the geologues remain in a standoff against Banro at Kadumwa. Both sides continue to use whatever is available to them—not least gold and contracts—to secure themselves and their interests before the future catches up with them.

Afterthoughts

Kathleen Davis (2008) has shown how the construction of the Middle Ages as a historical period, a past with specific characteristics, was crucial to the Euromodern project of sovereign state making. Insofar as Africa was seen, through the nineteenth-century modernist *camera obscura*, as medieval—for Hegel (2001), famously, "[only] on the threshold of the World's History"— its "feudalism" was the object of a paradox. On one hand, it was putatively a stage that the peoples of the continent should and would grow beyond. On the other, it was held to arise from their authentic, eternal cultures, out of which their indigenous forms of governance and customary law was imagined naturally to derive—and hence was expected to perdure. Forever.

The specter of the medieval, and its attendant paradox, is evident in the mix of fatalism and disdain that characterized Belgian interactions with *wami*. For the colonizers, Luhwindja and its residents belonged to a different space-time and were not, therefore, to be governed in the same manner as Europeans, nor should they come in contact with gold and the worldliness of which it is part. They required, instead, to be ruled by customary authority and kept away from the precious metal and its seductions. But— and here is the paradox-in-practice—the authority of *wami*, being enduringly feudal, lacked all credibility in Belgian eyes. It had to be domesticated by "modern" education, culminating in bureaucratic literacy, thus to render it rational and, most importantly, to keep it in check.

Either implicitly or explicitly, those directly involved in the recent events at Luhwindja also invoked the eternal medieval at various moments. Gilbert, for example, thought it important to work through the traditional authority of *bwami*, despite the fact that he saw it as outmoded, feudal; the historical rupture initiated by Banro's presence/present, he believed, would, for better or worse, ultimately end in a "modern" market-centered local economy. Recall, moreover, that the *mwami kazi* was said to have called her rival, Justin, a "Machiavelli" in her letter to the governor. Apart from all else, this makes plain the popular awareness of the condemnatory power of that name, one long invoked in the West, to represent the medieval antithesis of rational, enlightened rule. Justin was dubbed Machiavellian because, unable to see beyond his own tactical advantage, he allegedly courted whomever would strengthen his position at the expense of the sovereign state.

For their part, the people of Luhwindja evinced their own familiarity with the ways in which Europeans construct their modernity in relation to a dark past, even if they lacked direct knowledge of Euromodern understandings of feudalism: the conjoined threat of the *mwami kazi* and Banro have had to be domesticated by endless contracts, validated by official letters from a remote, neutral state authority—*not*, note, the parochial governor from nearby Kaziba but the more disinterested, abstract Ministry of the Interior. And when the self-proclaimed geologues identified themselves with practical science and bottom-up governance against the moribund, illegitimate tradition of *bwami*, they positioned themselves on the side of international law against the foreign company that had allied itself with the feudal *mwami kazi*. In so doing, they sent a clear message, to whomever was paying attention, that Banro and Esperance were on the wrong side of history. The strike and the barricade were the signifying currencies through which local people, especially but not only the leaders of the CODELU, hoped to influence events and communicate with the world outside, conjured into existence through international NGOs. Local discussion of these events evoked the French Revolution and other moments in Europe's past, and the CODELU explicitly distanced the *mwami* from Luhwindja's ancestors when they presented Banro with that painting of the cow.

In sum, ideas about feudalism have played a role in the way that kingship here was shaped during colonialism, domesticating it as the traditional embodiment of an outmoded, yet still present, time. The trope—feudalism, that is—was deployed by the different actors who seized Luhwindja as the stage on which the drama of World History was being played out. Patently, that drama belongs to a highly contemporary moment in the long story of global capitalism, one in which nation-states have largely lost whatever ability they might once have had to regulate their economies. In this age of "socially thin" extraction, competing rights and responsibilities are negotiated on the ground, with frequent reference to divergent histories, legal traditions, and ethical systems (Ferguson 2006). The recurrent, contrapuntal motifs of the medieval and the modern suggest that those involved are unwilling to interpret what is happening here as merely a Hobbesian struggle of all against all. Rather, the expropriation of people from their livelihoods is fashioning social forms, fields, and figurations—like the large, self-aware population of geologues and the world that has grown up around Banro— that speak to the possibility of another kind of future, another kind of society, another kind of politics. In this theater, the dramatis personae seize upon the offices and the legal powers of the state, wherever and whenever they can, in their efforts to move the promethean forces that swirl around them in various directions.

The temporality of *bwami* and its impacts on events in Luhwindja go well beyond the trope of the medieval. It also transcends the superficial politics of the present. For many years, *wami* have argued that they are connected to a spiritual realm rooted in the past, that this is the source of their power. The most successful ones, like Philemon, have bridged divergent temporal orders, co-opting gold into the temporality of the past while making bureaucracy and writing serve ancestral potency in the present. But recent events may have taken things a bit far, decreasing the sovereignty of *wami* until it becomes difficult for people to believe that they actually are the conduit to an ontological past—which, for some, is their only reason to exist. Now that this connection is broken, the *mwami kazi*'s performance of the customary has become farcical to many. Of course, it doesn't help that the ruler in question is "that witch from Kalehe." None of this is to argue that Gilbert was correct, that Banro has incited a revolution that has culminated in the demise of *bwami*. Rather than liberating people through the market, the company's operations have made everyone aware of the finitude of resources and the artisanal economy. This notion of an imminent end has led many to believe that they have to be endlessly creative, since soon they will not be able to depend on the earth in which customary authority is grounded. Here I want to stress that the labile, manifest politics of *bwami* really only make sense in their temporal configurations: a shifting back and forth among alternative pasts, alternative futures, and alternative worlds in the context of a fast-approaching finale. These temporal politics, or tempopolitics, are generative of new modes of thought and action—the collective strike, land seizures, peoples' governance, and the like—that have more to them than merely Machiavellian maneuvers. They portend new worlds in the making.

Notes

1. According to a Congolese legal expert, the law requires that three nonelected customary authorities be chosen by provincial parliamentarians to assist in ensuring that enacted statutes align with customary law. They have the same rights and responsibilities as other MPs.

2. To this day, local people remember a Peruvian man who gave a speech imploring Luhwindjans to remember that Banro is a corporation, not a development organization. There was, he said, nothing they could do to make a corporation care about them. The man was not seen around Luhwindja again.

3. I saw a letter from Banro—it was lying on the desk of a government office in Bukavu—that requested the state to remove the artisanals from Kadumwa by force. They did not.

References

Davis, Kathleen
    2008   *Periodization and Sovereignty: How Ideas of Feudalism and Secularization Govern the Politics of Time*. Philadelphia, PA: University of Pennsylvania Press.

Ferguson, James
    2006   *Global Shadows: Africa in the Neoliberal World Order*. Durham, NC: Duke University Press.

Geenen, Sara
    2011   Local Livelihoods, Global Interests and the State in the Congolese Mining Sector. In *Natural Resources and Local Livelihoods in the Great Lakes Region of Africa: A Political Economy Perspective*, An Ansoms and Stefaan Marysse, eds. London: Palgrave Macmillan.
    2015   Evident but Elusive: Practical Norms in the Congolese Gold Sector. In *Real Governance and Practical Norms in Sub-Saharan Africa: The Game of the Rules*, Tom de Herdt and Jean-Pierre Olivier de Sardan, eds. New York: Routledge.

Geenen, Sara, and Kara Claessens
    2013   Disputed Access to the Gold Sites in Luhwindja, Eastern Democratic Republic of Congo. *Journal of Modern African Studies* 51(1):85–108.

Geenen, Sara, D. Fahey, and F. Iragi Mukotanyi
    2013   The Future of Artisanal Gold Mining and Miners Under an Increasing Industrial Presence in South Kivu and Ituri, Eastern Democratic Republic of Congo: Discussion Paper. Antwerp: Institute of Development Policy and Management, University of Antwerp.

Geenen, Sara, and Jana Hönke
    2014   Land Grabbing by Mining Companies: Local Contentions and State Configurations in South Kivu (DRC). In *Losing your Land: Dispossession in the Great Lakes*, An Ansoms and Thea Hilhorst, eds. Oxford: James Currey.

Geschiere, Peter
    2000   Capitalism and Autochthony: The Seesaw of Mobility and Belonging. *Public Culture* 12(2):423–52.

Hegel, Georg
    2001   *The Philosophy of History*. Kitchener, Ontario: Batoche Books.

Mamdani, Mahmood
    1996   *Citizen and Subject: Contemporary Africa and the Legacy of Late Colonialism*. Princeton, NJ: Princeton University Press.

Williams, Raymond
    1975   *The Country and the City*. Oxford: Oxford University Press.

TWELVE

Third Contact

*Invisibility and Recognition of the Customary
in Northern Mozambique*

JUAN OBARRIO

Introduction

Following a devastating civil war and an eighteen-year Afro-Socialist experiment, the transition to democracy and rule of law in Mozambique that began in 1994 has been hailed by observers as a successful process of national reconciliation and politicoeconomic opening.

Yet in 2014, Mozambique held general elections under a formal "state of war," initiated by a statement from the RENAMO party that in early 2013 declared the peace accords broken. In the following months the RENAMO leadership relocated to a secret compound and their guerrillas launched scattered military operations in the center and north of the country.[1] Expert analysis of the renewed struggle usually emphasizes macro aspects of the transition, related to electoral politics, economic exclusion, or the composition of the armed forces and situation of demobilized combatants. More localized yet equally crucial forces, such as the political role of the customary in processes of war and peacemaking, tend to be occluded. In fact, the complex nature of political transition here contradicts the apparent blithe optimism of donors and central state reformers about the process of democratization over the last two decades. One of the most striking effects of dismantling of the socialist state and decentralizing governance has been the vigorous reemergence of the local level and its figures of traditional authority (see chapter 1, this volume).

In June of 2000, the Council of Ministers passed a decree that recognized customary chiefs as legitimate local agents of government (Sousa Santos et al. 2006; Bertelsen n.d.; Buur and Kyed 2005, 2006, 2007; Kyed 2007).[2] And yet customary authorities have been a controversial political issue since the colonial period. The same political party, FRELIMO,[3] that banned all traditional authorities, rituals, and beliefs after the 1975 revolution in the name of "antiobscurantist" socialist modernization, is currently reinstating as legitimate the very customary chiefs once decried as instruments of colonial power. These juridical reforms involve rewriting the fraught history of the country's northern region, and the complex play of strategic power relations at the national level (Sousa Santos et al. 2006; Meneses 2006). After the colonial and socialist periods, this constitutes, in the history of the Mozambican state, a "third moment" of articulation with the realm of the customary, one which attempts to synthesize previous conditions and redeploy these authorities and their imaginaries in the service of postsocialist policies and neoliberal processes of state legitimation.

Legal recognition of the customary in contemporary Mozambique illustrates the more general return of indigeneity in contemporary Africa, where tradition, custom, and territorialized conceptions of belonging have been reinvented, with authenticity and autochthony as central tropes. In the specific case of Mozambique, the hazardous ambiguity of this reemergence cannot be overstated (Bayart et al. 2001; Geschiere and Nyamnjoh 2000; Geschiere and Jackson 2006; Marshall-Fratani 2006).[4]

African Indigeneity

Articulations of the customary can only be understood in the African context by relating them to the history of state formation from the colonial period to the present (Dozon 2003; Young 1994). Extensive evidence demonstrates that in most of sub-Saharan Africa, local hierarchies of indigenous power were (re)constructed by colonial regimes through ethnographic inscription and juridical codification, giving rise to a system of customary authority, as well a plural legal grid, in terms of which populations were administered, violently settled, taxed, and mobilized as labor. Harsh discipline and social control were enforced in a *decentralized* regime of indirect rule through this realm of traditional local chieftaincies (Mamdani 1996; Chege 1997; O'Laughlin 2000).[5] Yet, these same political figures are being held up today in most of postcolonial Africa as a panacea for the achievement of decentralized, plural *democratic* cultures and the strengthening of civil society (West and Kloeck-Jenson 1999).

Colonial rule defined indigeneity in reference to naturalizing discourses of race, blood, and filiation and associated tropes of purity and authenticity. Indigeneity served to legitimate the foreign/African (and "citizen/ subject") binary—that is, the division between a small group of white or "assimilated" citizens and populations of native subjects, subdivided into territorialized ethnico-juridical groups, ruled by customary authorities (Mamdani 1996). The moment of independence saw the category of indigeneity redeployed in the nationalist project of "Africanizing" the state, which, rather than overturning the racial logic behind colonial sovereignty, inverted it.

In the case of Mozambique, the state made authenticity the grounds for an official ban on what the socialist regime defined as backward, "obscurantist" traditions—ritual, spiritual belief, local language, as well as traditional authorities, now dubbed as mere puppets of the colonial regime. The project of collective villagization was enforced by FRELIMO in the effort to break down traditional systems of kinship and labor, along with kin-based customary authority. Yet indigeneity continued to play a central mobilizing role in the period that spanned those two moments—exemplified in dramatic enactments of popular violence: the involvement of the customary and its authorities in the anticolonial war led by FRELIMO, for instance, and in the civil war between FRELIMO and the guerrillas of the Mozambican National Resistance, RENAMO. This historical context, in turn, created the contours of the third, contemporary moment.

Postwar reconstruction makes plain the paradoxical ways in which postmodern juridico-political frameworks engineer the return of legal regimes linked to colonial governance, where local imaginaries of political belonging—based on territoriality, blood, heritage, and sacred violence—are converted into political and economic resources and inserted into global political processes and markets (cf. Ferguson 2006; Hibou 2004; Geschiere 2009; see chapter 1, this volume). In Mozambique, as elsewhere in Africa, internationally led state reforms have involved the blending of "precolonial" norms (allegedly traditional kinship rules, or customary norms on issues of gender and generation) with contemporary legal forms (human rights, modern citizenship entitlements) as a potential escape from institutional impasse, or as part of the transition from armed conflict to the accountability required of modern democratic regimes (Mamdani 1996; Moore 1986; Chanock 1985; Shadle 1999; Snyder 1981; Cohen and Odhiambo 1992). Thus the recuperation of precolonial, customary practice in land tenure legislation passed in much of East Africa in the late 1980s and 1990s, or the transitional justice legislation that reinforced chieftaincy in Sierra Leone and Liberia, for example.

Conflicting and coalescing trends of nationalism, nativism, and neoliberalism operate on a field shaped by structural adjustment and transnational ventures of speculative and extractive capital that efface citizenship rights and weaken local governance. This politics exhibits a fundamental paradox, in which a postcolonial liberal democracy enforces a modernist legislation, endorsed as progressive and future-oriented, yet simultaneously embraces the immanent, violent legacies of colonialism entrenched within allegedly primordial forms of customary law and authority. In fact, the return of the customary also responds to local struggles and demands on the ground. What are the concrete effects of the inflection that custom produces on modern democratic regimes?

Within the hegemonic policies imposed globally in the last few decades, political and economic liberalization have sought to encompass diverse localities, customs, norms, rituals, and ideologies within unified "democracies," fostering arguments in favor of "legal pluralism," which reinforces the ethnicization of local identities and the fetishization of putatively ancient customary law. While some of these arguments are based on legitimate local demands, these endorsements of normative pluralism can undermine unitary models of citizenship and significantly complicate the criteria of social inclusion.

In line with this, through the staging of ceremonies of recognition and by way of legal-political reform, the Mozambican state has attempted to contain the multiple, proliferating normativities (religious or traditional authorities, for example, or forms of conflict resolution and ritual) under the single category of the customary, striving to subsume all prior historical moments into a continuous present leading toward future progress (Avineri 1974). This operation recuperates the central ideological dualisms of the colonial period and revitalizes a metaphysics of difference—including the subdivision of the population into regionalisms and ethnic identities—that has been characteristic of the reconfiguration of African nation-states as they have been articulated with contemporary global geopolitics (Mbembe 2002a, 2002b; Grovogui 1996).

Despite governmental efforts to embrace difference, social relations on the ground, deeply fragmented by violent experiences of late colonialism, early socialism, and war, have not been easily reconciled. Besides the contradictions of the state's ideological representations of the customary as crucial tool of postcolonial governance, an examination of concrete encounters and rituals of legitimization reveals the limits of the state's project of recognition. It also makes plain that the alleged foundation of the state sovereignty in the law does not hold when subjected to the test of its own petitions of principle (Comaroff and Comaroff 2003, 2006).

Indeed, juridical distinctions between private and public, foreign and national, or state and customary become blurred when applied to actually existing political contexts. What materializes is not a state apparatus, or a set of institutions, but rather a broad strategic field of power, in which distinct norms and alternate forms of sovereignty and citizenship struggle for expression, unfolding in an agonistic way. Let us explore an ethnographic instance of this process.

Rites of Sovereignty

"We have arrived in the capital of one of the invisible states," the administrator[6] says, with a half smile of satisfaction.[7] It is almost noon, and we are in a small village in the rural district of Macavelas,[8] not far from the Indian Ocean coast, in Nampula Province, northern Mozambique in June 2004. Emerging from a myriad of little mud huts and houses, a small crowd comes forward to greet us.

During the previous few days, the administrator had been talking to me about the ineffable political entities he called "invisible states." Like some kind of wild animal, he said—a large caterpillar in camouflage, concealing itself from the suspicious eyes of strangers—the existence of these assemblages is based on concealment, secrecy, dissimulation, silence: an oblique form of governance not assimilable within the categories of developmentalist discourse.

The administrator, the state's local representative, nominally rules over what is a contradictory space—a district that allegedly maintains the sovereignty of the state over a given territory, ruled by official laws. Local provincial courts are supposed to have jurisdiction over conflict and crime in this area. Yet something here escapes the juridical territorialization of the social: the unit includes within its borders deterritorialized remainders from other polities, other authorities, other rules.

The administrator, who had served in various rural districts in Nampula Province since the early 1990s, had "uncovered" the "invisible state" a few years earlier, during the immediate postwar and postsocialist transition. He explained how he had gained access to manifestations of these political structures after many a patient dialogue, numerous meetings, and the mobilization of many connections in search of trust and reciprocity. In a region where imaginaries of the state are weak and its legitimacy is feeble, and a province with a deep history of hostility toward centralized authority (precolonial, colonial, or socialist) and the strong presence of RENAMO, popular mistrust of the local administration was pervasive. According to the administrator, beyond the restricted space of influence of the precarious local state apparatus—a few dusty blocks around the center of the small town that serve as the seat of the district administration—the invisible state reigns. As the administrator put it: "They constitute the state where there is no state, at the base, at the level of the community." They are organized around necessities of subsistence, the provision of services, and the circulation of scarce economic resources that the local state cannot afford to provide.[9]

On the day when the administrator was going to make contact with this "invisible" entity in its own territory, he invited me to join his delegation, composed of administrators of subdistricts, and *regulo* (chief), Sukuta. The latter, the premier customary authority situated above eight lesser chiefs scattered throughout the area, had recently attained official recognition from the state as a local authority, henceforth to be included within local schemes of governance and made eligible for minor prerogatives.

We drive for two hours in a battered pick-up across the rural fields and hills where there was no road to follow, only blurred pathways. During the trip, the chief explains that the reason for our visit is the celebration of a local memorial ceremony held annually to honor Kupula Munu, a chief who had been leader of the communities in this area and a prominent fighter in the struggle against Portuguese colonialism in the early twentieth century (Newitt 1995).

Upon our arrival, a few prominent members of the community approach us, led by a man dressed in white, a local customary authority, who also holds a high rank in the "invisible" state. Behind him comes a woman, also dressed in white, taller, in her mid-forties, who is introduced as the queen (*pyamwene*) of these communities (the sovereign of the "invisible state," in the administrator's conception). She is a "niece" (by blood, or by political and kinship affinity) of the erstwhile chief Kupula Munu, now the actual power holder in this compound.

The main part of the ceremony is conducted at two tombs: the first, the smaller of the two, holds the remains of a relative of Chief Kupula; the second is the chief's own resting place. But before entering the area that surrounds the smaller tomb, the queen summons us. As though we are entering another spatiotemporal dimension, she orders us to remove our watches. Organizing a line, with herself at its head, she calls us forward, first the administrator, followed by one of his closest aides, then the main chief, Sukuta; myself; and others behind me. Inside, white and blue cloths hang from the ceiling. We sit uncomfortably, legs crossed, barely seeing one another through the dangling cloths. The queen begins to speak: slowly, softly, in a lilting half voice, she offers a musical lament, almost a prayer.

The queen is speaking in another's voice, through another's words, for she is merely an instrument of the Spirit. "It is not me who is talking, but the Spirit. It is the Spirit that commands me to utter these words. For the Spirit is crying," she says more than once. The dead chief's soul wants to speak his grief, express his anger and disappointment, the pain aroused from seeing his people suffer in solitude, abandonment, and disease. His anger is directed at the government, she-as-voice-of-the-Spirit says, for its agents have not fulfilled their so-often-repeated promises. She describes the Spirit's sadness and his awareness of the population's needs, enumerating a list that includes basic infrastructure: a school, water, cash ("the money from last year has already run out"). She explains the people's extreme isolation. "It is not me, it is the Spirit who laments because the government is very far away from us. Forgive me, please, if I speak bad Portuguese; it is because I live isolated, so far away."[10]

When the queen has finished, the administrator speaks in Makhuwa, expressing the government's willingness to reach out to the communities, reassuring its leaders as to the possibility of collaboration and the delivery of resources. He implicitly invokes future negotiations toward an alliance in which the government would provide gifts in return for the community's support. Afterward another official guest makes a short speech, this time in Portuguese. The queen then speaks again, bringing the ceremony to a close. This time, "development" is the keyword. She declares: "The Spirit complains; he does not feel well. The government must develop this area." Her words, and her tone of grief and quiet authority, unfold a story, weaving together the local and the central, the visible and invisible, all the while evoking the trinity of Spirit, Government, and Development.

One by one, visitors and locals file out of the tomb, leaving only the queen, the administrator, and me. Suddenly there is a subtle political shift. The queen leans toward the administrator and, making sure she cannot be heard, begins speaking to him in a low voice. There ensues a litany of complaints about the "invisible state's" internal politics. She focuses on the misconduct of a local chief, whose incompetence and malice, she says, are blocking all possibilities for development in the area. Barefoot, on our knees, we listen to the woman's whispered account of how badly the *mwenes* (chiefs, lords of the land), her own cousins, have behaved. That she, the great granddaughter of King Kupula, should be a witness to this! Suddenly, the political visitor, the state's representative, is pulled—as potential arbiter?—into the heart of this community's intimate power struggles (West 1998).

We leave the smaller grave and walk silently in a line towards Chief Kupula's tomb. An aura of sacredness begins to grow, a ceremonious calm descends on the group, and our movements become weighty. At the site of the white tomb we bend down on our knees to pass under the low door into the mortuary room. The cement building is gray inside, the darkness only broken by the sunlight filtering through a multicolored curtain hanging on the small front door. Before entering the space of the grave itself, the queen prays in a loud voice and addresses the Spirit, explaining who the visitors are and mentioning their ranks. We all clap rhythmically as she speaks. We will do it again after we leave the space of the tomb, as a sealing exercise of magic sound.

The tomb is made of cement with a roof of straw and nylon bags and with sunlight filtering through the threshold. Colorful women's dresses and other clothes hang from the roof. Just beneath where we are sitting lie the chief's remains. On the square tomb itself is spread a large white shirt; material dress for the immortal remains, prosaically connecting life and death. The flour scattered over the tomb, as well as several small bottles, accentuate this connection. Words bounce off the cement walls in eerie echoes. With so many of us crowded in, the atmosphere grows close, as if the slow speaking is gradually consuming the remaining air.

This is the climax of the ceremony, structured around the two mortuary spaces. The first moment had been intended as a sort of introduction, an intermediate, propitiatory time, held at the tomb of a lesser chief. This second moment is the moment of truth: the veracity of politics and negotiation, a spiritual authenticity. The speeches are made this time in Makhuwa. Another prominent member of the locality—a *mwene*—speaks, expanding on the community's need for money and infrastructure. He is followed by another local chief, then the queen and the administrator, before Chief Sukuta closes the séance with a prayer.

The tenor and intonation of the words spoken in the chief's tomb is bitter, sharper. The administrator, trying to explain the government's position and promising that donations will soon be delivered, sounds increasingly frustrated, especially after he is interrupted several times by complaints and slight rebuttals. This is the moment of power, of circulation, and of sacrifice. Beyond the queen's parochial introduction at the first tomb, other important community voices are heard, urgent and pressing, making more transparent the true significance of the invitation to the local FRELIMO state to attend this semi-secret ceremony: the airing of debts and gifts with a view to creating new political alliances.

At the end of the ceremony *Regulo* Sukuta[11] offers up a long prayer in Makhuwa, invoking Allah and the Spirit as interchangeable central forces.[12] The Muslim chief is a contemporary sign of a long regional history of ethnic and religious difference—and symbiosis. The prayer transports the king's spirit into a more inclusive, wider sacred space, one in which African local religion merges with Islam in a symbiosis that invokes a potentially new relationship that might now be inaugurated between the local, FRELIMO administration and the "invisible state." Before we file slowly out of the king's resting place, we place notes and coins in a *kofia*, a Muslim cap that is passed from hand to hand.

As we leave the tomb, the mood evaporates. Less than an hour has passed, and yet in the time-space of the tomb we have been tensely suspended on the edge of possibilities in the making, a liminal space where the states have spoken, demanding and acquiescing, shaping promises of things to come. Moving out of the sacred space, its elusive borders marked by numerous white hanging cloths, we emerge into another space and time. Just beyond the rocky entrance to the tomb stand a row of six chairs, would-be thrones for the administrator and his entourage, silhouetted against gray rocks and bright green trees and plants, like a theatrical stage. Every half word spoken, every silent move remains slow and ceremonious as each visitor begins to take her seat: the administrator in the center, his two closest aides at his side. We move suddenly into the next phase of this theologicopolitical event, this cementing of promises and pacts in what is a FRELIMO political rally.

These are testing political times in Mozambique. Six months after this event, a presidential election will take place. One of the obvious aims of the FRELIMO local administration in reaching out to the "invisible state" is to gain support from its subjects and its hierarchy of leaders. From the sacred ceremony thus emerges another ritual, both performances, like sides of the same coin, revealing distinct predicaments and possibilities of contemporary politics in Mozambique and the historical precedents that shaped them. During the rally, the local representatives of the FRELIMO administration urge the rural crowd to vote for the party that has been in power since independence. Yet underlying this secular, prosaic electoralism lies another enactment, one that recalls and commemorates the dreadful events of war.

First one to address the crowd is a lower order administrator of a sub-district (*chefe de posto*). Speaking in Makhuwa, he talks broadly about the community's needs, FRELIMO's work in the area, and the importance of registering to vote in the upcoming elections. He is followed by a Secretary in charge of local governance who explains to the crowd the new modalities of registration and voting. Then with solemn movements, the administrator stands up and takes a few steps forward. He smiles and shouts in the classic manner of FRELIMO rallies, but with an addition in honor of the dead chief:

Long live FRELIMO!
Long live Macavelas!
Long live King Kupula!
Long live National Union![13]

With theatrical gestures, he then addresses the crowd, weaving a narrative that links the local king with the history of FRELIMO's postcolonial struggle. Although he is fluent in Makhuwa, he speaks in Portuguese, an assistant translating in an act of political theatre that transposes the language of the state onto that of the "invisible state," figuring the potential of an alliance beginning to take shape.

"The life of this king constitutes a wonderful school for all of us. We are here to pay homage to the work that the chief performed for the district and the country," he begins. Around the legacy of the king's spirit, the administrator develops a political argument of broad implications, condensing many crucial moments of Mozambique's history over the past fifty years. The events of war are conjured as he speaks, disclosing a logic that relates wars of independence with civil wars, and both with the foundations of the current democratic state. At one point, he leans over, reaching toward someone sitting in the front row, asking him to hand over his voter registration ID card. "Kupula used to fight with his knives and spears. Today, Kupula's struggle and our independence must be defended with this weapon: our voter's ID."[14]

As he draws to a close, the administrator evokes development issues (Hanlon 1996). The gift must circulate: as moral or economic value, entering a circuit that allegedly describes a perfect circle and yet, as the queen's speech made clear, and as everybody seems to acknowledge, when referring to politics, money, or trust, this circle is constantly interrupted. The administrator's speech refers to projects, installations, provisions. He turns toward a man sitting to his left. An important member of his entourage, he is the owner of a cashew factory that will soon open in the area and will require sixty employees, principally young men. The community is urged to send their youth to work there.

Beyond his electoral rhetoric, the administrator develops a political reading of the past, a sort of shadow theater where, drawing on the political aura of a spirit of a precolonial chief at the heart of this community, he outlines a process of juridical transformation taking place: a new spirit of the laws (Obarrio 2006).

The culmination of the ceremony and the rally is a shared meal: as if to seal a reconciliation between the state, customary structures, and rural political communities. The administrator's aides busily fetch several pots of food and luxurious bottles of soda that they place on a colorful cloth spread on the ground. Then Chief Sukuta enters a mud house and brings out the queen's husband to introduce him to the administrator. He is a retired school teacher and old acquaintance of the chief, who emerges as a hidden link, conjoining trust and opening the possibility of the articulation between the state and these communities. The small group chats briefly and a promise of employment at the new factory for the queen's two daughters is made. All that remains now is to shake hands with the queen and the leaders of this other state. Then the administrator's delegation heads back to the district's capital.

History: Between State and Customary

I had witnessed a singular event, which could nevertheless be related to an extended series of acts taking place at the time, across the nation-state: minor spectacles in which the state recognized the legitimate authority of various customary chiefs (Buur and Kyed 2005, 2006; Goncalves 2005). In these sovereign rites, state liturgy was blended with local, customary ceremonies, resulting in a fusing of both political and religious contours. The underlying goals were similar: the articulation of political alliances with local governance to provide electoral purchase; the effort to co-opt rural polities and their sacred hierarchies, which in this region operate mostly as secret societies, based on kinship links or spiritual allegiance.

The main difference operating at this particular event, its singularity, was that it was also a monumental commemoration: the recognition, on behalf of the state, of the legitimate power and authority of a deceased chief. Almost worshipping the spirits of the dead, the local state was erasing decades of official policy, making an absolutely new gesture toward the relevance of the precolonial indigenous realm.

The ritual, with its religious contours and political rhetoric, signaled a unique moment that interrupted the flow of history and redirected its sense. This was the occurrence of a *third contact*, which actualized the modern history of indigeneity in the nation. Within a series of historical encounters, I have noted, two previous phases of exchange between state and customary—two moments of definition, control, and coercion of indigeneity—had taken place in modern times. The current third phase seems to blend various aspects of the two previous ones, through its reversals and aporias, toward a novel merging of past and future, or custom and law.

The *first contact*, we have seen, was the moment of effective colonial occupation, with its conquering and the reshaping of the customary, through the *Indigenato* regime (1930–1960); the *second contact* was the moment of postcolonial independence, of the socialist regime and its ban on the customary, understood as "obscurantist tradition" (1975–1992); the *third contact* marked the postwar transition to democracy, rule of law, and liberalization of the economy (1995–2005) and the reconfiguration of the local level as community. Let us examine these three phases in more detail now, as each of them constituted a redefinition of indigeneity, spanning together the colonial and postcolonial moments.

First Contact: Colonial *Indigenato*

The first contact between state and customary implied the colonial legal demarcation of indigeneity (O'Laughlin 2000; Hedges 2000; Meneses et al. 2006; West and Kloeck-Jenson 1999). This juridical context demarcated customary authorities' prerogatives and restricted indigenous rights. This dispensation is what the socialist regime later attempted to erase, and the contemporary democratic regime, in turn, aims to refigure it in a new light.

The *Indigenato*[15] regime was a juridical organization of the territory of the colony, which placed the native population under the sovereignty of customary chiefs (Pels 1996). It entailed a network of regulations that organized everyday life in the colony in terms of spatial, political, and ethnic segregation. Systems of education and labor, identification, and circulation, as well as harsh punishment and control, were intricately linked, set in motion by the force of law, which mobilized a shift from the condition of the slave to that of a "free laborer" under Portugal's fascist-capitalist conditions (Hedges et al. 1993; Isaacman 1996). Processes of classification relying on the category of indigeneity and its racialized, territorialized tropes perpetuated the diminished legal status of local African populations. In Mozambique, from the 1890s, chiefs were enrolled in the process of governance, first by concessionary capitalist enterprises, then by the colonial state, reproducing customary low in the process (Harries 1994).

Around the 1920s, the system of traditional authorities was adapted to the new official policy of indirect rule. The revised regime of 1929 classified the great majority of the Mozambican "indigenous" population into tribes, presupposing a common language and culture, where individuals were subjected to the authority of chiefs, defined as *autoridades gentilicas* (kin-based authorities). In the geographically marginal regions of the country, where effective occupation was weak, local chieftaincy became an extension of colonial rule. Alongside the process of producing traditional culture, customary law was codified by colonial functionaries and amateur ethnographers. This construction of a realm of "law outside the law" was essential for the consolidation of the colonial state apparatus. A tripod formed by ethnic provenance, territorialization, and ancestral authority was the stand upon which the subjection to customary law was sanctioned. Meanwhile, civil law regulated the lives of the citizens (settlers and *assimilados*) as well as disputes between foreign settler citizens—or the state— and the *indigenas*.

In 1944, a new colonial ordinance formally ascribed to chiefs the status of "assistants to the administration," and they became an integral part of the colonial state. Chiefs received a percentage of the hut tax that they collected and benefitted from the recruitment of labor and the sale of produce from mandatory agricultural labor. They also controlled land tenure in the indigenous reserves, zones ruled according to customary law, and ran their own police forces (*regulados*).

Throughout the colonial period, the local legitimacy of chiefs was fraught, subject to the arbitrary policies of indirect rule and its codification of the customary. While the legitimacy of chiefs was based on supposed filiation with local royal lineages, the Portuguese regime effectively appointed and deposed chiefs at will. In 1961, when Mozambique became an overseas province, the *Indigenato* regime was abolished. Yet while the status of indigeneity changed, the categorical distinction between indigenous population and settlers persisted. Those defined as *indigenas* became Portuguese citizens but remained subject to the customary law and the *regulos*, the latter becoming part of the local administration. By 1964, at the beginning of FRELIMO's guerrilla war, the abolition of the *Indigenato* regime had not in fact granted citizenship rights to the majority of the population. Instead, the colonial regime's counterinsurgency campaigns made the power of some customary authorities even more repressive. A decade later, Mozambique would gain its independence, but the customary would continue to shape the postcolonial political field in crucial ways, through local ritual, regional power, and war.

Second Contact: Afro-Socialism and Civil War

The trajectory of postcolonial chieftaincy during this second contact un-folded at the intersection of three axes: politics, economy, and violence (Dinerman 2006; Pitcher 2002; Lubkemann 2007). The project of social-ism, not merely as a modality of political organization but as a mode of production, marked the FRELIMO stance toward chieftaincy. In the 1980s in the north, the legitimacy and control that some chiefs still held signaled the political and economic relevance of these figures, despite a decade of repressive policies. In those regions, the FRELIMO regime co-opted some among the local authorities into "chiefs of production." The violence of the civil war was the other main vector that shaped the trajectory of customary authority, with many chiefs supporting the RENAMO guerrillas and mo-bilizing populations behind the promise of reinstating customary power once the rebels gained control of the nation. The axes of violence, politics, and economy formed the basis for a modernization project aimed at trans-forming the countryside through collective villagization, implemented by FRELIMO shortly after independence.

Villagization obeyed a double program of socialist governance of the rural areas: one face was aimed at addressing political economy, while the other engaged with juridico-political issues. The most crucial effect of vil-lagization for local governance was the attempt to dismantle the colonial system of customary authorities. At its first session after independence, the FRELIMO Council of Ministers abolished chieftaincy in a move aimed at carrying out a total transformation of rural society. Nonetheless, social structures based on kinship and hereditary succession never actually disap-peared after independence. FRELIMO's policies—such as collectivization, economic socialization, and the rejection of chiefs—would later be seen as the main causes for the support for RENAMO by vast rural populations—and their chiefs—in the center-north of the country.

The civil war (1977–1992) in the rural areas worsened an incipient divide between party-state structures and the rural population (West and Kloeck-Jenson 1999; Chan and Moisés 1998; Chingano 1996; Finnegan 1992; Hanlon 1984; Minter 1994). RENAMO guerrillas launched a war of sabotage, massacre, and terrorist destabilization, targeting infrastruc-ture and civilian populations. RENAMO also discovered the strategic value of establishing links with customary chiefs marginalized by FRELIMO. In many areas RENAMO used local structures of power as intermediaries in its own administrative hierarchy (Vines 1991). At some point, forced by the harshness of war and the precarity of its power and material base, FRELIMO also started establishing strategic alliances with chiefs in northern areas.

Through his fieldwork conducted in Nampula Province during the war in the 1980s, French anthropologist Christian Geffray (1990) offered a revisionist interpretation of the conflict that downplayed the importance of Cold War dynamics and South African intervention in favor of the importance of resistance by the masses to FRELIMO's policies regarding the customary, opposition coordinated by former chiefs in what came to be defined by experts as a "war of spirits" (Wilson 1992). Geffray's views were later adopted by sectors within FRELIMO and by Western donor institutions that, with the end of the Cold War, began exercising a deep influence in Mozambican governance in terms of the legitimization of customary authority.

Third Contact: Postcolonial Democracy

These prior periods of articulation and suppression were followed, then, by a third moment,[16] in which the postsocialist state reversed its previous commitment to the effacement of tradition within a context of negotiation with transnational donors and development agencies.

In the aftermath of the civil war, foreign actors—who had played a major role in brokering the cease-fire—argued that general elections were necessary to balance opposing militarized forces and render them both more accountable. Local elections would also allow "civil society" to evolve out of the centralized socialist FRELIMO state. An underlying assumption espoused by development agencies who supported state decentralization was that traditional authority would once more play a role in local governance within a representative democracy (Mamdani 1996; Bayart 2009; Comaroff and Comaroff 1999).[17] In the early 1990s, even before the war ended, sectors within FRELIMO, in alliance with donors, had already explored the potentialities of reviving customary chieftaincy. In 1991, the Ministry of State Administration organized a Ford Foundation-funded ethnographic research project on traditional authority that commissioned field research and held meetings with former chiefs and assemblies with local populations, generating an idealized, ahistoric view of "African authority." In 1994, before the first postwar general elections, the government passed legislation that was based on conclusions from that research project and addressed the devolution of various governmental functions to municipalities, legislation that allowed for traditional authority to be incorporated into local mechanisms of state governance. That project later became a USAID-funded unit, located within the Ministry of State Administration. Its work on administrative decentralization and chieftaincy before the elections of 1999[18] led to the Decree of 2000, which stipulated the recognition of community authorities, placing them on the same level as other local figures of power such as religious leaders or former socialist secretaries.

In this manner, the state rewrote decades of history by drafting new legal regulations and enacting gestures aimed at eliciting the allegiance of local communities—like ceremonies of chiefly recognition that resembled "ancient" spiritual rites. Encounters of state and the customary in northern Mozambique by way of theologico-political rituals—like the meeting at the tombs in the "invisible state," described above—brought together three distinct epochs—precolonial, colonial, postcolonial—within a single, ongoing temporality.[19]

The practices of repression and vassalization of local chiefs undertaken by the colonial state (1930–1960), as well as the policies of banning and deportation enacted by the socialist state (1975–1985), fostered a process of seeking out local authorities who were sympathetic to the state in otherwise hostile terrain. This process involved a dialectics of invisibility and recognition, a politics of visuality aimed at distinguishing friends from enemies, underneath layer upon layer of strategy, concealment, and distortion. Thus an optical form of power was enacted: a practice of staging a theatrical performance of state authority, rendering the state present and visible through rituals in which, as the protagonist of this stylized drama, it aimed at dialectically defining its elusive other—indigeneity, or the rural customary—as a ghostly antagonist (Scott 1997; Das and Poole 2004).[20]

As happened in the heyday of colonial rule, so in the middle of the first decade of the twenty-first century, a growing number of disputes occurred in the northern regions among kinship groups and individuals over legal succession to customary office and official state recognition, this amidst renewed pressures from the state. The chiefs were once again agents of local governance and control, tax collection and conflict resolution, as well as participants in economic development and the organization of voter registration and local elections. Disputes over the succession to customary authority were thus shot through with partisan angles of confrontation. The resurging ascendancy of chiefs was caught within struggles between FRELIMO and RENAMO, for instance. In fact, each instance of electoral political struggle restaged, in a lesser way, the contours of the civil war.

We have seen, in the rituals described above, how the state mobilizes symbolism drawn from various historic phases of violence–anticolonial struggle and civil war, as well as the Cold War[21]—in staging its contemporary democratic phase, which was itself the negotiated outcome of a violent conflict (Geffray 1990; Honwana 1997, 2002). Indeed, on the occasion of the performance of those rites, the speech of the local state representative traced a path from the state to "the community," depicting the upcoming election, in which the local community should choose "the party of peace" as the culmination of a long armed struggle beginning in the colonial period.

The ceremonies described above seemed to illustrate a suspended temporality that was prevalent throughout the nation in the middle of the first decade of the twenty-first century, created by historico-political forces that move simultaneously "progressively" toward the future and "backward" toward the past. The local state's approach toward the "invisible states" condenses several facets of the contemporary political moment and its coalescence of temporalities. The attempt to reach out to these polities illustrates the way in which the precolonial and the postcolonial are blended in the current political imagination. What was being reconsidered both at the level of the central state and at the level of local governance was the threshold between the two epochs: the very moment of national independence. It was at that juncture that the new nationalist regime attempted to break free from foreign domination and reform the state, while placing an emphasis on the transformation of local governance and the liberation of the indigenous, a key space in which colonialism had co-opted an ancient imagination of power enshrined in custom. The fate of the current reemergence of indigeneity, as well as its promise of freedom and emancipation, is directly related to the contemporary reconceptualization of what both the scope and the meaning of the precolonial actually were.

It could be argued that the relatively short period of colonial rule produced a rupture in history, a scission that arbitrarily established a previous time of the precolonial.[22] Today the state aims at politically defining the contemporary moment by reference to this spectral—present/absent—previous era, mobilizing the discourse of the law as a historicist narrative, in which the past is set to work in the present as an infinite, open-ended, and "flat" political temporality. Such is the meaning of the juridical rewriting of the historical past and the political mobilization of traditional authority, customary law, and spiritual ritual.

In this endeavor, tropes that were central to the colonial delimitation of the customary are given new life. The realm of indigeneity is constructed by the Afromodern urban sphere as a space of primitivism, deeply associated with nature itself. Custom is located by agencies of governance in a chain of significations associated to nature, kin, blood, local genealogy, and tradition—a series connected to a kind of spiritual authority, to "justice by reconciliation," and to a historicity that represents time as static: the eternal return of the same. Urban political elites portray customary authority—in policy, legislation, media—as infused with charismatic power, based on interaction with the spiritual realm, both spirits of the ancestors and those linked to natural resources. Amidst the democratic juridical reform of the state, the concept of the customary only began to regain currency in the early 1990s, in relation to land tenure reform. The capacity of the chief to distribute land also strongly relates this figure of authority to nature. The rural countryside, allegedly the true realm of the customary, has been recoded as the space of community, the new keyword for indigenous locality deployed by local and foreign development agencies (Berry 2001).[23]

The various political technologies at play in shaping the contemporary polity—legal discourse, political economy, public policy—certainly present neocolonial contours: decentralization; resurgence of chiefs as local government and enforcers of customary law; restrictions of citizenship rights; and a restructuring of the foundations of sovereignty. Remainders of state authority mingle with a montage of governmental practices exercised by an elusive "international community"—namely a compound of Bretton Woods institutions and various donor agencies (Macamo n.d.). At times, the figure that emerges is that of a latter-day protectorate, made up of national and transnational actors: a blend of postsocialist national(ist) elites and a neoliberal foreign assemblage of agencies. The reproduction of the realm of indigenous custom, which has connotations of a tabooed yet primordial authentic space, seems to be essential for the image that the Mozambican state projects to international agencies, which provide the majority of the national budget.

Indeed, a foreign vector intervenes at every level, shaping the outcome of political processes: from the development-oriented capital city, buoyed up by financial flows with obscure origins and effects, to the rural countryside of the customary villages. Such forces define macrolegal reforms at the central level, design the reemergence of the customary as local community, and adjudicate conflict over land tenure (Merry 2003). This transnational element is even present, we have seen, at a remote locality in the north, where a spiritual ceremony takes place, to be followed by an attempt by the local state to reconcile itself with an indigeneity that had been neglected for decades. The customary, or at least those of its layers made visible by the state, is annexed through a double bind of simultaneous political inclusion and exclusion. The rule of law of modern liberal democracy, the constitution, absorbs the plurality of differences under an absolute universal positive norm. This political context represents for both the local political postcolonial elites, and for their international humanitarian and developmentalist tutors, a perfect canvas on which is depicted the classical myth of a social contract emerging out of states of war and states of nature (Hall and Young 1997). The chief reemerges today as embryonic incarnation of this new commonwealth, as an inverted replica of the state apparatus, or a small Leviathan (Obarrio n.d.).

Spirit Level

The morning after our excursion to the invisible state, the administrator, some of his aides, the chief, and I met at the chief's house, at the small district capital. The house was located next to a small mosque, and near a local state post, outside which people were queuing, waiting to register to vote in the upcoming general elections.

The men had gathered to seal what had been evoked the day before. We went outside the house, kneeling around the grave of the chief's father. The space of this third tomb would host another conjunction of religious sentiment and political manoeuver, both a continuum and a rupture with respect to the ceremonies held the previous day.

Two key characters stood face to face, two figures who, throughout the last hundred years of history, had incarnated an agonistic relation of power in the locality: the administrator and the customary authority. Indeed, in this region, the reproduction of history had been based on the fluctuating alliances and struggles between a representative of the local (colonial, postcolonial) state and a chief. The rule of law of the liberal-democratic regime had brought these two former adversaries together, standing side by side at the edge of the grave that kept the mortal remains of the chief's father.

Among a few other people, the sheikh of the small mosque was also present. Yet it was the chief who first raised his arms and prayed. This time, his plea was made in both Makhuwa and Portuguese. Once again, the prayer was addressed both to Allah and the Spirit, eliciting a syncretism of the various histories of locality and the translocal expansion of Islam into the current historical meaning of the "customary." The chief prayed to the spirits for the soul of his father, who had also been a *regulo*, within a long family line of "customary" hierarchies. In his prayer the chief narrates that his father had been part of King Kupula's forces who had battled against the colonizer.

Chief Sukuta prays to the Spirit. Each invocation is a flowery display of historical references: dates and places where struggles, negotiations, strategies, rebellions, and alliances took place, ending with a reference to this town, to the dead chief, to his grave. It is a sacred speech, which evokes death as a main political marker of this area's history. The chief asks the Spirit to watch over his father's soul, so that it can illuminate current life in the district; to hold him close, so that his son's work for the People of the region will be guided by the Spirit itself, mediated by the father's soul.

Chief Sukuta prays, his arms raised as the speed and tone of his grave, dark voice escalates. The plea to the Spirit seems to endow kinship with a sacred aura, relinking two fundamental pillars of the legitimacy of "traditional" authority, overlooked by the current juridical recognition. The prayer, imploring the Spirit to descend and become a powerful force in this locality, evokes a key aspect of chieftaincy, its meditation with an otherworldly space populated by invisible forces and the elements. The chief is a secular political interface between local state and "community," working in prosaic development, fiscal, and electoral issues. Yet the legitimacy of his authority is based as much on negotiations established both with profane state authorities as well as with a world of supernatural powers.

The renewed influence of chiefs had been increasing since the final stages of the war in the late eighties, when the governor of the province established collaborations with "customary authority" in which *regulo* Sukuta participated. In the past, certain chiefs had exerted influence in sporadic ways, through kinship links, on the party cells and local socialist state units. Yet broad sectors of the population in this region celebrated the governmental ban on chiefs, broadly viewed by their "subjects" as arbitrary, violent local tools of colonial rule. There was a widespread adherence in the North of the country to early FRELIMO policies regarding education, health, and development, until around 1979, when the harshness of war and scarcity, as well as the effects of collective villagization, undermined that earlier support. This political tension was present at the scene that brought together the state delegation and the chief.

Now the chief is finishing his prayer at his father's grave. The plea ends with a reference to his current contingent ally, the administrator, inviting him to speak. Kneeling in front of the cement grave, the administrator presents a blend of prayer and political reverence: referring to the dead man with almost worshipful veneration. He alludes to the dead chief and thanks the Spirit for the work currently being undertaken by his son, the chief.

The administrator's words appear duplicitous, conveying a fictive message on the history of relations between the socialist state and the "customary." Yet the message accomplishes the performative effect of opening a potential space of agreement. The few words that the officer utters in the lonely twilight are at the same time an act of mourning, a prayer, a political speech. Moreover, his words seem like small archival pieces from the kaleidoscope that is the history of the region, in which at any given conjuncture, due to the dynamics of war, politics, law, the economy, or "development," men and women exchange places, masks, customs, arms, or banners, creating new social configurations.

The administrator declares his gratitude for the chief's collaboration with local governance and asks the Spirit for support for his own local administration. Finally, he requests help toward the victory of FRELIMO's current presidential candidate in the incoming general elections, "so the government can continue with its task of development." The teleological discourse of progress (democracy, development) embraces "tradition," carrying it toward the completion of its historical logic.

The names of the party and of the presidential candidate—who will visit this town in just a few days' time—echo in the void of the approaching night, and then there is only silence. The administrator stands up after he has finished his prayer. Yet one more person has to speak for the séance to be complete. Finally, the sheikh of the nearby mosque closes his eyes and prays in Arabic to Allah. After this short prayer we shake hands and it is all over.

The Politics of Secrecy

Yet as we witnessed in the ritual meeting at the tombs in the Macavelas district, where the state sought to reconcile itself with its indigenous other, something ethereal emerges in the encounter between them, an element of local power that exceeded the alleged transparency of administrative practice and state regulation. Indeed, the religious and political lines of that partly sacred, partly profane circuit of reciprocity carried traces of (sanctified, secret) norms that could not be absolutely enclosed by the current (secular, transparent) rule of law. Traces of spirituality, violence, and exchanges with otherworldly realms, which were constitutive of chieftaincy in the region, exceed political calculation and the legal regulation that attempts to accommodate the customary within a negotiated peace process and the new democratic regime.

The vernacular territory of a shadowed "invisibility" appears, in the eyes of state officers, to erect one trench upon another in the ideological warfare against the assault of the state, that is, different barriers to prevent the codification by official optical devices. This takes place within a historical condition of segmentary formations opposing the surveillance, control, and repression of different versions of the state, from Portuguese indirect rule up to the FRELIMO postindependence programmatic reforms and the civil war. Local communities attempt to reap the spoils of precarious development programs and commercial investment and still elude the mechanisms of control attached to them.

At the moment of third contact, the claims of the state to fully subsume indigeneity and thus congeal it into an apparatus of government confronted its limits. The visibility and legibility of indigeneity is occluded by secrecy, and the recognition of its legality and political legitimacy is interrupted by mutual suspicion.

Recall that during his speech outside the tombs, the local administrator in Nampula spoke of the construction of a cashew factory that would offer employment to the local community. The construction had begun well, months earlier, the Portuguese owner hiring many workers from amongst the town's youth, who started cutting down trees. Suddenly one morning, there was an accident. A tree fell on one of the young workers, injuring him badly. That, the administrator later told me, got the machinery of the invisible state going. Rumors that this particular project was not respecting the spirits started circulating widely. The managers of the factory had not performed all the due ceremonies and more accidents were surely forthcoming. The administrator described in detail how many of the young workers, sons of prominent members of the "invisible state," were fearful and soon stopped going to work altogether, and shortly, construction of the factory ground to a halt. Several weeks later, the Portuguese owner approached the administrator, explaining his predicament and asking for help. The administrator then contacted the authorities of the "invisible state," and after lengthy discussions, an agreement was reached in order to resume work that involved the performance of a series of sacrifices to spirits and the exchanges of material gifts and money.

The alleged invisibility of these states is thus an ambiguous attribute, whose potential political meanings and effects disseminate endlessly. Just as the urban representations of the customary ignore the dynamic nature of these polities and their fashioning through colonial violence, this label of invisibility was also a sleight of hand of a struggling local state. The perception of secret organizations of local leadership is part of the structure of the postcolonial state and its (re)construction of indigeneity. Obviously, from the point of view of rural populations, there is nothing invisible about their structures and norms, their figures of power and internal struggles, even if their leadership operates as secret societies. Their interactions with other instances of power partake of the fabric of everyday life and the ongoing reconstruction of local political fields.

At the same time, they stand as a sort of repository of alternate histories, memories that materialize in the face of current dangers (Benjamin 1992), challenging the state's historicist move or being put to work in the painstaking reconstruction of life in common. They are the real, yet spectral, double of the customary that is constructed both by the central state and by the foreign development industry. The purported invisibility that effaces them is predicated on the silent coded commandments that circulate within their ranks. Beyond those limits, secrecy is a law and sacredness a narrative that together fabricate both a structure and a history. They do so through performances of a camouflaged, mimetic nature, as the administrator's metaphors made clear, or through well-rehearsed political choreographies that alternatively enclose and disclose its mysterious orderings, such as the event that had paralyzed the production of a factory.

The state's recognition[24] of norms and forms of power at the local level implied an optical acknowledgment (Comaroff and Comaroff 2004; Povinelli 2002; Oomen 2005; Crais 2006) that only attained one level of the officially recognized customary. The official recognition of a legally reformed indigeneity advances a representation of customary authorities and law as genuinely traditional and bearing a legitimacy that would reside almost outside of historical time. But as the rituals analyzed above show, a seemingly endless conflict takes place between the state and the customary. The obscure outcome of the negotiations performed at those ceremonies shows that it is a struggle of suspicion and secrecy, of mutual rejection and pursuit. It is a war of positions in which the present constructs a certain past, toward the juridical self-fashioning of the state through the creation of a border zone that separates it from the customary as its alleged other. The dialectical circuit that merges the various levels and epochs produces a leftover. The field of the vernacular—its sacredness, its secrecy, its history of violence—cannot be fully assimilated into the juridical recognition of the customary enforced by the modernist secular state and transnational agencies.

Conclusion

The historical legacies of colonial indigeneity reveal its profound ambiguity as a foundation for new, more democratic forms of political life. Fetishized by national and transnational actors alike as the authentic precolonial customary, it is based on contemporary interpretations of a mythologized past and bolstered by new legislation attending to local culture, rights, and diversity in the wake of the decentralization of the state and the deregulation of markets and land property. Thus accredited, it functions as an unexamined ground for the legitimacy of newly recognized forms of local power exercised on behalf of the state.

As our encounter with the "invisible state" makes plain, the revitalization of indigeneity in the neoliberal moment uncovers fractures and ruptures that escape postcolonial governmentality and its totalizing aspirations. Yet this does not necessarily imply the failure of state power or the weakening of elite domination. Instead, the politics of recognition reveals the centrality of structures of autochthony and its tropes for the reconstruction of the state in Africa (see chapter 1, this volume). The political conundrums of this process are exposed in the state's bid for hegemony and legitimacy, relying as it does upon a political history branded by violence and a contradictory interplay between bylaws with potential for emancipation and fierce, authoritarian statutes from the past that collide with human rights and international law.

Thus, the return of the customary in Africa should be analyzed within a shift in forms of governance and modes of domination of the state (Coronil 1997; Das and Poole 2004; Mitchell 1990; Ferguson 2001), the latter understood not as an apparatus but rather as an extended ensemble of relations, giving rise to new sites of negotiation and conflict among international agencies and transnational capital, urban elites and local holders of power, whose political outcome appears to be dangerously uncertain.

Notes

1. "Mozambican ex-rebels Renamo in police clash," *BBC News*, 4 April 2014, http://www.bbc.com/news/world-africa-22031922, accessed 20 July 2014.
2. The decree creates a sort of "postsocialist tradition," so to speak, locating chiefs as legitimate traditional authorities at the same level as other local figures of power, such as former socialist secretaries, or neighborhoods or religious leaders, all defined under the rubric of "community authorities." Decreto 15/2000, Boletin da Republica, 20 de Junho, Maputo, Publicacao Oficial da Republica de Mocambique. On the decree, see Boaventura de Sousa Santos (2006); on the historical conundrums of customary authority, see Buur (2006) and Buur and Kyed (2005).
3. FRELIMO abandoned Marxism-Leninism at its 5th Congress (1989). A new generation of high-ranking officers has since emerged, yet the leadership at the level of the Central Committee remained the same as that which led the postindependence process. Joaquim Chissano remained the president for nineteen years following the death of historic revolutionary leader Samora Machel in 1986. His successor, Armando Guebuza, who won two general elections after 2005, was the first minister

of interior after independence. In 2014, the FRELIMO candidate Filipe Nyusi became the first Mozambican president who did not fight in the war of independence.

4. See the evidence presented in the special issue on autochthony in *African Studies Review*, edited by Geschiere and Jackson (2006).

5. This essay elaborates on the analysis of colonial refashionings of the customary through indirect rule (and of "decentralized despotism") by Mahmood Mamdani, seeking to move beyond some of its less flexible historical and ethnographic aspects. See also the debate among Mamdani, Cooper, Austen, and Ferme in *Politique africaine* (1999). In order to study a proliferating array of vernacular spaces and avoid some of Mamdani's dichotomies (citizen/subject, state/customary), I follow elaborations offered by Gayatri Spivak (2000). For the specific case of Mozambique, see the debate between Mamdani and Bridget O'Laughlin (2000) in *African Affairs*.

6. Mayor of a district.

7. The "invisible state" is a phrase used by local state officials; indeed, a rhetoric of invisibility and suspicion regarding indigenous forms of power—undetectable by the sensory apparatuses of the state—had wide currency among such local officers at the time of my fieldwork.

8. The name of the district has been changed.

9. I consider the administrator's account to be in line with descriptions of the dynamics of resilient precolonial rural semi-secret political structures in the former Portuguese colony of Guinea-Bissau, in Forrest (2003). On the rooting of African states in rural structures of filiation, power, and accumulation, see Bayart et al. (1992).

10. This refers to the multiple forms of distance—political, material, and symbolic—existing between the local state and the communities. This separation had been intensified by war, when the customary to a large extent fought against the state in the center-north of the country. Invisibility here does not refer merely to the political concealment of the community and its authorities but also to their being unapproachable through lack of physical access.

11. Later on, the chief would reveal himself as the one who actually engineered the encounter between the local state and this community in the context of this ceremony.

12. Approximately 20 percent of the Mozambican population are Muslims. Mozambique has had a strong Islamic presence since the arrival of Arab sheikhs and traders in the north of the territory in the twelfth century. In provinces like Nampula, indigeneity and customary authority are synonymous with Islam in its African form.

13. These remarks condense a whole history of political reversal: the officer's speech blends a range of references that would have been unthinkable a few years earlier but are sensible in light of the more recent recognition of indigenous authority. Thus he makes reference to FRELIMO government alongside mention of an ancient local customary chief, a prominent member of the lineage system that FRELIMO had opposed and attempted to dismantle after independence.

14. The speech presents the current democratic regime as a transposition of the previous situation of war. FRELIMO and RENAMO, former enemy war camps, competed in 2003 for the democratic vote, which also meant struggling over the chiefs' loyalty in a province where chiefs have shown a strong support for RENAMO since the civil war. The speech superimposes this history over the canvass of the anticolonial war led by FRELIMO, which had Nampula Province as one of the main battlefields. The "customary" played a crucial role in both instances of war.

15. The *Indigenato* regime was ideologically parallel with the French colonial Code de l'Indigenat (1888–1947), which had established the subaltern juridical status

of natives of French colonies through taxation and *corvee* labor. The *Indigenato* followed the guidelines of British and French indirect rule, although it also created a small sector of "assimilated" native subjects, who enjoyed certain citizenship rights.

16. The notion of a "third contact" alludes to a triad of moments of collusion between state and customary and is also a reference to Michael Taussig's conceptualization of a "second contact" in the negative dialectics between colonizer and colonized, in which the latter mimes and instrumentalizes the images of the former in order to regain symbolic power. In the third moment, the Mozambican state attempts to reincorporate the political imagination of chieftaincy it had previously banned and execrated (Taussig 1993).

17. This ideological move implied a reconfiguration on behalf of the state and foreign donor agencies of rural customary authority as part of an incipient civil society. In contrast, the terms of democratic inclusion in Africa are overdetermined by the legacy of the colonial divide between rural indigeneity and urban citizenship.

18. See, for instance, the essentialization of indigeneity espoused by the project's director Irae Lundin (1988). I thank Irae Lundin for discussing some of her views on autochtony with me during an interview in Maputo in 2000.

19. The notion of "becoming," and of entangled temporalities in contemporary Africa more generally, has been developed by Achille Mbembe (2001).

20. The local category of "invisible" states could also be linked to an "optical unconscious of the state." My reflection on the political as a nontransparent realm, and governmentality as a "dialectics of seeing," alludes to Walter Benjamin's intuitions. On Benjamin, see Krauss (1993) and Buck-Morss (1989).

21. See the classical ethnography by Henri Junod (1962) on Tsonga in Southern Mozambique.

22. The period of effective occupation by the Portuguese colonial state (1930–1975) was preceded by a precolonial era of imprecise limits. Should the precolonial be defined as a period before the implementation of Portuguese control and rule by European companies (1880s), or before 1498, the moment of the arrival of Vasco da Gama on the Mozambican coast and his encounter with Arab chieftaincies in the 1500s?

23. "Communities are individual juridical persons like corporations, and they know their spatial limits very well," a high-ranking program officer from an international development agency told me during an interview held in Maputo in 2003. I had observed that often, what was being demarcated as "customary communal land," based on "historical continuities," was actually, according to archival evidence, the territory of chiefdoms established by the Portuguese colonial regime.

24. On the "limits of recognition" in the context of legal pluralism in Mozambique, see Sousa Santos et al. (2006). For a parallel example of settler colonialism in Australia, see the work of Elizabeth Povinelli (2002).

References

Abrams, Philip
    1988 Notes on the Difficulty of Studying the State. *Journal of Historical Sociology* 1(1): 58–89.
Avineri, Schlomo
    1974 *Hegel's Theory of the Modern State*. Cambridge: Cambridge University Press.

Bayart, Jean-Francois
    2009   *The State in Africa: The Politics of the Belly*. Cambridge: Polity Press.
Bayart, Jean-Francois, Peter Geschiere, and Francis Nyamnjoh, eds.
    2001   Autochtonie, démocratie et citoyenneté en Afrique. Special issue, *Critique Internationale* 1(10).
Bayart, Jean-Francois, Achille Mbembe, and Comi Tolabour
    1992   *La politique par le bas en Afrique noire: Contributions à une problématique de la démocratie*. Paris: Karthala.
Benjamin, Walter
    1992   Theses on the Philosophy of History, Thesis VI. In *Illuminations*. London: Fontana.
Berry, Sara
    2001   *Chiefs Know Their Boundaries: Essays on Property, Power and the Past*. London: James Currey.
Bertelsen, Bjorn
    n.d.   Co-Opting Tradition? State Strategies of Controlling an Unruly Field in Mozambique. Paper presented at Afrikaseminaret, Department of Social Anthropology, University of Oslo, 21 October 2008.
Buck-Morss, Susan
    1989   *The Dialectics of Seeing: Walter Benjamin and the Arcades Project*. Cambridge, MA: MIT Press.
Buur, Lars
    2006   New Sites of Citizenship: Recognition of Traditional Authority and Group-Based Citizenship in Mozambique. *Journal of Southern African Studies* 32(3):563–81.
Buur, Lars, and Helene Maria Kyed
    2005   *State Recognition of Traditional Authority in Mozambique: The Nexus of Community Representation and State Assistance*. Uppsala: Nordiska Afrikainstituter.
    2006   Contested Sources of Authority: Re-claiming State Sovereignty by Formalising Traditional Authority in Mozambique. *Development and Change* 37(4):847–69.
    2007   State Recognition of Traditional Authority in Mozambique: The Legible Space between State and Community. In *State Recognition and Democratization in Sub-Saharan Africa*, L. Buur and H. M. Kyed, eds. New York: Palgrave Macmillan.
Chan, Stephen, and Venâncio Moisés
    1998   *War and Peace in Mozambique*. New York: St. Martin's Press.
Chanock, Martin
    1985   *Law, Custom and Social Order: The Colonial Experience in Malawi and Zambia*. Cambridge: Cambridge University Press.
Chege, Michael
    1997   Review of *Citizen and Subject: Contemporary Africa and the Legacy of Late Colonialism*, Mahmood Mamdani. *African Studies Quarterly* 1(1). https://asq.africa.ufl.edu/files/Book-Reviews-Vol-1-Issue-1.pdf.
Chingono, Mark F.
    1996   *The State, Violence, and Development: The Political Economy of the War in Mozambique, 1975–1992*. Brookfield: Avebury.
Cohen, David W., and E.S. Atieno Odhiambo
    1992   *Burying SM: The Politics of Knowledge and the Sociology of Power in Black Africa*. Portsmouth, NH: Heinemann.
Comaroff, Jean, and John L. Comaroff
    2003   Reflections on Liberalism, Policulturalism, and ID-ology: Citizenship and Difference in South Africa. *Social Identities* 9(3):445–74.

2006   Introduction. In *Law and Disorder in the Postcolony*, J. Comaroff and J. L. Comaroff, eds. Chicago: University of Chicago Press.

Comaroff, Jean, and John L. Comaroff, eds.
1999   *Civil Society and Political Imagination in Africa: Critical Perspectives*. Chicago: University of Chicago Press.

Comaroff, John L., and Jean Comaroff
2004   Criminal Justice, Cultural Justice: The Limits of Liberalism and the Pragmatics of Difference in the New South Africa. *American Ethnologist* 31(2):188–204.

Coronil, Fernando
1997   *The Magical State: Nature, Money, and Modernity in Venezuela*. Chicago: University of Chicago Press.

Crais, Clifton
2006   Custom and the Politics of Sovereignty in South Africa. *Journal of Social History* 39(3):721–40.

Das, Veena, and Deborah Poole, eds.
2004   *Anthropology in the Margins of the State*. Santa Fe, NM: SAR Press.

Dinerman, Alice
2006   *Revolution, Counter-Revolution and Revisionism in Postcolonial Africa: The Case of Mozambique, 1975–1994*. London: Routledge.

Dozon, Jean-Pierre.
2003   *Frères et sujets: la France et l'Afrique en perspective*. Paris: Flammarion.

Ferguson, James
2001   Transnational Topographies of Power: Beyond the 'State' and 'Civil Society' in the Study of African Politics. In *The Anthropology of Politics: A Reader in Ethnography, Theory, and Critique*, J. Vincent and D. Nugent, eds. Oxford: Blackwell.
2006   *Global Shadows: Africa in the Neoliberal World Order*. Durham, NC: Duke University Press.

Finnegan, William
1992   *A Complicated War: The Harrowing of Mozambique*. Berkeley, CA: University of California Press.

Forrest, Joshua
2003   *Lineages of State Fragility: Rural Civil Society in Guinea Bissau*. Athens, OH: Ohio University Press.

Geffray, Christian
1990   *La cause des armes au Mozambique: Anthropologie d'une guerre civile*. Paris: Karthala.

Geschiere, Peter
2009   *The Perils of Belonging: Autochthony, Citizenship, and Exclusion in Africa and Europe*. Chicago: University of Chicago Press.

Geschiere, Peter, and Stephen Jackson
2006   Autochthony and the Crisis of Citizenship: Democratization, Decentralization, and the Politics of Belonging. Special issue, *African Studies Review* 49(2):1–8.

Geschiere, Peter, and Francis Nyamnjoh
2000   Capitalism and Autochthony: The Seesaw of Mobility and Belonging. *Public Culture* 12(2):432–53.

Goncalves, Euclides
2005   Finding the Chief: Political Decentralisation and Traditional Authority in Mocumbi, Southern Mozambique. *African Insight* 35(3):64–70.

Grovogui, Siba
1996   *Sovereigns, Quasi-Sovereigns, and Africans: Race and Self-Determination in International Law*. Minneapolis, MN: University of Minnesota Press.

Hall, Margaret, and Tom Young

1997   *Confronting Leviathan: Mozambique since Independence.* Athens, OH: Ohio University Press.

Hanlon, Joseph

1984   *Mozambique: The Revolution under Fire.* London: Zed Books.

1996   *Peace without Profit: How the IMF Blocks Rebuilding in Mozambique.* London: James Currey.

Harries, Patrick

1994   *Work, Culture, and Identity: Migrant Laborers in Mozambique and South Africa, c. 1860–1910.* Johannesburg: Witwatersrand University Press.

Hedges, David

2000   *O sul e o trabalho migratorio.* In *Historia de Mocambique,* vol. 1, C. E. Serra, E. Medeiros, and J. Moreira, eds. Maputo: Livraria Universitaria, Eduardo Mondlane University.

Hedges, David, Aurélio Rocha, Aurélio Medeiros, Gerhard Liesegang, and Arlindo Chilundo, eds.

1993   *Historia de Mocambique,* vol. 3, *Mocambique, no auge do colonialismo 1930–1961.* Maputo: Eduardo Mondlane University.

Hibou, Beatrice, ed.

2004   *Privatizing the State.* New York: Columbia University Press.

Honwana, Alcinda

1997   Healing for Peace: Traditional Healers and Post-War Reconstruction in Southern Mozambique. *Peace and Conflict: Journal of Peace Psychology* 3(3):293–305.

2002   *Espíritos vivos, tradições modernas: Possessão de espíritos e reintegração social pós-guerra no sul de Moçambique.* Maputo: Promédia.

Isaacman, Allen

1996   *Cotton is the Mother of Poverty: Peasants, Work and Rural Struggle in Colonial Mozambique, 1938–1961.* London: Heinemann.

Junod, Henri

1962[1926]   *The Life of a South African Tribe,* vol. 1, *Social Life.* New Hyde Park, NY: University Books.

Krauss, Rosalind

1993   *The Optical Unconscious.* Cambridge, MA: October Books and the MIT Press.

Kyed, Helene Maria

2007   State Recognition of Traditional Authority: Authority, Citizenship, and State Formation in Rural Post-War Mozambique. PhD dissertation, Roskilde University.

Lubkemann, Stephen

2007   *Culture in Chaos: An Anthropology of the Social Condition in War.* Chicago: University of Chicago Press.

Lundin, Irae Baptista

1988   Traditional Authority in Mozambique. In *Decentralisation and Municipal Administration: Descriptions and Development of Ideas on Some African and European Models,* I. B. Lundin and F. J. Machava, eds. Maputo: Friedrich Ebert Stiftung.

Macamo, Elisio

n.d.   How Development Aid Changes Societies: Disciplining Mozambique through Structural Adjustment. Paper presented at CODESRIA 11th General Assembly, Dakar, Senegal, 2005.

Mamdani, Mahmood

1996   *Citizen and Subject: Contemporary Africa and the Legacy of Late Colonialism.* Princeton, NJ: Princeton University Press.

2000   Indirect Rule and the Struggle for Democracy: A Response to Bridget O'Laughlin. *African Affairs* 99(194):43–46.

Mamdani, Mahmood, Frederic Cooper, Ralph Austen, and Mariane Ferme
1999   Debat Autour d'un Livre. Mamdani (Mahmood), *Citizen and Subject: Contemporary Africa and the Legacy of Late Colonialism*. *Politique africaine* 73:193–211.

Marshall-Fratani, Ruth
2006   The War of 'Who is Who': Autochthony, Nationalism, and Citizenship in the Ivorian Crisis. *African Studies Review* 49(2):9–43.

Mbembe, Achille
2001   *On the Postcolony*. Berkeley, CA: University of California Press.
2002a   African Modes of Self-Writing. *Public Culture* 14(1):239–73.
2002b   On the Power of the False. *Public Culture* 14(3):629–41.

Meneses, Maria Paula
2006   Traditional Authorities in Mozambique: Between Legitimization and Legitimacy. In *The Shade of New Leaves: Governance in Traditional Authority, a Southern African Perspective*, M. O. Hinz and H. K. Patemann, eds. Berlin: Lit Verlag.

Meneses, M. P., J. Fumo, G. Mbilana, and C. Gomes
2006   The Traditional Authorities. In *Law and Justice in a Multicultural Society: The Case of Mozambique*, B. de Sousa Santos, J. C. Trindade, and P. Meneses, eds. Dakar: CODESRIA.

Merry, Sally Engel
2003   Review: From Law and Colonialism to Law and Globalization. Review of *Law, Custom and Social Order: The Colonial Experience in Malawi and Zambia*, Martin Chanock. *Law and Social Inquiry* 28(2):269–90.

Minter, William
1994   *Apartheid's Contras: An Inquiry into the Roots of War in Angola and Mozambique*. London: Zed Books.

Mitchell, Timothy
1990   Everyday Metaphors of Power. *Theory and Society* 19:545–77.

Moore, Sally Falk
1986   *Social Facts and Fabrications: "Customary" Law in Kilimanjaro, 1880–1980*. Cambridge: Cambridge University Press.

Newitt, Maylyn
1995   *A History of Mozambique*. Bloomington, IN: Indiana University Press.

Obarrio, Juan M
2014   *The Spirit of the Laws in Mozambique*. Chicago: University of Chicago Press.
n.d.   A Matter of Time: The State of Things in Mozambique (forthcoming)

O'Laughlin, Bridget
2000   Class and the Customary: The Ambiguous Legacy of the *Indigenato* in Mozambique. *African Affairs* 99(394):5–42.

Oomen, Barbara
2005   *Chiefs in South Africa: Law, Power, and Culture in the Post-Apartheid Era*. New York: Palgrave Macmillan.

Pels, Peter
1996   The Pidginization of Luguru Politics: Administrative Ethnography and the Paradoxes of Indirect Rule. *American Ethnologist* 23(4):738–61.

Pitcher, M. Anne
2002   *Transforming Mozambique: The Politics of Privatization, 1975–2000*. Cambridge: Cambridge University Press.

Povinelli, Elizabeth
    2002   *The Cunning of Recognition: Indigenous Alterities and the Making of Australian Multiculturalism.* Durham, NC: Duke University Press.
Republic of Mozambique
    2000   *Report: Decreto 15/2000, Boletin da Republica, 20 de Junho, Maputo.* Publicacao Oficial da Republica de Mocambique.
Scott, James
    1997   *Seeing Like a State: How Certain Schemes to Improve the Human Condition Have Failed.* New Haven, CT: Yale University Press.
Shadle, Brett L.
    1999   'Changing Traditions to Meet Current Altering Conditions': Customary Law, African Courts, and the Rejection of Codification in Kenya, 1930–60. *Journal of African History* 40(3):411–31.
Snyder, Francis
    1981   Colonialism and Legal Form: The Creation of 'Customary Law' in Senegal. *Journal of Legal Pluralism* 19:49–90.
Sousa Santos, Boaventura de
    2006   The Heterogenous State and Legal Pluralism in Mozambique. *Law and Society Review* 40(1):39–75.
Sousa Santos, B., J. Trindade, and M. P. Meneses, eds.
    2006   *Law and Justice in a Multicultural Society: The Case of Mozambique.* Dakar: CODESRIA.
Spivak, Gayatri Chakravorty
    2000   From Haverstock Hill Flat to US Classroom: What's Left of Theory? In *What's Left of Theory? New Work on the Politics of Literary Theory,* J. Butler, J. Guillory, and K. Thomas, eds. New York: Routledge.
Taussig, Michael
    1993   *Mimesis and Alterity: A Particular History of the Senses.* New York: Routledge
Vines, Alex
    1991   *RENAMO: Terrorism in Mozambique.* Bloomington, IN: Indiana University Press.
West, Harry
    1998   'This Neighbor is Not My Uncle!': Changing Relations of Power and Authority on the Mueda Plateau. *Journal of Southern African Studies* 24(1):143–60.
West, Harry, and S. Kloeck-Jenson
    1999   Betwixt and Between: 'Traditional Authority' and Democratic Decentralisation in Post-War Mozambique. *African Affairs* 98(393):455–84.
Wilson, Ken
    1992   Cults of Violence and Counter-Violence in Mozambique. *Journal of Southern African Studies* 18(3):527–82.
Young, Crawford
    1994   *The African Colonial State in Comparative Perspective.* New Haven, CT: Yale University Press.

ACKNOWLEDGMENTS

This project began when the African Studies Workshop at Harvard convened a conference in April 2014 to explore the present and future of chiefship and the customary. This volume is its harvest, augmented by three essays written subsequently at the invitation of the editors.

The conference would have been impossible without the unstinting support of the Center for African Studies at Harvard—and, specifically, of Caroline Elkins (Oppenheimer Faculty Director Emeritus), Susan Cook (executive director), Maggie Lopes (associate director), and Elise Noel (former staff coordinator of the African Studies Workshop); also of Alma Medina, our research and administrative assistant. To all of them is owed a deep debt of gratitude.

CONTRIBUTORS

LAUREN ADROVER is a sociocultural anthropologist who works on cultural production, commodification, and political economy in Ghana. She received her PhD from Northwestern University in 2014. Her dissertation, "Festival Encounters: Value Logics and the Political Economy of Cultural Production in Ghana," analyzes the relationship between cultural production and Ghana's shifting political economic landscape since colonialism. Her essay "Branding Festive Bodies: Corporate Logos and Chiefly Image T-Shirts in Ghana" appeared in *African Dress: Fashion, Agency, Performance* (2013).

JOCELYN ALEXANDER is professor of commonwealth studies at the University of Oxford. She is a historian of southern Africa whose work has focused on politics, state making, war, and memory over the last century. Her current research concerns the history of political imprisonment in Zimbabwe. In addition to numerous essays, she is author of *The Unsettled Land: State Making and the Politics of Land in Zimbabwe, 1893–2003* (2006) and coauthor of *Violence and Memory: One Hundred Years in the "Dark Forests" of Matabeleland* (2000).

SARA BERRY is a retired professor of history at Johns Hopkins University. She has done research on land, development, agrarian change, political economy, and socioeconomic history, with primary emphasis on Nigeria and Ghana. Her books include *Fathers Work for Their Sons: Accumulation, Mobility, and Class Formation in an Extended Yoruba Community* (1985), *No Condition is Permanent: The Social Dynamics of Agrarian Change in Sub-Saharan Africa* (1993), and *Chiefs Know Their Boundaries: Essays on Property, Power, and the Past in Asante, 1896–1996* (2001).

BENOIT BEUCHER is a researcher at the National Foundation for Scientific Research, Université Libre de Bruxelles, and a member of the Institute of African Worlds. He has published widely on the history of West African societies under French colonialism, the relationship between knowledge and power, the politics of ethnicity, the history of the state, and the dynamics of Mossi kingdoms in Burkina Faso, on which he has a forthcoming book, *When the Men Eat Power: An African Nobility Facing History*. His essays have appeared in *Sociétés politiques comparées* and *Politique africaine*.

MBONGISENI BUTHELEZI is a research manager at the Public Affairs Research Institute in Johannesburg, South Africa. Until recently, he was a senior researcher at the University of Cape Town in the Archive and Public Culture Research Initiative. He also held appointments at the Centre for Law and Society and in the Department of English at the same university. His research focuses on customary leadership in South Africa. He holds a PhD in English and comparative literature from Columbia University.

JEAN COMAROFF is the Alfred North Whitehead Professor of African and African American Studies and of Anthropology, and an Oppenheimer Research Fellow, at Harvard University. She is also an honorary professor at the University of Cape Town. Her research has centered on the making and unmaking of colonial society, the nature of the postcolony, and the late modern world as viewed from the Global South. Her publications include *Body of Power, Spirit of Resistance: The Culture and History of a South African People* (1985) and, with John Comaroff, *Of Revelation and Revolution* (2 vols., 1991 and 1997), *Ethnography and the Historical Imagination* (1992), *Millennial Capitalism and the Culture of Neoliberalism* (2000), *Law and Disorder in the Postcolony* (2006), *Ethnicity, Inc.* (2009), *Theory from the South: Or, How Euro-America is Evolving Toward Africa* (2011), and *The Truth about Crime: Sovereignty, Knowledge, Social Order* (2016).

JOHN COMAROFF is the Hugh K. Foster Professor of African and African American Studies and of Anthropology, and an Oppenheimer Research Fellow, at Harvard University. He is also an honorary professor at the University of Cape Town. His research and extensive published work has centered on the making and unmaking of colonial society, politics and law in Africa, and the late modern world as viewed from the Global South. He is coauthor of *Rules and Processes: The Cultural Logic of Dispute in an African Context* (1981) and the books with Jean Comaroff listed above.

SUSAN COOK is executive director of the Center for African Studies, Harvard University. Her research, on traditional leadership and the anthropology of the corporation, focuses on the Royal Bafokeng Nation in South Africa, where she also served as an advisor to the *kgosi* (king). Her journal articles include "The Business of Being Bafokeng: Corporatization in a Tribal Authority in South Africa," *Current Anthropology* (2010), and "Chiefs, Kings, Corporatization, and Democracy: A South African Case Study," *Brown Journal of World Affairs* (2005). She also edited *Genocide in Cambodia and Rwanda: New Perspectives* (2006).

LAUREN COYLE is assistant professor of anthropology at Princeton University. Her research interests include legal and political anthropology, critical theory, mining and capitalism, and ritual and symbolic power, with a focus on Ghana. She has a PhD in anthropology from the University of Chicago and a JD from Harvard Law School. Her current book in preparation is entitled *Fires of Gold: Law, Land, and Sacrificial Labor in Ghana*. Her essays have appeared in *Telos, Transition,* and *Rethinking Marxism,* and in an edited volume, *Corporate Social Responsibility? Human Rights in the New Global Economy* (2015).

MARIANE FERME is professor of anthropology at the University of California, Berkeley. Her research focuses on materiality and everyday life in Sierra Leone, on the political imagination, and on transitional justice institutions, particularly the Special Court for Sierra Leone. Her publications include *The Underneath of Things: Violence, History, and the Everyday in Sierra Leone* (2001), essays in *Cahiers d'études africaines, Politique africaine, Journal of Material Culture, Humanity,* and *Anthropological Quarterly,* and chapters in several edited volumes.

PETER GESCHIERE is professor of anthropology at the University of Amsterdam, fellow of the Royal Netherlands Academy of Sciences, and coeditor of the journal *Ethnography*. He has done historical and anthropological research in West Africa and published widely on citizenship, belonging and exclusion, and witchcraft and politics in Africa and elsewhere. In addition to *The Modernity of Witchcraft* (1997), *Perils of Belonging: Autochthony, Citizenship, and Exclusion in Africa and Europe* (2009), and *Witchcraft, Intimacy, and Trust: Africa in Comparison* (2013), he has published numerous essays. He is also supervisor of the project Islam in Africa for the NWO (Netherlands Organization for Scientific Research) program on The Future of the Religious Past.

JUAN OBARRIO is associate professor of anthropology at Johns Hopkins University. He holds a PhD from Columbia University and has conducted fieldwork in Mozambique on law, custom, violence, and magic. He is currently working on healing, politics, and religion in West Africa and is the author of *The Spirit of the Laws in Mozambique* (2014) and *Matter of Time: State of Things and Secrecy in Northern Mozambique* (forthcoming). His recent essays include "Remains: To Be Seen: Third Encounter between State and 'Customary' in Northern Mozambique," *Cultural Anthropology* (2010), and "Beyond Equivalence: The Gift of Justice (Mozambique 1976, 2004)," *Anthropological Theory* (2010).

DINEO SKOSANA is a doctoral student in politics at the University of the Witwatersrand. Her current research investigates the relationship between heritage and mineral policy in South Africa, addressing the question of how recent legislation has shaped local political processes—specifically, the politics of death—in a coal mining community in Mpumalanga Province. She has previously conducted research on chieftaincy and local governance in Mokopane, Limpopo Province. Her scholarly interests span indigenous politics, governance, policy, culture and heritage, and land claims.

JAMES SMITH is professor of anthropology at the University of California, Davis. His research interests include the cultural politics of time, artisanal mining and resource extraction, religion and the occult, and vernacular understandings of development in Africa. He is currently working on the social life and political economy of coltan mining in the Democratic Republic of the Congo and is author of *Bewitching Development:*

Witchcraft and the Reinvention of Development in Neoliberal Kenya (2008), coauthor of *Email from Ngeti: An Ethnography of Sorcery, Redemption, and Friendship in Global Africa* (2014), and coeditor of *Displacing the State: Religion and Conflict in Neoliberal Africa* (2012). His articles include "Tantalus in the Digital Age: Coltan Ore, Temporal Dispossession, and Movement in the Eastern DR Congo," *American Ethnologist* (2013), and "Snake Driven Development: Nature, Culture, and Religious Conflict in Kenya," *Ethnography* (2006).

INDEX

Page references in italics refer to illustrations

AbaThembu, 2

acephalous societies (tribes without rulers), European appointments of chiefs for, 10–12

Adrover, Lauren, 31. *See also chapter 9, this volume*

African empires, 9, 41n16

Africanist archaeology, and study of precolonial states, 41n17

African National Congress (ANC), 228n8; focus of mobilization on urban areas, 113–14; lack of legislation on role of chiefs in postapartheid state, 115; land reform program, 97; perception of future of Inkatha Freedom Party, 125; shift to view of customary authorities as "voter banks," 21, 62, 80, 87, 114; writing of customary leadership into new constitution, 87, 129n5

African political systems, historicity of, 9–13

African Political Systems (Fortes and Evans-Pritchard), 2, 8–9

Afrobarometer, 206n93

agribusiness, 179nn8–9; and chiefly authority over land, 14, 16, 19, 94; and conflicts in rural chiefdoms, 169–71

Ahidjo, Ahmadou, 70

Akan: *Adae* festivals, 265, 269n16, 269n20; Akan goldweights, 267n8; beads and *kente* linked to chiefship of, 244n13;

and *Fetu Afahye*, 31–32, 231; importance of gold in cosmology of, 250–52; influence of Akan chiefs, 232–33; languages and regional dialects and attributes, 244n3; migration of, 101n25

Akwapim Twi dialect, 244n3

Akyeampong, Emmanuel, 265

Alexander, Jocelyn: on chiefly authority both alternative to and adjunct of state, 21; on durability of chiefship, 9; on flexibility of chiefship, 2; on provenance of chiefly legitimacy, 26; on "return" of chiefly authority, 24–25. *See also chapter 5, this volume*

Alvord, E. D., 136

amaMpondo: last of Xhosa-speaking groups to be brought under colonial rule, 217; remittances from migrant laborers as most important source of household income, 217; respect of workers for king, 213, 221, 225, 227; slain workers at Marikana platinum mine, 30, 211

amaXhosa king, coronation of in 2015, 20–21, 22–23, 215

"American chiefs," 2, 26

"Analysis of a Social Structure in Modern Zululand" (Gluckman), 29

Anglo American (South African conglomerate), 87